The Artist and the Built Environment

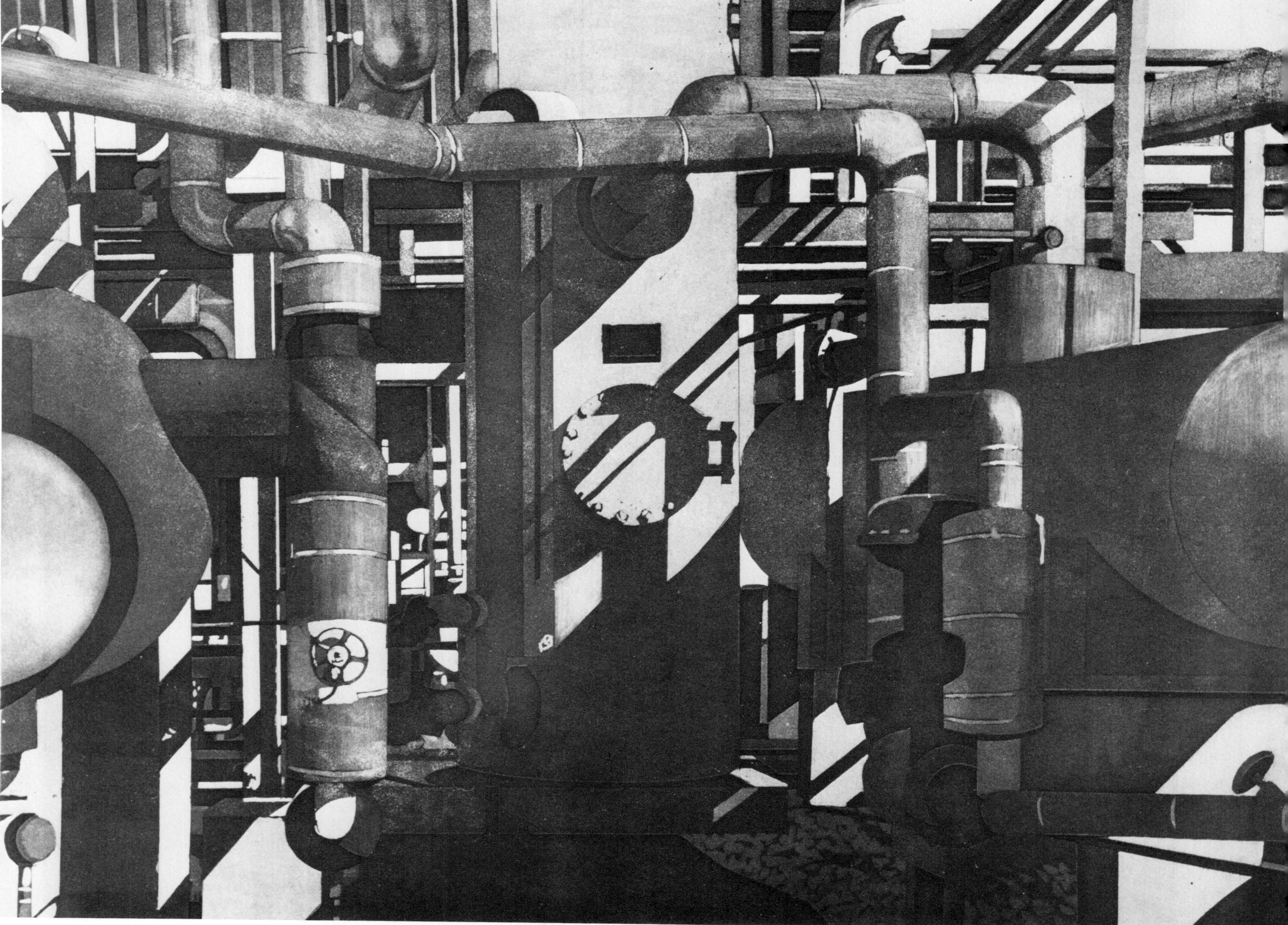

Donald Stoltenberg

The Artist and the Built Environment

DAVIS PUBLICATIONS, INC.
Worcester, Massachusetts

Frontispiece: *Compressor,* 1979.
Etching and aquatint on paper, 17½" × 23½".
Sidney Hurwitz.

All illustrations not otherwise credited are by the author.

Acknowledgment:

Maurice Utrillo, *La Porte Saint Martin.* Copyright by SPADEM, London, 1980. See page 2.

Walter Greaves, *Battersea Reach.* Copyright by A.D.A.G.P., Paris, 1980. See page 117.

Andre Derain, *The Pool of London.* Copyright by A.D.A.G.P., Paris, 1980. See page 121.

Printed in the United States of America
Library of Congress Catalog Card Number:79-53779
ISBN:0-87192-118-9

Composition: J.S. McCarthy Co., Inc.
Printing and Binding: Kingsport Press
Graphic Design: Jane Pitts

1 2 3 4 5 6 7 8 9 10

CONTENTS

ACKNOWLEDGMENTS

My thanks to:

Sid Hurwitz for the steady encouragement he has given to this project, for the use of his work, exposure of his working methods, and especially for the time and effort he contributed to gather material for this book.

Ralph MacKenzie for his fine photographic craftsmanship and keen eye in catching the essentials and nuances of the works in progress shown.

Ken Bernstein and Greg Hein.

George Nick and Flora Natapoff for allowing their working spaces to be invaded and for their individual contributions to the examples of method and realization shown in this book.

Larry Webster for his photographic series and developing painting of the railroad bridge.

Davis Publications, and in particular, Jerry Stashak for his continuing support and Martha Akstin and Beth Lyle for their assistance.

INTRODUCTION

There is a new preoccupation with the built environment—the buildings, transportation, and engineering works around us. Industrial archaeology, preservation, and conversion of old structures to contemporary uses indicate a new awareness of the urban landscape, the effect it has upon us, and the richness that it can contribute to our lives. There is a growing appreciation of the anonymous buildings and structures of the industrial revolution with their accumulated layers of history and use. Veneration has come to great engineering works of the past, such as the Eiffel Tower and the Brooklyn Bridge. Though constructed from small components in contrast to the smooth, monolithic forms of our own time, they still stir us with their scale and power.

It is the artist's function to examine, digest, and interpret our surroundings, to give us ways in which to react to them, evaluate them, and, in various ways, to come to terms with them. The artist can point out beauty where there seems to be none, can intensify moods or qualities that reveal the means to see, enjoy, and appreciate our conditions. The artist can help us to digest or grasp the welter of confusing and diverse forms that our increasingly built-up environment throws at us.

Included in this book are artists who have responded to this theme either for the span of their working lives, such as Canaletto or Sheeler, or for periods of it, such as Demuth or Burchfield, or some who at a moment in their careers have made a significant statement, such as Turner or Soutine. The response may be direct, requiring on-location work with constant reference to the motif, studio work, sketches, photographs, and repeated visits to the motif. At the other extreme, it may be work executed far away in time and place from the subject—a statement distilled through memory and interest.

Organization of this book is by subject matter rather than by chronology or style. Having come through a period when the subject was devalued as an object of importance to the viewer and even to the artist, it is worthwhile now to regain a broader view and to examine the subject matter itself. Examples have been chosen to show how artists of different periods, temperaments, and backgrounds have approached similar subjects or even the same motif. This was done to discover their attitudes, their individual selections from the many aspects in a given subject, their intensification or exaggeration of some of its characteristics, and the suppression or elimination of other qualities in order to make a visual point. They are showing the viewer something about the subject that has never before been noticed or appreciated.

This, then, is a sampling of what past and contemporary artists have done with the theme of the built environment. When possible, descriptions of the approaches and techniques of past painters have been included, especially when stated in their own words. The working methods of several currently active artists are followed in greater detail as they react to, analyze, and finally synthesize a painting or drawing.

Emphasis has been put on craft which is of considerable importance in understanding the individual artist and the artist's state of mind. There were some problems. Artists, understandably, are often unwilling to stop during the course of their work to explain the reasons for what they are doing. The purpose was to follow the flow of uninterrupted activity that results in a fully realized work. The photographer, too, had to try to capture key actions without intruding. If it were not feasible to stop at intervals while the work was progressing, the working thought processes were reconstructed after completion of the painting. As a result, some of this documentation is from the outside in: observing, noting, and photographing in a log-fashion how a work was physically developing. Some was from inside out: remembering thoughts, problems, solutions, and decisions made while working. The conclusion inevitably formed that the how or why a work develops as it does is an elusive thing. It is hoped that what has been put down here will show how some artists who work with the built environment set about their tasks and interpret it in their various ways.

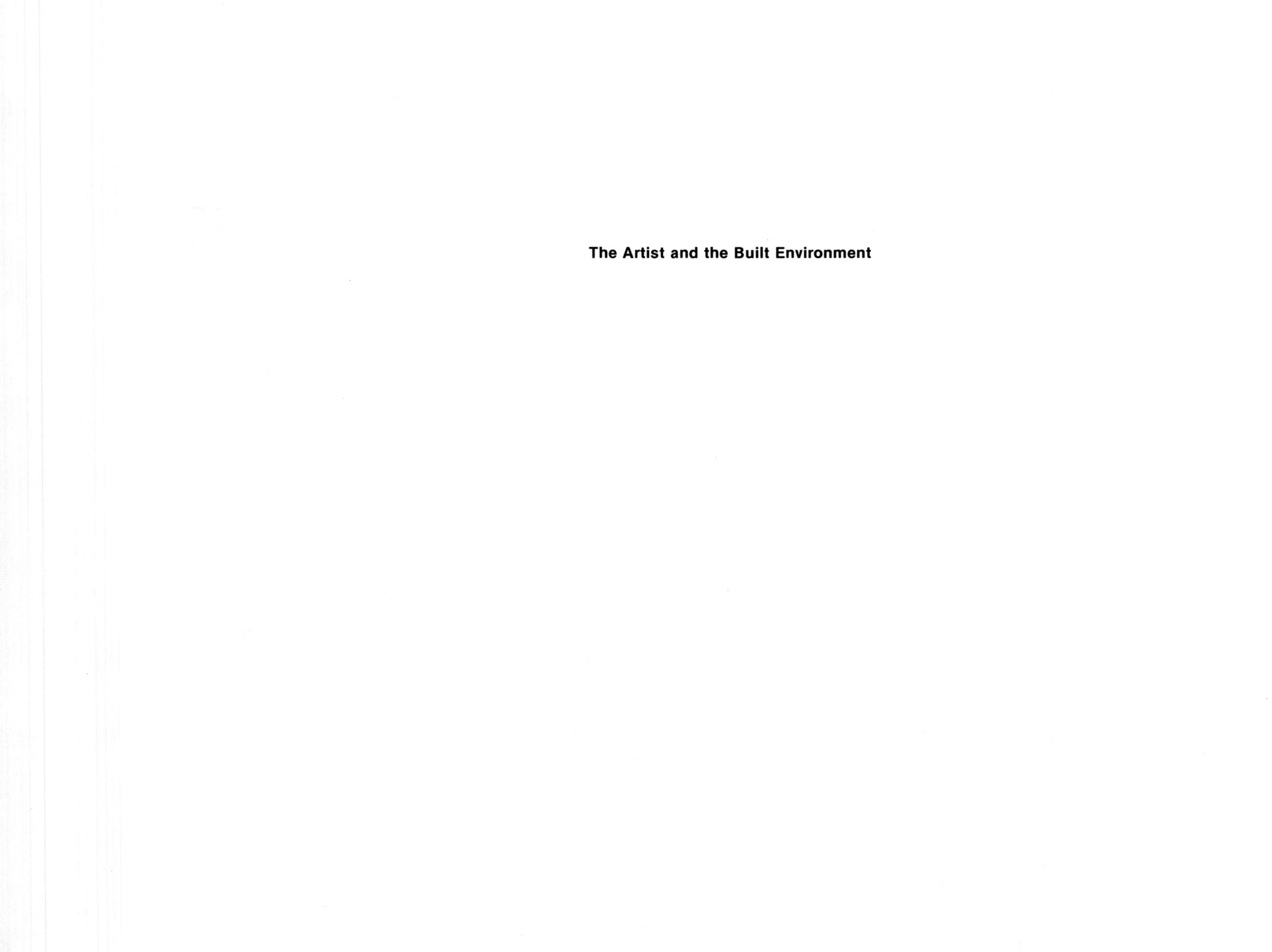

The Artist and the Built Environment

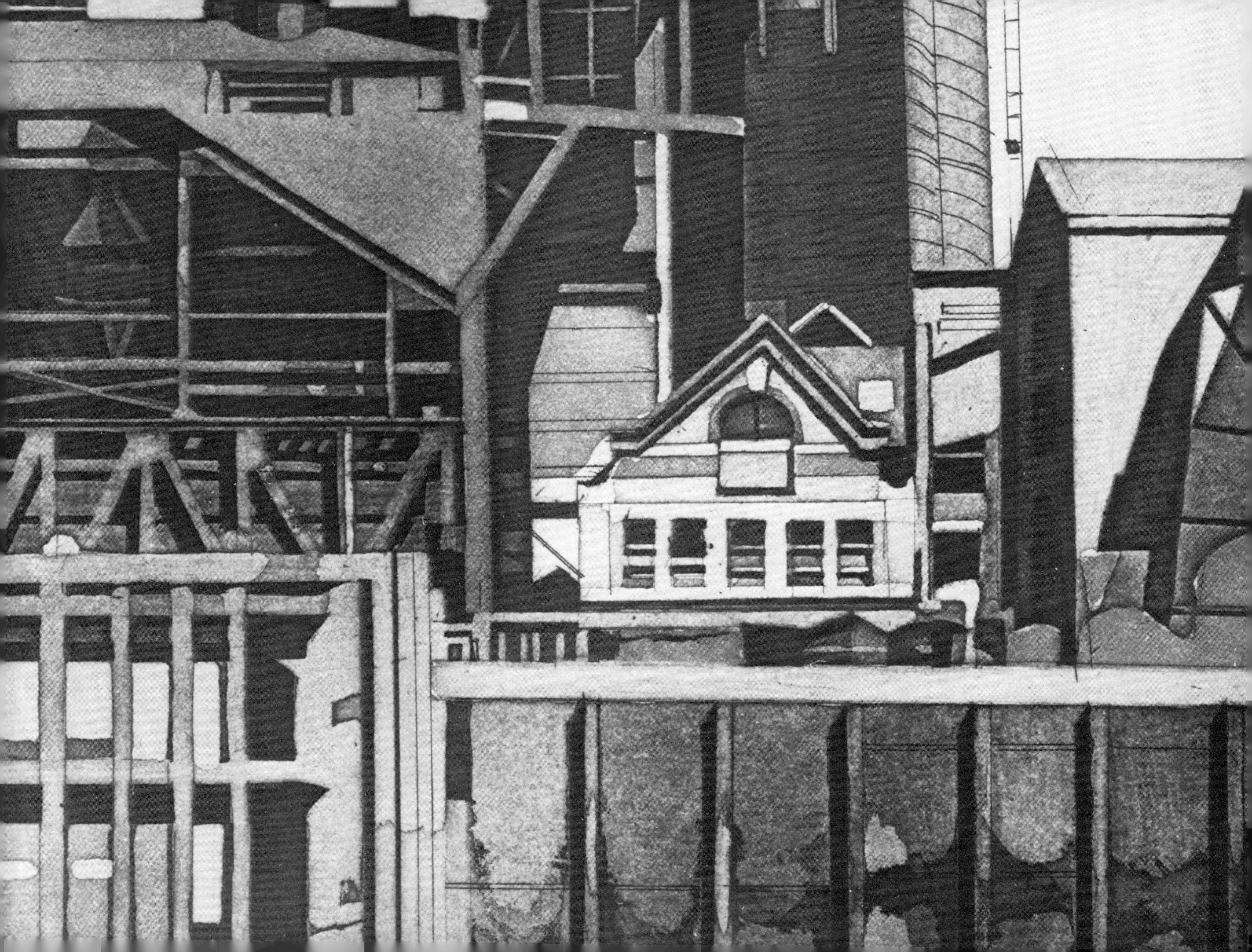

CHAPTER ONE

Cityscapes

In this detail of *Power Station*, there is one of those contrasts that makes the urban environment so surprising and rich in character: a gable-roofed public house virtually engulfed in the giant scale of the warehouses and industrial buildings that surround it. Once it is recognized, as seen in the complete print of this Thames-side scene, it becomes the visual and psychological focus of the whole composition.

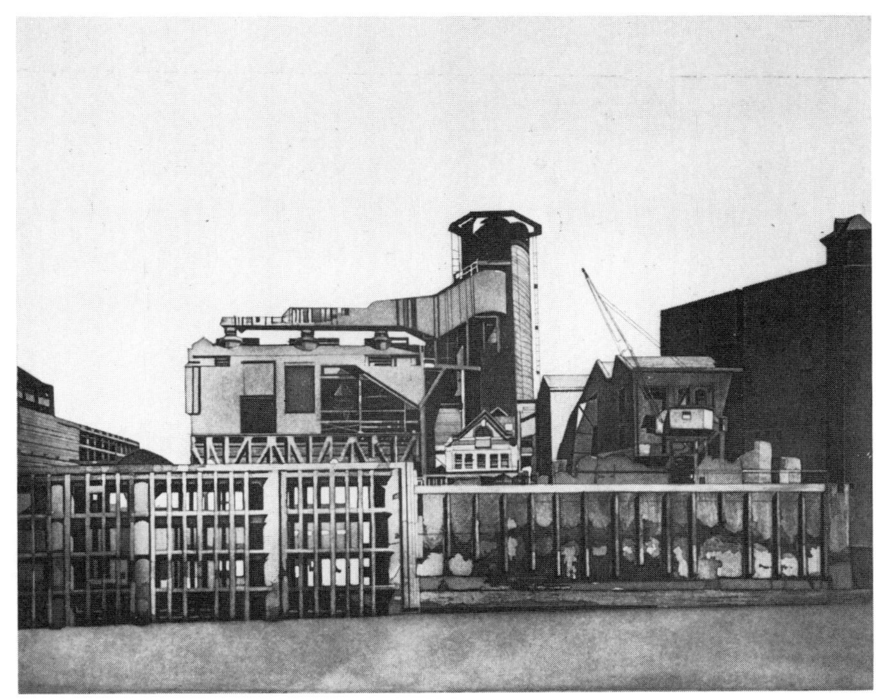

Thames Series II—Power Station, 1975. Etching and aquatint on paper, 20″ x 24″. Sidney Hurwitz.

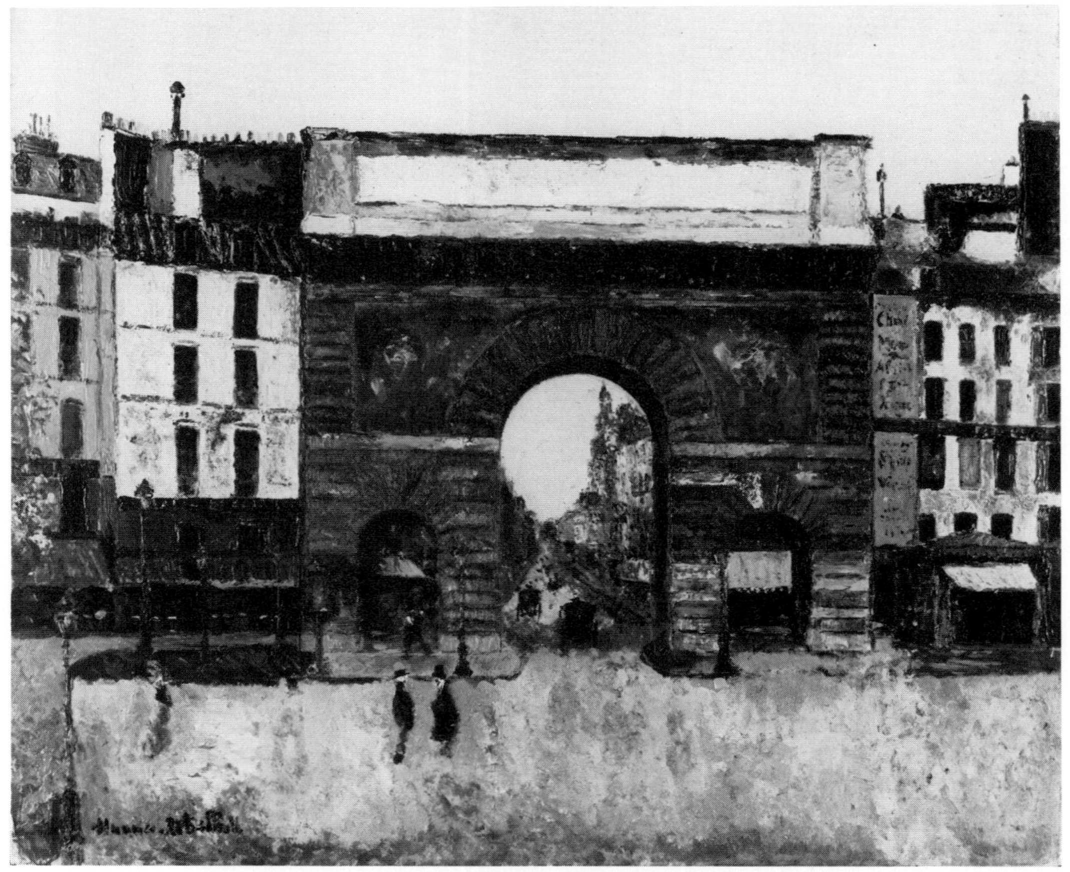

***La Porte Saint Martin*, c. 1910. Oil on board, 31½" x 27¼". Maurice Utrillo. Courtesy, Tate Gallery, London.**

This triumphal arch, erected in 1674 to commemorate a battle victory by Louis XIV, was painted by Utrillo during his White Period (c. 1907-1914) when he was at the peak of his powers. It shows how Utrillo used his impasto technique to build firm, solidly constructed masses and to suggest detail without actually defining it, as in the receding street through the arch.

In spite of the alcoholism that plagued him for most of his life, he managed to produce a large body of work, including a memorable series of the buildings and streets of Montmartre and interpretations of some of the great French cathedrals. At first, he set up his easel in the streets in front of his chosen motifs. After approximately 1909, however, all his paintings were done in his studio, often from postcard views.

An instinctive painter, Utrillo had a remarkable ability with the physical properties of the medium. Sometimes mixing plaster and eggshell with his paints, he achieved a range of luminous, milky whites, pearly grays, and pale blues often contrasted with deep greens, glowing reds, and rich, velvety blacks. At his best, he was able to build strong architectural orchestrations of texture, tone, value, and color combined with atmosphere and intense mood. For Utrillo, the buildings he painted had individuality and souls which he sought to express.

Many artists have found stimulating form and atmosphere above and behind the street facades of the city. The view opposite, painted in the latter part of 1885 from the window of Van Gogh's rented room, shows the functional, unadorned aspects of the cityscape with its chimney extensions, lean-to additions, and random outbuildings. Van Gogh twisted and curved his painted lines and shapes to intensify the mood of a gray, wintry, urban subject.

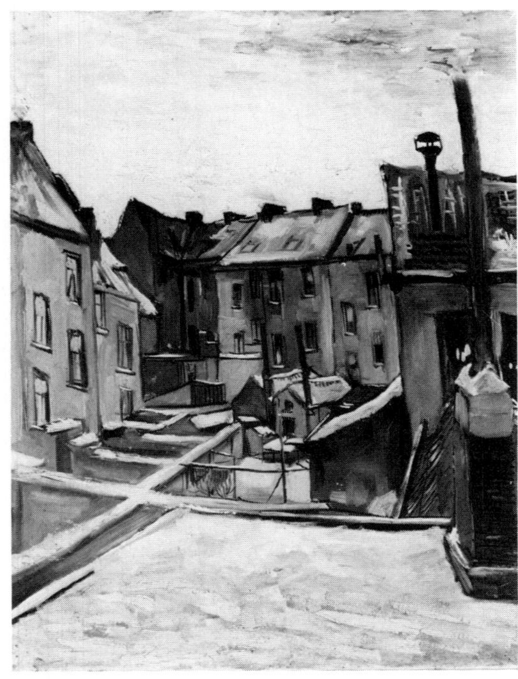

***View from Vincent's Room—Antwerp*, 1885. Oil on canvas, 17½″ x 13″. Vincent Van Gogh. Courtesy of the Vincent Van Gogh National Museum, Amsterdam.**

"One never paints what one sees or thinks one sees; rather, one records with a thousand vibrations, the shock one has received . . . . " (DeStael). In his painting of Paris, the roofs are schematized into heavily troweled blocks of paint. From underneath, a rim of strongly contrasting color is occasionally allowed to show. Pale blues and pinks in the continuous sky area contrast with the patches of light and dark blues, grays, browns, and reds below it. The painting as an object is emphasized by the textured surface of thick paint and the avoidance of any hints of linear perspective. The viewer is left to project into the composition the space that is only implied. From this comes an arresting tension. The painting works as a physical equivalent to the reality of the city roofscape. In his short life, DeStael developed a simplified but powerful and original vision which has expanded our perceptions.

***The Roofs*, 1952. Oil on board, 78″ x 59¼″. Nicolas DeStael. Musee National d'Art Moderne, Centre National d'Art et de Culture G. Pompidou, Paris.**

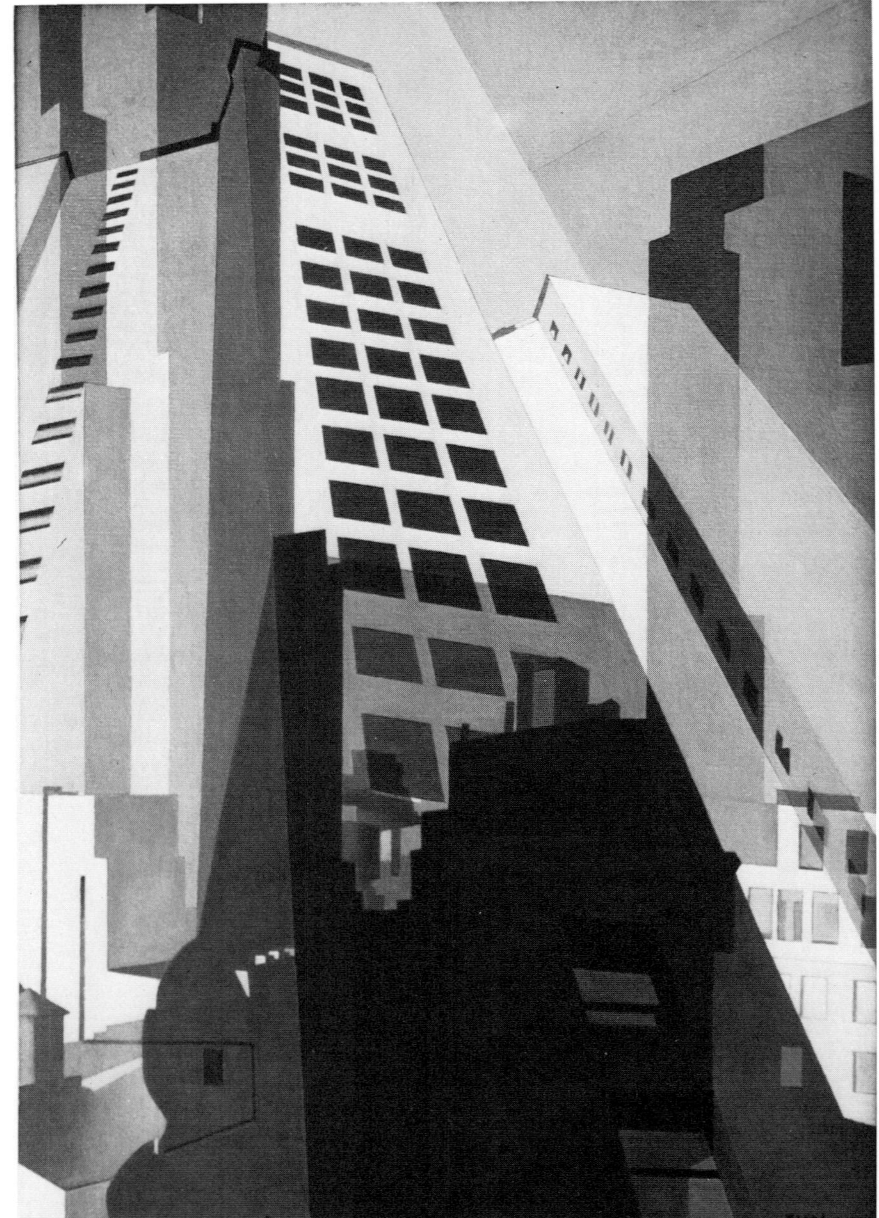

New York #2, 1951. Oil on canvas, 27" x 18⅛". Charles Sheeler. Courtesy of Munson-Williams-Proctor Institute, Utica, New York.

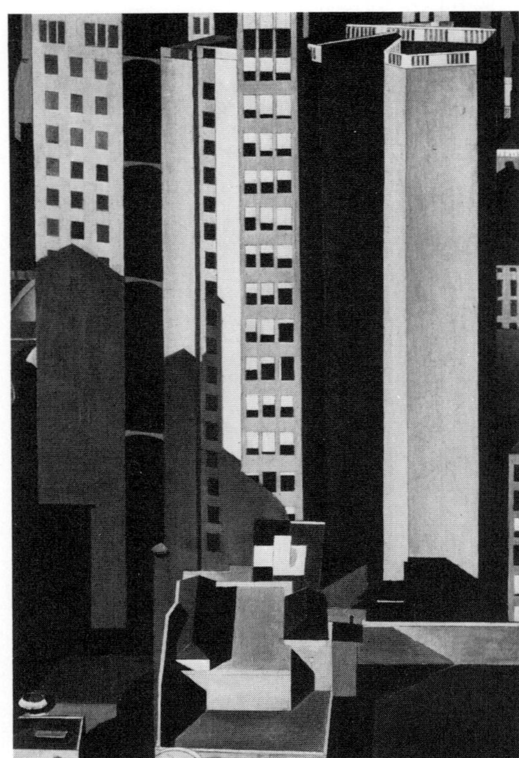

Offices, 1922. Oil on canvas, 20" x 13". Charles Sheeler. The Phillips Collection, Washington, D.C.

More than thirty years and a vastly different concept separate these two works relating to the same subject by Sheeler, yet both have his purified form and geometric clarity. *Offices* has a rigid structure in taut vertical balance with the edges of its planes sharply defined by deep shadows. In *New York #2*, the planes slant and go off in divergent directions. Superimposed photographic negatives were the basis of the multiple viewpoints and prismatic transparencies that bring dynamic movement to this painting.

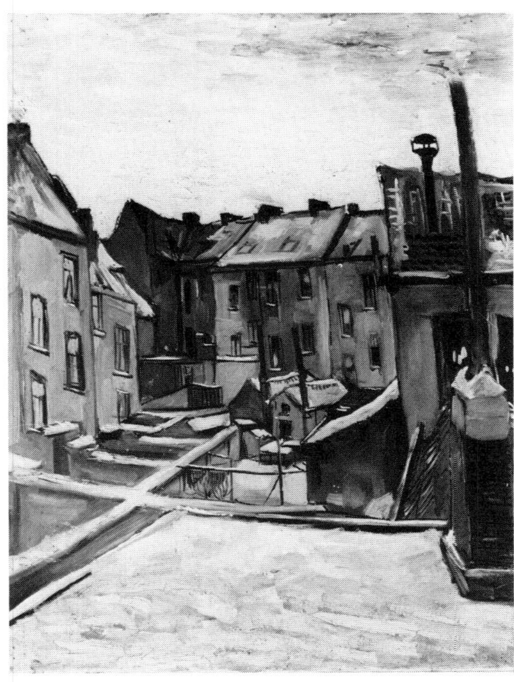

***View from Vincent's Room—Antwerp*, 1885. Oil on canvas, 17½" x 13". Vincent Van Gogh. Courtesy of the Vincent Van Gogh National Museum, Amsterdam.**

"One never paints what one sees or thinks one sees; rather, one records with a thousand vibrations, the shock one has received . . . . " (DeStael). In his painting of Paris, the roofs are schematized into heavily troweled blocks of paint. From underneath, a rim of strongly contrasting color is occasionally allowed to show. Pale blues and pinks in the continuous sky area contrast with the patches of light and dark blues, grays, browns, and reds below it. The painting as an object is emphasized by the textured surface of thick paint and the avoidance of any hints of linear perspective. The viewer is left to project into the composition the space that is only implied. From this comes an arresting tension. The painting works as a physical equivalent to the reality of the city roofscape. In his short life, DeStael developed a simplified but powerful and original vision which has expanded our perceptions.

***The Roofs*, 1952. Oil on board, 78" x 59¼". Nicolas DeStael. Musee National d'Art Moderne, Centre National d'Art et de Culture G. Pompidou, Paris.**

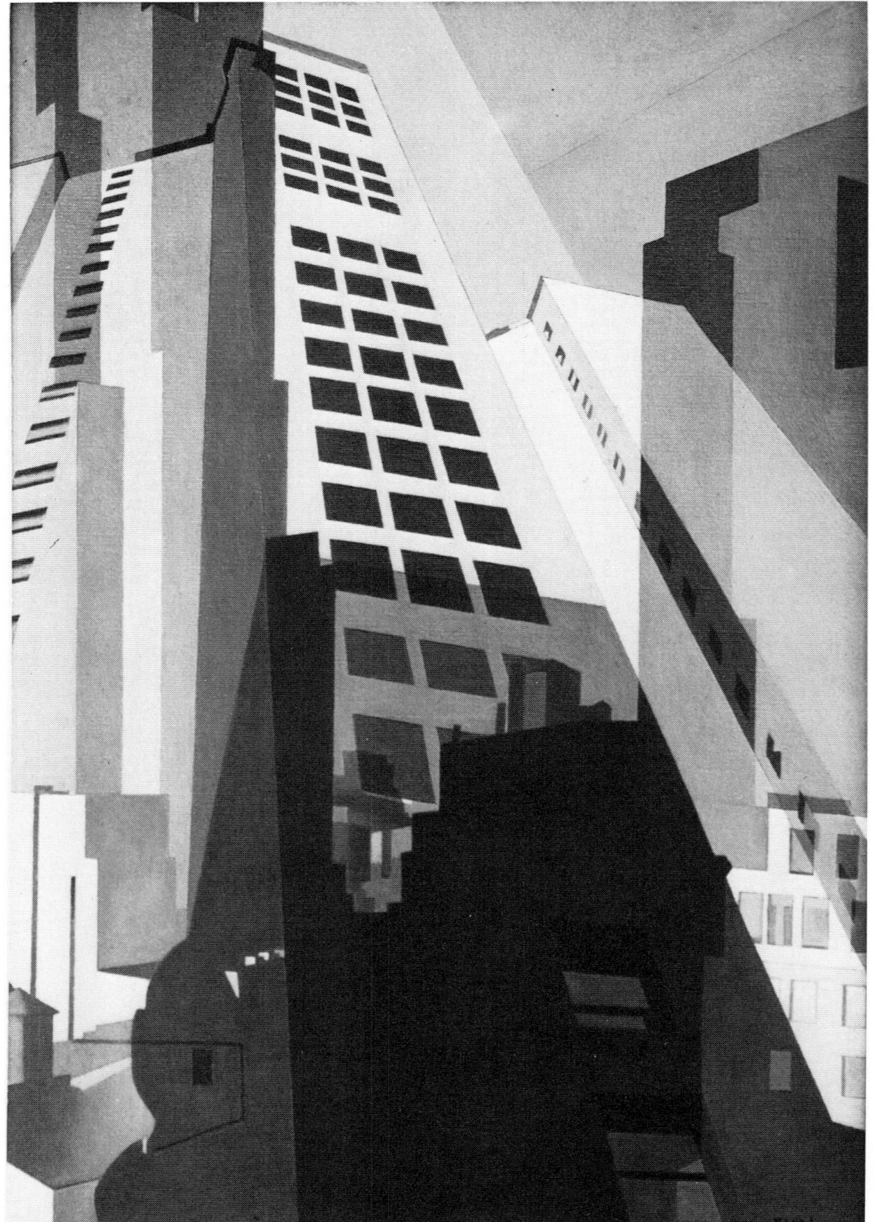

New York #2, 1951. Oil on canvas, 27″ x 18⅛″. Charles Sheeler. Courtesy of Munson-Williams-Proctor Institute, Utica, New York.

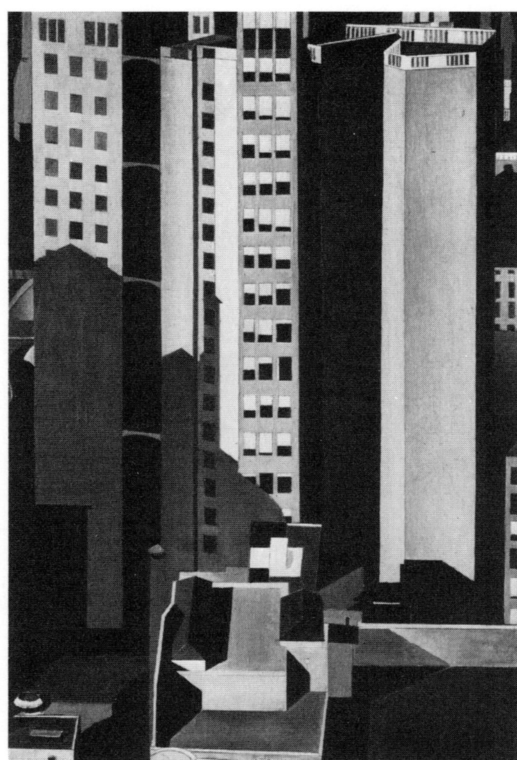

Offices, 1922. Oil on canvas, 20″ x 13″. Charles Sheeler. The Phillips Collection, Washington, D.C.

More than thirty years and a vastly different concept separate these two works relating to the same subject by Sheeler, yet both have his purified form and geometric clarity. *Offices* has a rigid structure in taut vertical balance with the edges of its planes sharply defined by deep shadows. In *New York #2*, the planes slant and go off in divergent directions. Superimposed photographic negatives were the basis of the multiple viewpoints and prismatic transparencies that bring dynamic movement to this painting.

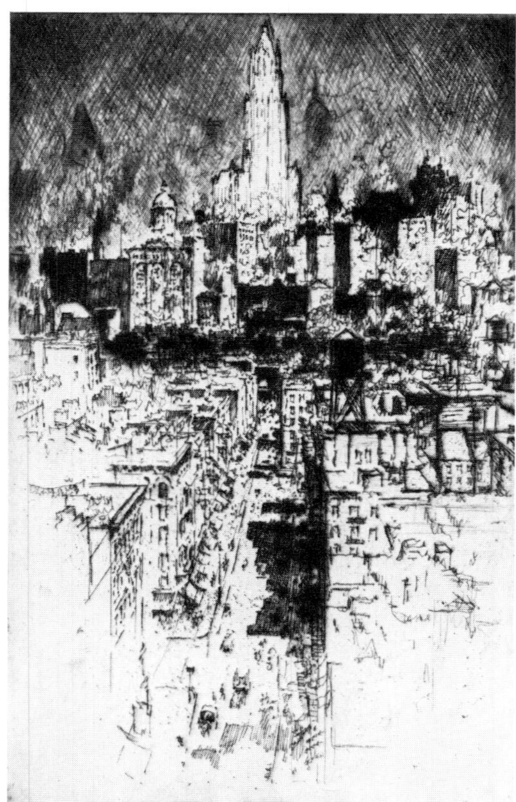

Up to the Woolworth, **1915. Etching, 11⅞″ x 7¾″. Joseph Pennell. From the collection of The Library of Congress, Washington, D.C.**

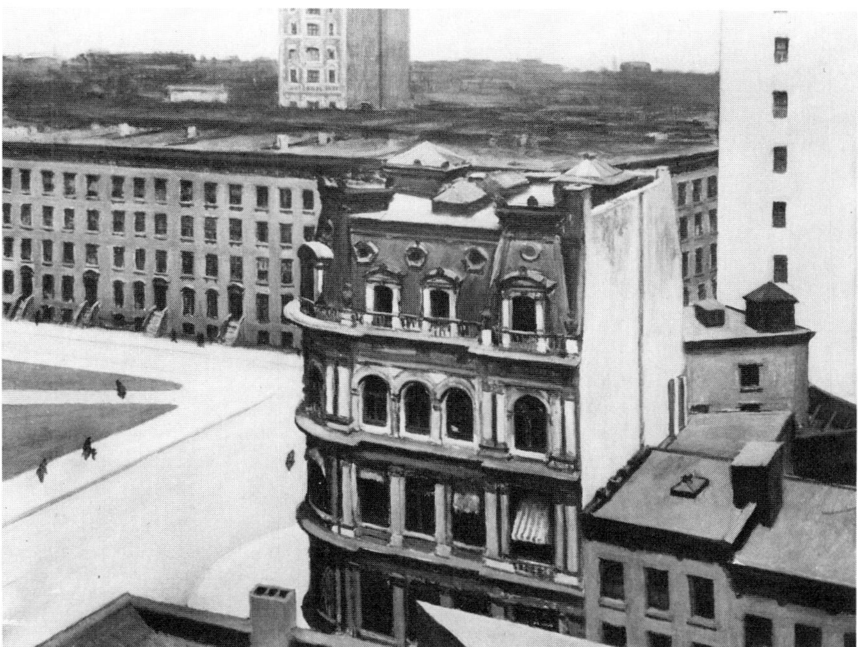

The City, **1927. Oil, 28″ x 36″. Edward Hopper. Courtesy of the Museum of Art, University of Arizona, Tucson, the C. Leonard Pfeiffer Collection of American Art.**

Joseph Pennell considered the New York skyline "the most wonderful view in the world" and he did numerous etchings of it from 1906 to the end of his life. In his famous World War I poster, *That Liberty Shall Not Perish*, he pictured it in flames with a bomb-shattered Statue of Liberty in the foreground. This lively, Impressionist cityscape uses a cross as its compositional anchor. Its line technique may owe something to Whistler, whom Pennell knew and admired.

Edward Hopper's ability to capture the spirit of a building or an architectural style was remarkable. By simplification and elimination of any detail that does not contribute to the mood, he has given the French Empire-style building in the center foreground a striking monumentality and presence. Similarly, there is a lonely majesty about the building at the center top of the picture that towers over a sea of flat roofs. Note how those roofs are merely suggested; hints are given for the viewer to complete.

Most of his early work was painted "after the fact", as he would say. Later, his oils were studio-painted from memory and observation. These tended to be composites rather than transcriptions of a particular motif. As the years went on, he spent more and more time carefully choosing subjects and planning the composition. He would make many on-location sketches of details and then develop the overall composition in a larger drawing. These sketches were not carried too far, as he feared he might copy them rather than the concept in his mind. He preferred to work out a picture on the canvas: painting, scraping off, and repainting. Towards the end of his life, this process took as long as a year whereas many of his early oils were finished within a week.

Beneath the El, **1973. Watercolor on paper, 13½" x 18".**

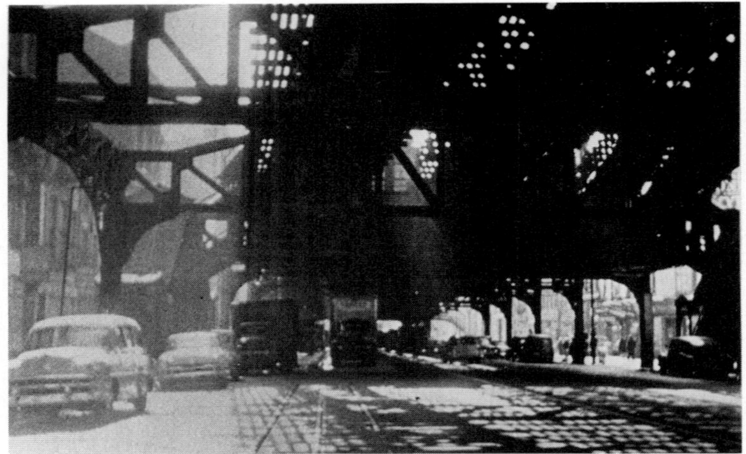

Photograph of New York's vanished Third Avenue El, taken in the early 1950s.

An important feature in some older American cities was the elevated railway. The el still survives, notably in Chicago where it defines the Loop. Although it did produce noise and darkened streets, it also created a sense of excitement. Its steel structure wound through the city between tall buildings, rising, dipping, and curving as it responded to features in the cityscape. For the visually minded, it offered a variety of delights: a lacy and high structure that broke light into millions of geometric shapes. At station stops, it widened to encompass pitched-roof waiting rooms and elaborately articulated covered stairways. From below, it was a fantastic black sculpture which caused light to break into shafts and myriad dots, casting zebralike patterns on the streets and traffic.

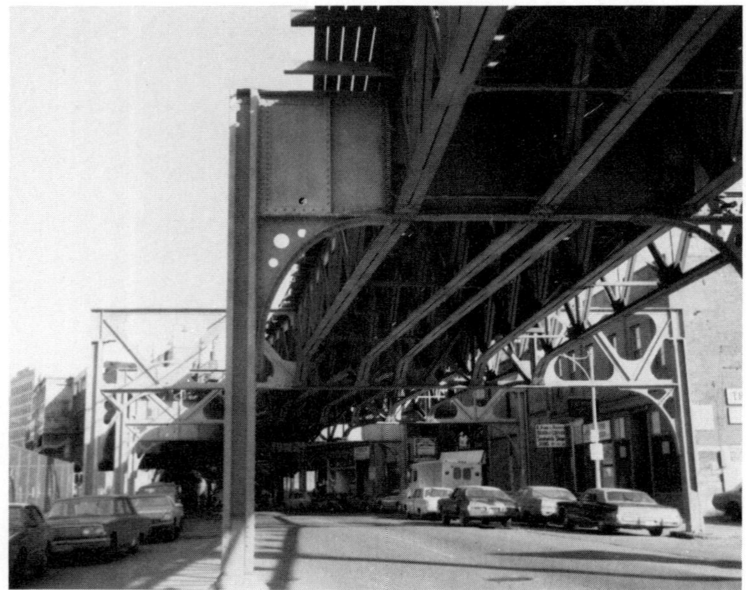

Photograph, Boston's South End, 1978.

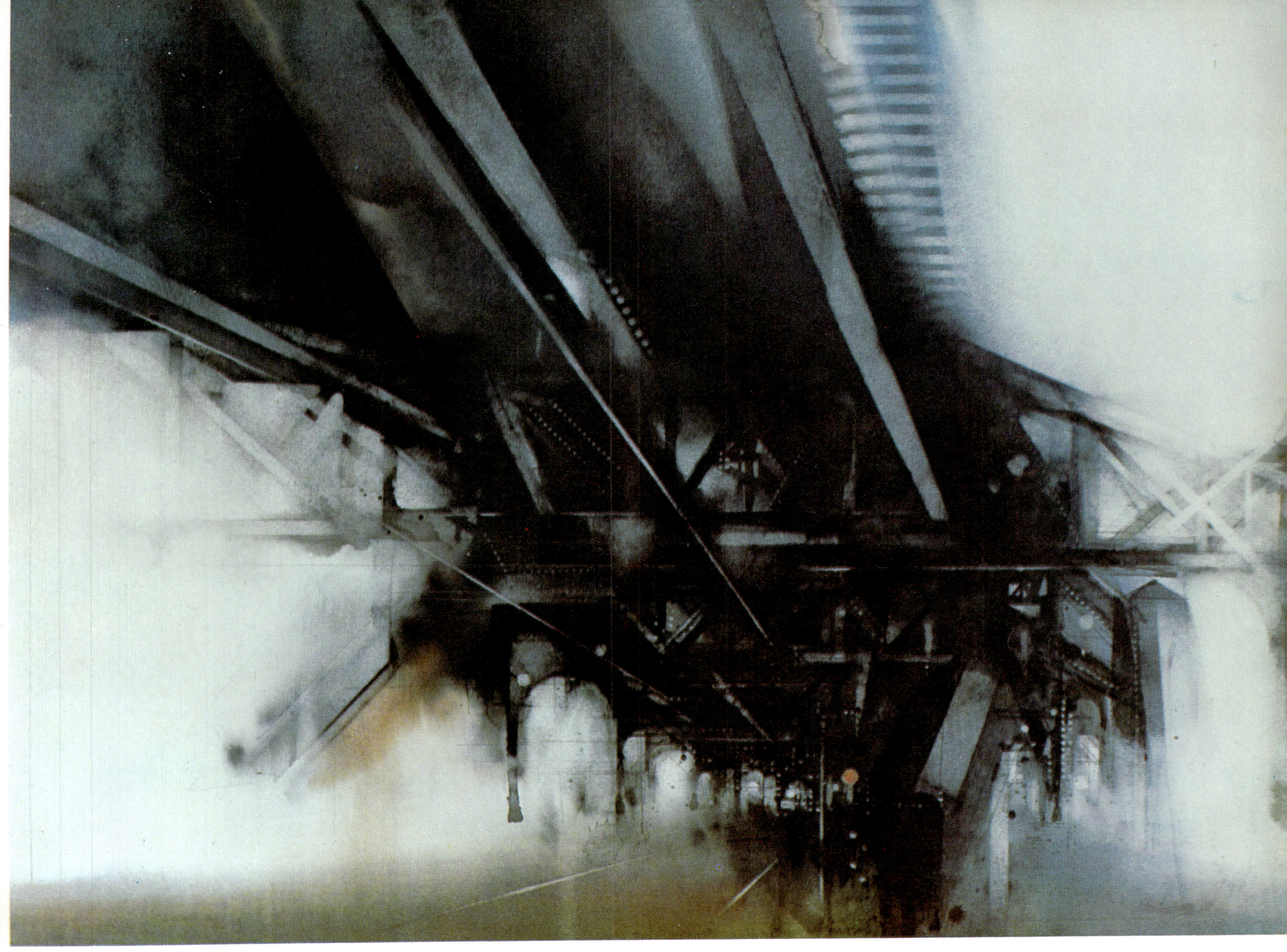

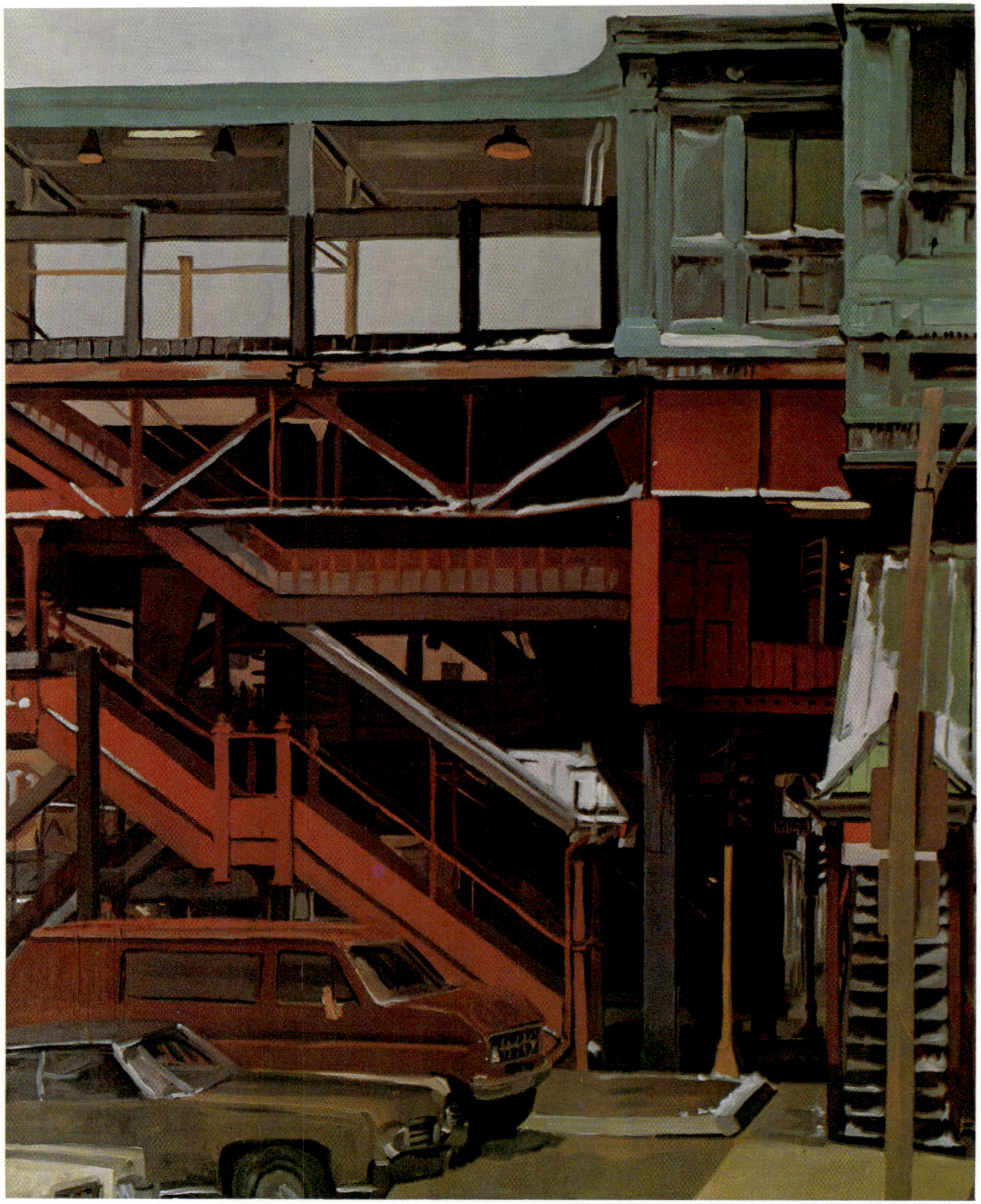

Dover Street Station, **Boston, 1978. Oil on canvas, 40″ x 48″. George Nick.**

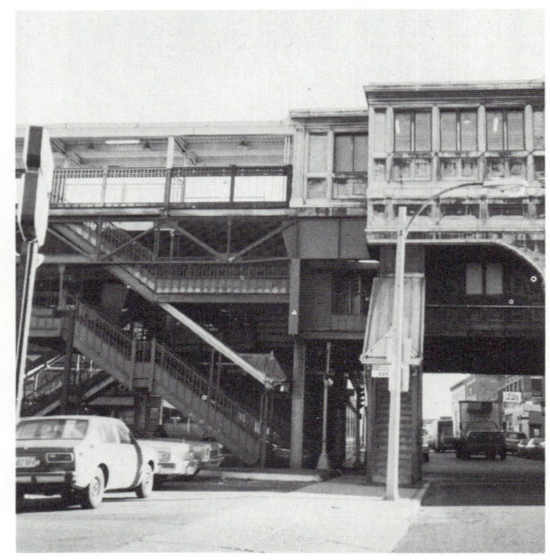

One morning in the latter part of 1978, George Nick parked his mobile studio on Dover Street in Boston. With the back window facing the el station, he began this painting. He returned to the same spot at the same time on many mornings to develop and complete it.

George Nick has said, "I always feel the act of painting reveals the observation. I trust my instincts and rarely feel I either understand why I have selected a certain subject or what the painting will look like. The process of painting reveals what I am studying so carefully and the surprise development of the piece which in turn delights me."

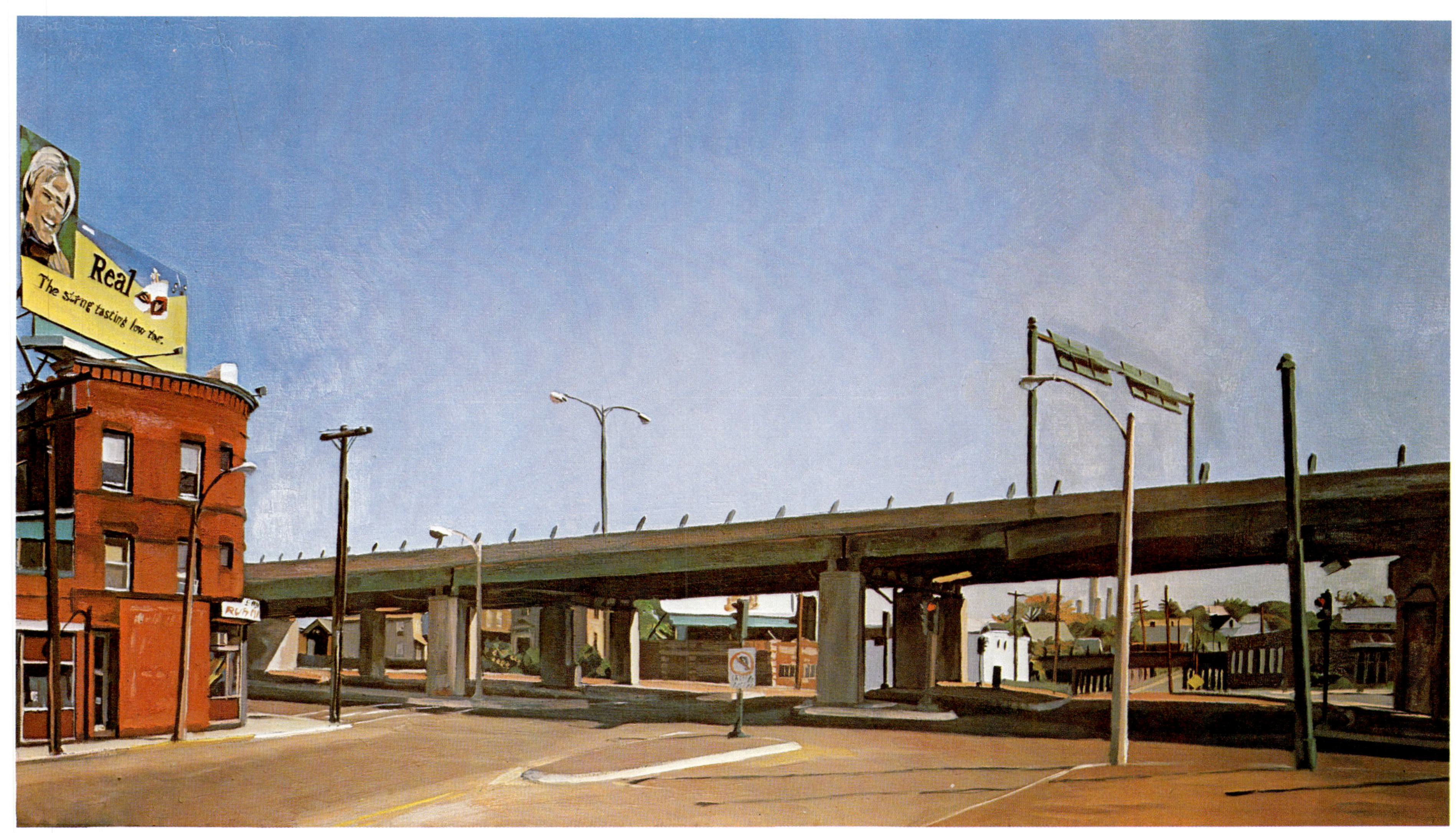

McGrath Highway Bridge, Somerville, 1978. Oil on canvas, 34″ x 60″. George Nick.

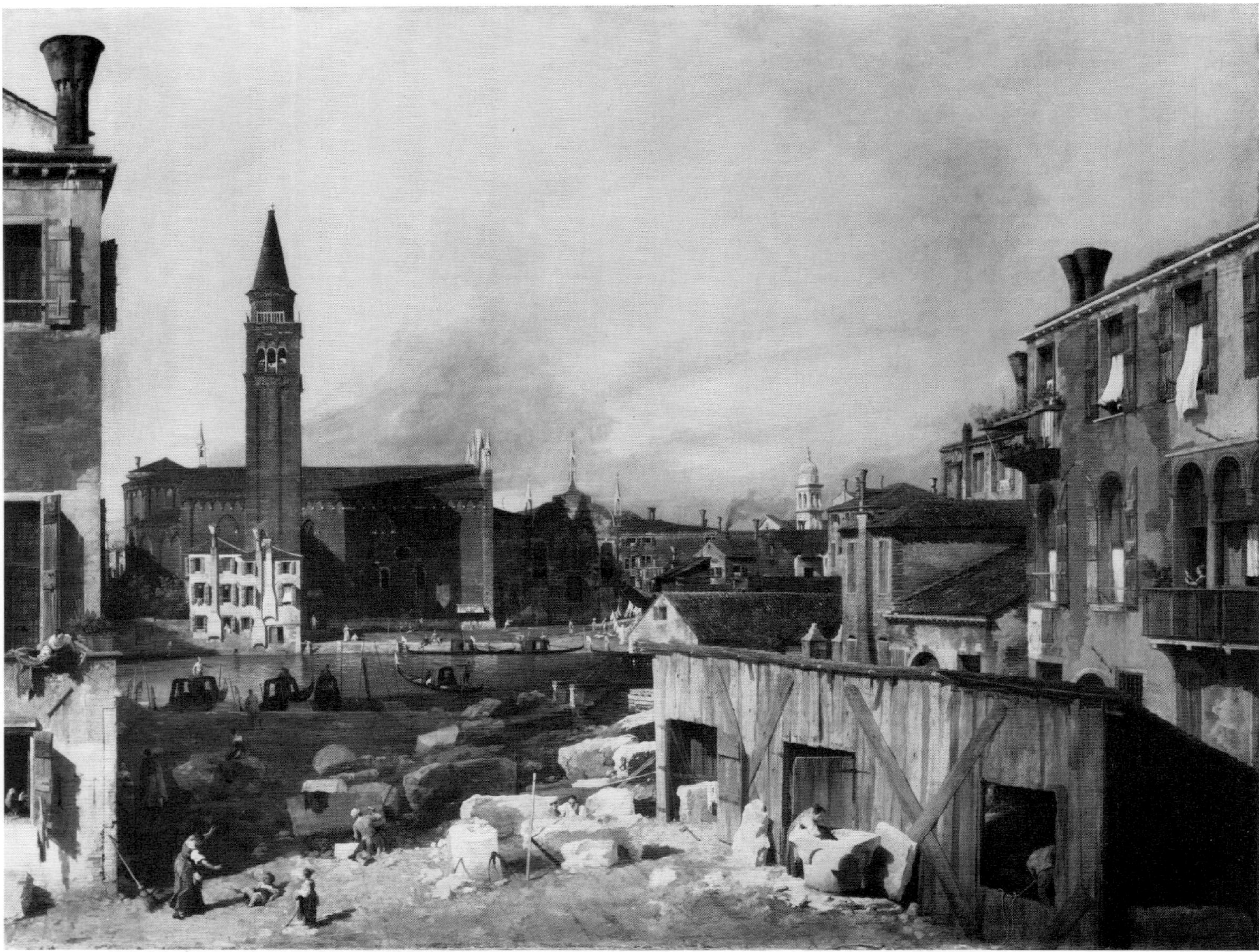

***The Stonemason's Yard*. c. 1730. 64⅛" x 48¾". Antonio Canaletto. Courtesy of the Trustees of The National Gallery, London.**

This view across the Grand Canal in Venice represented accurate, detailed topographical painting, and was early proof that a landscape could be a work of art expressing depth of feeling. Light was crucial to Canaletto's special vision. In his early work, he employed the romantic chiaroscuro evident in this painting. In later works, light is handled in a more descriptive and clearly defined way. Mechanical aids, such as the camera obscura, brought reality to his views, but it was his manipulation of light and shadow that brought life to them. In *Stonemason's Yard*, the passages of light and dark playing across the buildings, sharpening or softening contours, forcing parts forward or into recession result in an orchestration of space, form, and atmosphere.

Canaletto used his considerable talent to delineate the great cities of Venice and London in pictures which persuaded the viewers to see the cityscape in a new way.

This highly romantic panorama (right) is painted in a thin, stained, veillike manner more often associated with watercolor than with oil. The subtle composition depicts the intricately structured complexity of the city through suggestion rather than explicit delineation. Blurred hints of detail are given to the viewer to complete.

By dragging the dark shapes of windows and chimney pots vertically, a counterpoint is set up with the tree trunks at left and the towers, spires, chimneys, and domes in the distance. Softly painted edges of roof caps, cornices, and chimney tops seem to catch the light and give the picture a glowing luminosity. This is again focused on and intensified by the reflected light on the surface of the river Seine.

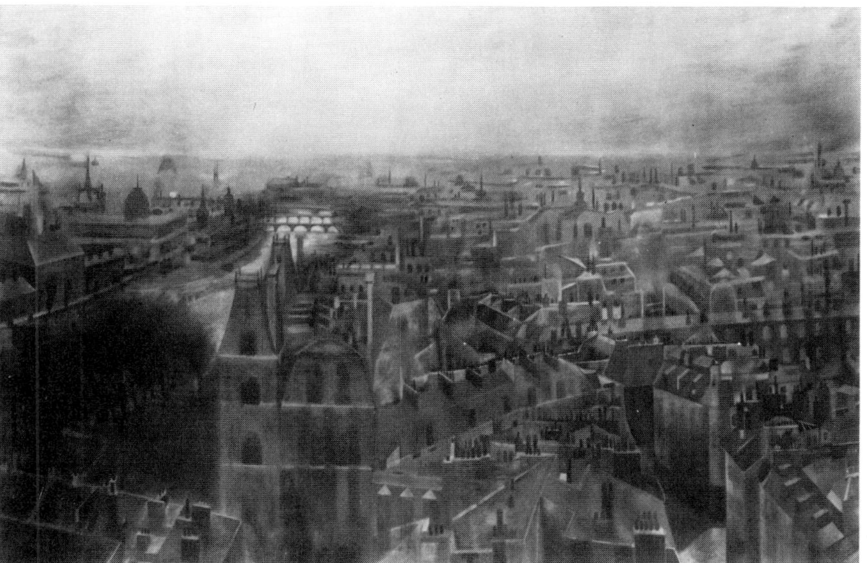

***Paris*, 1949. Oil on canvas, 42″ x 62″. Loren MacIver. Courtesy of The Metropolitan Museum of Art, New York, the George A. Hearn Fund.**

"Always the mass, the whole, that which particularly strikes us. Never lose the first impression by which we are moved. . . . Give in to the initial impression. If we have really been touched, the sincerity of our feelings will be communicated to others." Corot's words express the attitude which could produce this painting in such sensitive, caressing brush strokes, and clear, warm light. Although simply handled, the effect of rich architectural detail and a lyrical portrayal of the texture and color of earth, stone, water, and sky are present. It is a more bucolic Paris than we know today, one through which the Seine seems to meander, not yet controlled by straight, stone quays.

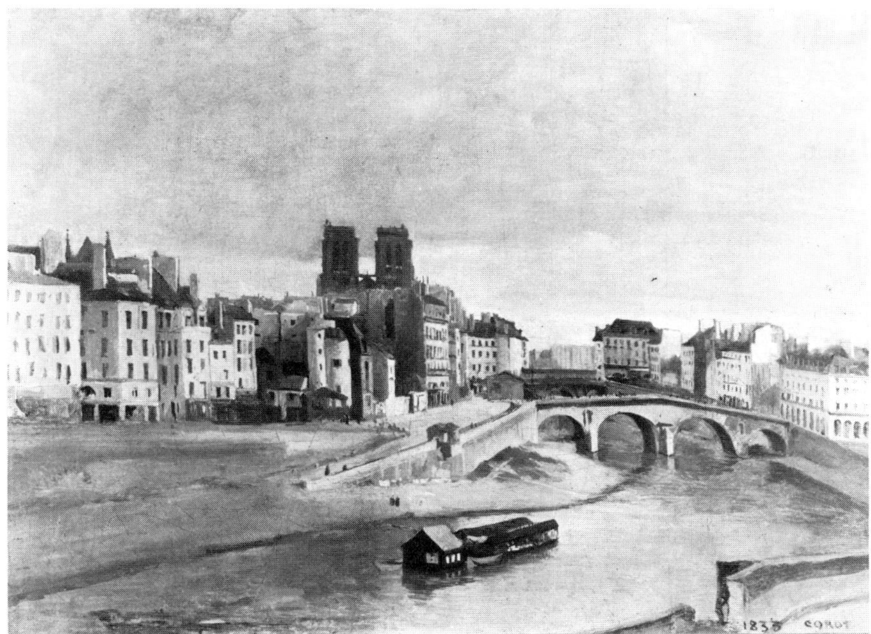

***La Seine et Le Quai des Orfevres*, 1833. Oil on paper, 24¾″ x 18⅛″. Camille Corot. Courtesy, Musee Carnavalet, Paris. Photograph by Lauros-Giraudon.**

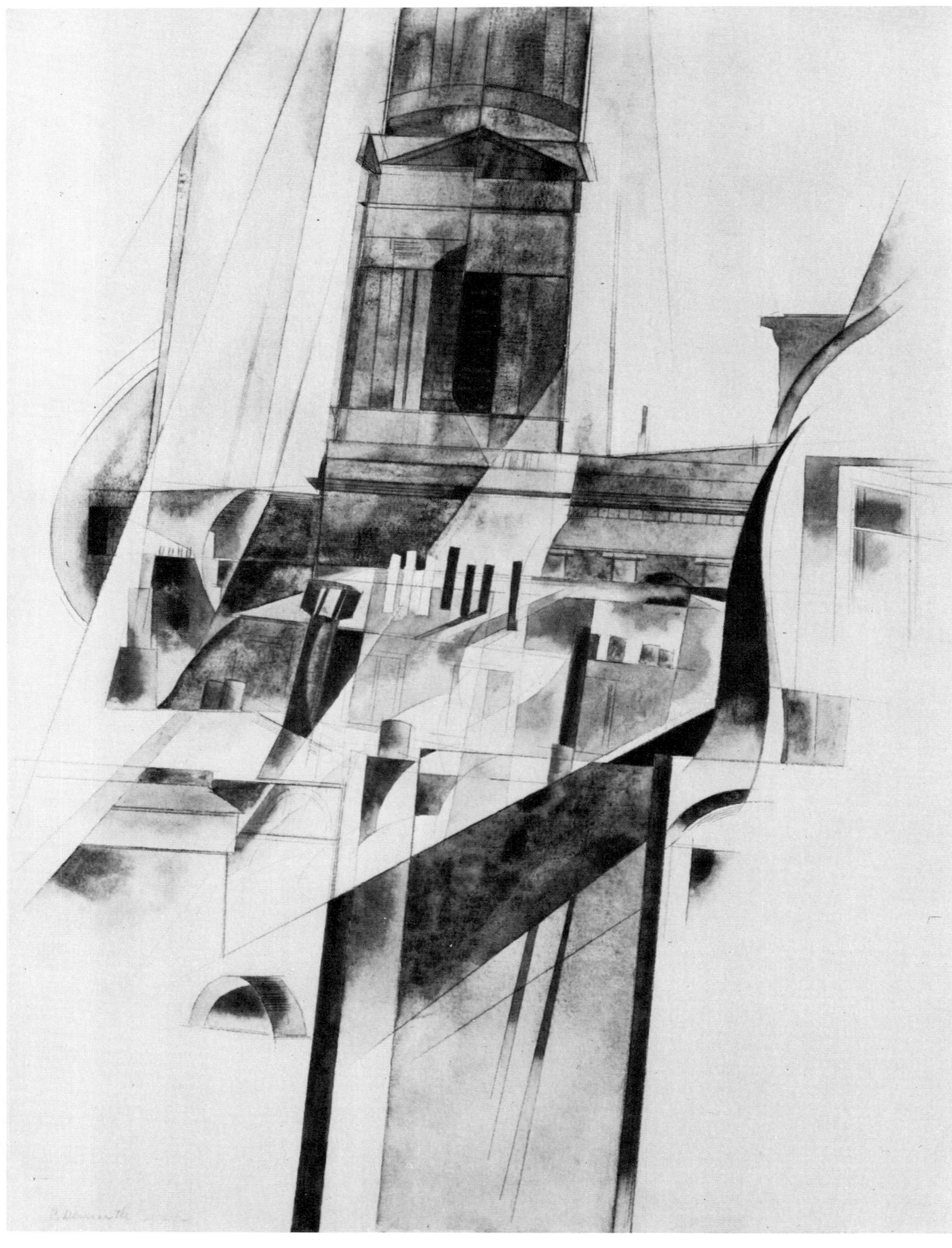

***Church and Steeple*, 1921. Watercolor on paper, 14¼" x 10⅞". Charles Demuth. Courtesy of The Brooklyn Museum, the Dick S. Ramsay Fund.**

Watercolor was a favorite medium of Demuth's and he excelled in it. Unlike his oils, in which paint covers the entire surface, Demuth's watercolors are vignetted and float, anchored, if at all, to certain points at the edge of the paper. He allowed the white paper to remain as a vital contribution to his compositions. The Cubist lines of force, multiple viewpoints, and fractured planes are all here, handled with a spare, elegant, knifelike crispness.

Demuth came from Lancaster, Pennsylvania, where he grew up in the shadow of a fine Wren-inspired colonial church tower. It seems likely that this early exposure to the white-painted wooden architecture of America led him to the numerous studies he later made of buildings in Lancaster, Bermuda, and New England.

"I have to live some time in a place before I can begin producing genuine expressions of my reactions to the place." It was the gritty, industrial towns of eastern Ohio and western New York in which Burchfield lived all of his life that provided the subject matter which he painted intensively during his middle period (1919 to 1943). The weathered nineteenth century houses with their sagging porches, stained clapboards, stark windows, and sharply silhouetted roof lines caught his interest. To these somber motifs he brought some of his Expressionist intensity which characterized the periods of fantasy before and after this middle period. With an overpowering, poetic mood, his paintings record the shapes, forms, and details of the eastern factory town architecture. He said, "If I presented them in all their garish and crude pretentiousness and unlovely decay, it was merely through a desire to be honest about them."

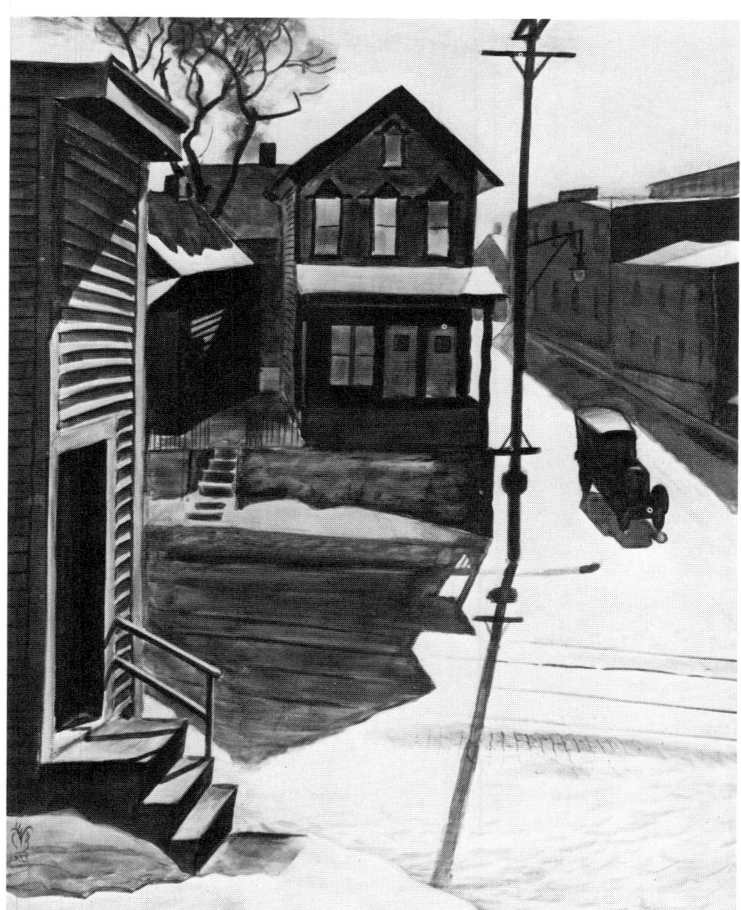

Ice Glare, 1933. Watercolor, 30¾″ x 24¾″. Charles Burchfield. Courtesy, Whitney Museum of American Art, New York.

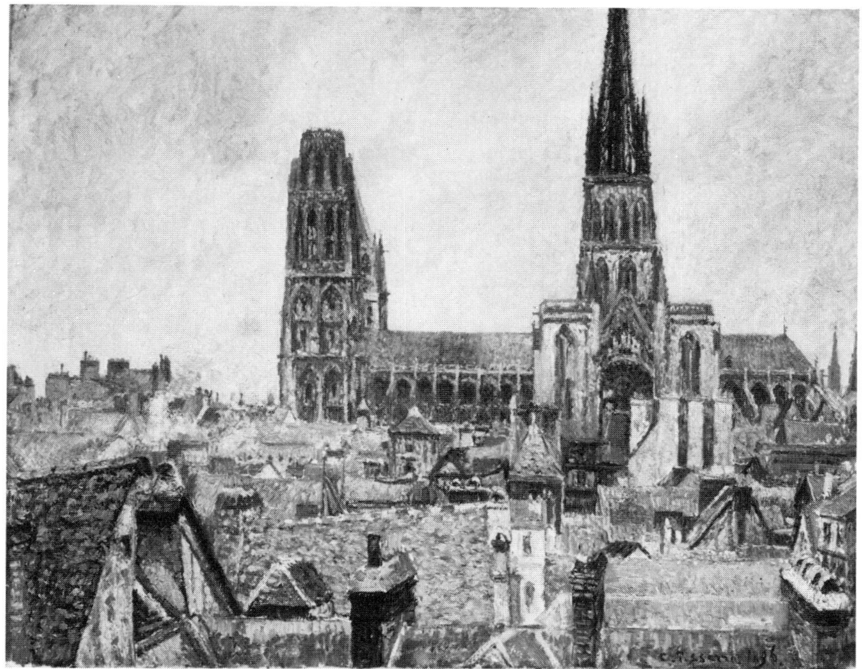

The Roofs of Old Rouen, 1896. Oil on canvas, 28½″ x 36″. Camille Pissarro. Courtesy of The Toledo Museum of Art, Toledo, Ohio. Gift of Edward Drummond Libbey.

Painted towards the end of his life, this lateral view of the great cathedral of Rouen shows Pissarro's keen observation of light and atmosphere. While the surface flickers with the broken color and the vigorous sketchlike brushwork of Impressionism, the architectural integrity of the subject remains firm underneath it.

The special appeal of this motif is in the geometric shapes, planes, and scale changes of the buildings surrounding the harbor. The large forms in the foreground contrast to similar but miniaturized forms within the intricate band across the background.

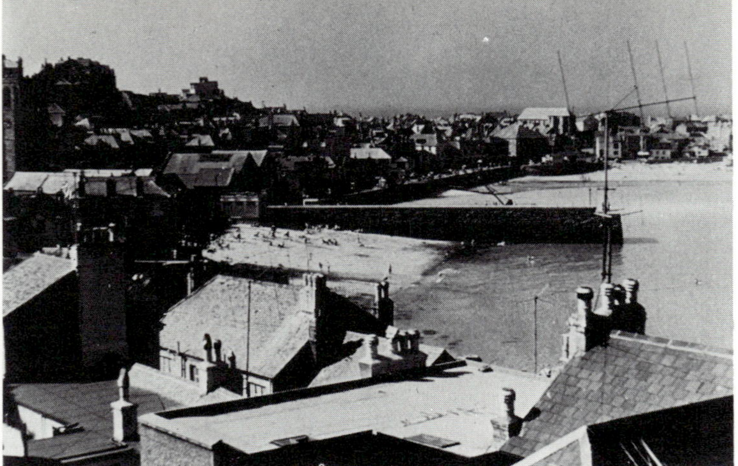

***Saint Ives Roofs and Harbor*, 1979. Watercolor on paper, 13″ x 20″.**

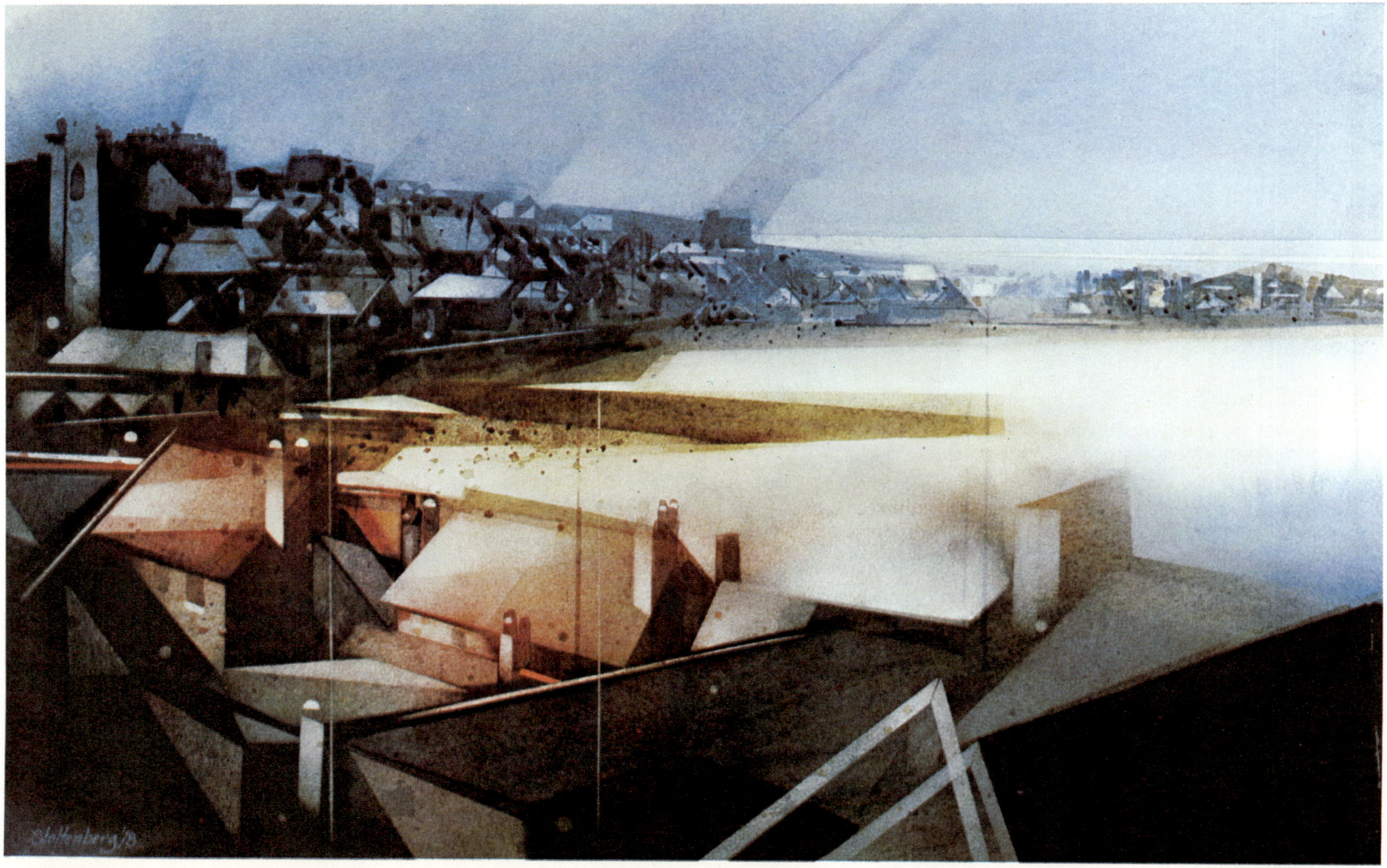

The scene is reduced in the drawing to a pattern of lines that correspond to the edges and corners of the buildings. It emphasizes the rich pattern of shapes by abstracting them out of tone and color.

The small (lower right) watercolor submerges the drawing in favor of a flowing movement of lights and darks. After roughly sketching the forms in pencil, water was sponged over the entire surface. The watercolor pigment was allowed to flow, being confined only in a very general way, so that the roof shapes would seem to float. Tones were massed to form a large C-shape. The dark shadows, walls, and roofs were put in while the paper was still wet to prevent any hard edges. After drying completely, masks were used to sponge out lights, chimneys, gables, and the strip of water at the far side of the harbor.

The emphasis in the larger watercolor is on the geometric forms, taking a cue from the sharp shapes in the sun and the shadow of roofs, walls, chimneys, sea walls, and pier. The color and light are an exaggeration of those found in the motif. Perhaps the greatest distortion occurs in the values in which the lights are grouped in a horizontal shape across the middle of the composition, with the strongest contrasts being saved for the roofs and chimneys at the middle left. The aim was to emphasize the glowing warmth of the harbor by giving a darker, cool contrast above and below it.

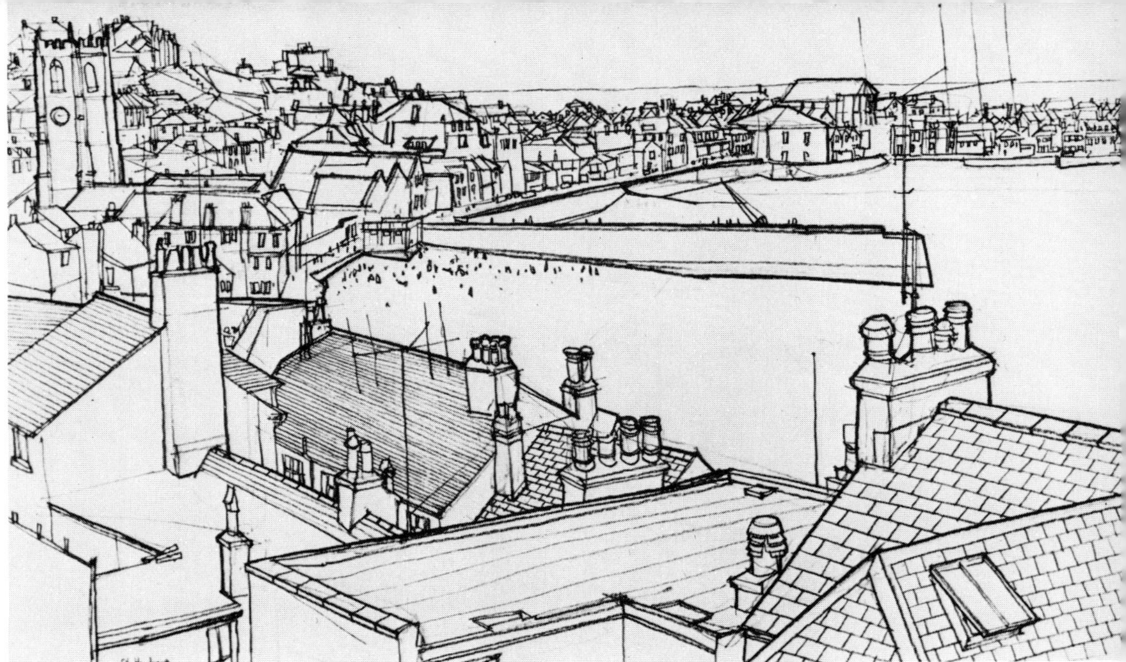

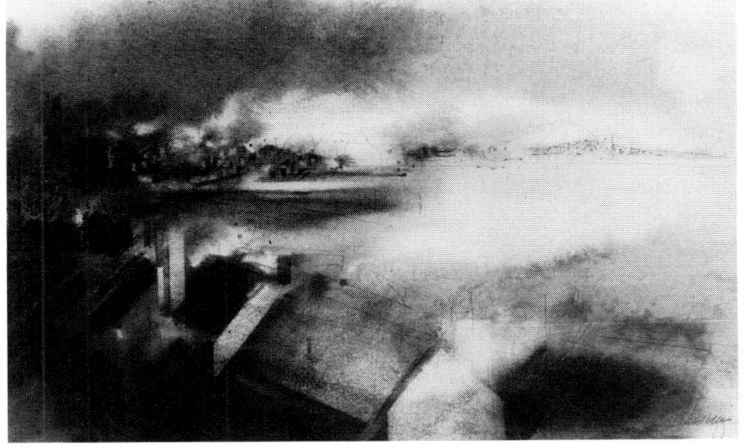

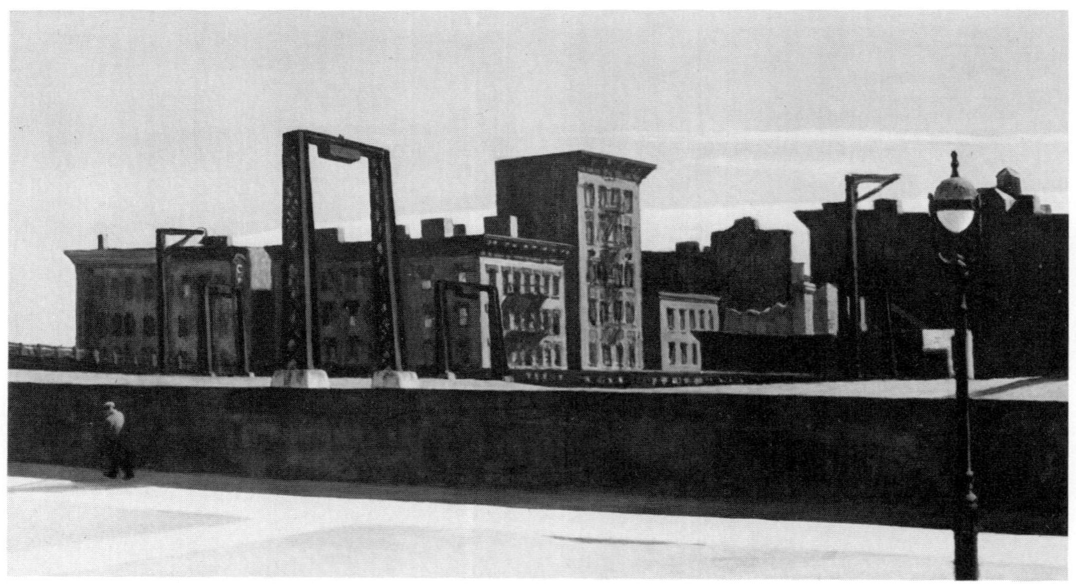

Manhattan Bridge Loop, 1928. Oil, 35″ x 60″. Edward Hopper. Courtesy of The Addison Gallery of Art, Phillips Academy, Andover, Massachusetts.

"I spend many days usually before I find a subject that I like well enough to do, and spend a long time on the proportions of the canvas, so that it will do for the design, as nearly as possible, what I wish it to do. The very long horizontal shape of this picture, *Manhattan Bridge Loop*, is an effort to give a sensation of great lateral extent. Carrying the main horizontal lines of the design with little interruption to the edges of the picture is to enforce this idea and to make one conscious of the spaces and elements beyond the limits of the scene itself.

"The picture was planned very carefully in my mind before starting it, but except for a few small black-and-white sketches made from the fact, I had no other concrete data, but relied on refreshing my memory by looking often at the subject . . . . The color, design, and form have all been subjected, consciously or otherwise, to considerable simplification.

"My aim in painting has always been the most exact transcription possible of my most intimate impressions of nature." (Edward Hopper)

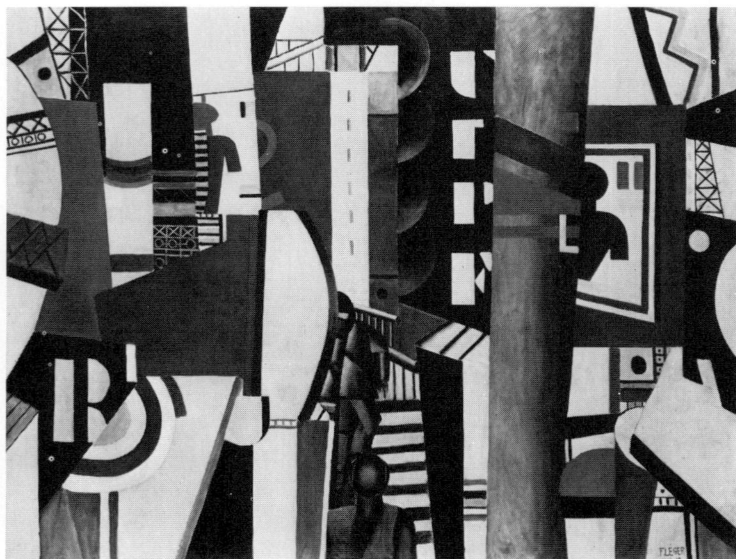

The City, 1919. Oil on canvas, 91″ x 117″. Fernand Leger. Courtesy of the Philadelphia Museum of Art, The A. E. Gallatin Collection.

Leger was a Cubist painter before the First World War. He was profoundly affected by his years at the front in contact with modern precision engineering. His forms and colors became influenced by machinery with its brightly code-painted pipes and ducts. The immediate impetus for *The City*, painted just after the war, was the Place Clichy, site of the largest advertising posters in Paris. It is a synthesis of the most dissonant and modern bits and pieces of the city reassembled into a patterned abstraction. Avoiding any reference to perspective space, it does seem to relate to the layered fragments of posters commonly seen on city walls.

In this dynamic cityscape, the steep San Francisco streets are compressed as if seen through a telescope. The usual devices for establishing distance in a landscape—diminishing scale, converging and vanishing perspective lines, atmospheric weakening of sharpness and color—are minimized. Instead, streets and houses become blocks of color piled up on one another, overlapping, and forming planar abstractions which are essentially two dimensional. As the eye discovers the three-dimensional subject, a stimulating conflict occurs and the mind tries to reconcile the two. The viewer is forced to see the cityscape in a new way. As Thiebaud said, "Common objects become strangely uncommon when removed from their context and ordinary ways of being seen."

If the concept of this painting is supercharged, so too is its execution. Emphasis on the physicality of oil paint authoritatively applied makes the reality of walls, roofs, and pavements tangible. Color is raised in pitch, particularly at the edges of planes and where obliquely seen walls become intensified chromatic lines. Lines of all kinds—wires, poles, pipes, and lane markings—thrust, crisscross, define, and stiffen. Awareness is heightened as the eye explores and recognizes familiar urban forms juxtaposed in new and unfamiliar combinations.

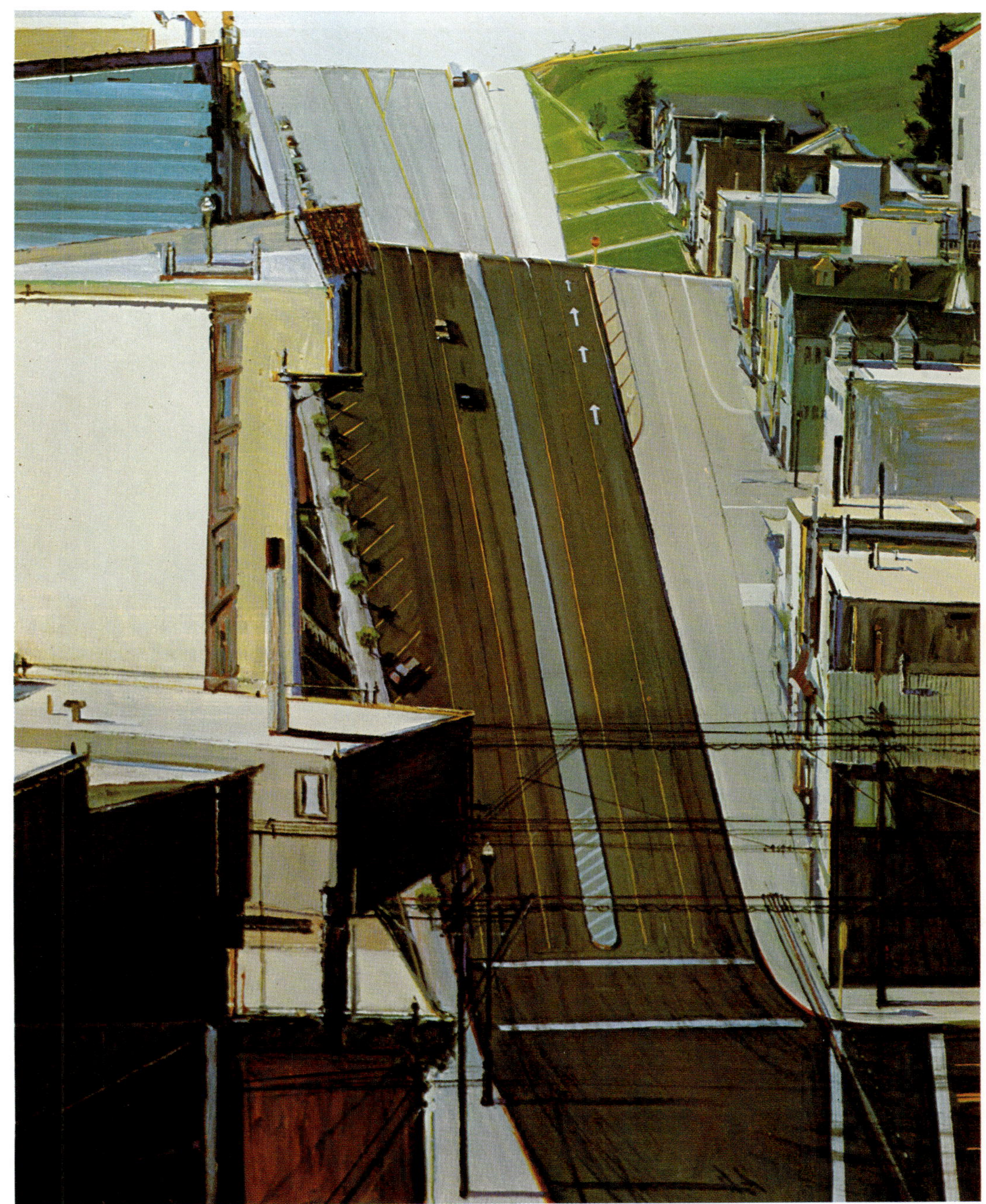

***Down from Twin Peaks*, 1977. Oil on canvas, 16″ x 22″. Wayne Thiebaud. Photograph courtesy of the artist.**

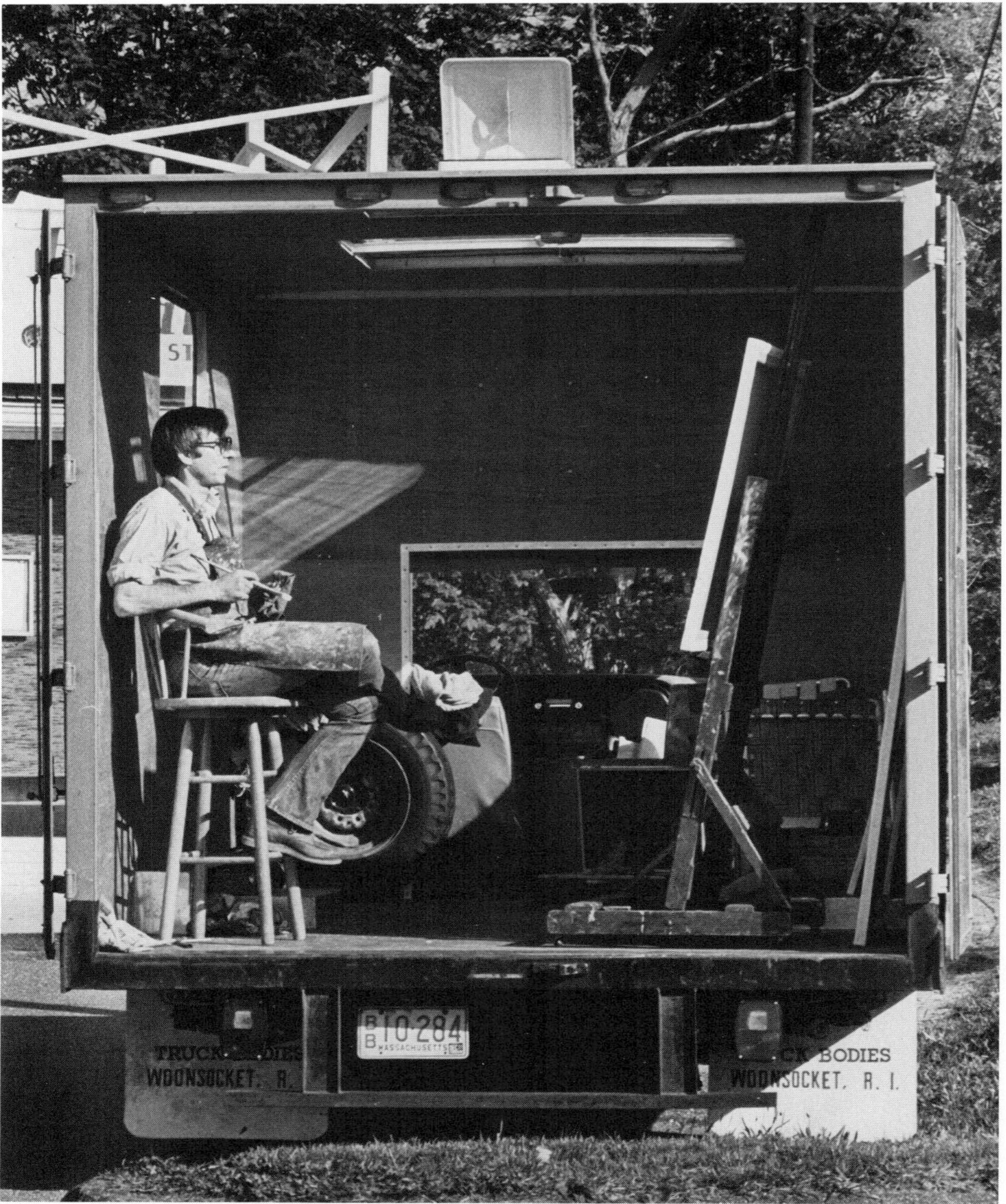

CHAPTER TWO

Buildings

George Nick is a painter who works only on location. He has no studio in the usual sense. Rather, he works from inside a specially fitted van, or if that is not possible, in the open on a portable easel. The subject of the oil painting is always in front of him for immediate reference; he never works away from the motif.

Light is of primary importance to Nick. Once he has chosen a subject seen under a particular light, he will return to work on it only when those conditions are the same. He notes the exact time of day and returns for subsequent sessions an hour before and works until an hour after that time. Five or six paintings of different subjects which show various times of day and weather conditions are always in progress. With these five or six options available, Nick always has at least one painting on which he can work.

Depending upon size, treatment, or complexity of the subject, paintings may require from one to sixteen sessions to complete. The painting *Houses of Chatham Light*, the creation of which is documented here, was completed in a remarkably short single session of three and one-half hours.

In the first stages of work, Nick's attention is primarily on the motif. As he becomes more familiar with it, his concentration begins to shift to the painting. At some point, he is divided equally between the two. He devotes more attention to the painting as it nears completion, and the motif is used only for information on which to improvise. The painting has finally developed a completely separate identity of its own.

Case study of the painting, *Houses at Chatham Light*, by George Nick

On 20 May 1977 at midday, when shadows change more slowly than at any other time, George Nick parked his van with the rear window facing the chosen motif: the roadside in Chatham on Cape Cod. At that time, Nick was going through a period of doing one session paintings. He felt the need to work spontaneously, wet in wet, and wanted to "deal with accidents more openly and directly." He was attempting to combine the slow and meticulous control of his earlier works with the new, looser paint configurations of this style. This approach is "riskier, involves taking more chances and is not as often successful, but the discoveries made are worth it . . . achieving things never anticipated or known before."

It was with this attitude that Nick approached the three houses at Chatham Light. In the very short time of three and one-half hours, he chose the motif, analyzed it, made decisions regarding what to include, leave out, emphasize or simplify, and executed a complete visual statement of what he saw and felt. Hundreds of decisions were made. Many were automatic, the result of years of working out similar problems. Each new subject brings with it its own particular challenges and these are handled instinctively and directly. The result is a work which has a firm underlying structure with a loose, painterly surface that takes full advantage of the particular qualities of oil paint.

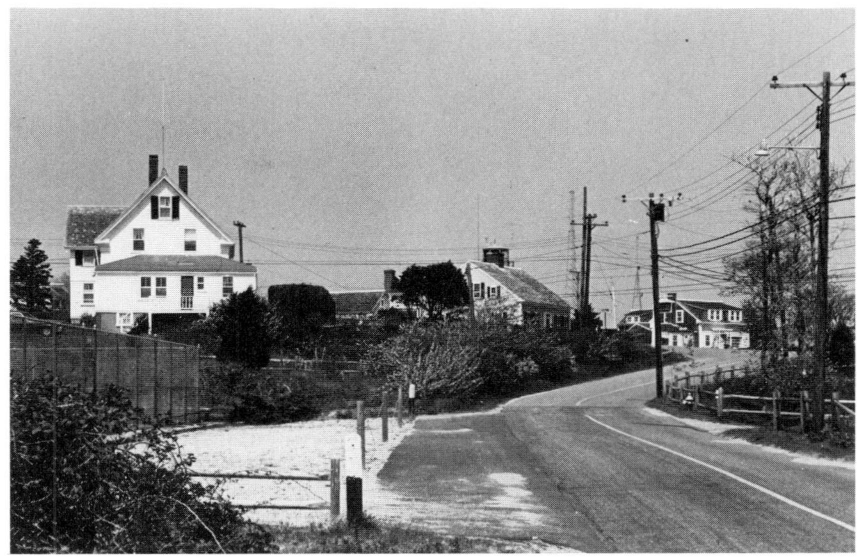

(12:00 P.M.) The motif as seen from the exact point from which it will be painted. Nick liked the character of the buildings, their relation to one another, how they were set at different levels, and, most importantly, how the light hit them. He was also interested in the contrasts of sandy foreground, foliage, buildings, and sky. The entire scene struck him as a particular combination that he had never before tackled. The problem was to tie it together into an organic whole, to give it an identity. Like a puzzle with interlocking pieces, how will it fit together?

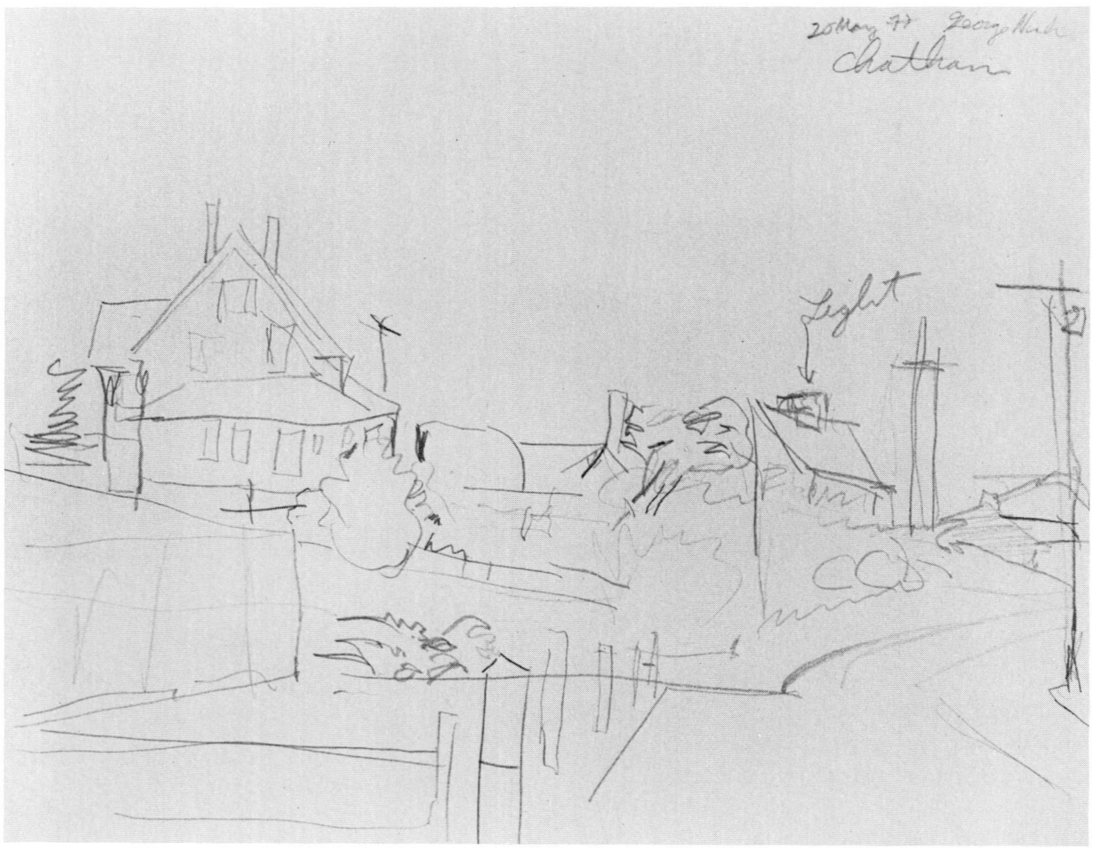

Preliminary pencil drawing. Nick calls this a "physical mark towards an idea, a scribble to get to know the subject." It helps him to work out what will be in the painting and it will not be referred to again.

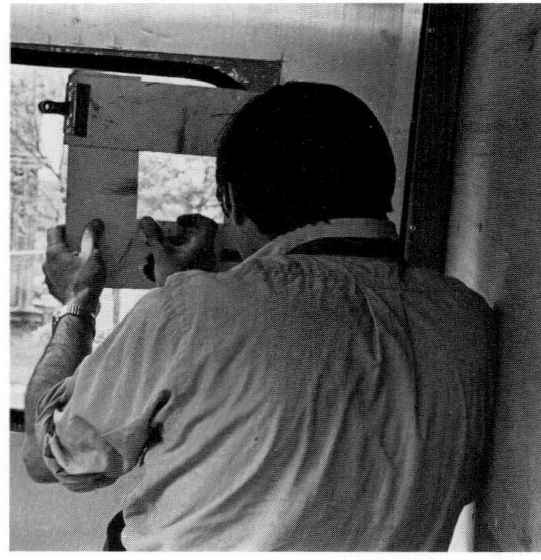

(12:40) Nick uses a viewfinder made of two L-shaped pieces of cardboard that can be clipped together to form rectangles of various proportions. In this case, it is a 3 x 4 ratio, the same as the 36″ x 48″ canvas that he will use. Seen through the viewfinder, the three-dimensional world is translated into two dimensions. It makes it easier to see the shapes, activity, rhythms, mood, colors, and composition; the dynamics of how forms relate to the edge and how close the house should be to it; the amount of sky that should be included; the relative importance and size of areas. A comparison to the finished painting will show the many compositional changes that were made. Nick did not like the bush in the left foreground; he brought the large house very near the left edge of the canvas and the rail fence to the bottom edge. The rail fence at the right side of the road is eliminated. The road itself is flattened in the foreground and compressed, as is the entire motif, to emphasize the land rise, crest-of-hill effect.

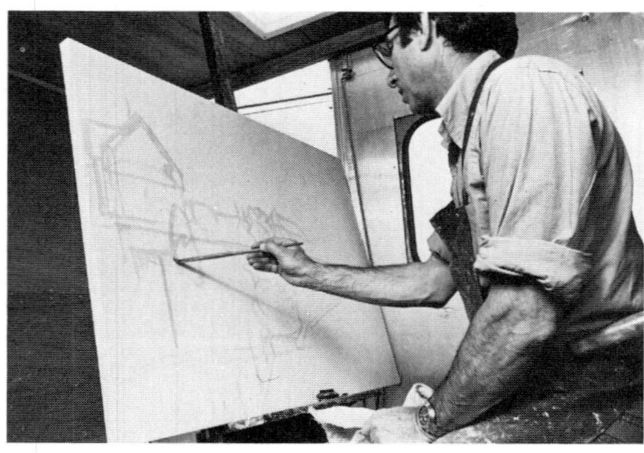

With a bristle brush, the first drawing in a light blue turpentine wash is done on the primed canvas.

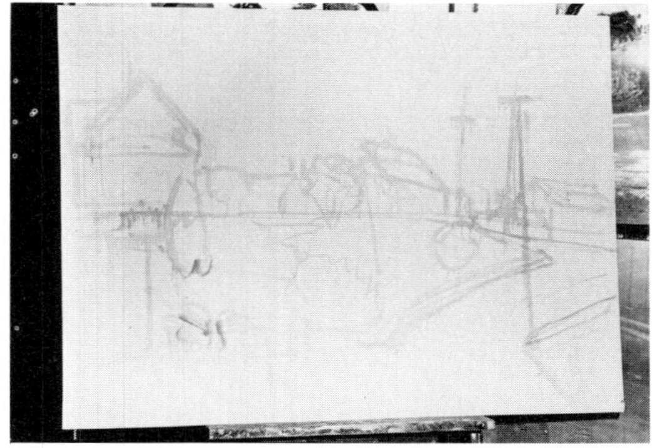

The preliminary wash drawing on the canvas.

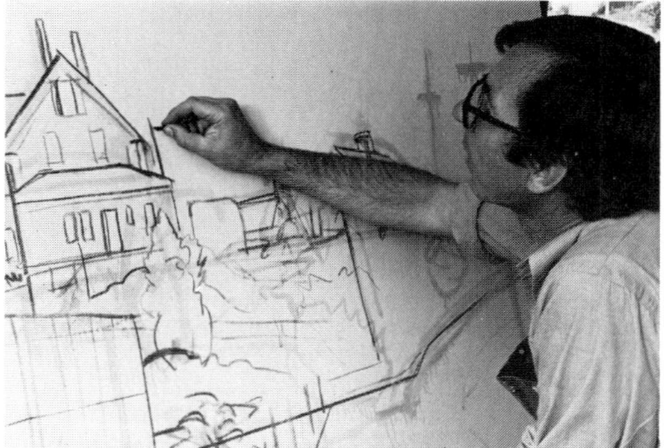

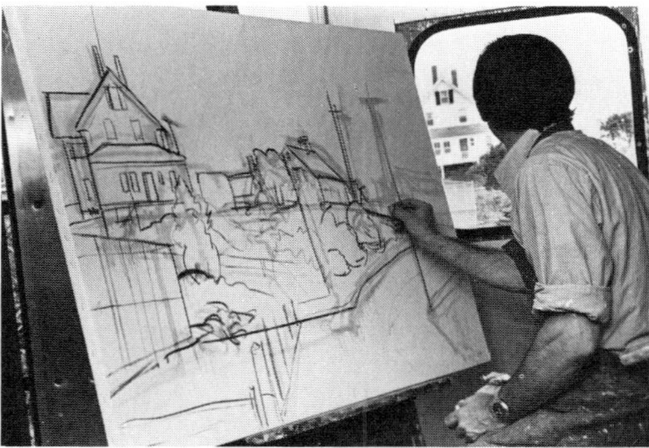

(12:50) Using a soft charcoal stick, Nick articulates and details the drawing. Since this can easily be erased or changed, the drawing is kept open as he gradually defines the shapes.

(1:10) The completed drawing. The composition and design are now well established, but may be modified during the painting process.

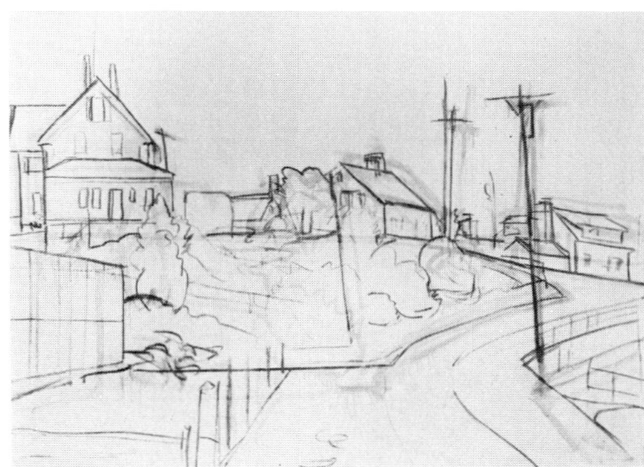

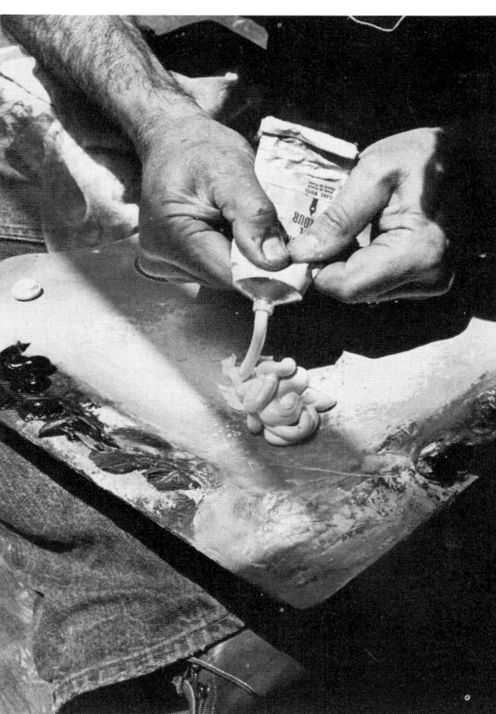

(1:10) Laying out the oil paints on the palette. Cadmium yellow medium, yellow ochre, cadmium reds (light, medium, and deep), alizarin crimson, dioxazime purple, permanent greens (light and deep), thalo blue, raw umber, and ivory black are arranged around the edge. A larger amount of flake white to be used in mixing tints is put near the middle. A metal cup of medium, made of one-half linseed oil, one-quarter turpentine, and one-quarter damar varnish, is clipped to the edge of the palette. This will be used to soften the paints' consistency and to keep them from drying to a dull finish (sinking in).

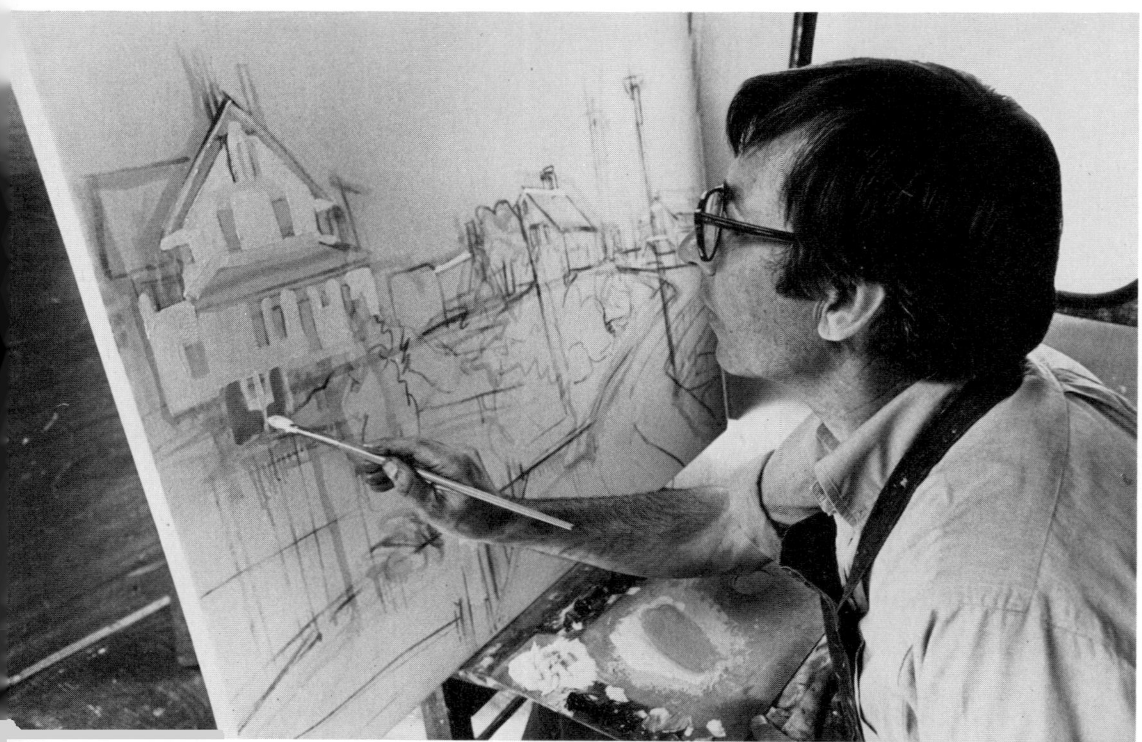

(1:20) The first application is of white paint. This is brushed onto the roof ridge caps, post tops, and walls of the large house at the left. To keep the light colors clean, Nick generally works from light to dark in the painting.

(1:30) Light blue is brushed on the large house's shadows and gray green is painted on its roofs.

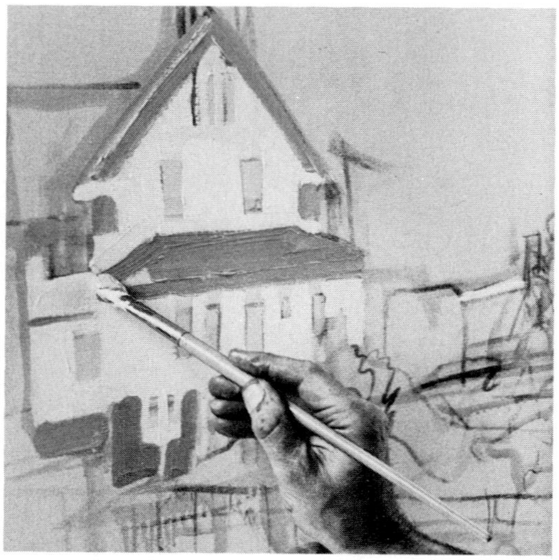

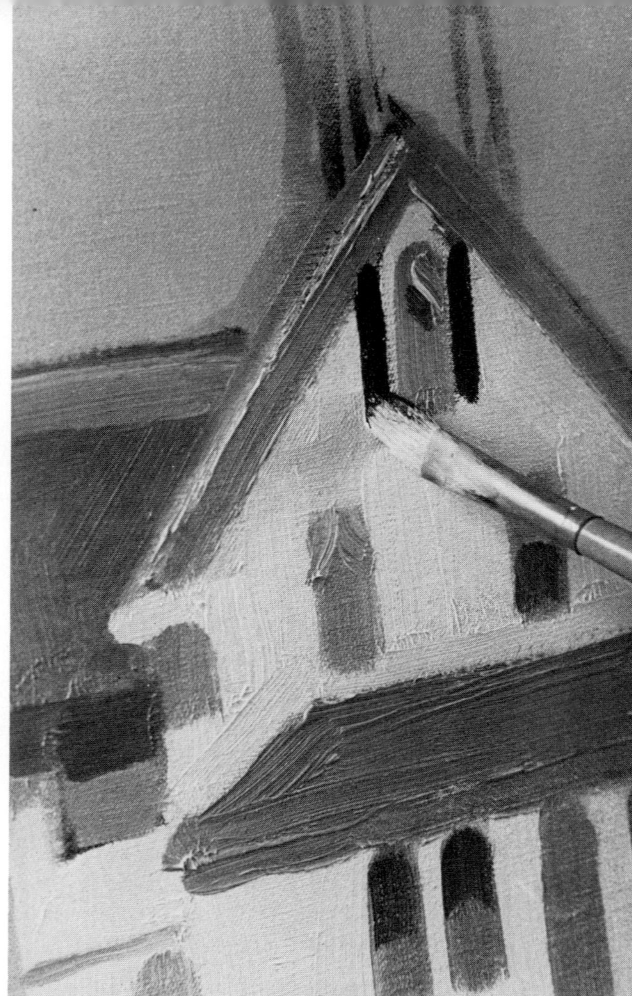

(1:40) A single brush stroke of dark gray is used for each shutter. The same color is used for the shadow under the porch of the large house. This jump ahead to dark was done to quickly establish the identity of the full form, a way of moving the painting.

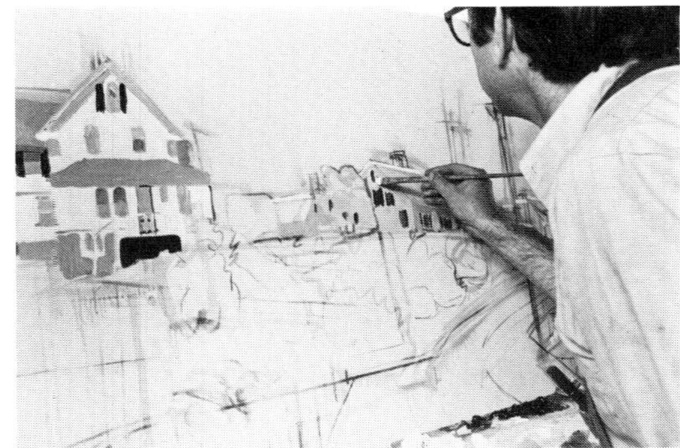

A gray green defines the walls of the middle house. Nick initially worked on the two houses because he was confident about how they should be painted. They are now established as a secure foundation upon which to build the rest of the painting.

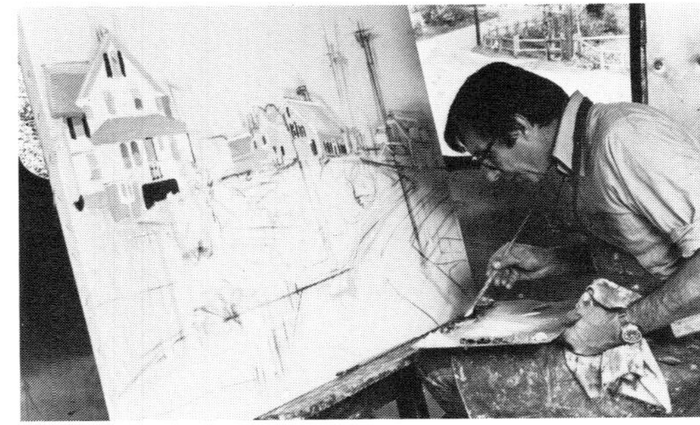

Mixing paint on the palette. Painting with one or two brushes (flats, filberts #8, #10, or #12), Nick picks up color from the edge of the palette and mixes it in the center before he brushes it onto the canvas. He is able to quickly achieve an infinite range of colors. When changing colors, heavy paint is removed from the brush with a palette knife; the remainder is removed by dipping the brush into the medium and wiping it with a cloth.

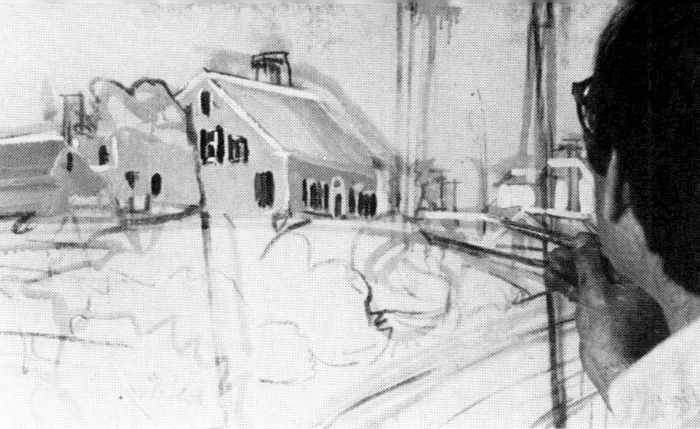

Work is begun on the house on the far right.

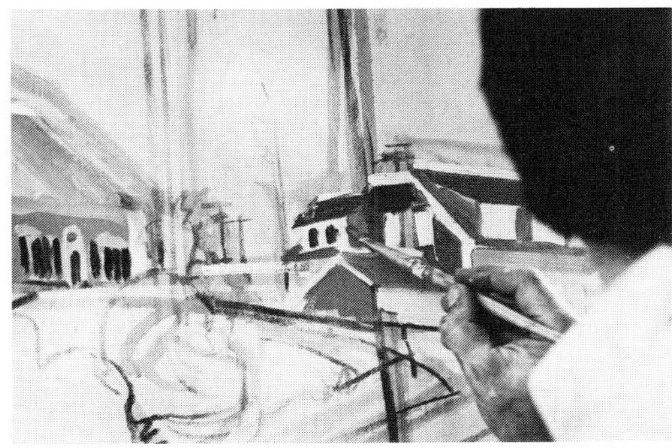

(1:50) The front walls are painted yellow with various grays on the shingled side walls and roofs. A reddish brown is painted on the chimney.

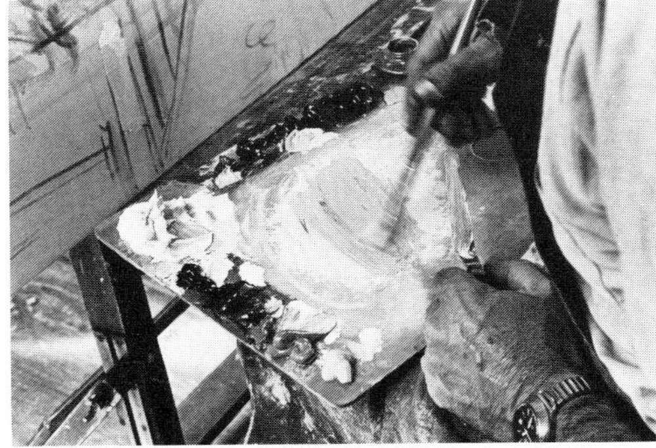

A flat brush is used to mix a tint on the palette.

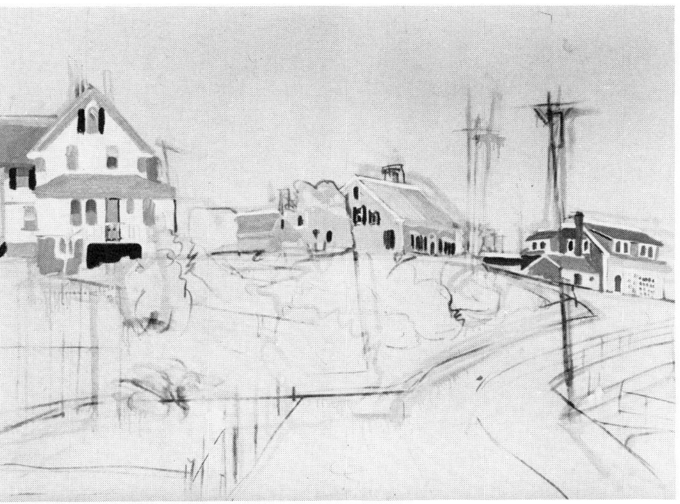

State of the painting at 2:00 P.M.

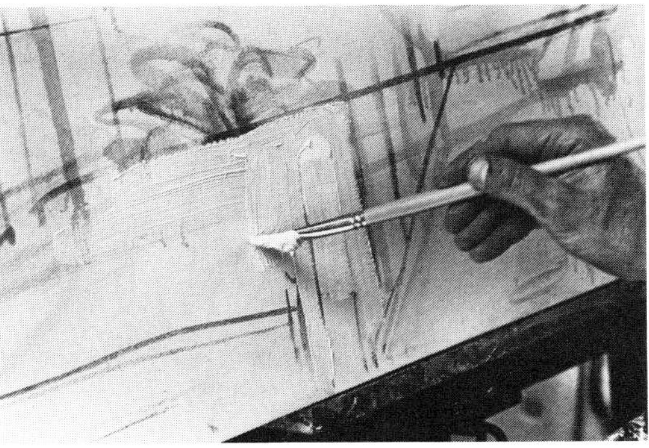

(2:05) The sandy area in the left foreground is painted in a cream tone. Feeling that the foliage area in the center of the composition will be the most challenging, Nick is painting the surrounding areas first to establish reference points.

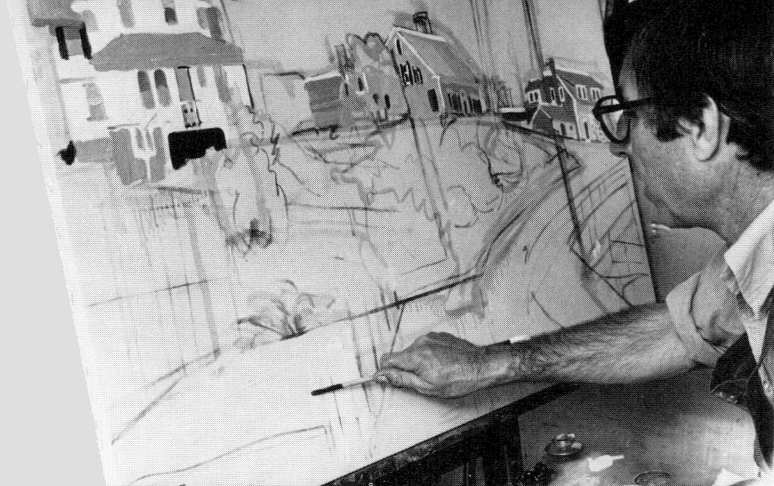

The handle of the brush is used to score lines through the wet paint to the charcoal lines which define the fence posts. Nick will sometimes use his fingertip to pull a color across an edge or to remove a small area of paint.

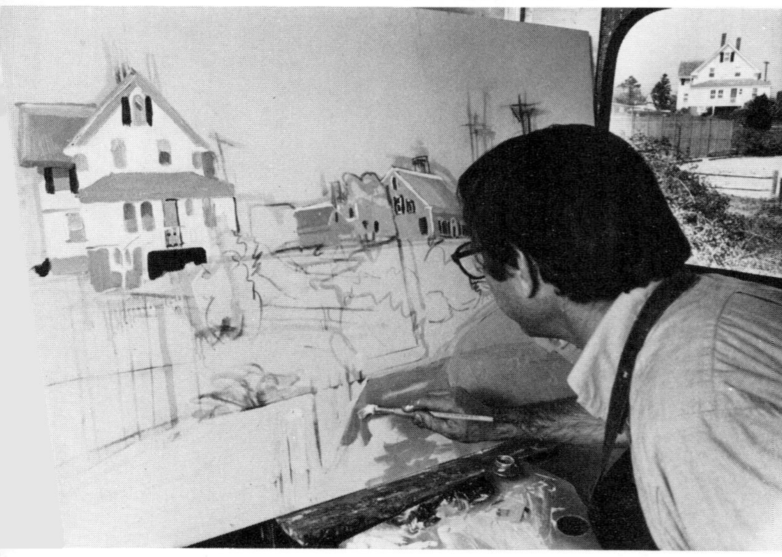

(2:15) The foreground road and parking area are painted in gray green.

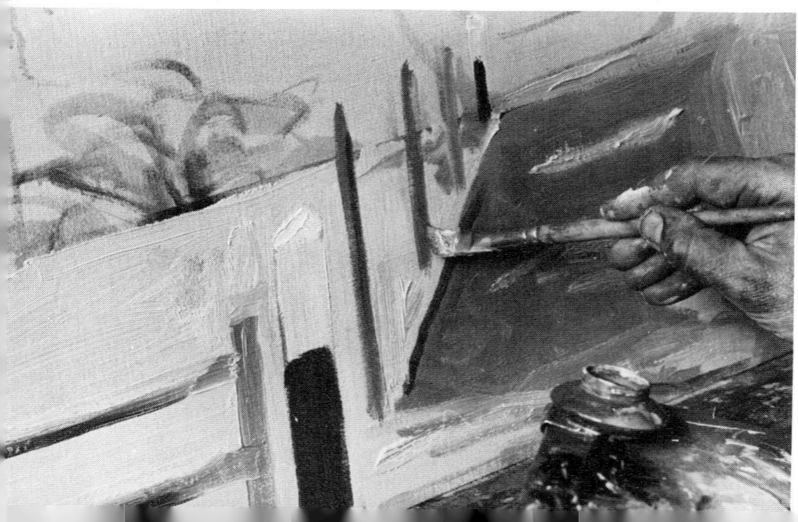

Fence posts alongside the paved area are brushed in.

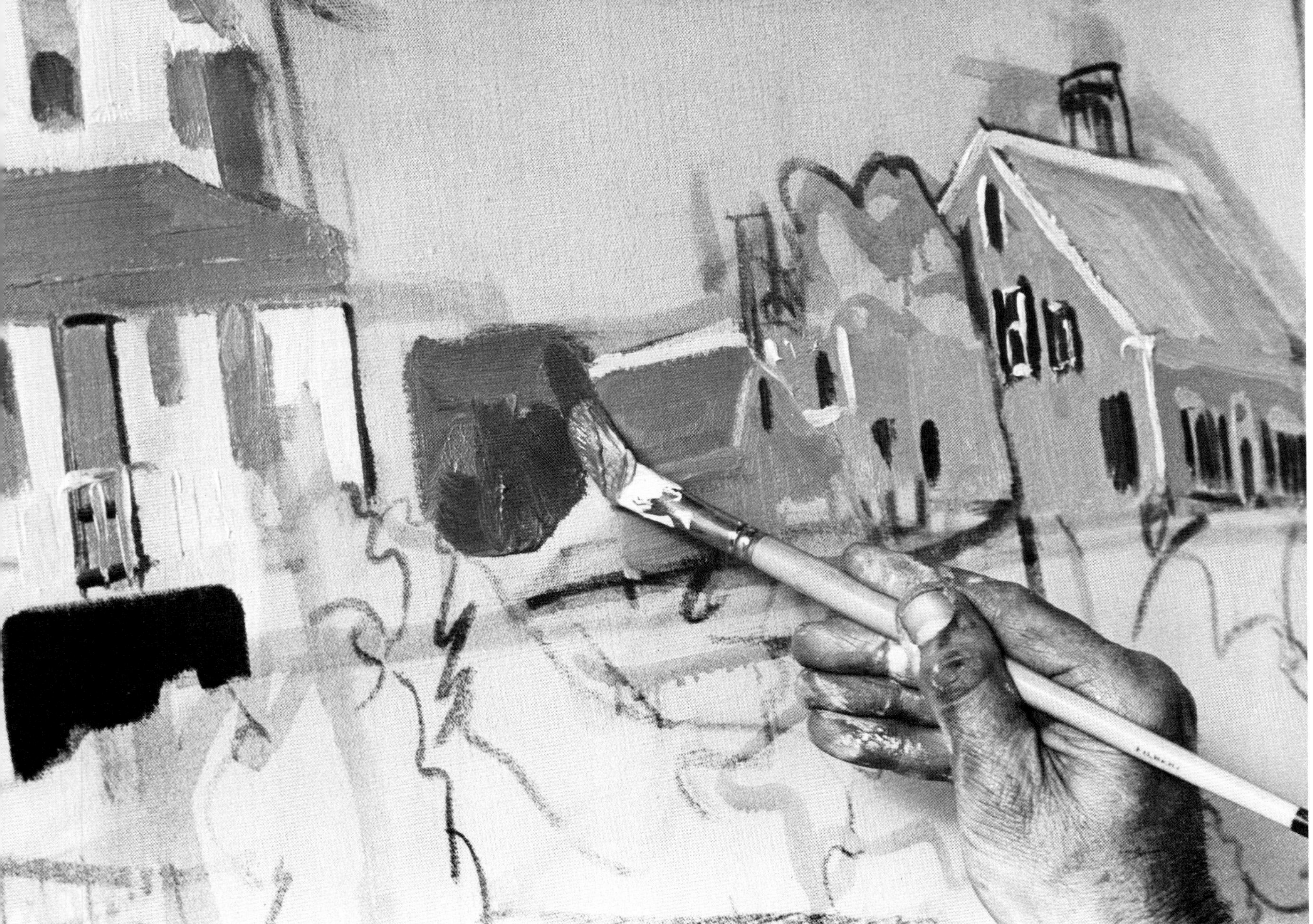

(2:30) The first foliage is painted.

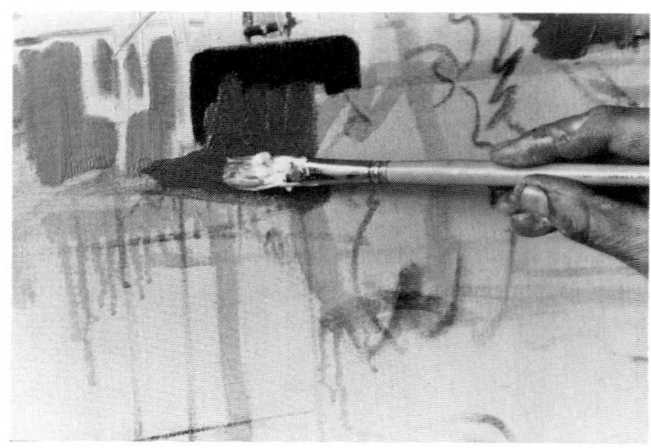

Brown paint is brushed in to make the foliage under the large house's porch. It can be seen that the brush is charged with a lighter color as well as the color being applied.

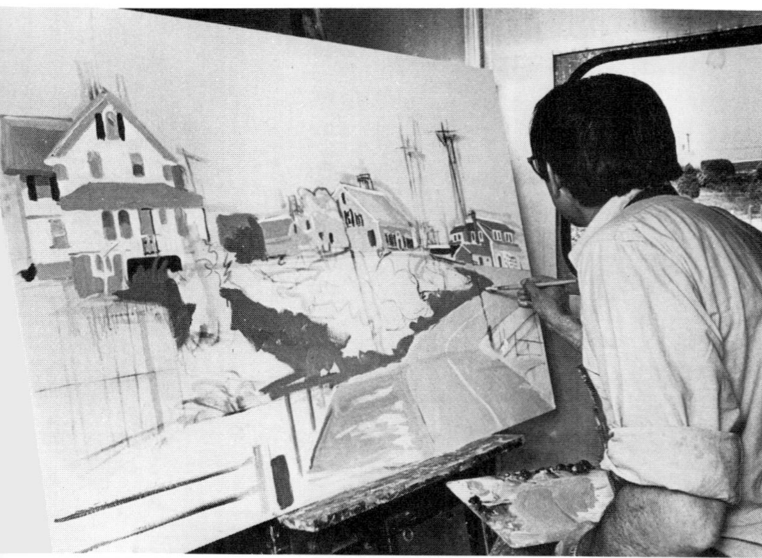

The roadside is painted in a warm green. Nick is working around the edge, gradually going inward to the center of the foliage.

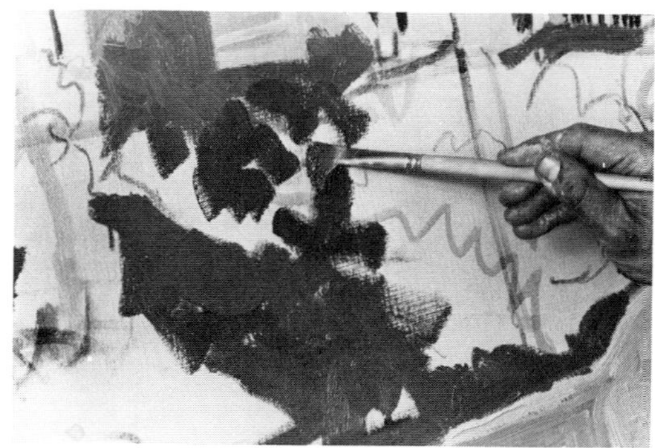

Coming closer into the center, Nick puts in blotches of local color: reds, ochres, browns, and greens. In what he feels is a complicated situation, Nick will put in large masses first, building detail on top of them with a stabbing technique.

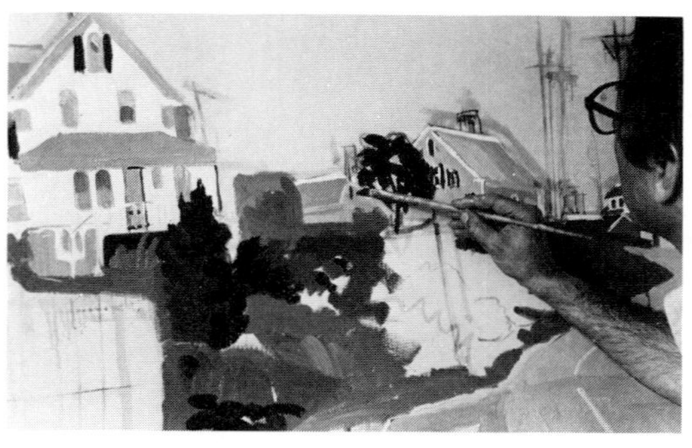

Tree foliage is put in with dark greens, sometimes almost black, to match what Nick sees in the motif.

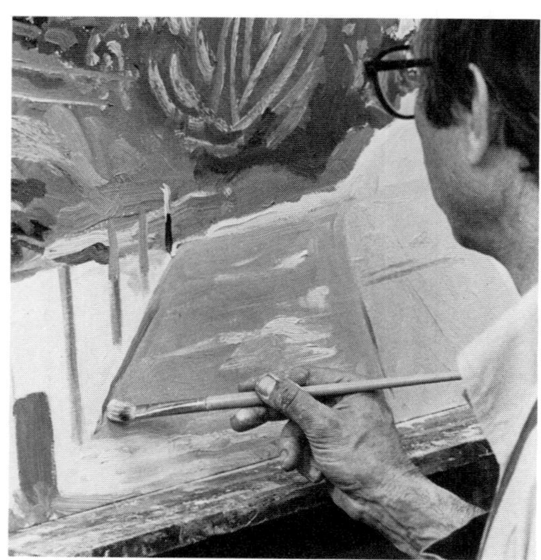

(3:05) The paved parking area is repainted, one of the few examples of refinement in this very direct work. Above this area can be seen the just completed foliage. The growth patterns of bushes and shrubs have been superimposed over simple masses of color in bold brush strokes. This makes a textural contrast to the buildings, paving, and sky.

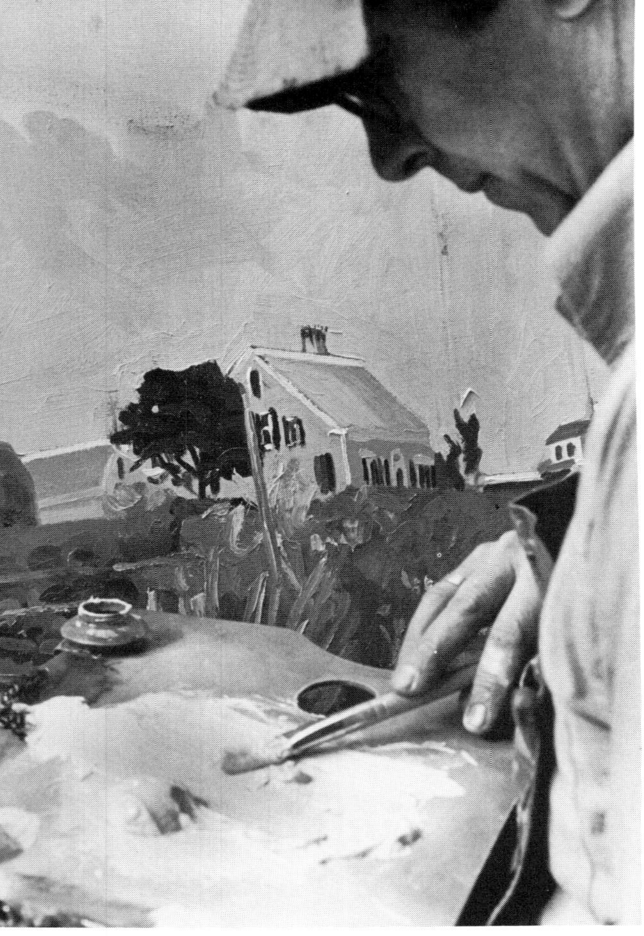

(3:15) For the sky, a light blue of flake white, thalo blue, and the medium is mixed on the palette. The light blue is brushed onto the sky area. For the sky at the left which "felt rosy", some cadmium red is added to the mixture. Similarly, cadmium yellow medium was added for other areas. The result is that the sky does not remain flat, but pulsates with temperature changes. Nick tends to use colors for their emotional effect and thinks of them in terms of warms and cools rather than in hues. This emotional consideration determined the amount of sky that was included in the painting.

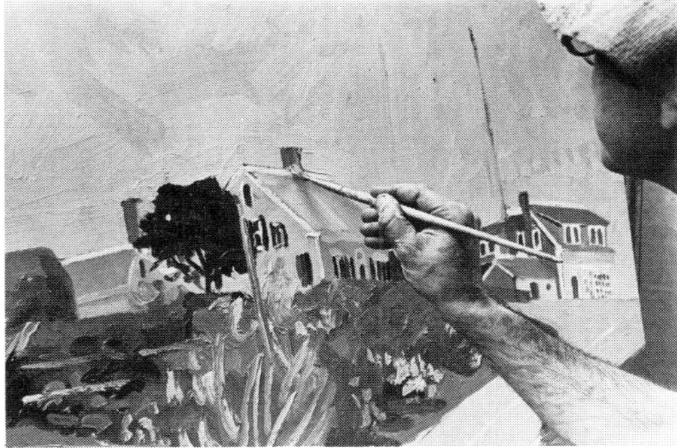

(3:35) Red orange is applied to the chimneys of the middle house, the large house, and on one side of the chimney of the small house. A darker value of the same color is used on the shadowed sides of the chimneys.

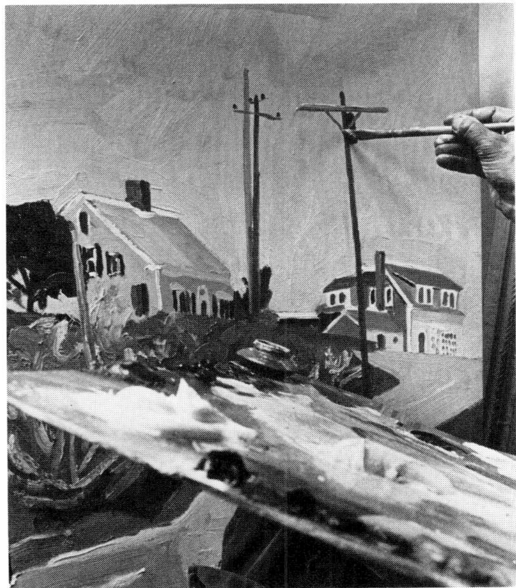

(3:40) Utility poles are superimposed over the sky.

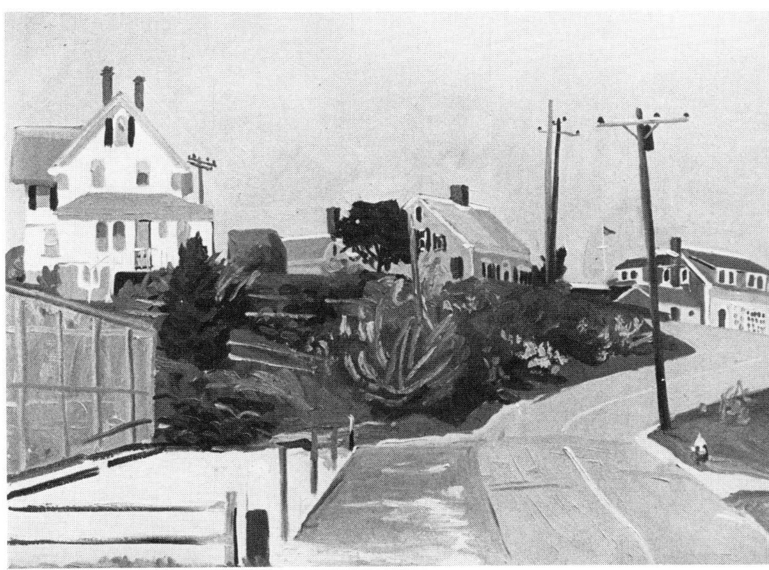

(3:50 P.M.) The painting is finished.

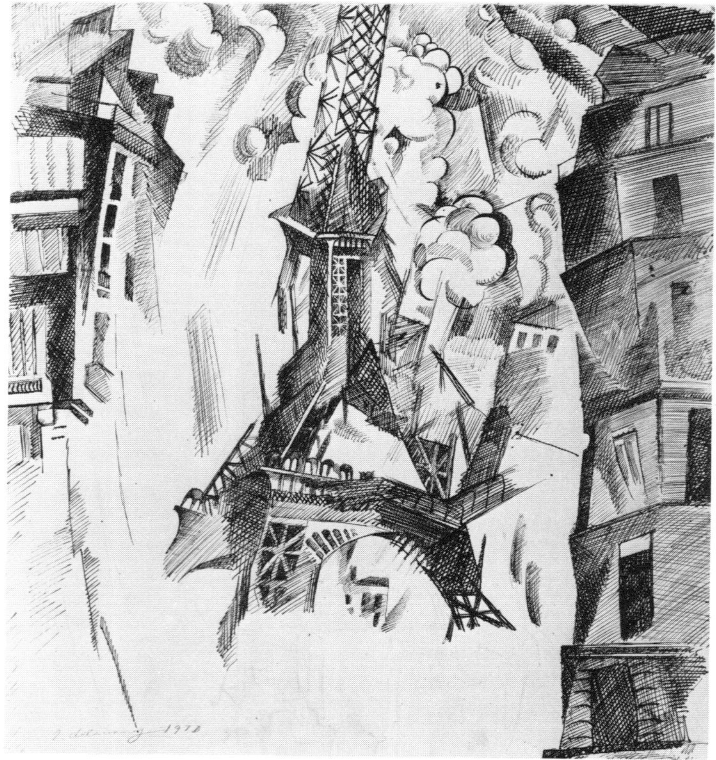

The Tower, **1910. Pen and ink, 21¼″ x 19¼″. Robert Delaunay. Collection, The Museum of Modern Art, New York, the Abby Aldrich Rockefeller Fund.**

These two dramatic studies of the Eiffel Tower marked a new way of representing the spatial reality of the modern city. Delaunay did many Cubist analyses of the subject in a variety of media. In an effort to develop a new vision which incorporated time and motion, the Cubists shattered form and incorporated many viewpoints in the same composition. Juxtaposed here are low, high, inside, outside, close, and distant views that are mixed with cloud shapes to create a new type of shallow, but dynamically structured, pictorial space. Cubism was a revolution in perception so profound that the built environment has never since been seen in the same way.

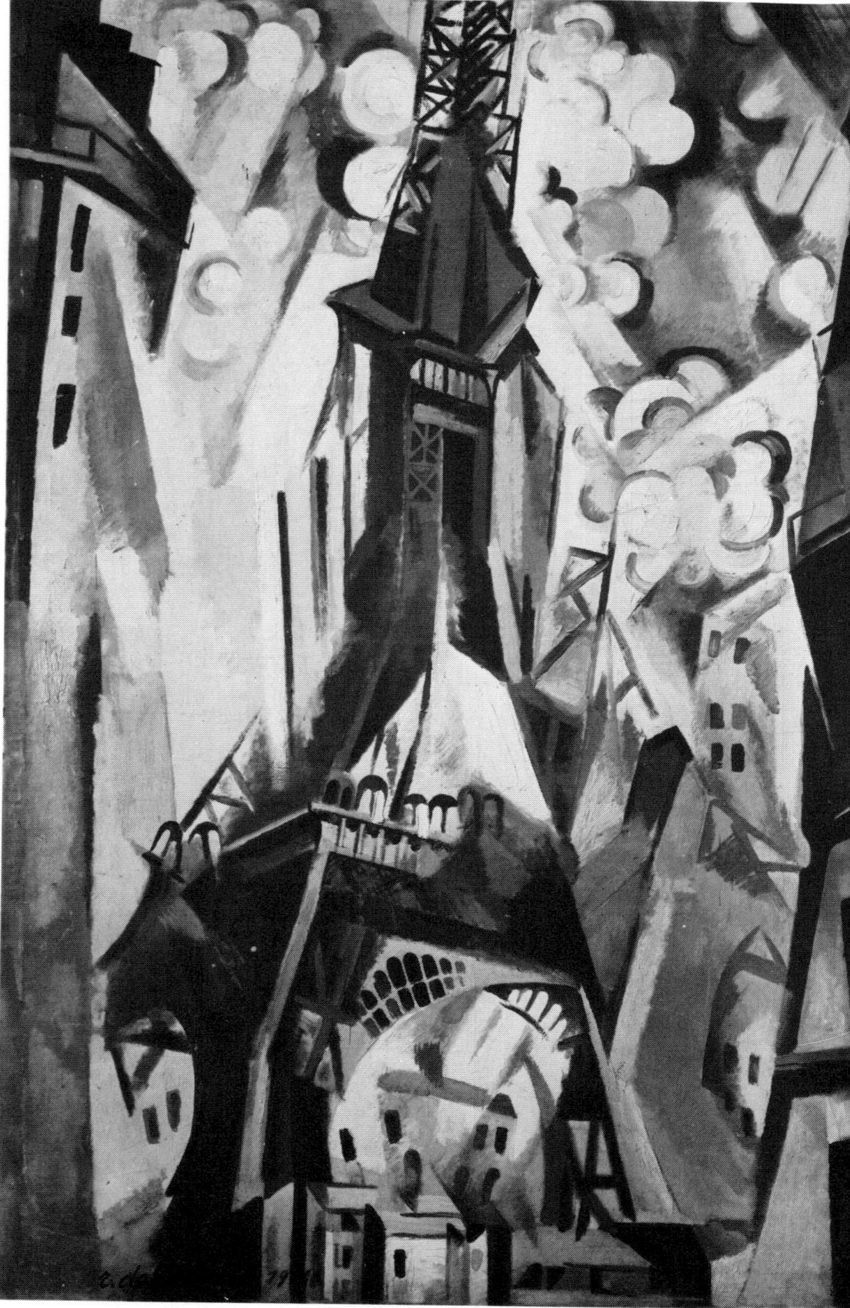

La Tour Eiffel, **1910-1911. Oil, 69″ x 51″. Robert Delaunay. Courtesy of the Kunstmuseum Basel and The Emanuel Hoffman-Foundation.**

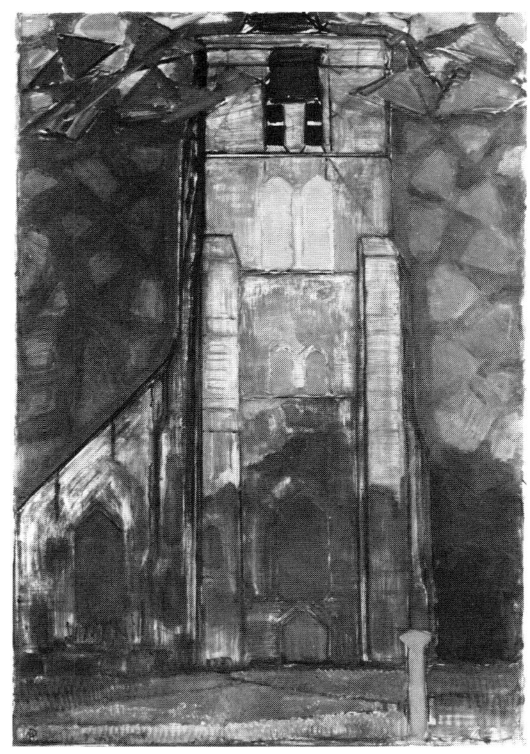

Church Tower at Domburg, **1910-1911. Oil on canvas, 29½" x 45⅝". Piet Mondrian. Courtesy, Haags Gemeentemuseum, The Hague.**

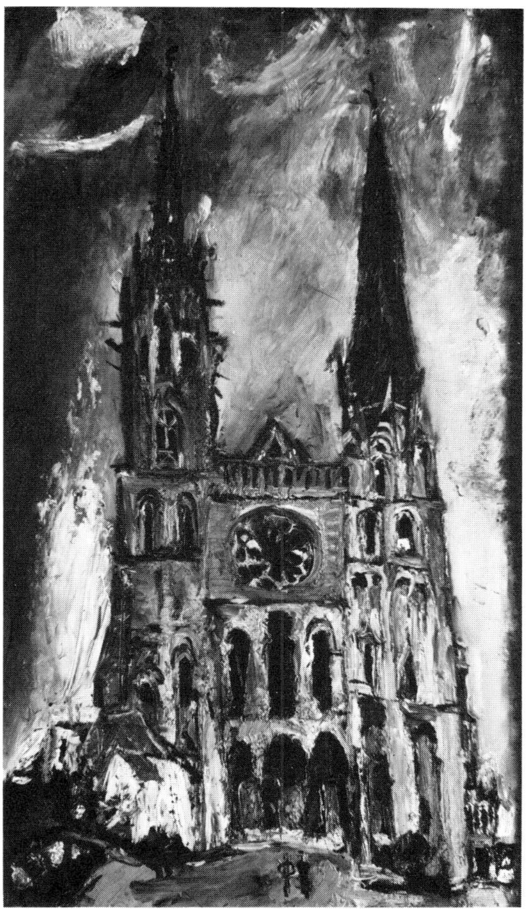

Chartres Cathedral, **1933. Oil on wood, 36" x 19¾". Chaim Soutine. Collection of The Museum of Modern Art, New York. Gift of Mrs. Lloyd Bruce Wescott.**

When Mondrian painted this church tower, he had been influenced by the French Nabis who used flat applications of tone. Their spokesperson, Maurice Denis, said, "We must never forget that a picture, before being a warhorse, a nude woman, an anecdote, or whatnot, is essentially a flat surface covered with colors arranged in a certain order." In this painting, Mondrian's emphasis on the vertical/horizontal elements foreshadows the use of grids in his later, mature style. The emphasis on pictorial structure and the forceful use of light and color create an especially effective architectural statement.

In the early 1900s, Utrillo painted a similar view of this great French cathedral in a vigorous but more monumental mood. Much earlier, Corot had done a serene, golden, more distant view of it. In this tempestuous version, Soutine painted the foreground, doors, and lower roofs of the cathedral in reds and red orange, with bright green foliage around it. As the eye goes up to the spires and the sky, the color becomes cooler in gray greens and blues, but bits of red paint still show through. It is as if the interior is consumed with fire which is just beginning to show outside. Everywhere is the electric, nervous brushwork, the tipping, tilting forms of the Expressionist.

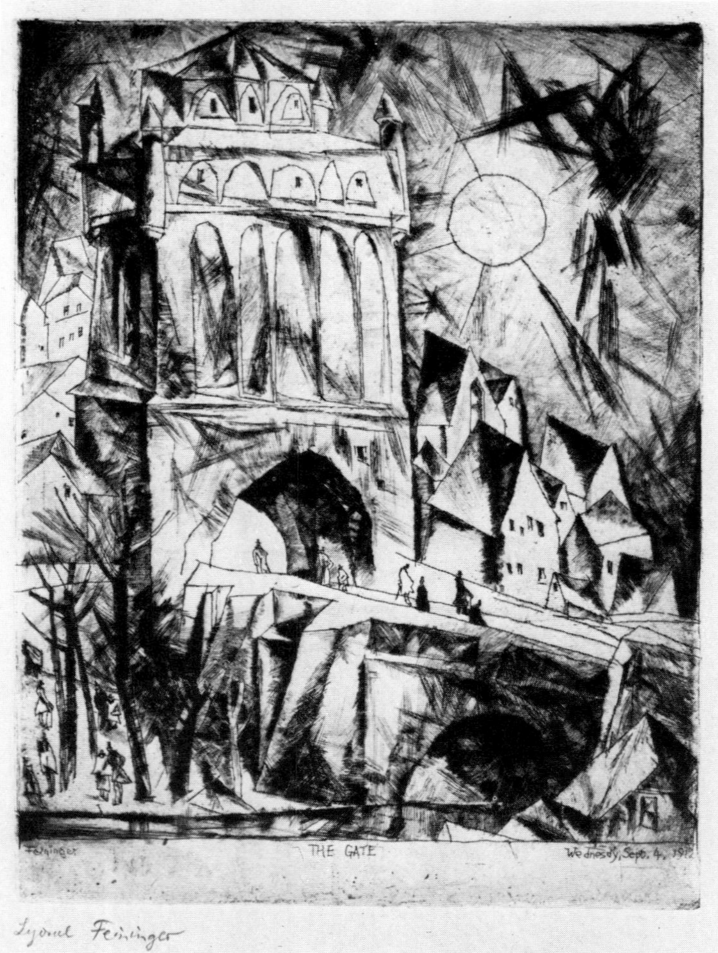

***The Gate*, 1912. Etching and drypoint, $10\frac{11}{16}$" x $7\frac{13}{16}$". Lyonel Feininger. Collection of The Museum of Modern Art, New York. Gift of Mrs. Donald B. Strauss.**

In 1911 the American born, German-trained illustrator and artist, Lyonel Feininger, was exposed to Cubism on a visit to Paris. From then on, he used the Cubist techniques of fragmentation and planar organization to dematerialize the ships, steeply gabled houses, Gothic towers, tall buildings, and narrow streets, which he loved to paint, into crystalline luminous compositions. *The Gate* shows how Feininger's distinctive angular treatment of the roofs, gate tower, and bridge of a medieval town produces a highly charged, emotional effect.

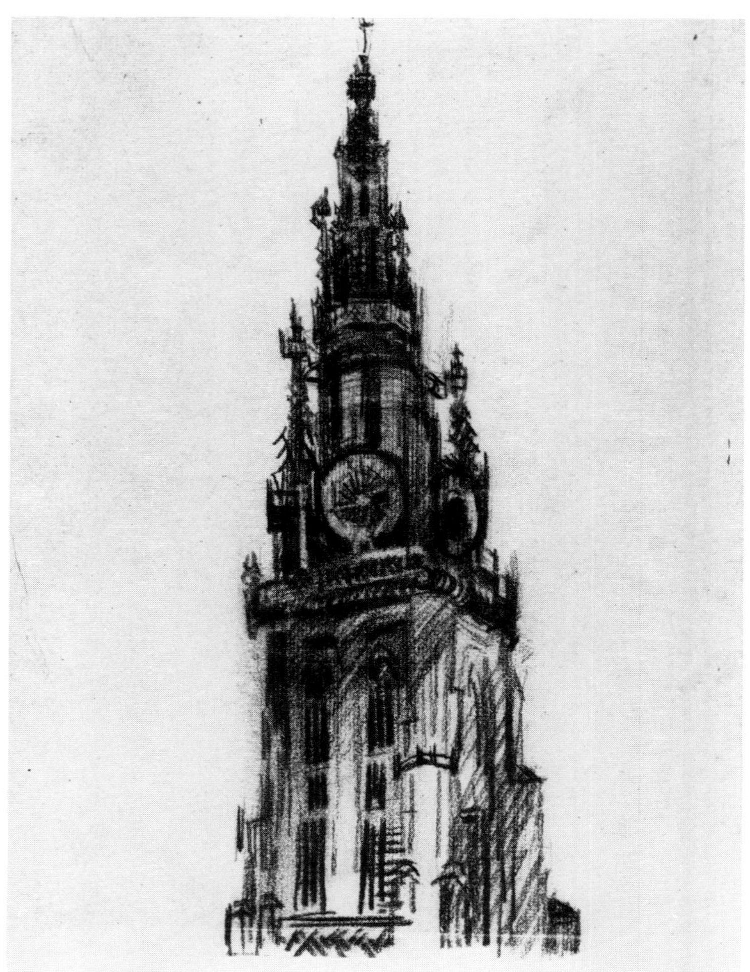

***The Tower of the Cathedral in Antwerp*, 1885. Black crayon on Ingres paper, $11\frac{1}{2}$" x $8\frac{1}{4}$". Vincent Van Gogh. The Vincent Van Gogh National Museum, Amsterdam.**

Vincent Van Gogh had a wide range of subject matter. He has left us many drawings and paintings of buildings, cityscapes, bridges, and boats done in his idiosyncratic, intensely emotional style. During the winter of 1885, he worked in Antwerp and among the subjects that came under his scrutiny was the cathedral tower. This drawing shows the intensity of his feeling that distorts and sets slightly off balance, giving a lively tension to the rigid Gothic architecture.

When Marin returned to the United States in 1912 from a long stay in France, he was struck by the burgeoning vitality of the new buildings going up in lower Manhattan. "I have just started some Downtown stuff," he said, "and to pile these great houses one upon another with paint as they do pile themselves up there so beautiful, so fantastic—at times one is afraid to look at them but feels like running away."

Fortunately, Marin stayed to produce some of the most explosive visual documents of the modern cityscape ever done. Among them was an extensive watercolor and etching series of the new Woolworth Tower, then the tallest building in the world. "I see great forces at work, great movements; the large buildings and the small buildings; the warring of the great and the small; influences of one mass on another greater or smaller mass. . . each subject in some degree to the other's power. . . ."

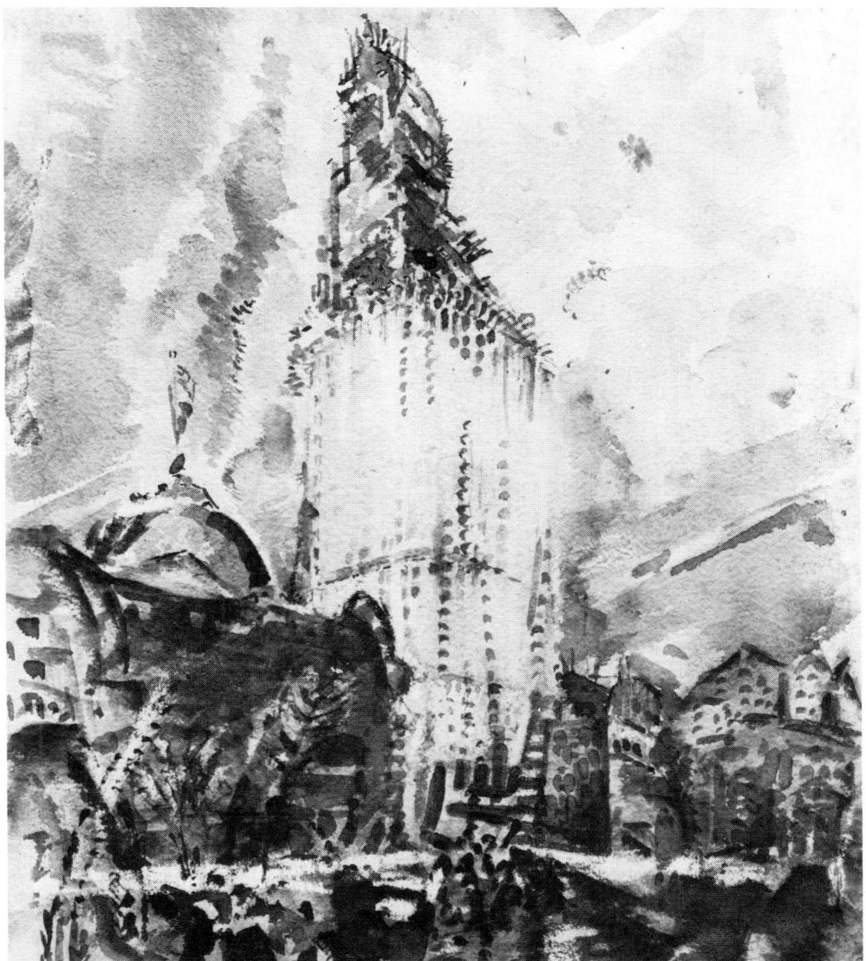

Woolworth Building #28, 1912-1913. Watercolor, 15¾" x 18¾". John Marin. Collection of the National Gallery of Art, Washington, D.C. Gift of Eugene and Agnes E. Meyer.

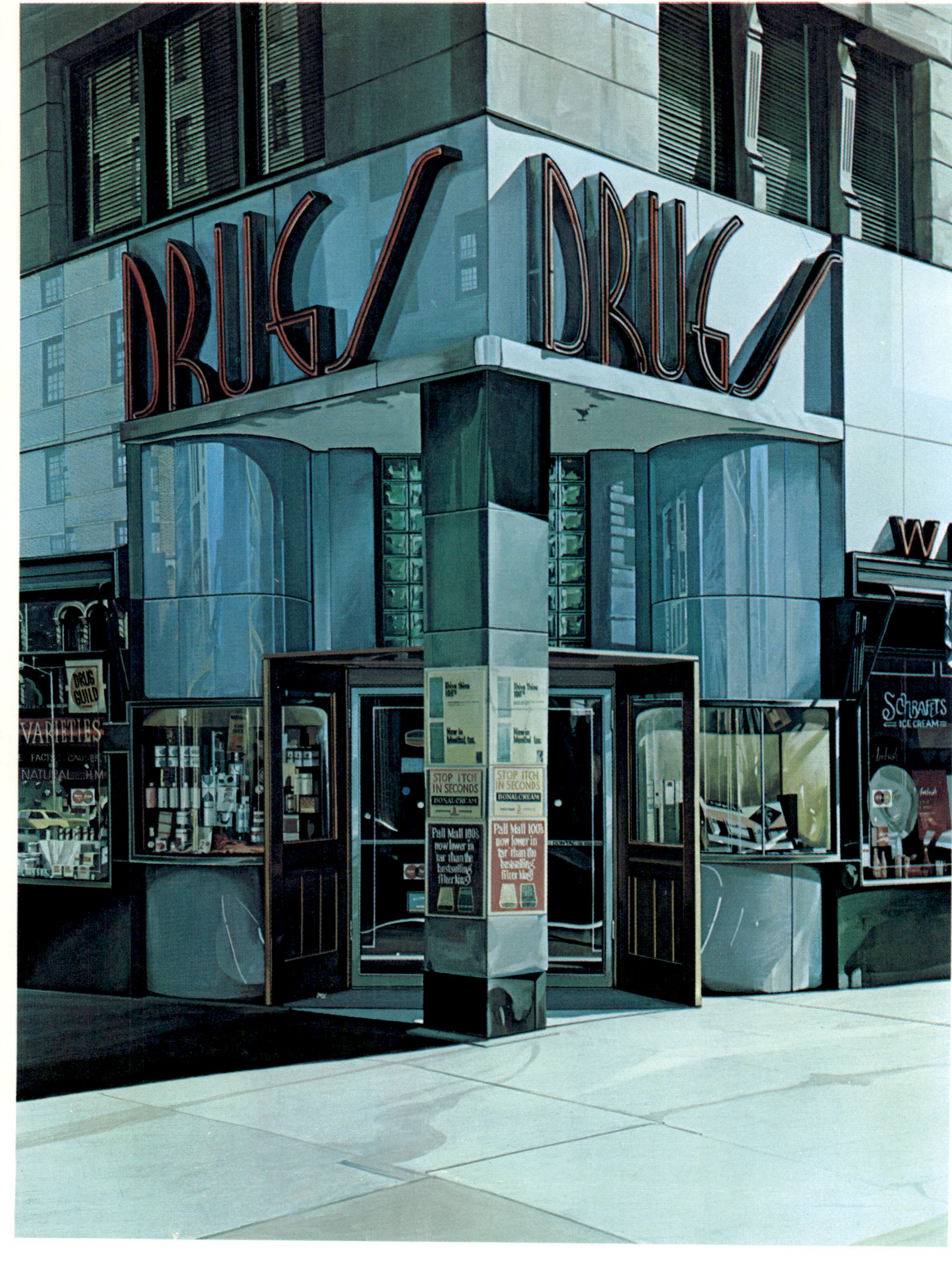

Photography is an important tool for Richard Estes in creating his ultra-realist paintings. He takes numerous random color photographs of the city (generally on Sundays in New York). He prints these himself, and if he sees something that interests him, he will return to that scene and photograph it again. Many photographs are required to give him all of the information that he needs. He selects a particular viewpoint, a reflection, a light effect, a detail which will be combined in a single painting.

Working in his studio on a stretched canvas, he loosely blocks in the basic composition with diluted umber acrylic paint. Then comes the lights and darks, working from larger to smaller forms. Consulting his photographic enlargements, he simultaneously develops the entire painting in acrylics until it looks superficially complete. He spends more time overpainting in oils to get just the right quality of depth and range of color. It is a slow, calculated process, often involving changes, additions, and subtractions. Finally, he arrives at that balance where all of the parts are of equal interest and importance to hold the painting together.

Reflections are a particular preoccupation for Estes. In this painting, the architectural features of surrounding buildings are mirrored in the many glazed surfaces of the drugstore.

***Drugstore*, 1970. Oil on canvas, 60″ x 44⅜″. Richard Estes. Collection of The Art Institute of Chicago.**

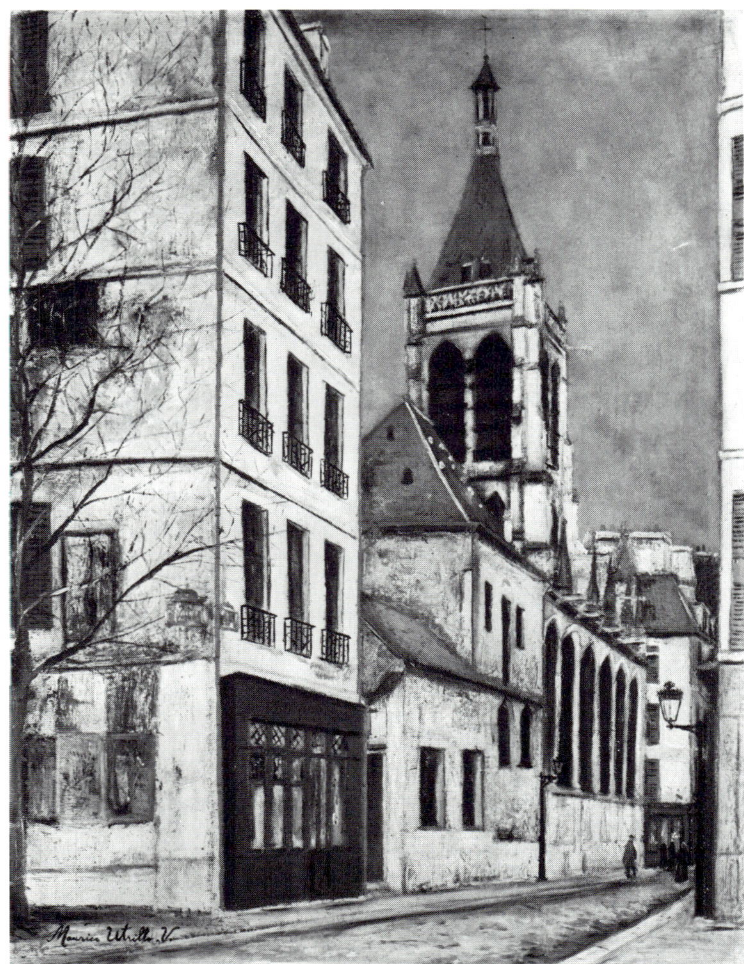

***The Church of Saint-Severin*, 1886. Oil on canvas, 28¾" x 21¼". Maurice Utrillo. Courtesy of the National Gallery of Art, Washington, D.C., the Chester Dale Collection.**

Utrillo once said, "I enjoy painting churches, even if they are second-rate." Saint-Severin, a Gothic jewel in the Latin Quarter of Paris, is certainly not second-rate. It has provided the motif for one of Utrillo's strongest compositions which combines firm construction with poetic feeling. The treatment of the bell tower especially shows his sensitivity to architecture through paint.

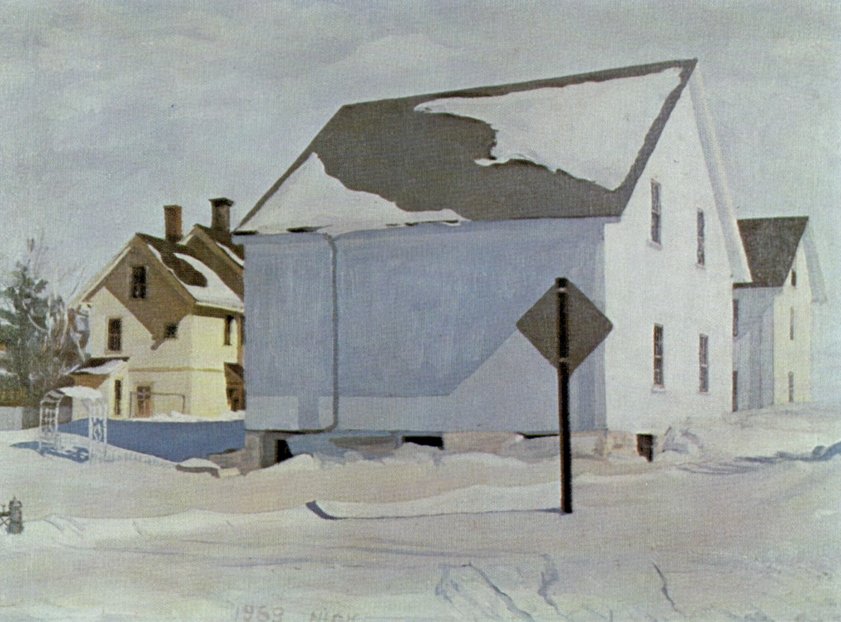

***After the Blizzard of 1969*. Oil on canvas, 20" x 27". George Nick.**

Domestic buildings such as these in Lexington, Massachusetts, occur frequently in George Nick's work. He has written, "The architecture I paint is closely associated with the carpenter training I had with my father when I was a child."

CHAPTER THREE

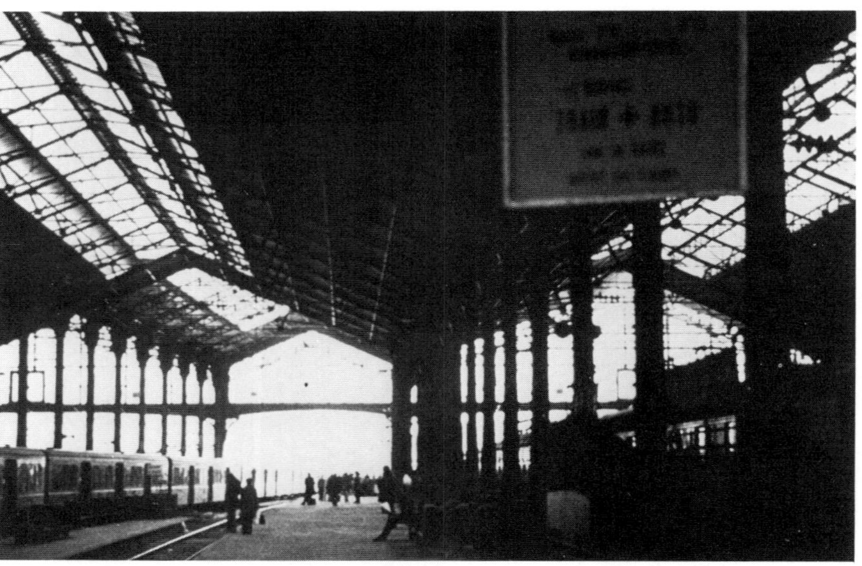

Interiors

Case Study of the painting, *The Railway Station*

Sharp angles of light and shadow, converging lines of perspective, a multiplicity of shapes and forms under the complex roof of a metal and glass structure, all leading to a glare of light beyond the confines of the building—these are the qualities that attract and strike me when I experience the interior of train sheds. The impulse for this painting is the collective impact of many stations, but it was triggered by a visit to one, the Gare Saint Lazare in Paris.

These two sketches were made late one cold afternoon during the intervals between trains' arrivals and departures with their streams of hurrying passengers. Because of the complicated subject, I decided to do a double page (8¼" x 11½") drawing to include as much detail as possible. The principle characteristic was the effect of a basically dark interior broken by patches of light in a three to one ratio. I also wanted to stress the lines of the roof, tracks, and trains that converged and led to a band of glowing white light at the horizon. The intricate structure of the roof was broken with angular shapes of light from the gable ends and the skylights. Patterns of light intersected with dark structural lines. Light leaked into the dark interior through myriad geometric openings, spotlighting objects and surfaces, but leaving much in deep, velvety, dark shadow. The smaller drawing, one page of a 4⅛" x 5⅞" sketchbook, was done from a slightly lower angle along a platform between two trains. This emphasized the triangular and diamond shapes of light which formed something like a large V.

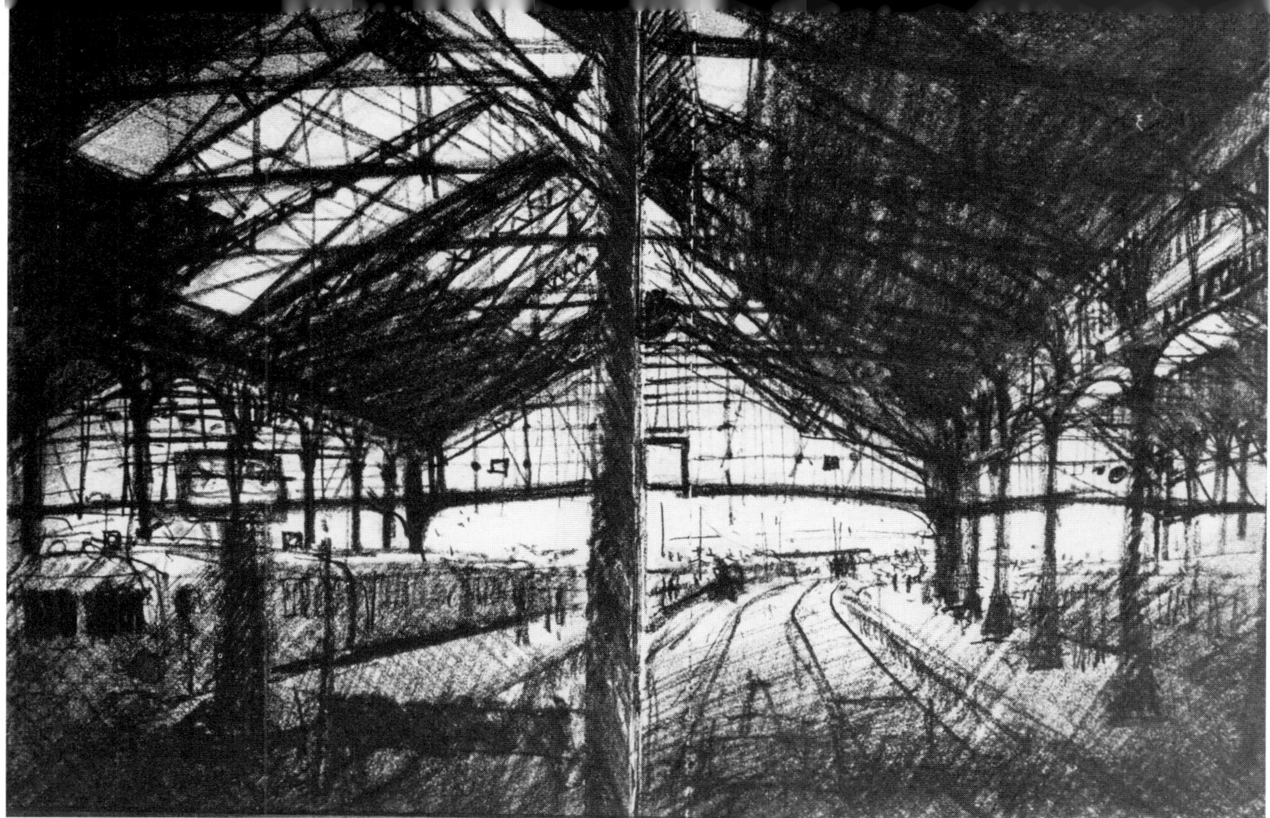

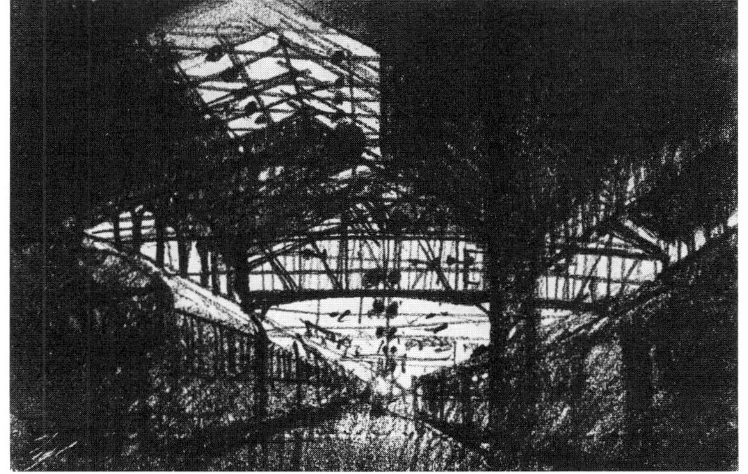

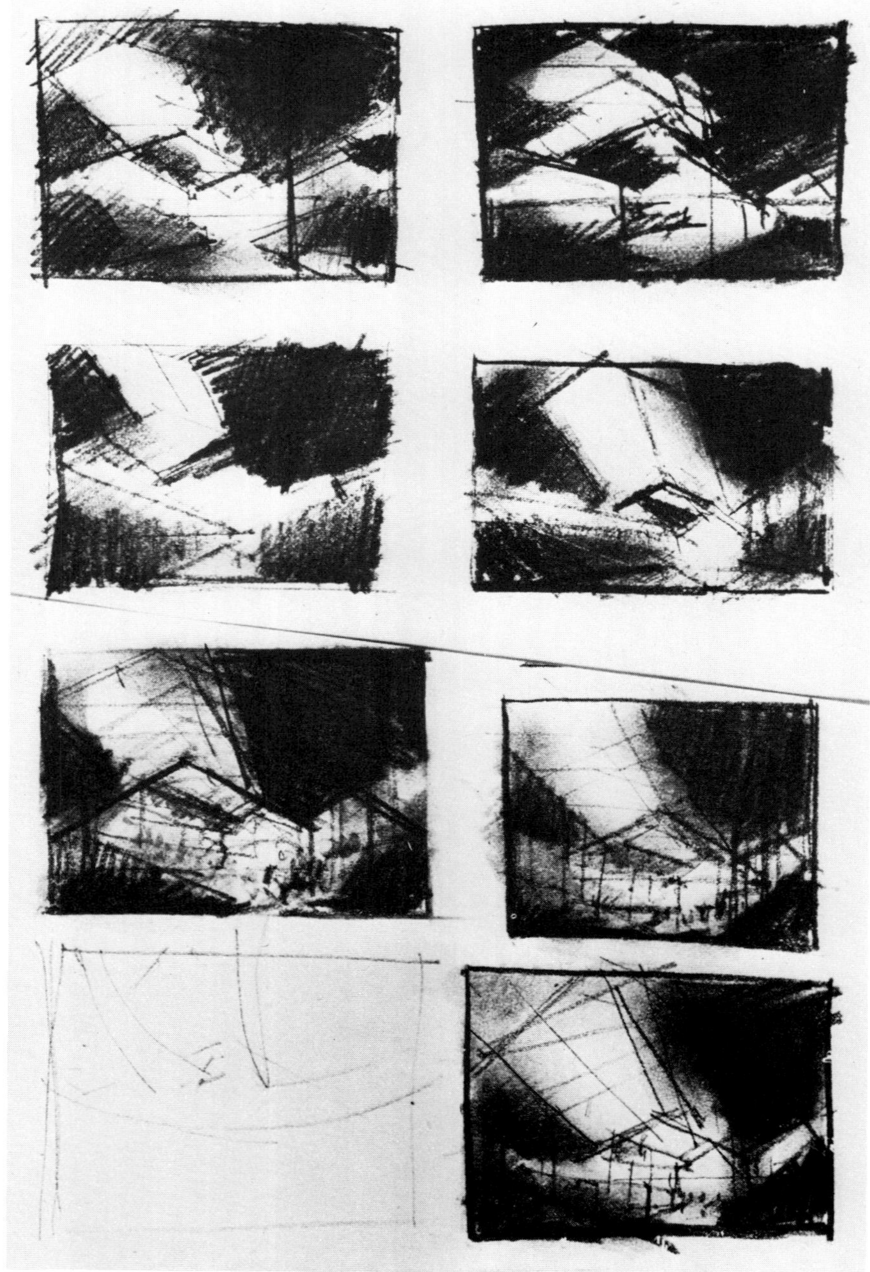

Thumbnail sketches

I made many thumbnail sketches from the two drawings to explore a variety of compositions. Sometimes one characteristic was dominant and pushed to its limit. Sometimes parts of both drawings were combined. By making the sketches small and simple, I could sift out the best from the many possibilities.

Sketch 1. This combines features of the drawings and the photograph. Diamond shapes of light and dark interact and focus on the white shape at the lower center.

Sketch 2. The light shapes group together within the dark background.

Sketch 3. The light areas converge from all four sides to lead the eye to a distant point at the lower center.

Sketch 4. A combination of sketches 2 and 3. This leaves the edges dark and brings the light areas into an irregular cross which converges at the lower right center.

Sketch 5. A more detailed development of sketches 3 and 4. This sketch pulls the light areas into a V. It indicates the columns receding into the distance and includes some foreground detail.

Sketch 6. The light areas form an arrow-shape pointing down to the lower right.

Sketch 7. I again used the arrow-shape. The light areas are more consolidated by the darkening of the upper left-hand corner.

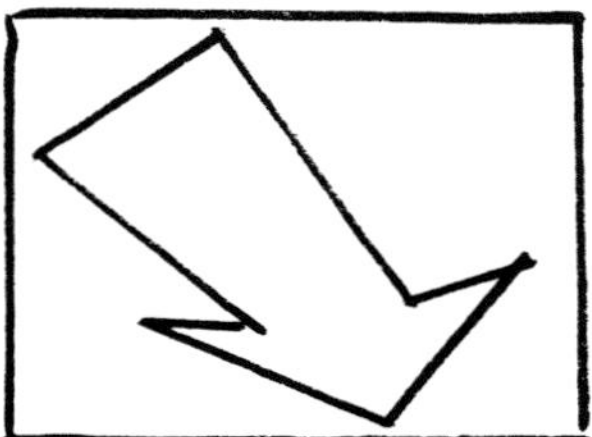

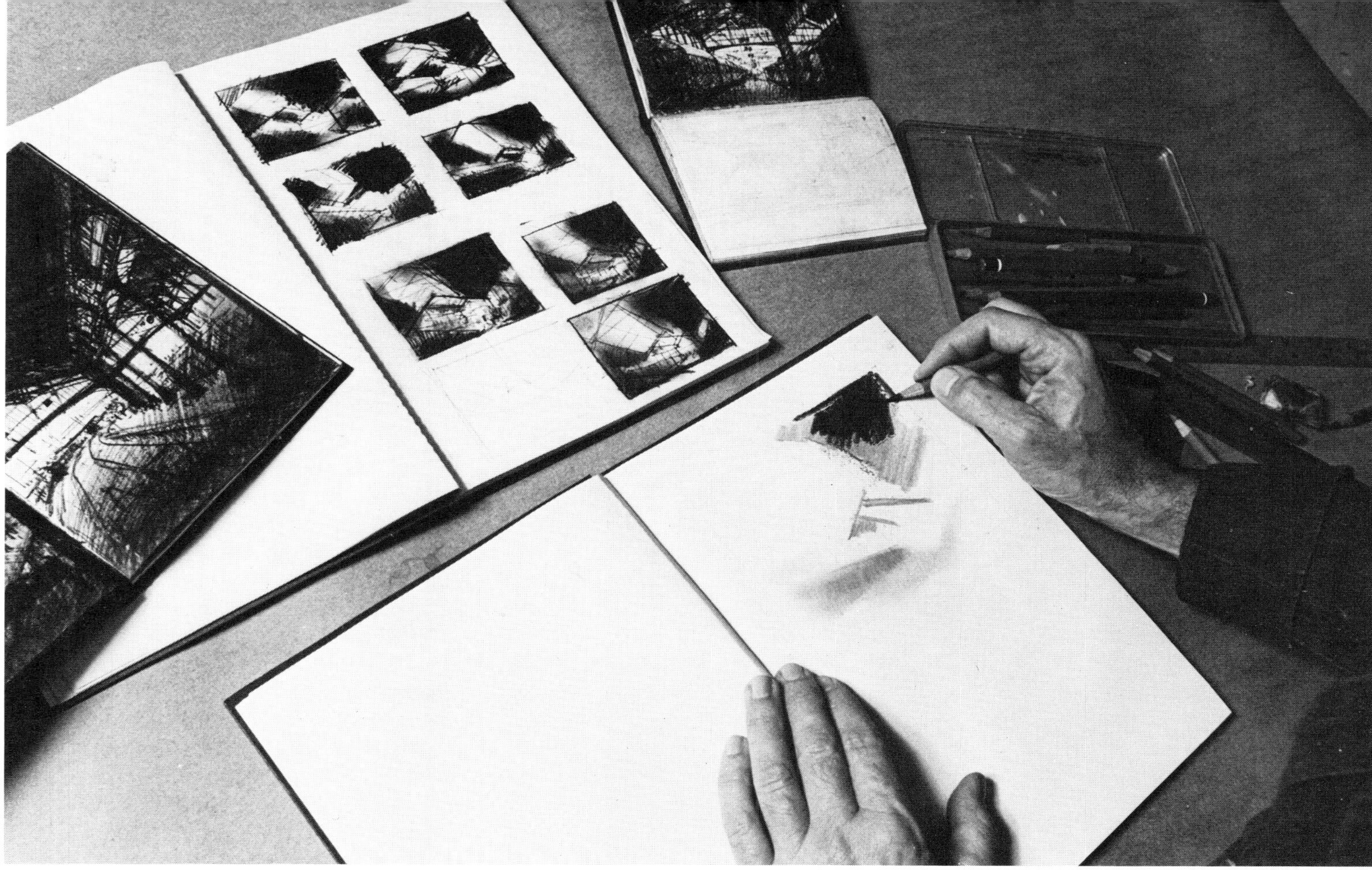

The final preliminary sketch

With the two drawings and the seven thumbnail sketches in view, I made a final preliminary drawing in pastel pencil and charcoal. This was based primarily on the seventh thumbnail sketch, but some parts of the others were included. I was careful of the proportion (three to four) in this drawing. Although mostly concerned with the light shapes, dark areas, and overall composition, I did refer to the two sketchbook drawings for details such as the roof structure and column spacing.

The values were worked out: pure white is concentrated at the far end of the train shed, graying down as it points out to the four sides of the picture plane. All four corners are dark; the largest dark area is at the upper right, the second largest is at the upper left, the third is at the lower left, and the smallest area is at the lower right. A small patch of dark is near the center. Stated simply, the composition is a light diamond within a dark rectangle. The two light lines in the top half of the composition help to define this diamond-shape. The light areas within the drawing roughly form an arrow pointing to the lower right, as in thumbnail sketches 6 and 7.

Bright hues of red, yellow, and blue radiate from the white focus at lower right and darken as they reach the edges of the picture plane. Blues dominate the upper two-thirds: light blue in the skylights to blue back at the corners. In the lower one-third, the dark corners are brown. A red area forms the train at left center, and below the white, ochre darkens to brown at the edge. These colors, forms, and other qualities do not necessarily relate to the Gare Saint Lazare, but come from filtered

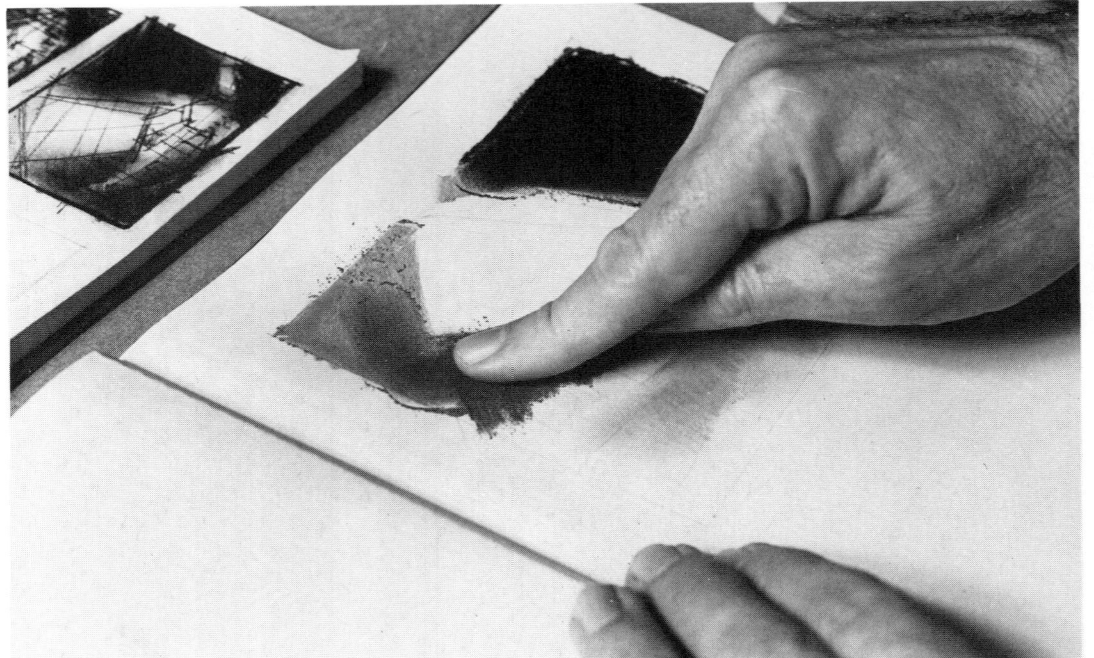

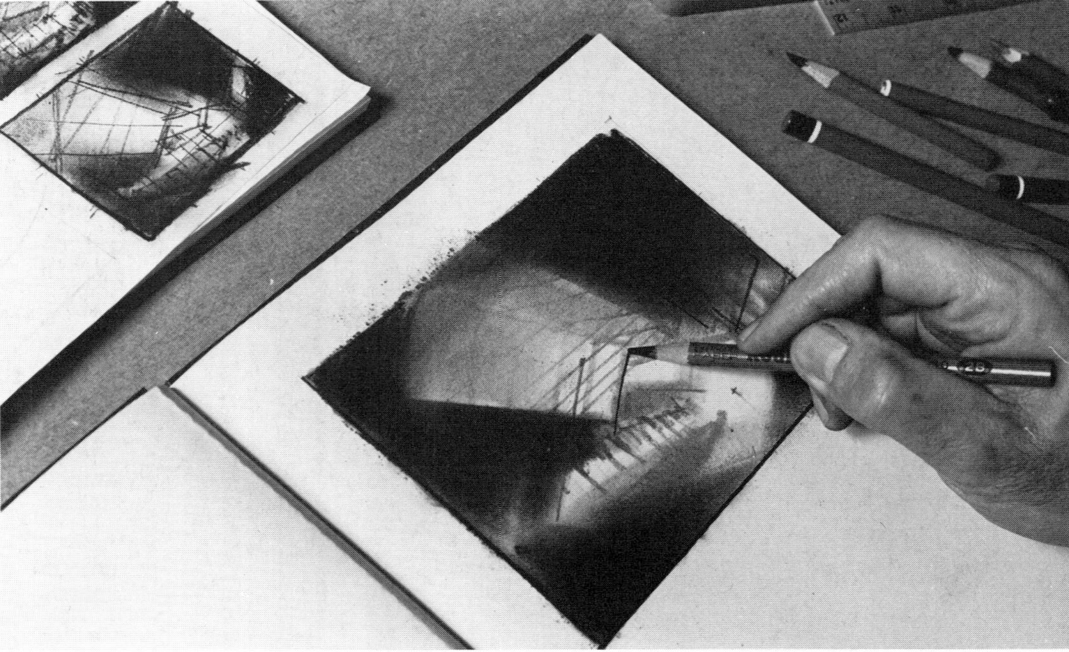

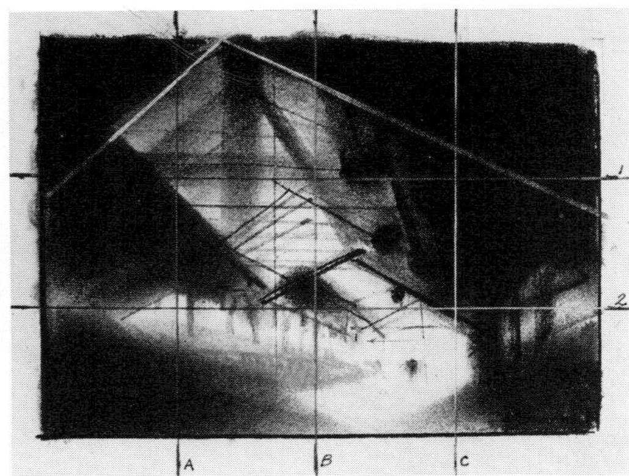

memories or feelings of other stations. The glowing bright colors that are picked out by the shafts of light from the skylights illustrate this merging of present reality and past recollections.

The thumbnail sketches and the final preliminary drawing were done with a good deal of finger smudging. Sometimes, I erased to obtain a white. Lines were put in to either strengthen the drawing or for sharp contrast.

The preliminary sketch does provide the broad outlines of the projected painting and may avoid basic compositional problems. It is planned as a help, not as a limitation, and it will be discarded if a change of approach seems appropriate during the course of the painting.

Squaring-up. In order to enlarge the drawing, I drew a grid of five lines: three vertical (A, B, C), and two horizontal (1, 2). This grid divides the drawing into twelve squares.

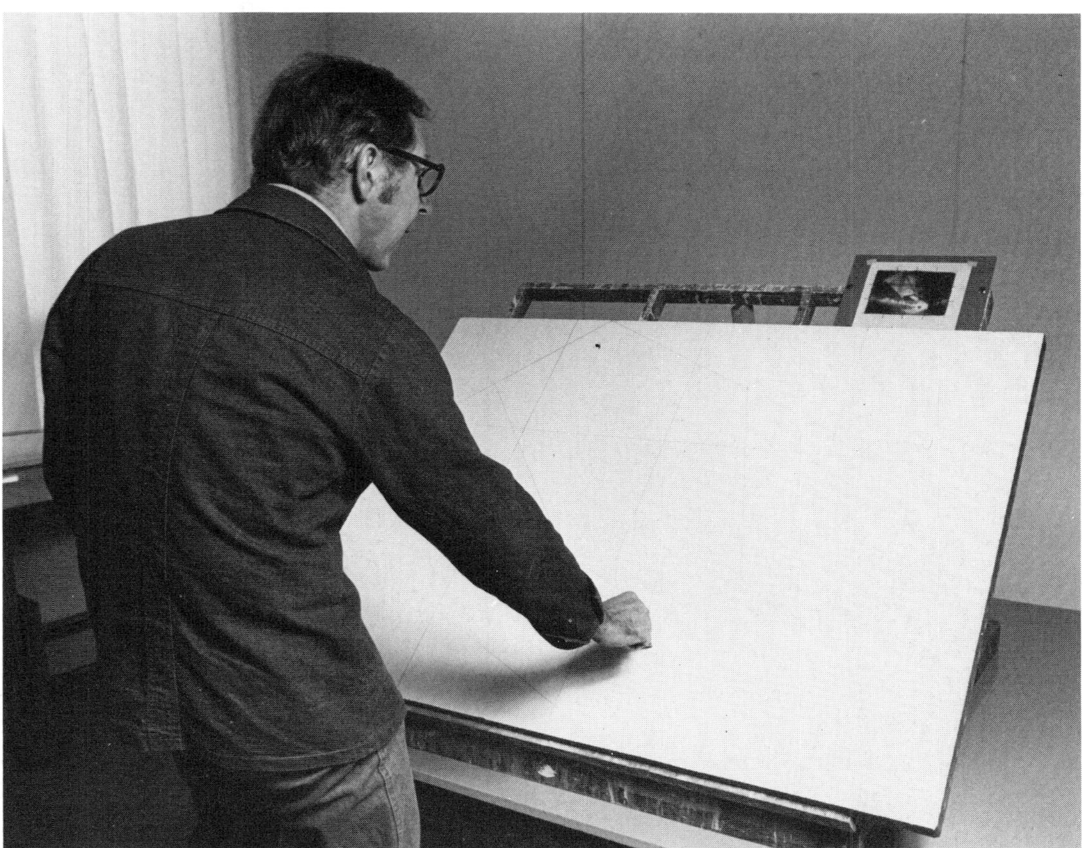

The acrylic underpainting

The stretched canvas. Because the drawing is proportioned three high to four wide, a textured canvas was stretched to the dimensions of 36″ x 48″. Using a knife, I covered the canvas with two coats of acrylic gesso.

Scaling-up. With a pencil, the canvas is divided into twelve equal squares to correspond to the twelve squares on the drawing. With the drawing in view, I plotted the basic lines of the composition on the canvas. This is done by defining the beginning and end points of each line and connecting them with a pencil line. For instance, the roof line runs from the top to the right edge of the sketch. The top of this line intersects the top edge of the sketch in square 2, about one-third the distance from line A to line B. The end of this line intersects the right edge of the sketch in square 8, about one-third the distance from line 1 to line 2. The rest of the compositional lines were plotted in the same fashion.

If the drawing had been more complicated, a smaller grid of forty-eight squares might have been used. The more squares, the more tedious is the plotting of points, even though the accuracy is improved. A similar, but more expensive and time-consuming method is to take a 35mm slide of the drawing and project it on the stretched canvas. Make sure that the edges of the drawing correspond to the edges of the canvas, and then trace the lines onto the canvas.

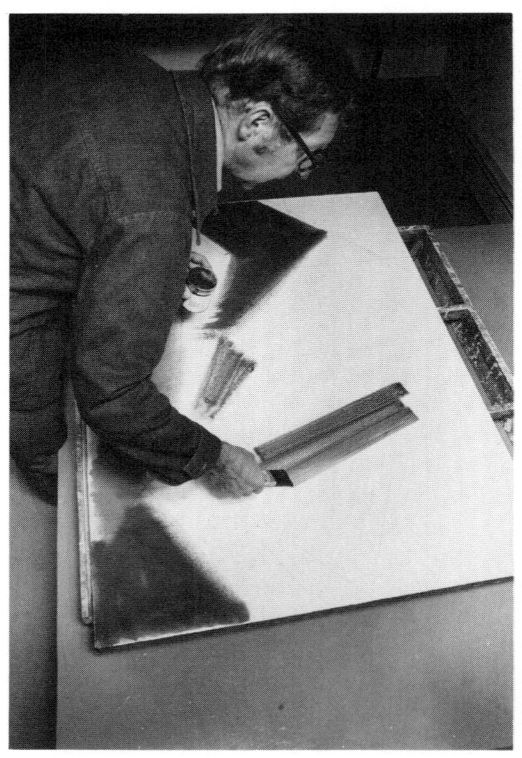

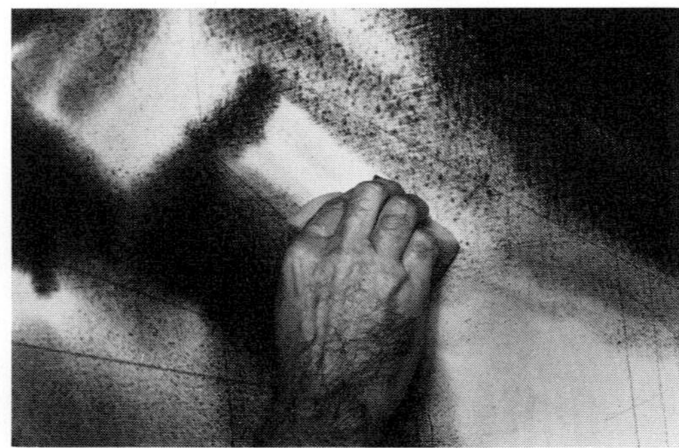

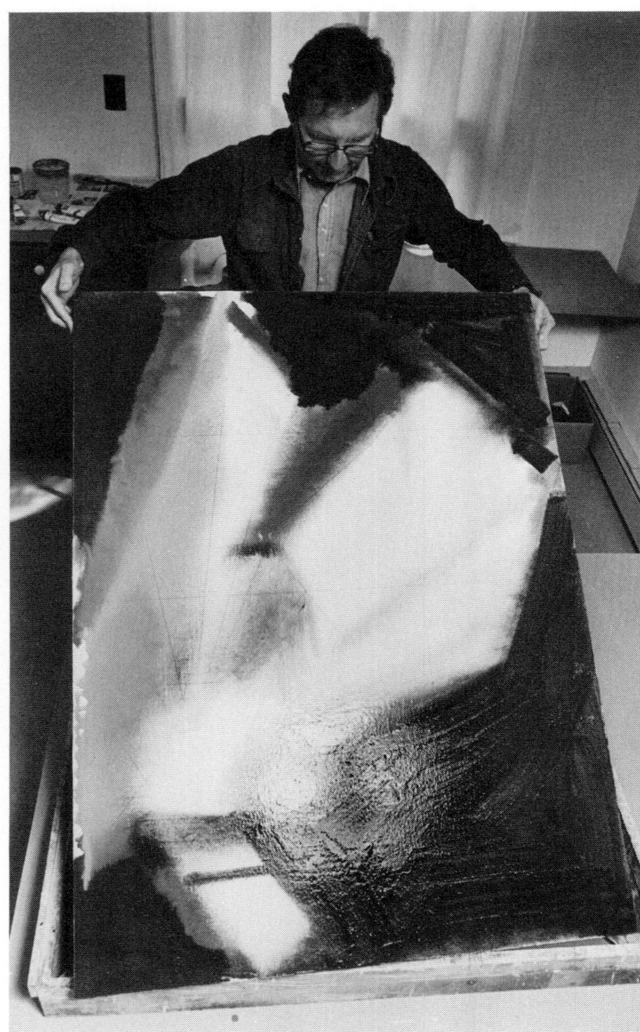

The first application is a series of colored acrylic washes that correspond to the pastel and charcoal tones of the preliminary drawing. I made a fluid mixture (one part pigment to two parts water) in separate cans for each of the four basic colors: raw sienna, cadmium red, thalo blue, and burnt sienna. I sponged the entire surface of the canvas to make it shining wet. Working from the lightest (raw sienna) to the darkest color (thalo blue), I applied the paint to the wet canvas with one-inch, flat nylon brushes. The canvas is kept horizontal while the paint is applied. Between applications, however, I often tilt it to allow the colors to mingle and run, achieving the soft effect of the drawing. Control is exerted by tilting, sponging off paint that has invaded a white area, and reapplying paint where it has become too weak. When the desired colors and tones are achieved, the canvas is left in a horizontal position on the easel to dry. Some additional mingling will occur as the painting dries. Also, because the colors will weaken just as in a wet-worked watercolor, overstate them during application.

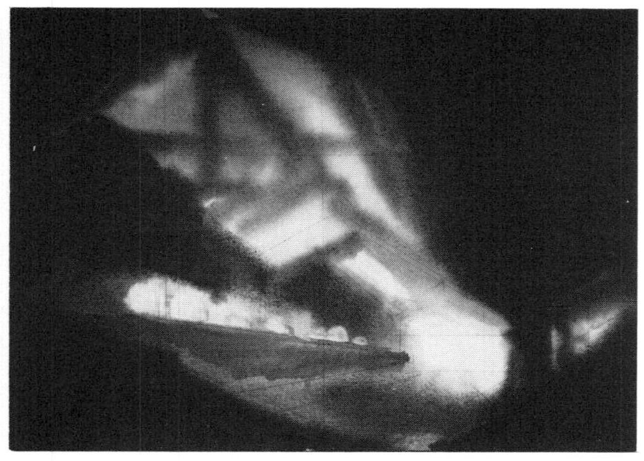

The completed first stage of acrylic underpainting.

Knifing on acrylic paste. The next stage is to apply thicker, smoother surfaced, and more sharply defined areas with a knife to contrast with the washes. This continues the development of form and drawing, and begins the complexity that will characterize the finished painting.

For the first application, I prepared a mixture with a painting knife of one part gel medium to two parts modeling paste on a piece of scrap cardboard. To make the mixture opaque white when it dries, I added a small amount of white acrylic paint. If the mixture is too thin, add powdered white pigment. This is applied with a knife or a sponge to areas of the painting through masks and stencils.

Masks and stencils. The letter and number stencil sheet is commercially available. The circles, simple geometric shapes, and rows of arches and dots are made from stencil paper using punches, a cutting compass knife, and a straight edge. These will be used in the acrylic and oil painting stages. They can be used over again if the paint is wiped off after use. More fragile, single-use masks can be made from newspaper. These are exceptionally useful for very large shapes. Masks and stencils provide a quick, precise means of applying painted shapes and to remove areas of wet paint (subtractive painting). Masking tape is also used to create a variety of sharply defined lines, edges, and shapes.

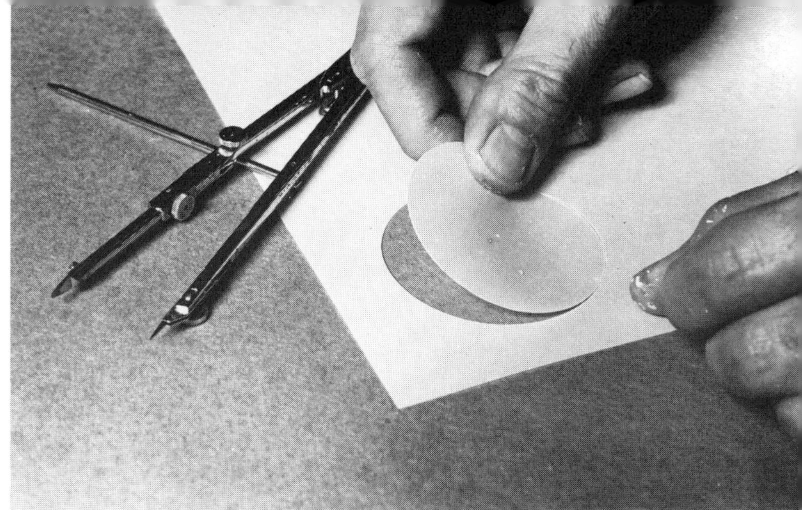

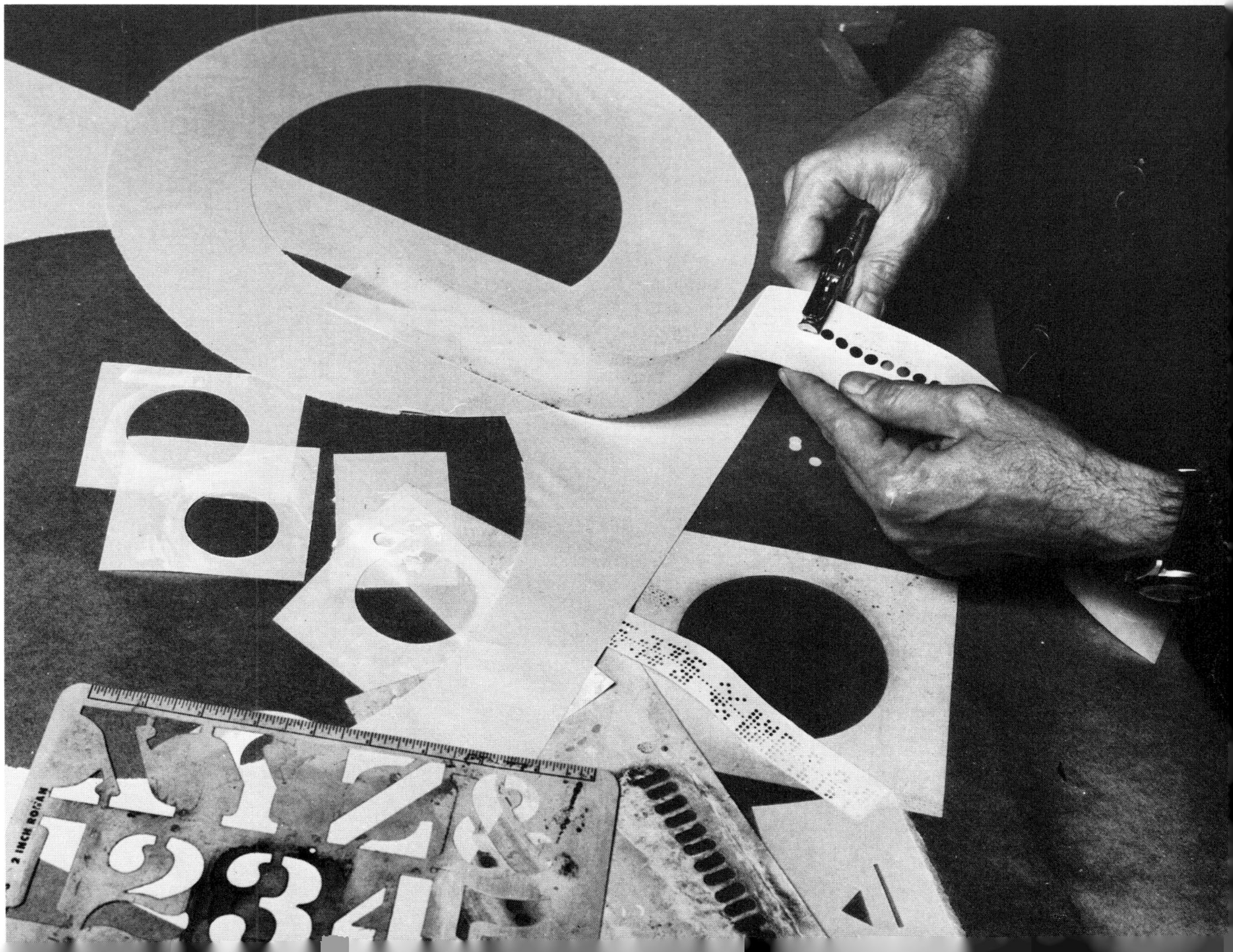

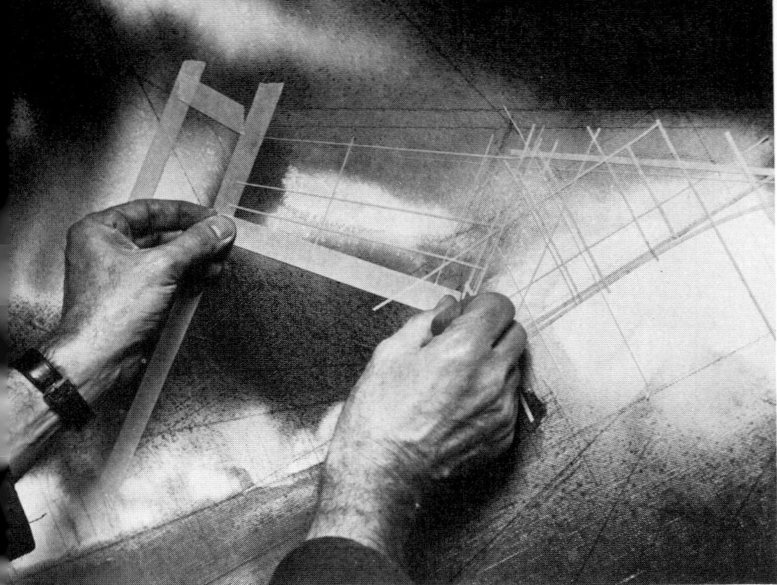

I first worked on the gable end of the train shed and the adjoining skylight in the far end of the roof. To define the bars between the panes of glass, a series of narrow strips of masking tape is cut and pressed onto the painting in a grid pattern. Wider strips of tape are used to define the outer limits of these areas. The acrylic paste mixture is then knifed on within the wider tapes. After the paste has been built up to a thickness of approximately one-sixteenth of an inch and smoothed out, carefully lift off the tapes. The result is a well-defined pattern of triangles and rectangles in low relief.

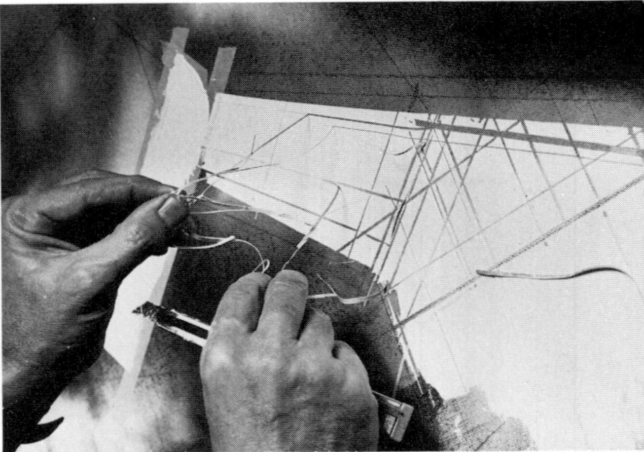

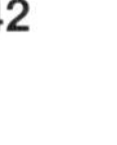

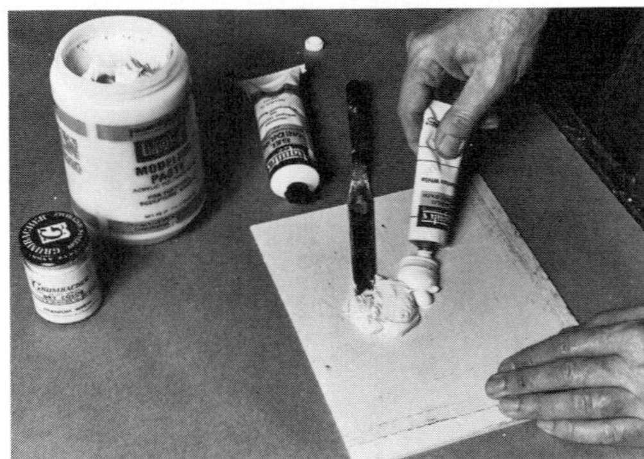

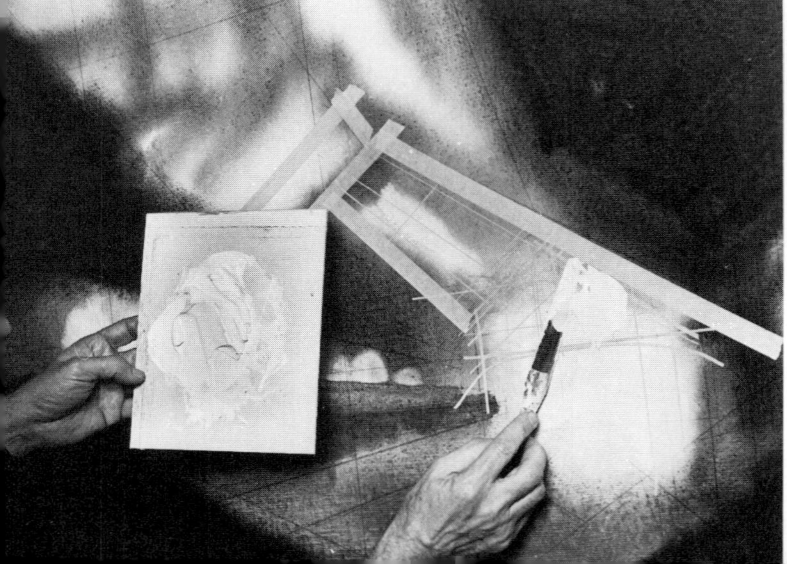

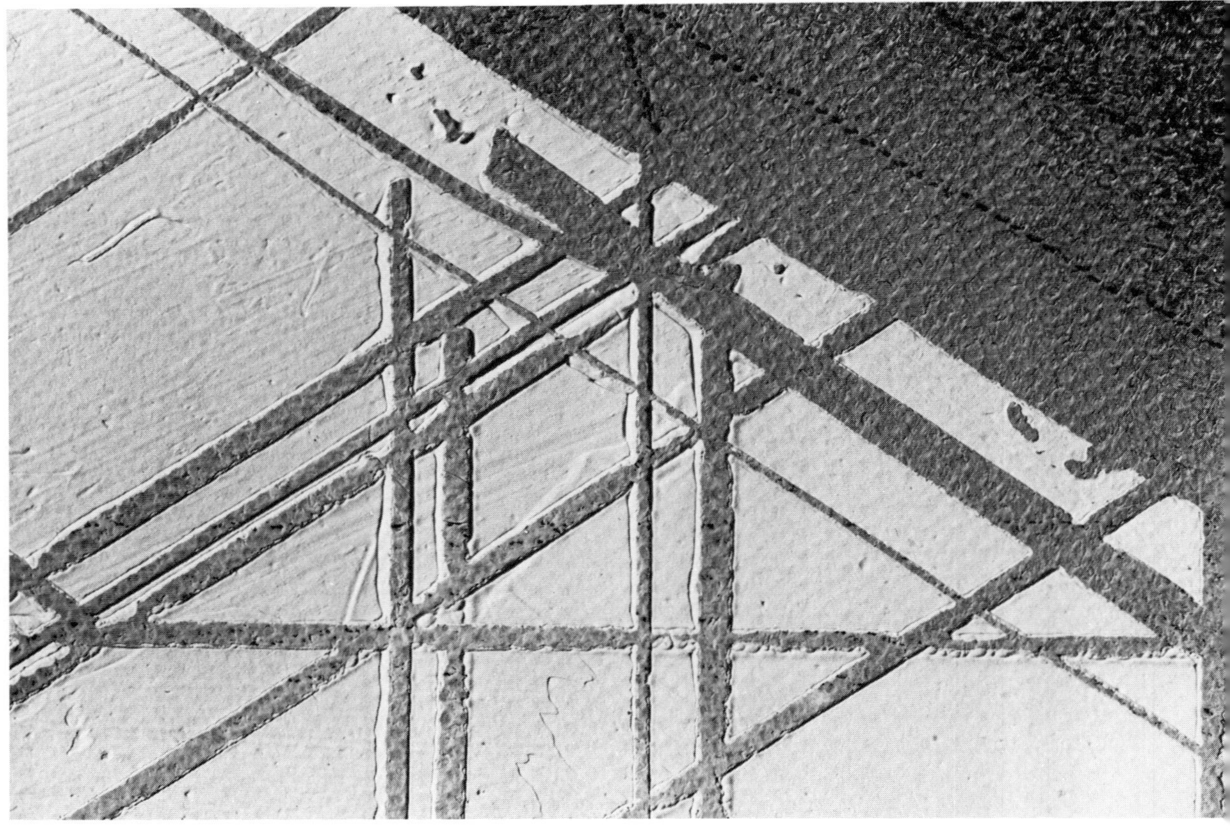

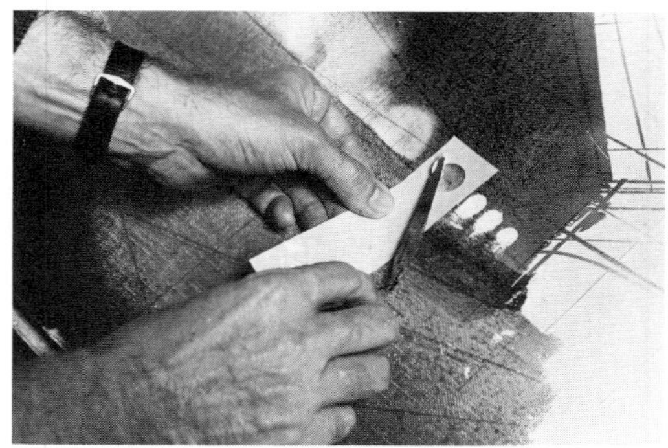

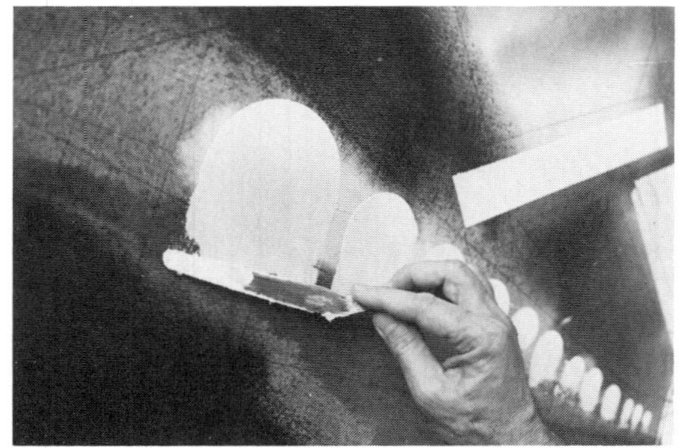

A row of circles which increases in size from the center to the left edge of the painting is added. This defines the light arches between the columns above the train at the left side of the train station. After the paste has been pressed through the circle masks and while it is still wet, I dragged it downwards toward the bottom of the painting, extending it and changing its shape from a circle to an archway. Other shapes of white paste are placed on for the skylight.

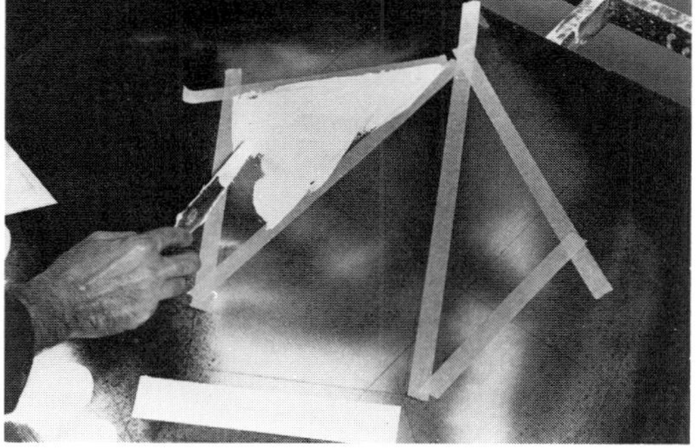

Another batch of paste colored with cadmium red acrylic paint is used to make a long triangular patch which indicates the train receding into the distance. Blue and then brown will be applied to the large dark areas of the roof, the foreground corners, and the dark columns at the right.

The completed second stage of the acrylic underpainting is below.

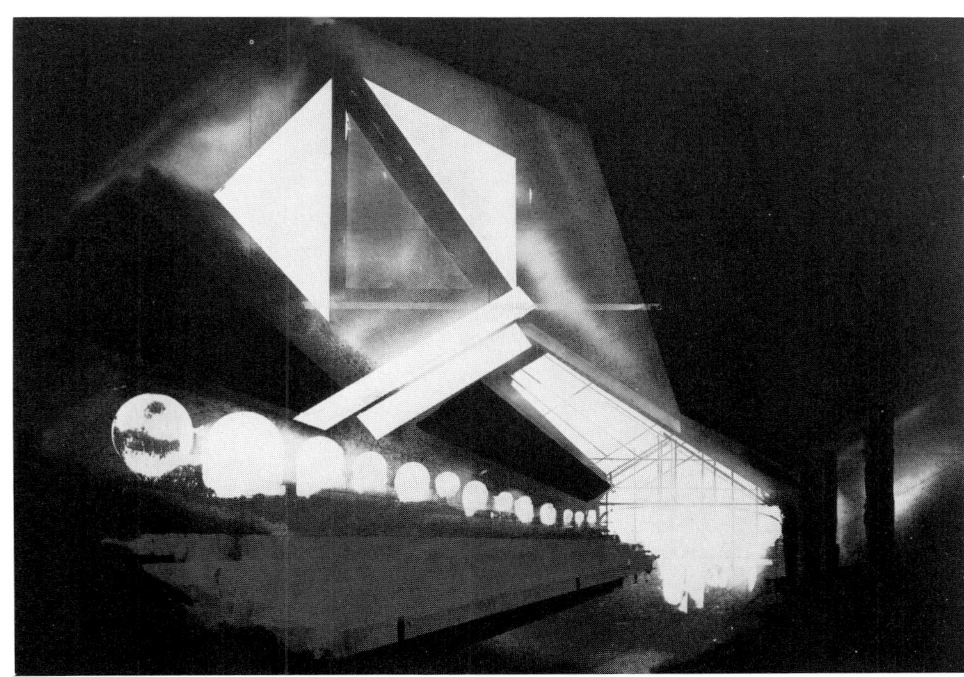

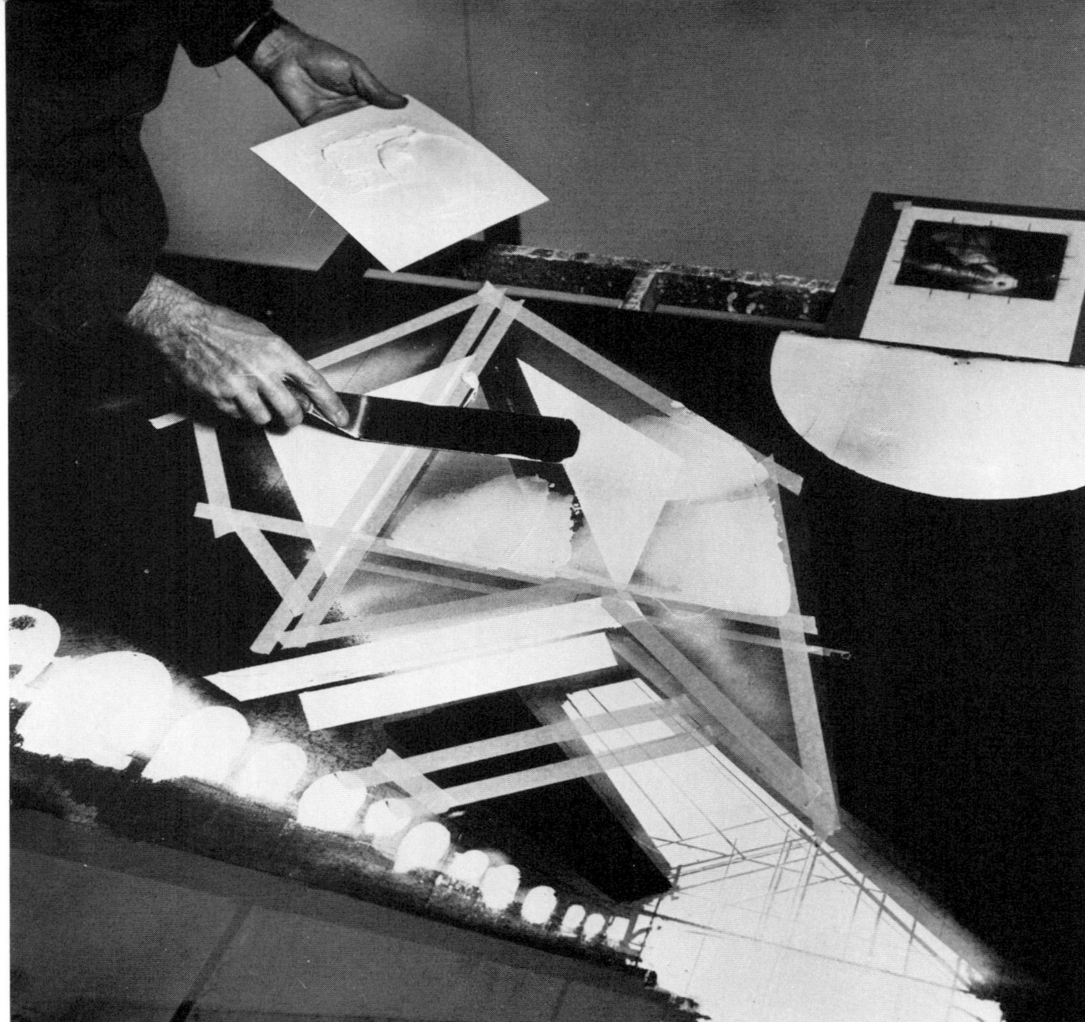

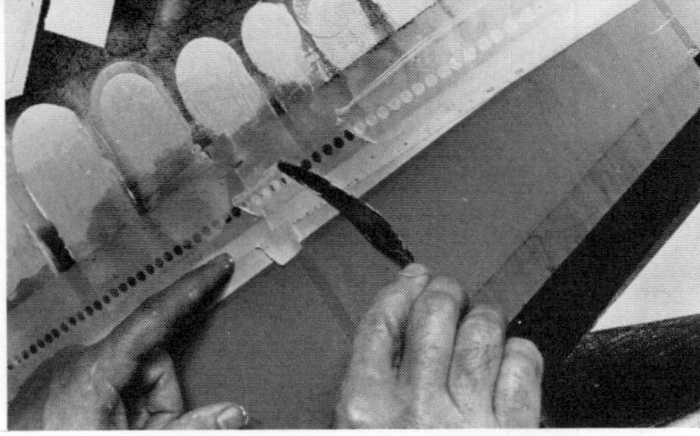

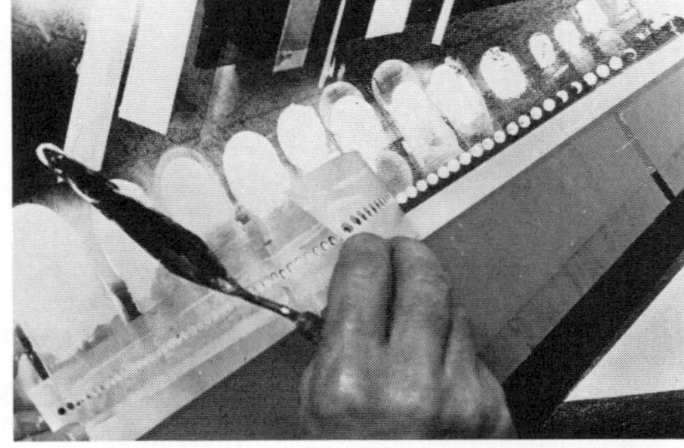

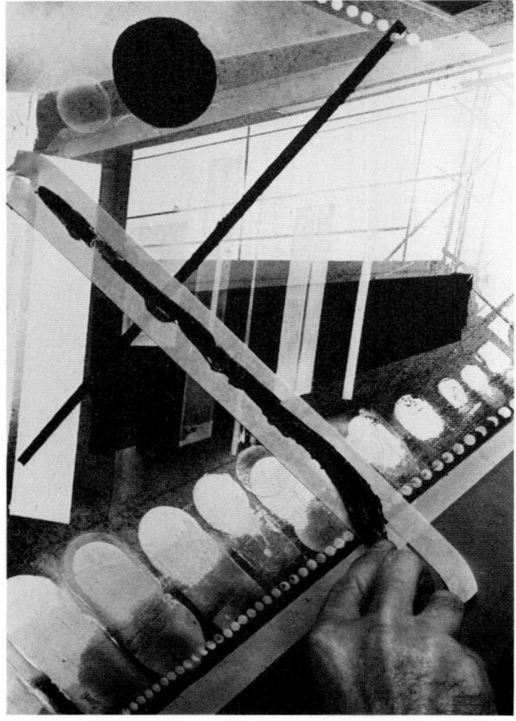

For the third stage, I made a semitransparent acrylic paste to further define the form and space. This will begin to suggest the ambiguities that will come from transparencies and overlappings. By using a mixture of modeling paste and gel, almost transparent shapes are positioned to weave in and out of the opaque white shapes to pull them all together. I used a large spatula knife to apply these areas. Rows of small lights are created through the use of a hand-punched stencil. The upper right roof line, the perspective lines that define the trains in the foreground, and the roof of the train at the left are all put in with masking tape and paste. The large light discs at the upper right are knifed in with circle stencils cut from newspapers.

A dark disc and lines are put in to further define the roof structure.

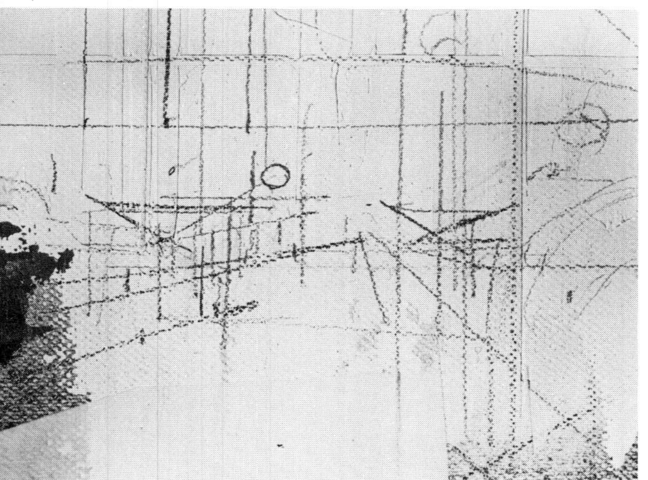

With a pencil, detail is added at the horizon line under the far end of the roof. Using small stencils, I knifed on white acrylic paste to produce a textured pattern of shapes at what will be the focal point of the painting. Circles and rectangles of thick paste are worked into the triangular gable end of the roof.

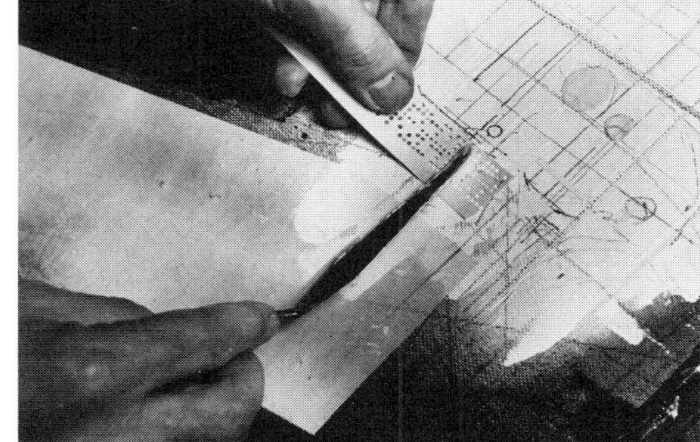

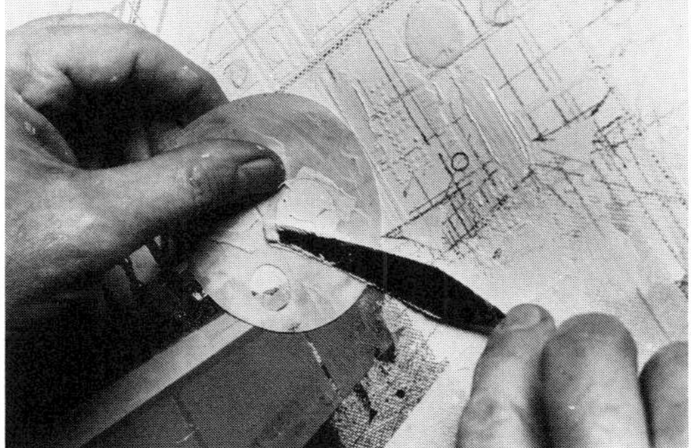

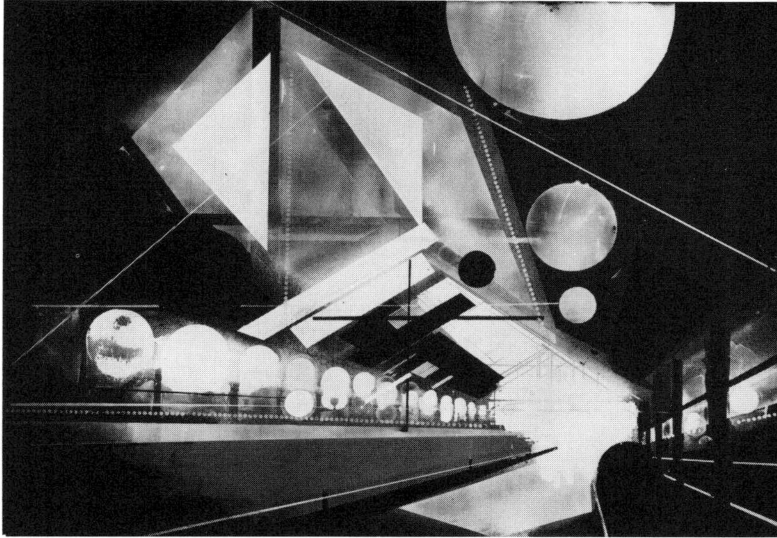

The completed third stage of the painting: the acrylic underpainting is finished. After drying for a few hours, the oil painting phase will begin.

The preceding steps might have been done with oil paint, but extensive drying time between applications would have been required due to the thickness of some areas. The acrylic paste and paint provide a faster means to achieve a similar effect. Collage materials could also have been incorporated because the acrylics act as an adhesive and sealer if cloth or paper are used. In this painting, the built-up edges, lines, and raised and depressed areas will provide a receptive surface for the oil paint washes.

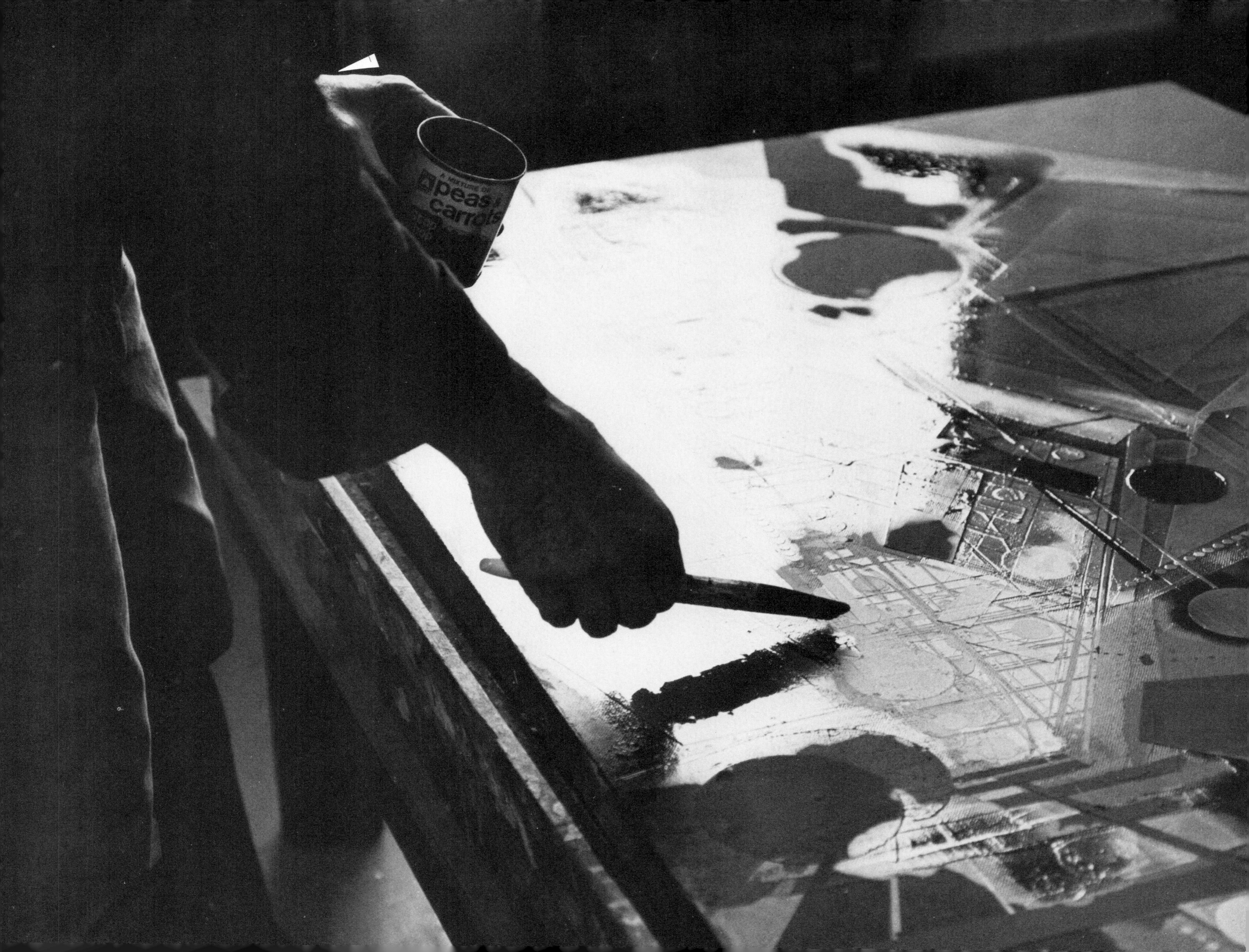
A MIXTURE OF
peas
carrots

The oil painting

The first step is the use of thin turpentine washes (one part oil paint to six parts turpentine). Beginning with a solution of raw sienna, and using a one-inch flat brush, I sometimes dropped, sometimes brushed it onto the surface of the painting. The fluid color runs into the low areas, lines, and hollows, creating a drawing network and giving form to what was just a light colored texture. The same thing is done in other areas in thalo blue. The strongest effect with this technique is in the light gable end of the train shed and just below it. A white turpentine wash is applied to some of the dark areas of the painting. This white wash is also used to soften those areas that have a hard, light and dark contrast.

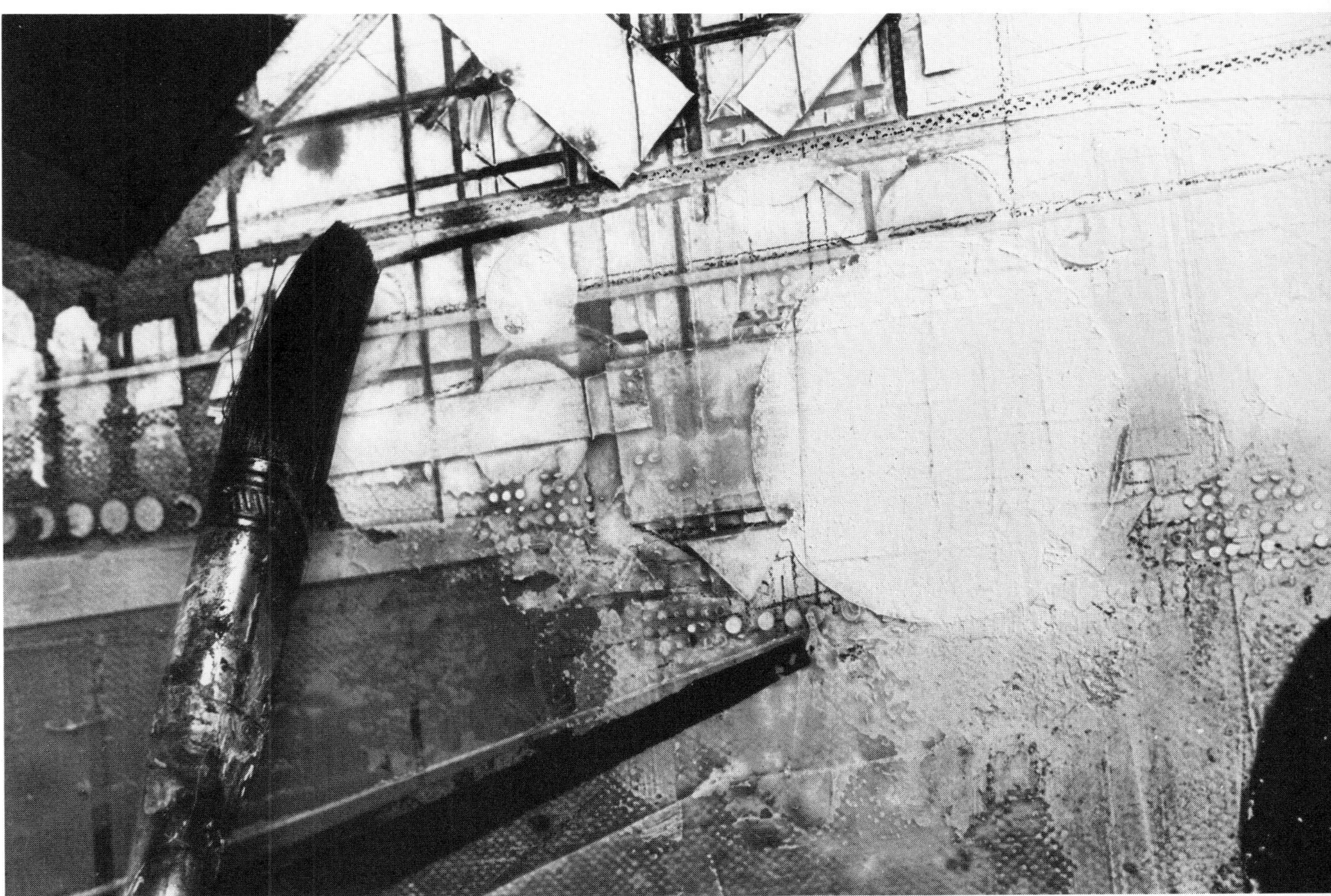

Using sponges, stencils, and masks, I next applied thin layers of oil paint. From a paper palette, thalo blue paint is picked up and applied with a foam rubber sponge. A small amount of turpentine is added to the sponge to make the paint spread more easily. Two strips of masking tape mark off a wide vertical blue stripe which runs from the top to the bottom at left center of the painting. By pulling the paint-charged sponge across in this way, a semitransparent blue film is applied which allows the shapes underneath it to show through. Similar stripes are put in other parts of the roof and in the entire upper right and left corners.

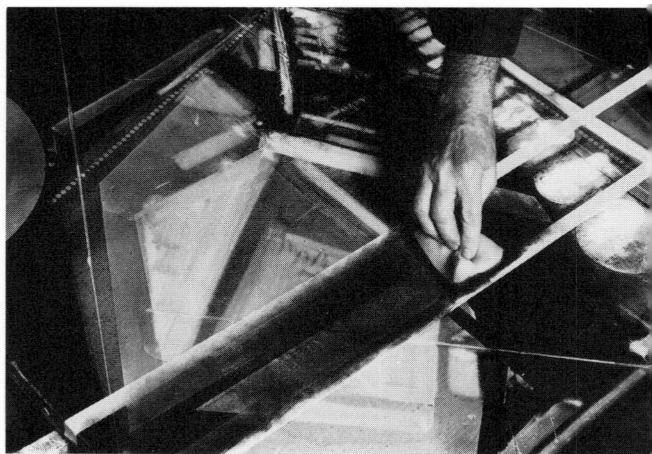

The same procedure is followed with burnt sienna, filling the two lower corners of the painting. If a gloss is desired in the dried paint film, a mixture of linseed oil, damar varnish, and turpentine in equal parts should be used on the sponge instead of plain turpentine.

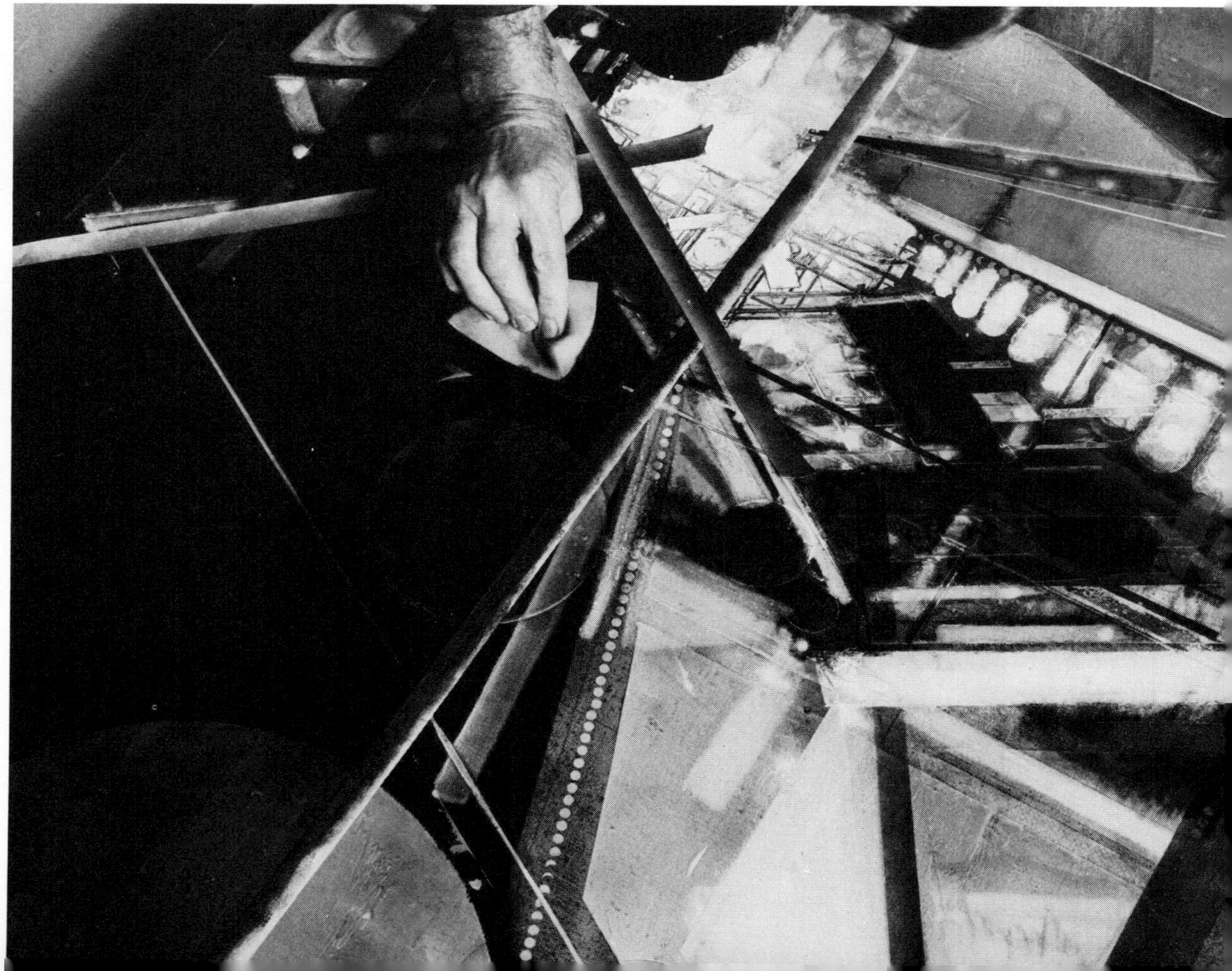

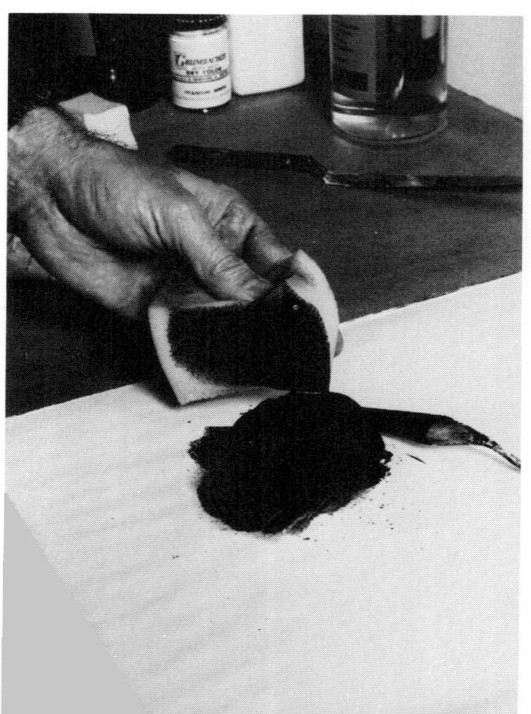

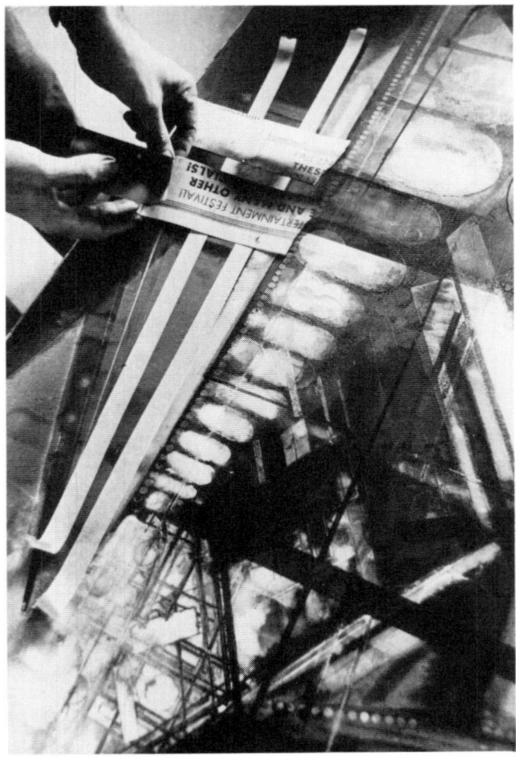

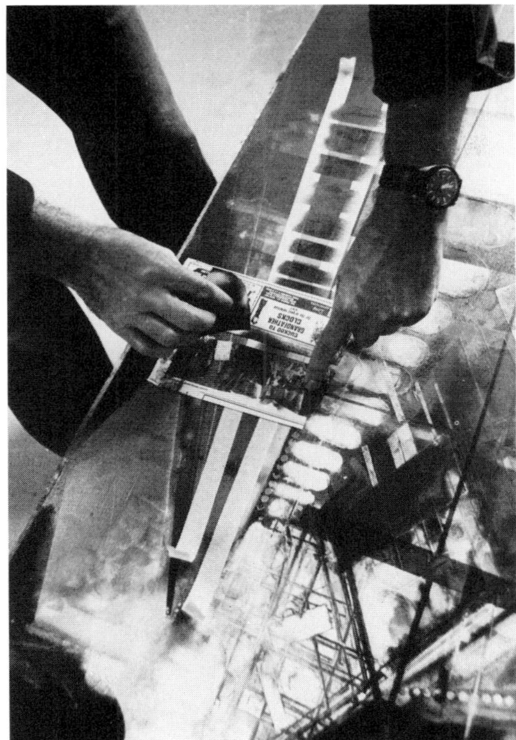

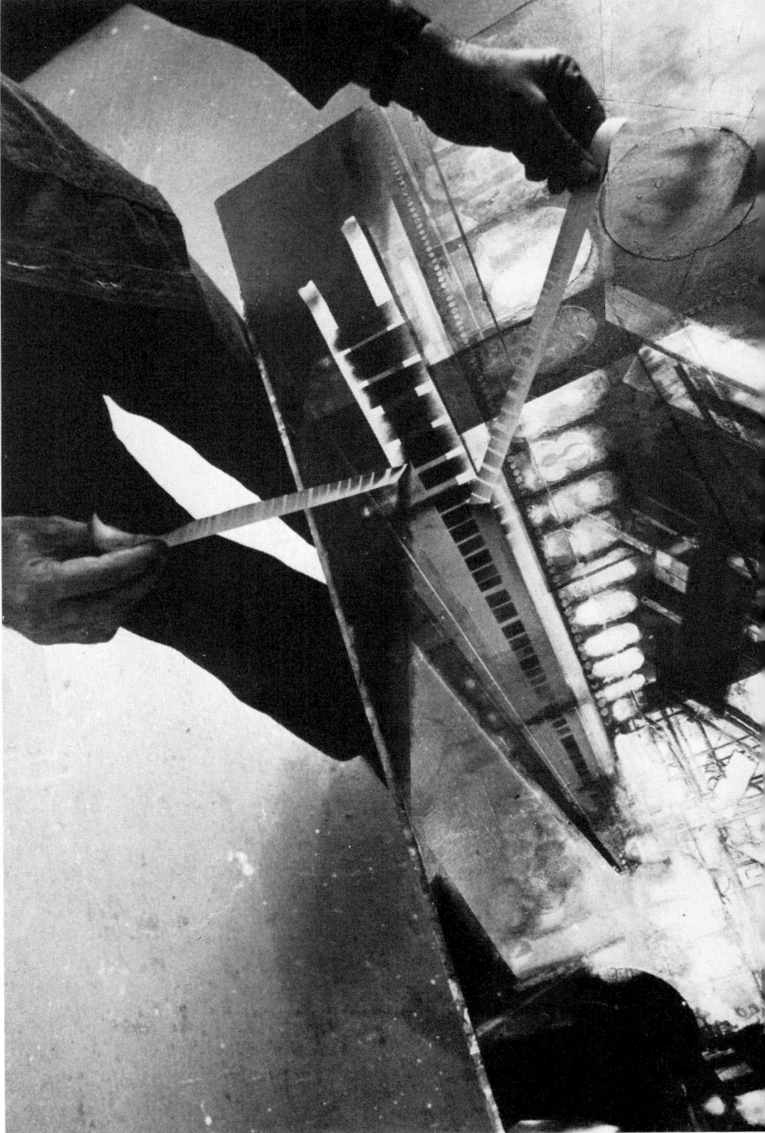

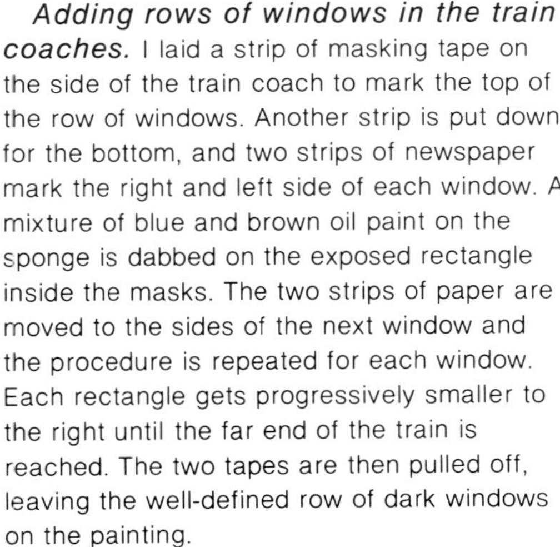

Adding rows of windows in the train coaches. I laid a strip of masking tape on the side of the train coach to mark the top of the row of windows. Another strip is put down for the bottom, and two strips of newspaper mark the right and left side of each window. A mixture of blue and brown oil paint on the sponge is dabbed on the exposed rectangle inside the masks. The two strips of paper are moved to the sides of the next window and the procedure is repeated for each window. Each rectangle gets progressively smaller to the right until the far end of the train is reached. The two tapes are then pulled off, leaving the well-defined row of dark windows on the painting.

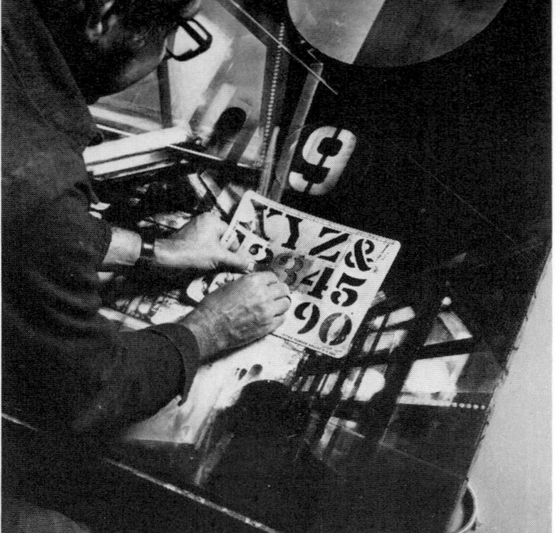

Light colored (raw sienna mixed with white) numbers were sponged on through a stencil. In like manner, other light shapes were put in: the headlight in the lower right foreground, roof lines, discs of light over the train and at the end of the train shed.

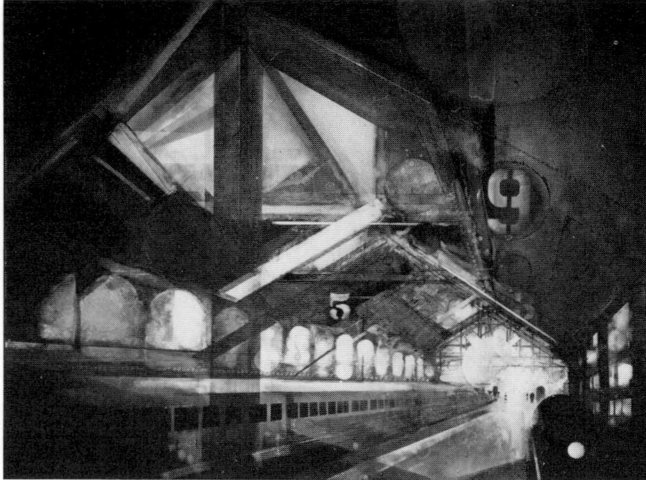

The painting at this stage shows a general softening of tonalities and the addition of more specific details.

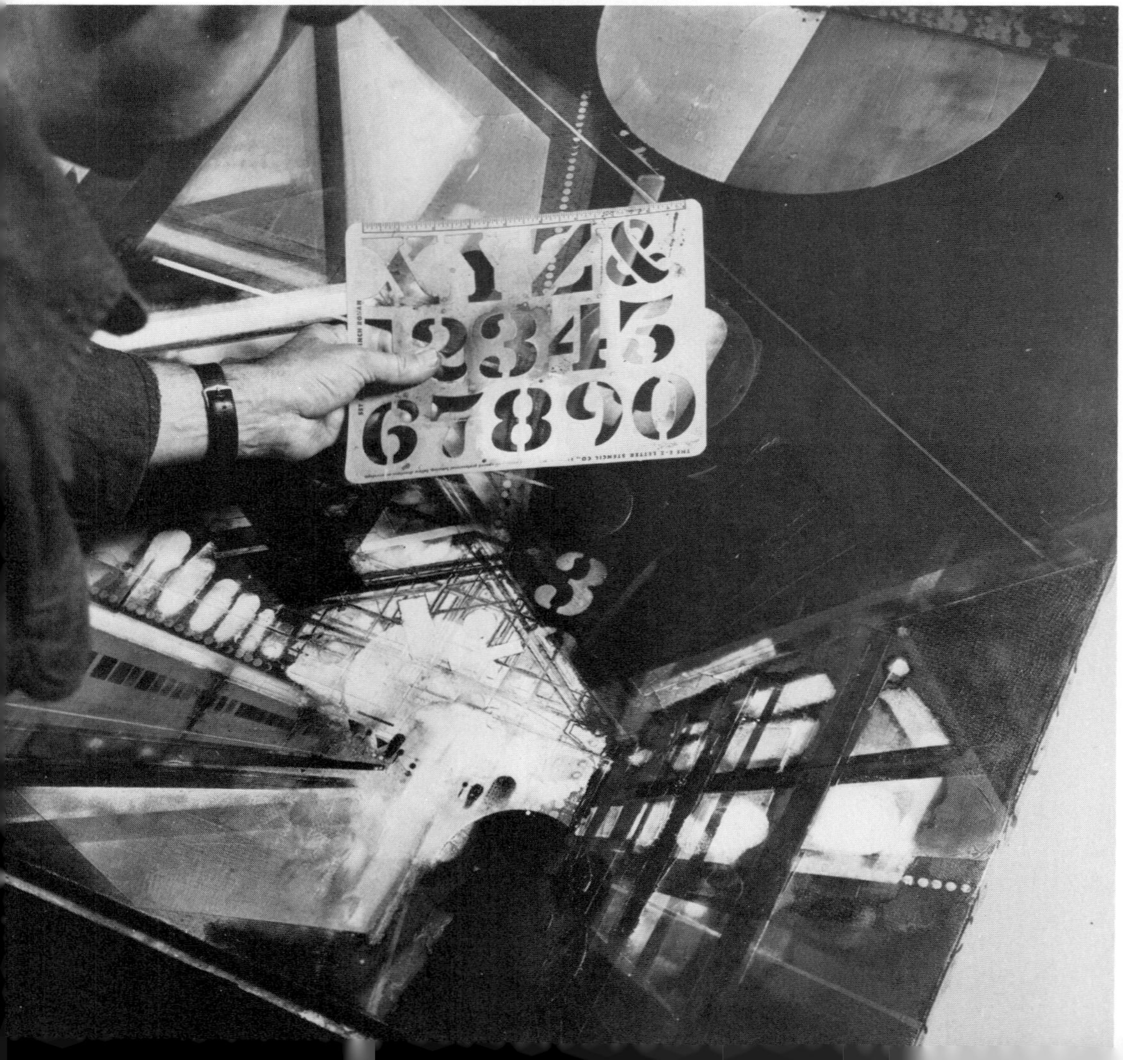

Adding sharp detail. The next step is to apply paint with the brush and ruling pen. A small pointed brush charged with fluid paint defines and adds to the columns supporting the roof. The dragged brush stroke contrasts to the sharp geometry of the masked lines. A wider flat brush charged with dark paint is used to roughly suggest figures on the platform in the lower right foreground. As the painting progresses, its character shifts between sharp and geometric and soft and romantic. Whenever it seems to be going too far in one direction, it is pushed back to the other.

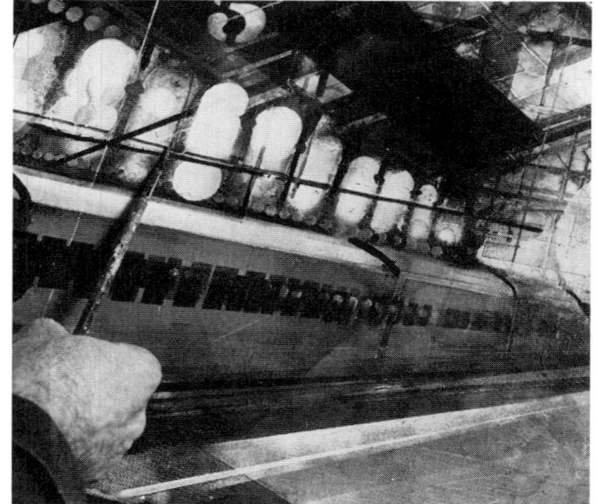

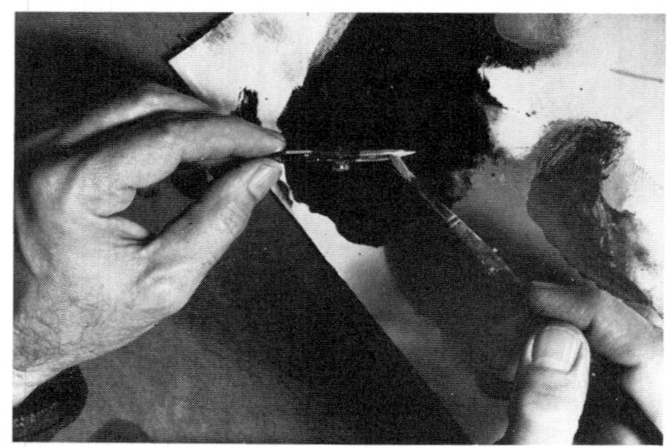

Using a pointed brush, the ruling pen is charged with fluid, light, oil paint (thinned with turpentine). With a drafting triangle as a guide, a light line is ruled under the train windows. Another light line is dragged with the pen across the skylight area.

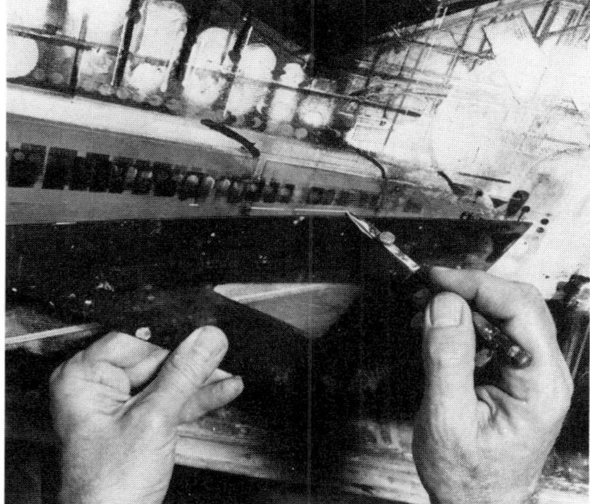

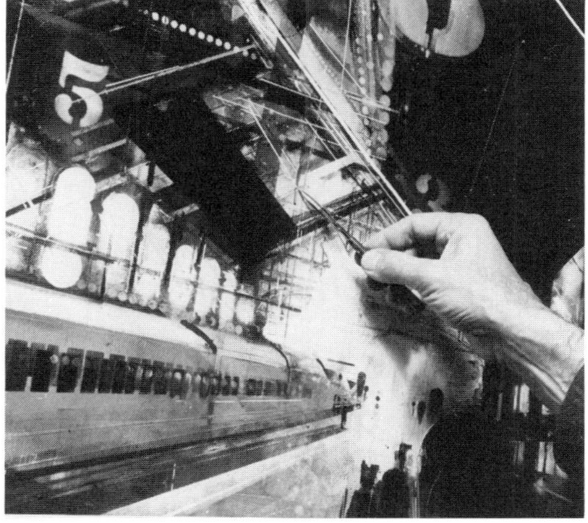

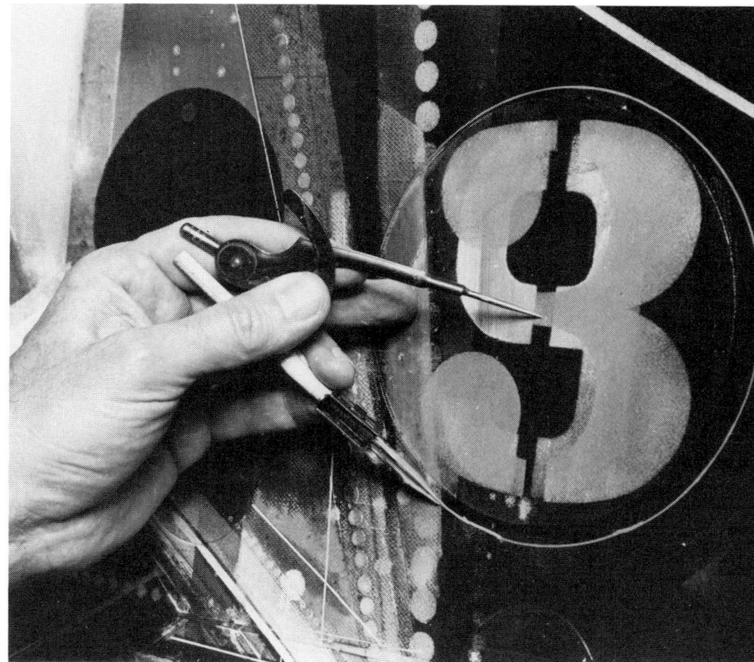

Using a ruling pen compass, various sized circles are drawn to reinforce the background circles or to add small detail on the light, distant horizon.

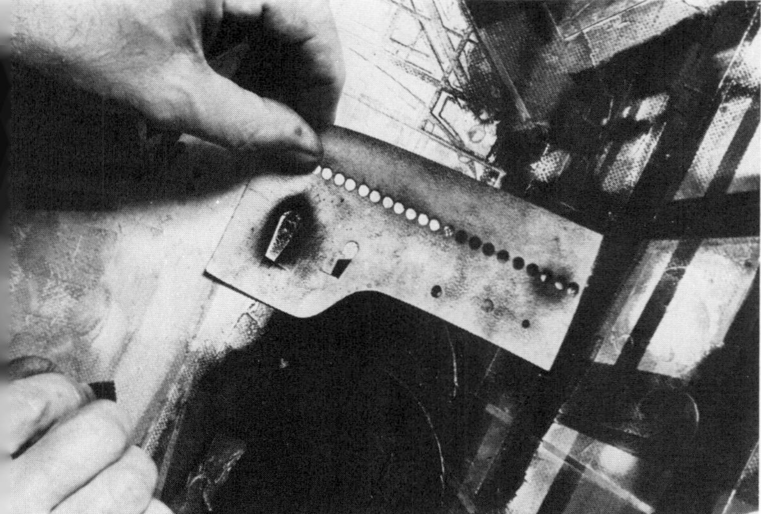

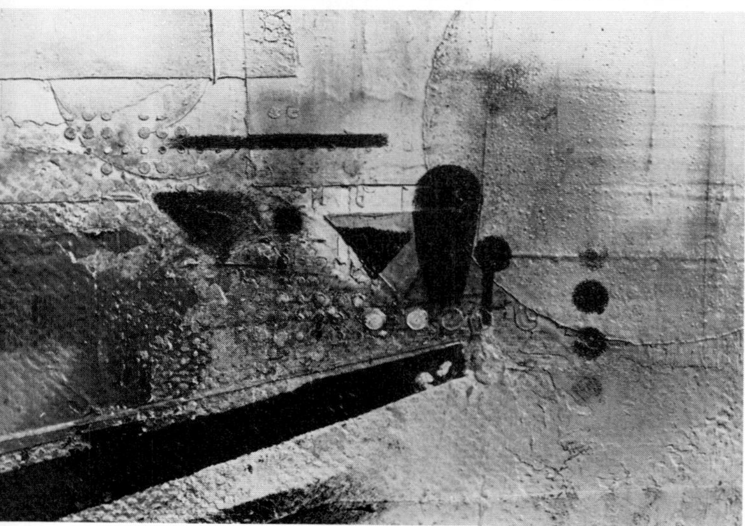

Sponge and stencils are used with cadmium red and raw sienna to add strong but very small shapes in the deepest part of the painting.

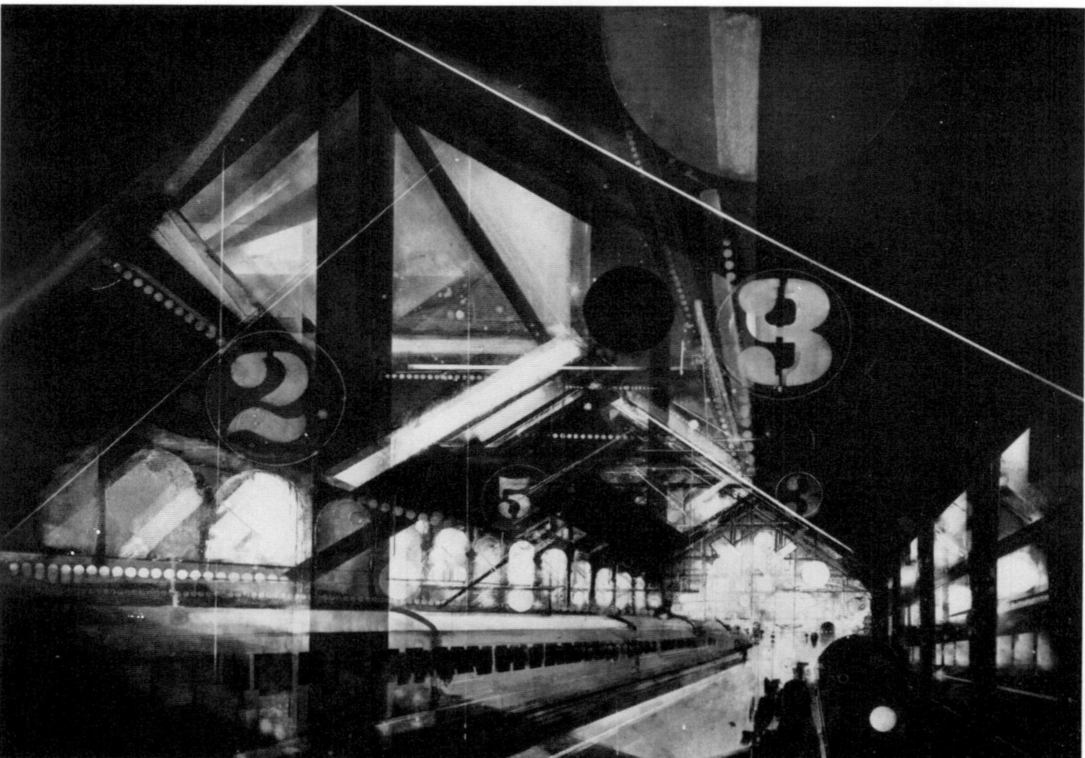

The painting at this stage contains most of the essential forms, but the important adjustment of values, tones, and points of emphasis is yet to come.

Reworkings. The last phase is the most challenging. It is the point at which the painting should come alive so that the total *is* greater than the sum of its parts. It is the adjustments: lighter here, darker there; softer edges, sharper edges; more detail, less detail—just the right balance of all the elements. Sometimes it seems that the right combination is just one step away; that just one more small alteration is all that is needed to make the whole snap into place and achieve the rightness that can be felt rather than explained. So, the small alteration is made, but still something is wrong. Another change is made; the roof is darkened with a transparent blue tone. It helps, but not enough. The arches are too regular, too defined, and a tone is applied over them to push them back into the shadows. Then they seem somehow empty, and a row of hanging lights is added.

The same sort of reworking took place on the train coaches. The rows of windows were nearly sponged out with red tones, and transparent white shafts of light were brushed over them. Then some of the windows were brought back again, this time with upper and lower openings. Similarly, the white focal point of the painting was reworked, made busier with ruled lines, patches of white impasto and finally pulled together by sponging on a large white disc and knifing on a smaller white circle with thick paint.

Tedious as they may seem, these reworkings add a quality to the painting. The effect of partially or totally hidden shapes and details gives a richness and dimension. A tension is set up between these stages in the growth of the painting, and tension has much to do with the impact and staying power of a work of art. Tensions of various kinds: the tension of spatial ambiguity, as when the exact position of a column or arch is unclear or when a space can be read in more than one way; the tension of surface, as when a distant area which had been drawn in has receded from the surface but is brought back with texture; the tension when small scale makes a form recede but warm color and sharp contour make it advance; the tension when some painted shapes are vague, but have enough suggestion of form for the viewer's eye to articulate them as figures.

The finished painting provides a set of visual clues which the viewer adds up, thus participating to make a complete visual experience. In this case, it was the space, light, color, forms, atmosphere of *The* railway station—not any in particular, but an ultimate, universal place of memory and feeling. (See color reproduction on page 56.)

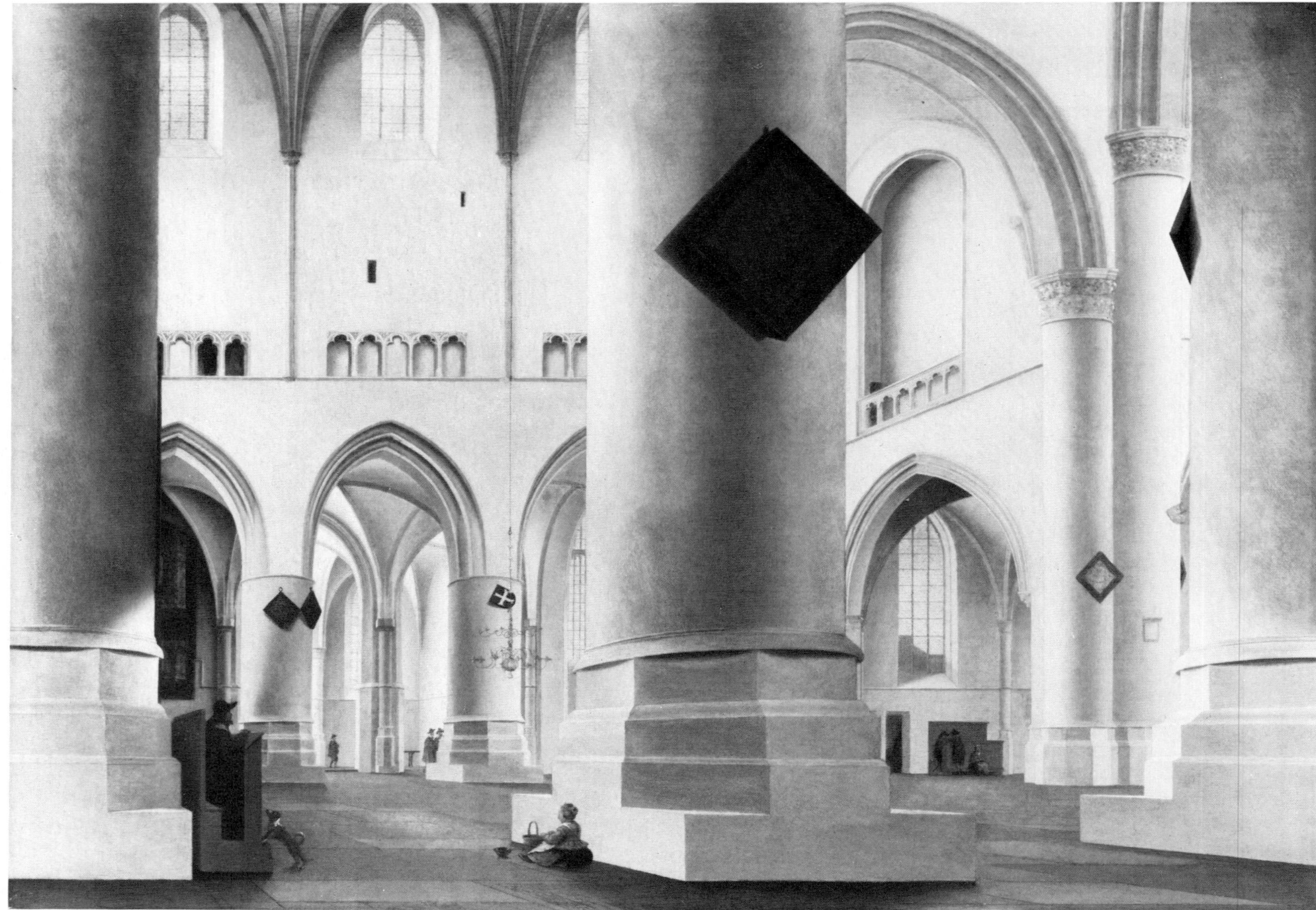

Interior of St. Bavo, Haarlem, **1636-1637. Oil on wood, 32⅛" x 23$^{7}/_{16}$". Pieter Saenredam. Courtesy of the Trustees of the National Gallery, London.**

It has been said that no one could paint a bare wall like Saenredam. This seventeenth-century Dutch painter is responsible for some of the most remarkable portraits of architecture ever made. His cool, light-filled interiors incorporate an almost unbelievable range of whites. Concave and convex volumes, constantly changing spatial intervals and complexities work on a descriptive and abstract level. He drew his subjects meticulously and then painted them with clarity and delicacy, eliminating everything that was not essential to the mood that he had set out to capture.

The subject in this large painting is a pedestrian bridge under the skylighted roof of a large, London railway station. It is a study in diagonals: the composition takes its cue from the roof structure, repeating it in the bridge railings, and echoing it in the band of activity at the bottom of the picture. The loose, sketchy technique acts as counterpart to the firmly drawn composition.

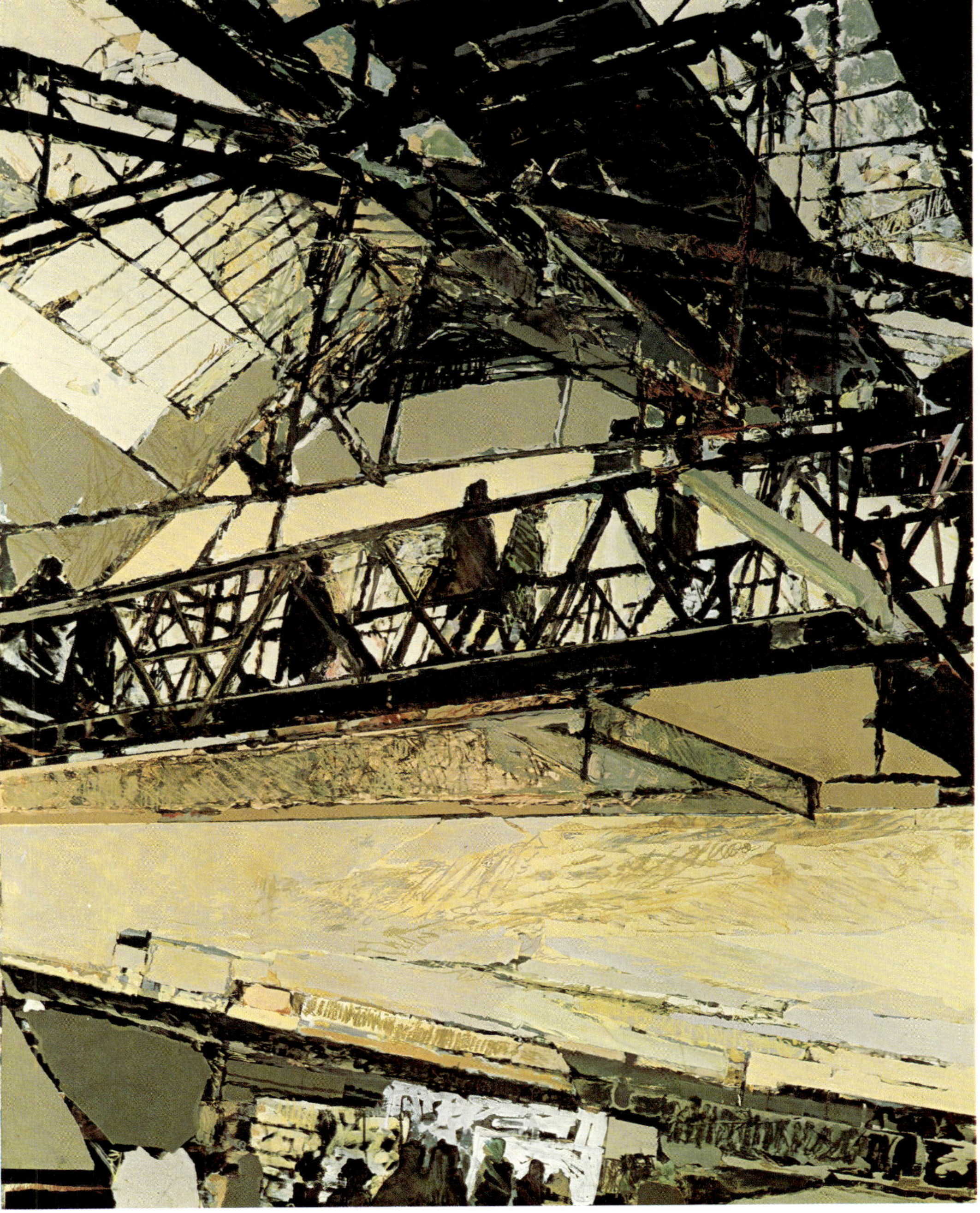

Catwalk, 1976. Acrylic, pastel, and collage on canvas. Flora Natapoff. Photograph by Greg Heins.

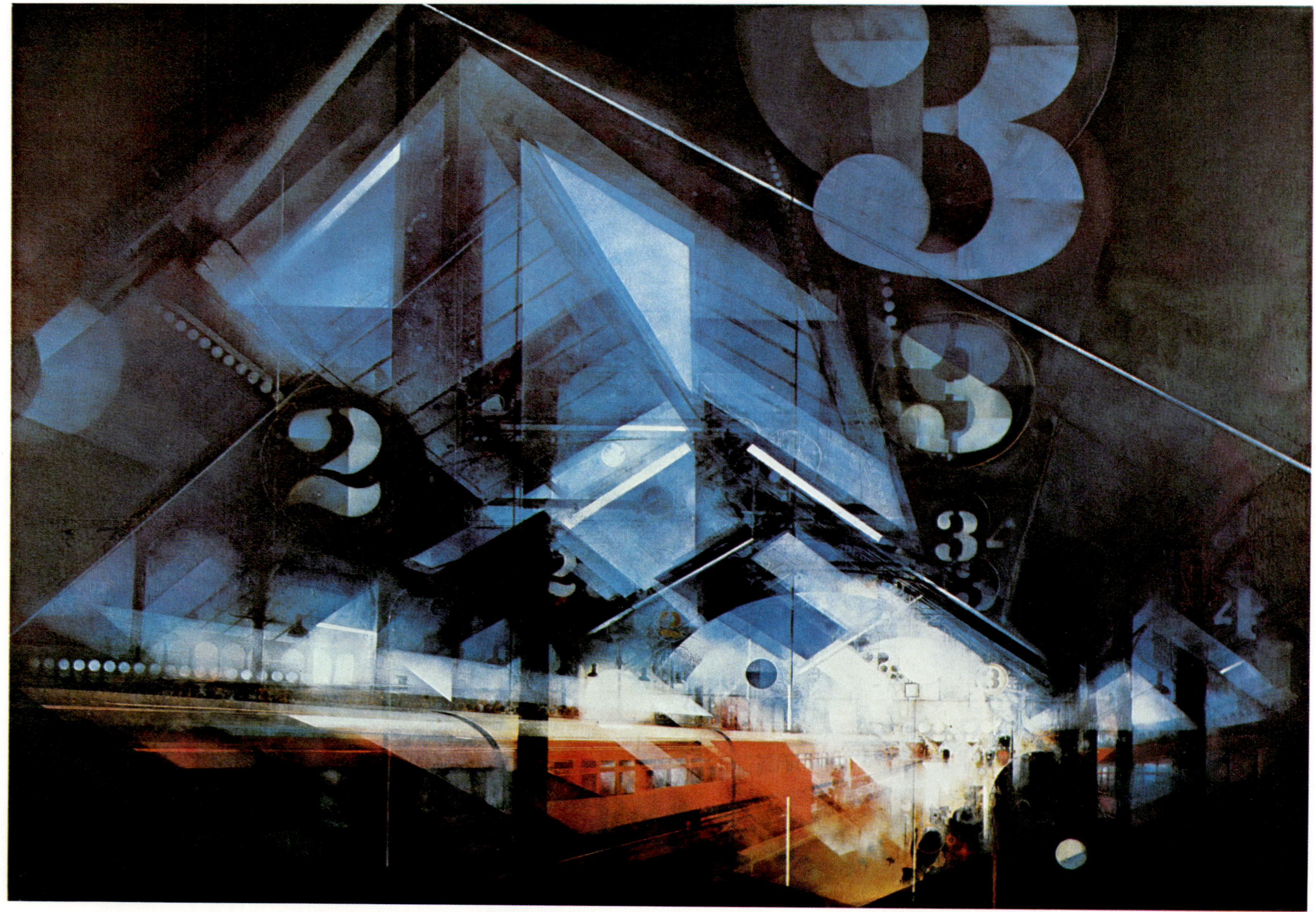

The Railway Station, 1978. Acrylic and oil, 36″ x 48″.

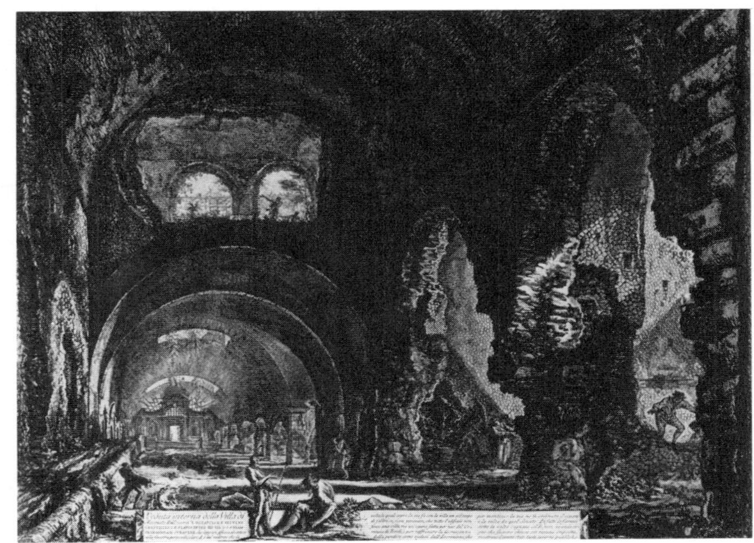

Veduta Interna della Villa di Mecenate, **1764. Etching, 18½" x 24¼". Giovanni Battista Piranesi. Photograph by Ralph MacKenzie.**

Trained as an architect, Piranesi's strong interest in buildings found an outlet in powerful black-and-white etchings. He studied Roman ruins and Baroque structures from a variety of viewpoints and under all lighting conditions, including moonlight, looking for the effects which would best portray the beauty he found in them. His remarkable visual memory allowed him to work directly on his plates with only rough shorthand notes made on site for reference. Through the manipulation of viewpoints, exaggerated perspective, and imaginative chiaroscuro, he achieved a heightened sense of poetic grandeur. Proof of his imaginative distortions can be found by comparing some of his prints to the motifs which still exist and trying to match his viewpoint.

In this print, one in his series of Roman views, the interior of the ruined villa is given gargantuan proportions through the placing of tiny human figures at key points, such as in the two arches at upper left. The effect is intensified by the skillful use of veils and shafts of light which penetrate the dark vault.

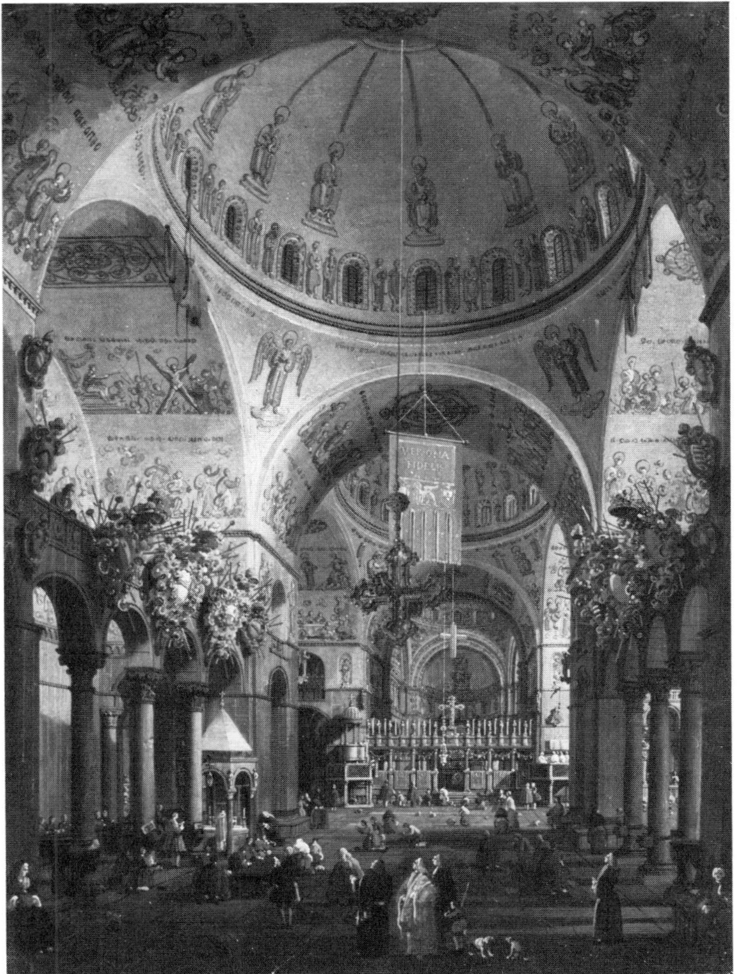

Interior of Saint Mark's, Venice, **c. 1756. Oil on canvas, 17⅞" x 12⅜". Giovanni Antonio Canaletto. The Montreal Museum of Fine Arts, bequest of Miss Adaline Van Horne.**

This small painting by Canaletto is done in his later, more precise style. It captures the rich color and detail of the basilica's splendid Byzantine interior with its massive arches, domes, and golden twelfth and thirteenth century mosaics.

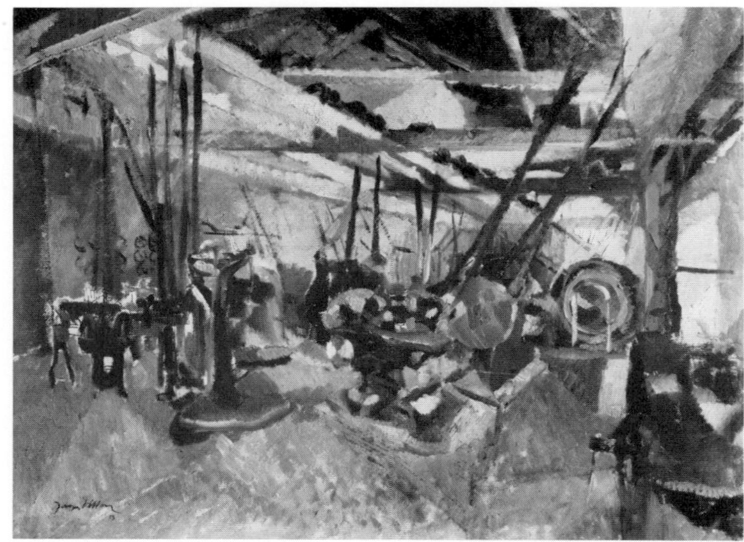

The Machine Shop, **1913. Oil on canvas, 36½" x 29". Jacques Villon. Courtesy, The Phillips Collection, Washington, D.C. Photograph by J.H. Schaefer & Son.**

In 1913 Jacques Villon was employed in a mechanic's workshop in Asnieres, France. For two years he used this workshop as a theme for a series of paintings and graphic works. Thirty years later, in 1946, 1947, and 1955, he returned to the motif. Villon was fascinated by machines and did other series on airplanes, concrete mixers, cranes, and threshing machines. His art was a methodical analysis, a rearrangement and refinement of natural forms into architectonic compositions of rhythm and light.

Although the early version (above) is the most literal interpretation of the three, a geometry of lines and planes from the pulleys, belts, wheels, and architecture of the workshop creates a pictorial structure. Somewhat Fauve in treatment, it does show the raw material from which the later, more abstract, works were constructed.

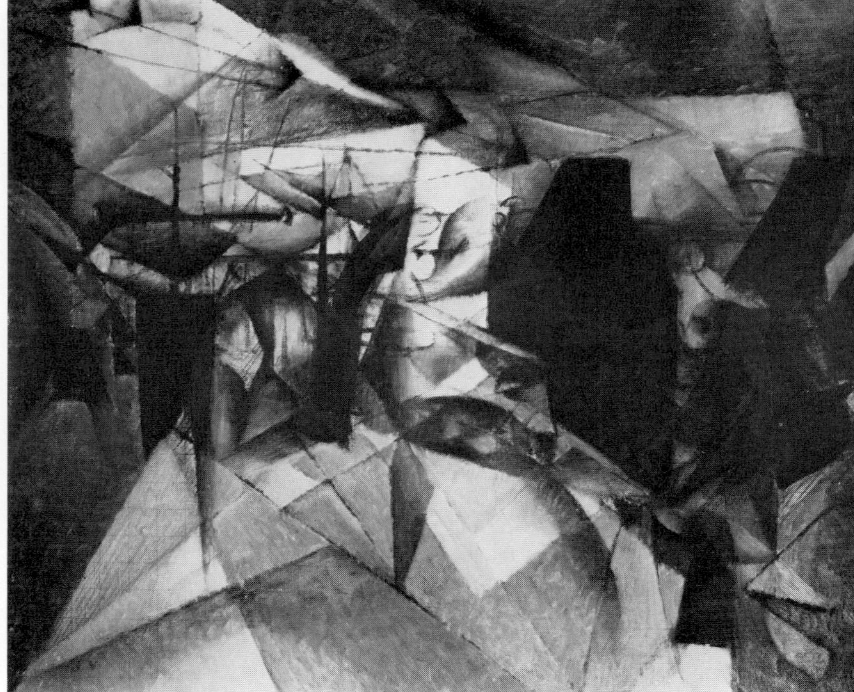

The Workshop of a Mechanic, **1914. Oil on canvas, 36½" x 38¾". Jacques Villon. Courtesy, The Columbus Gallery of Fine Arts, Columbus, Ohio.**

A year later, light and dark planes are distilled from the patterns of window light and shadows cast by the belts and machinery. Most altered is the space which has become more Cubist in its shallow intricacy and constant reference to the flatness of the picture plane. A romantic light is produced by the rhythmic progression of glowing planes, which build to their strongest contrast against the dark planes at the center of the composition.

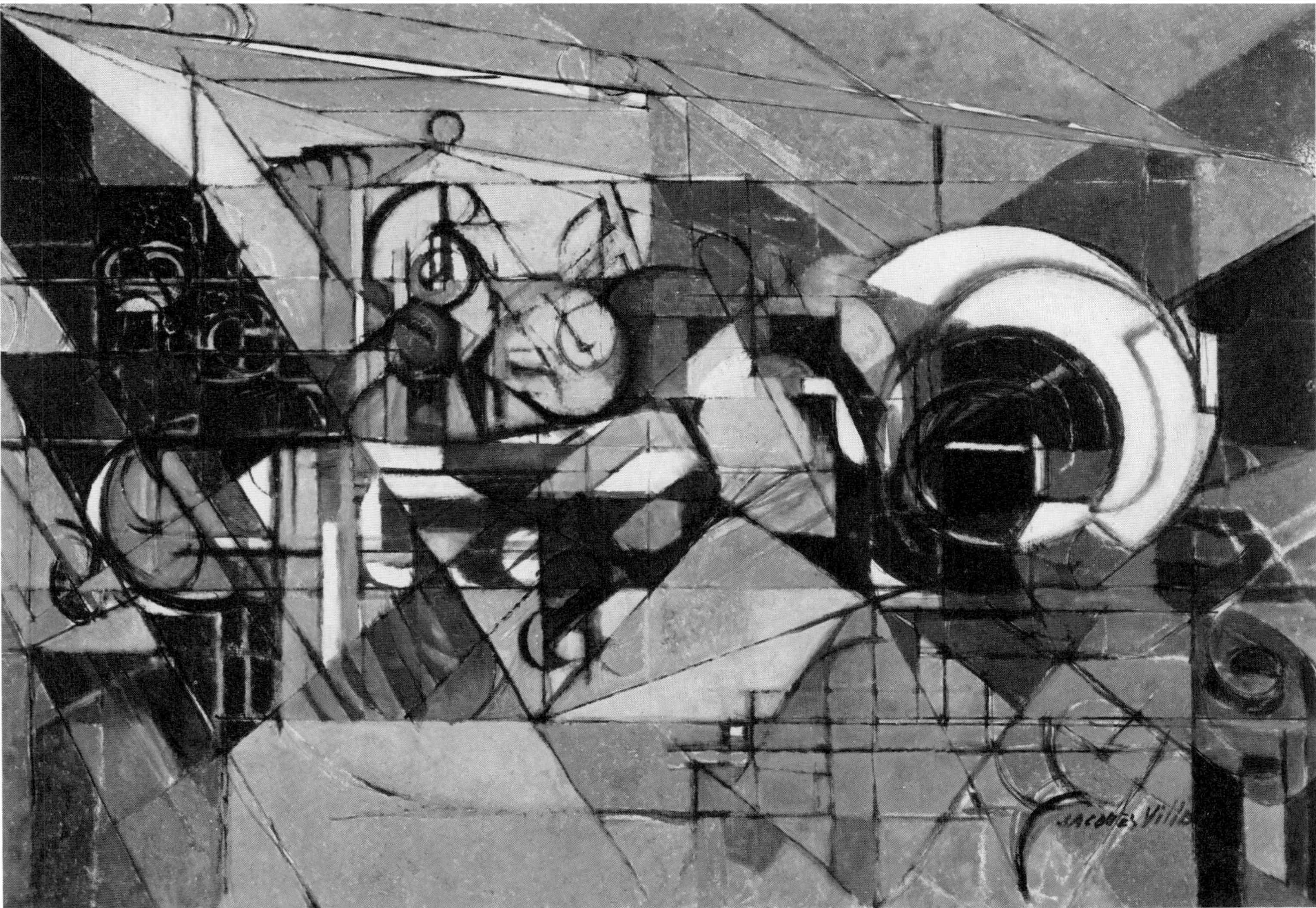

***The Little Machine Shop*, 1946. Oil on canvas, 46⅜" x 31⅞". Jacques Villon. Courtesy, The Phillips Collection, Washington, D.C.**

Done in Villon's mature style, space is further flattened and more rigidly controlled by a linear grid into which the machine forms are fitted. The wheels which had almost disappeared are now reasserted and are locked into tension with the straight lines. Light is no longer atmospheric, but glitters as it describes the facets of the sharply fractured surface. Common to all three versions is the rhythmic pattern of triangles which translates literal forms into a coherent, abstract geometry.

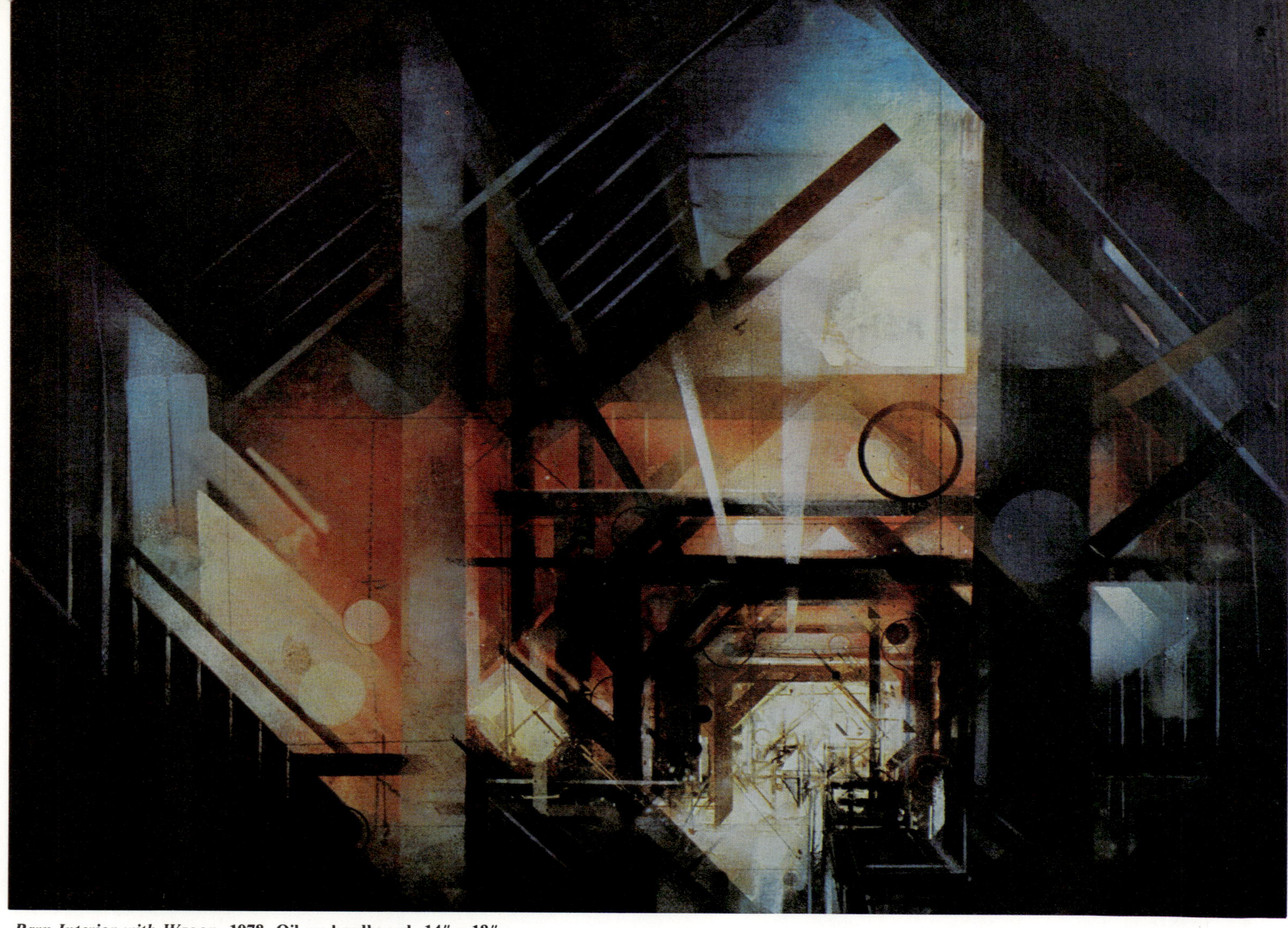

***Barn Interior with Wagon*, 1978. Oil on hardboard, 14″ x 18″.**

Light enters through gaps between barn boards and open doors, glaring off of the floor and from behind the timber posts, beams, and wind braces. Light is reflected off of the rafters and is seen through a hay wagon's wooden bars. These qualities from many barn interiors are recalled and combined. One of a series of watercolors and oils exploring this subject, the painting is about light and color as modulated by the timbered structure.

CHAPTER FOUR

Construction and Demolition

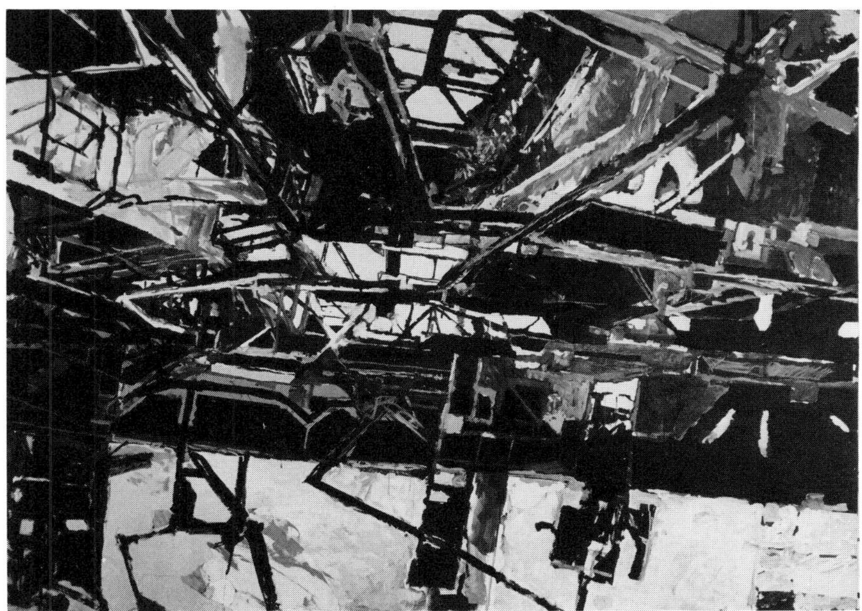

Factory and construction paintings by Flora Natapoff

Flora Natapoff has used a partially wrecked factory as the theme for an extensive series of acrylic drawings and collage paintings. The rough-hewn, bold vitality of these works parallels the jagged character of the subject. In the larger pieces, light and shadow are fragmented into staccato patterns. These create richly intricate forms and spaces that are sufficiently ambiguous to allow the viewer some latitude in how they are read.

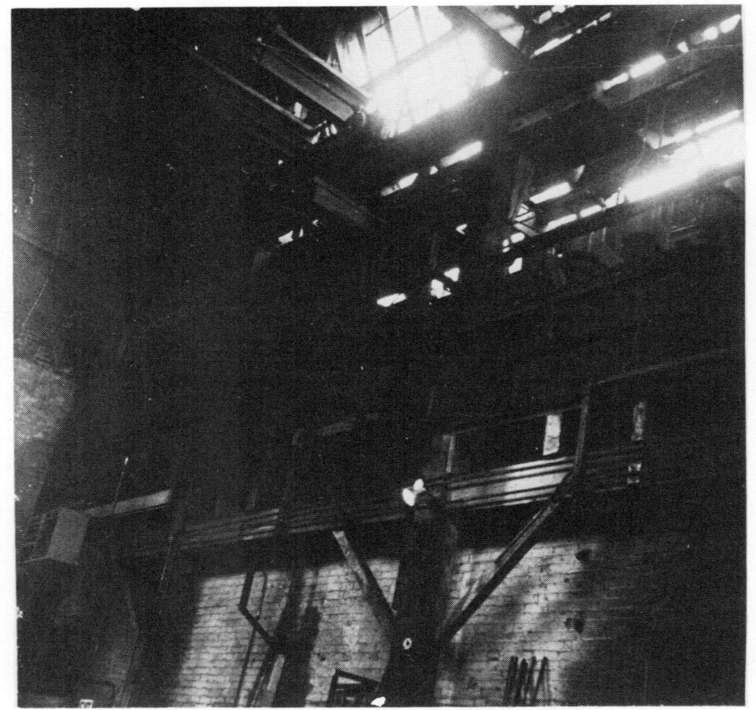

Photograph of the interior of a partially demolished shoe factory in Watertown, Massachusetts, that has served as the basis for many of Natapoff's drawings and paintings.

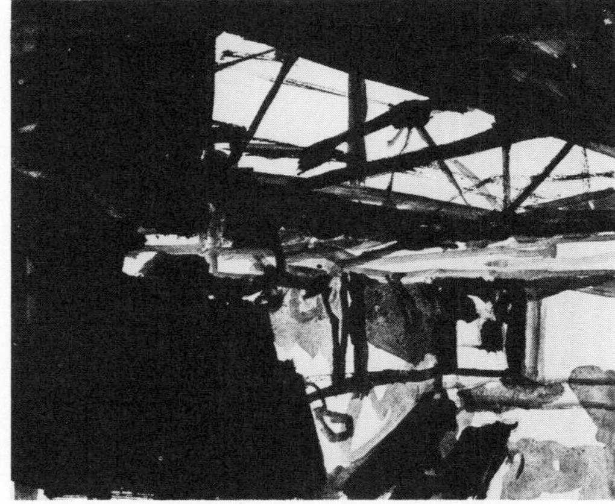

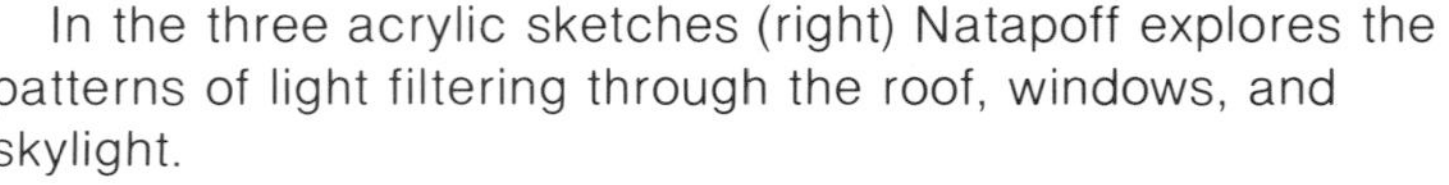

In the three acrylic sketches (right) Natapoff explores the patterns of light filtering through the roof, windows, and skylight.

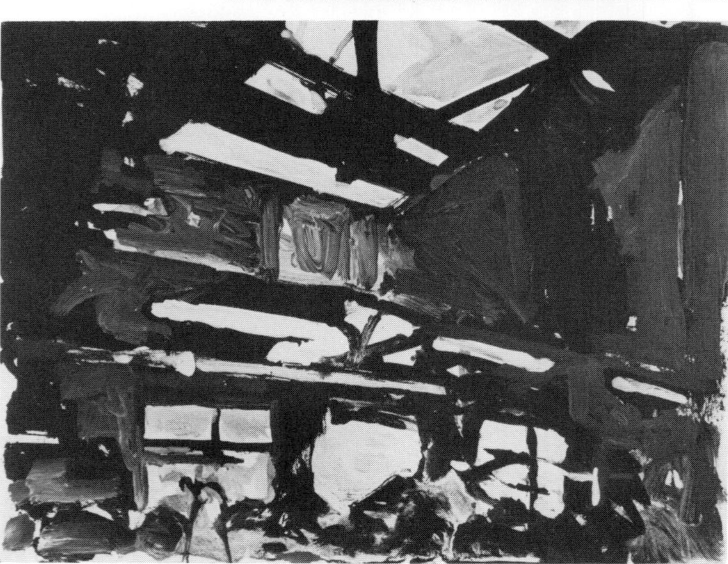

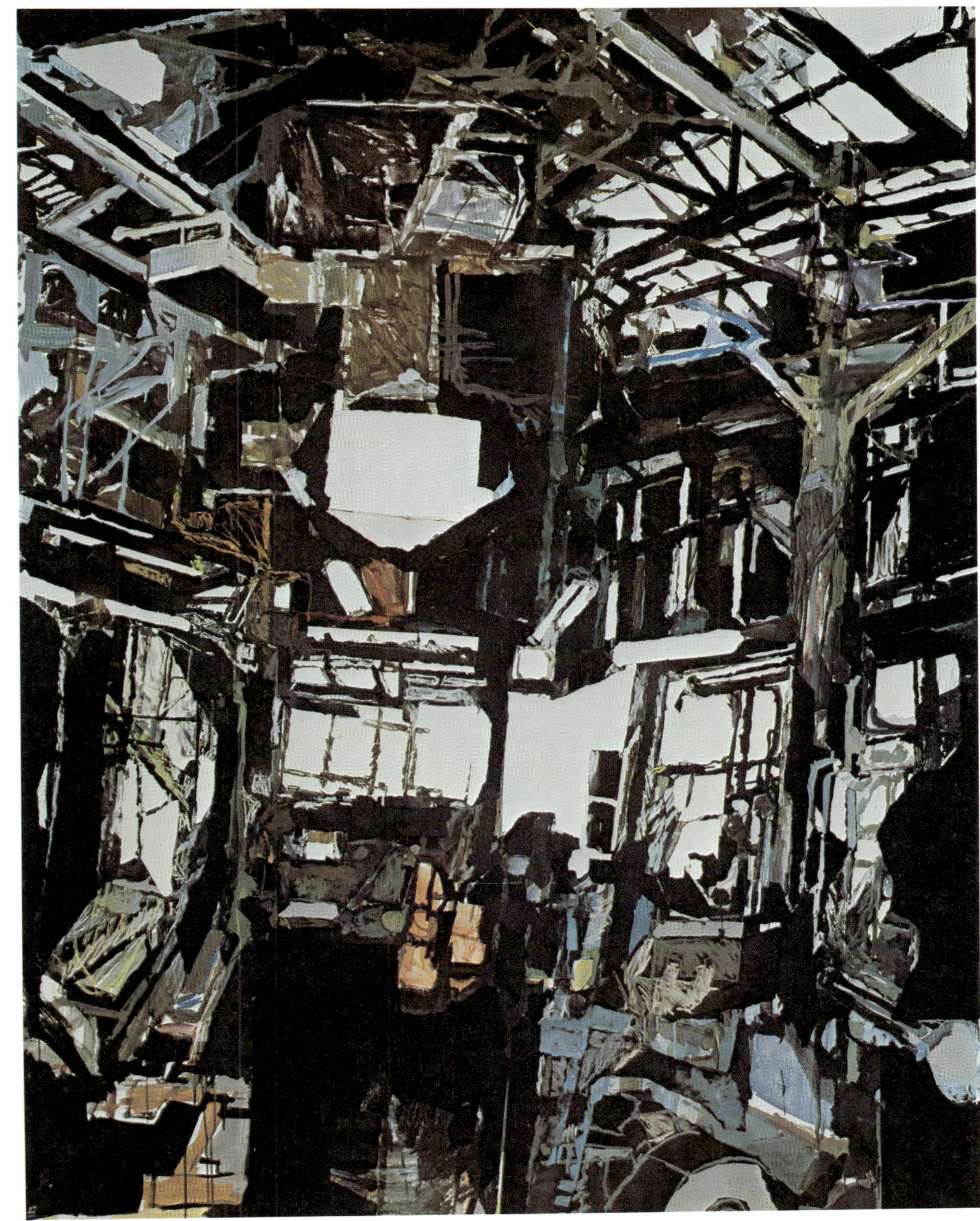

Factory Interior, 1974. Acrylic, pastel, and collage on canvas. 95″ x 72″. Flora Natapoff.

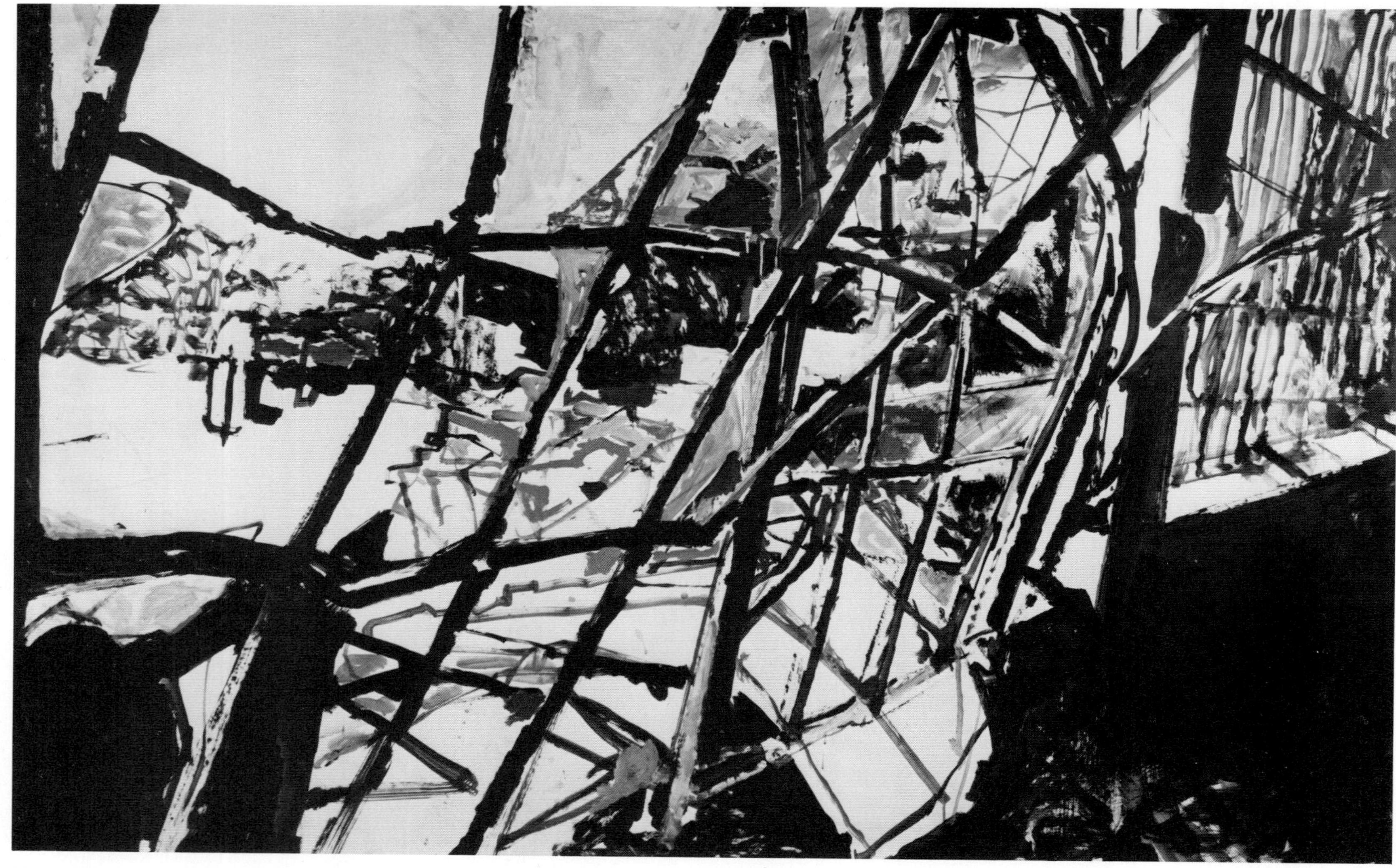

***Broken Window*. Acrylic drawing, 54″ x 84″. Flora Natapoff.**

The twisted window frames fragment the outside forms in this drawing of a factory building.

While in Paris during the summer of 1978, Flora Natapoff was attracted to a particular construction site. The shining white new building was in stark contrast to the mellow grays of the old buildings that surrounded it. She explored the scene with her camera and did a series of charcoal pencil drawings from the resulting photographs. Three drawings from this series are shown here.

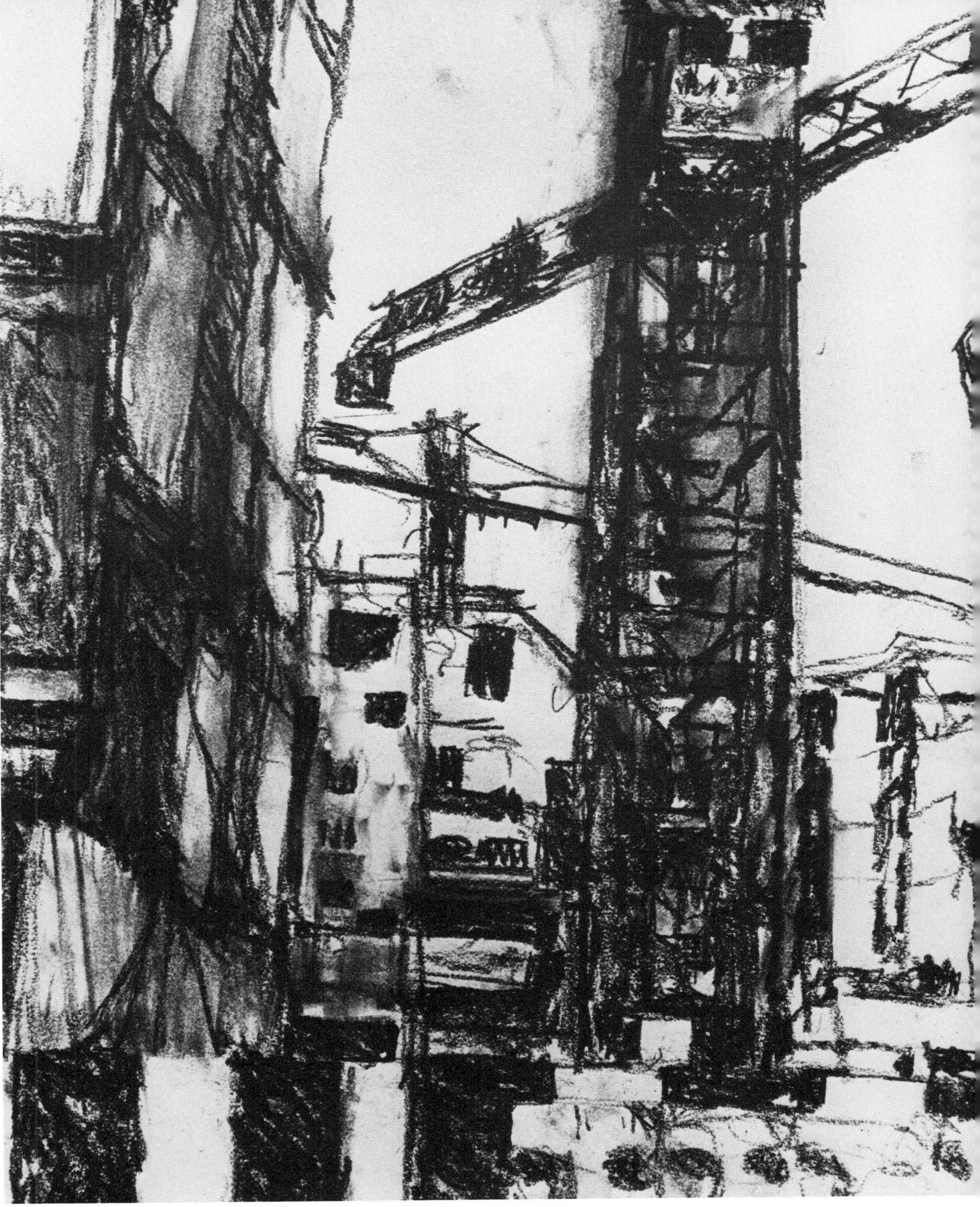

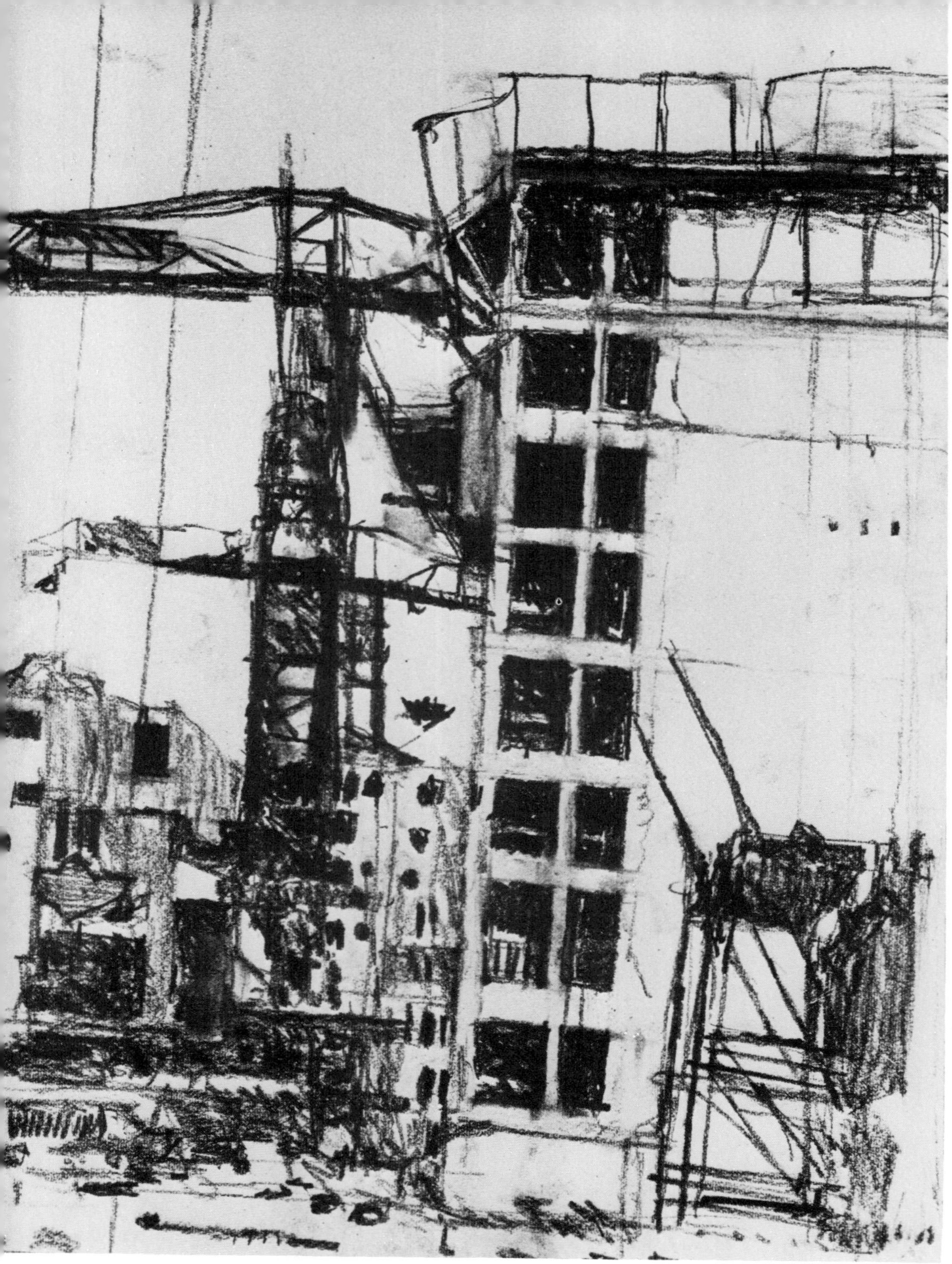

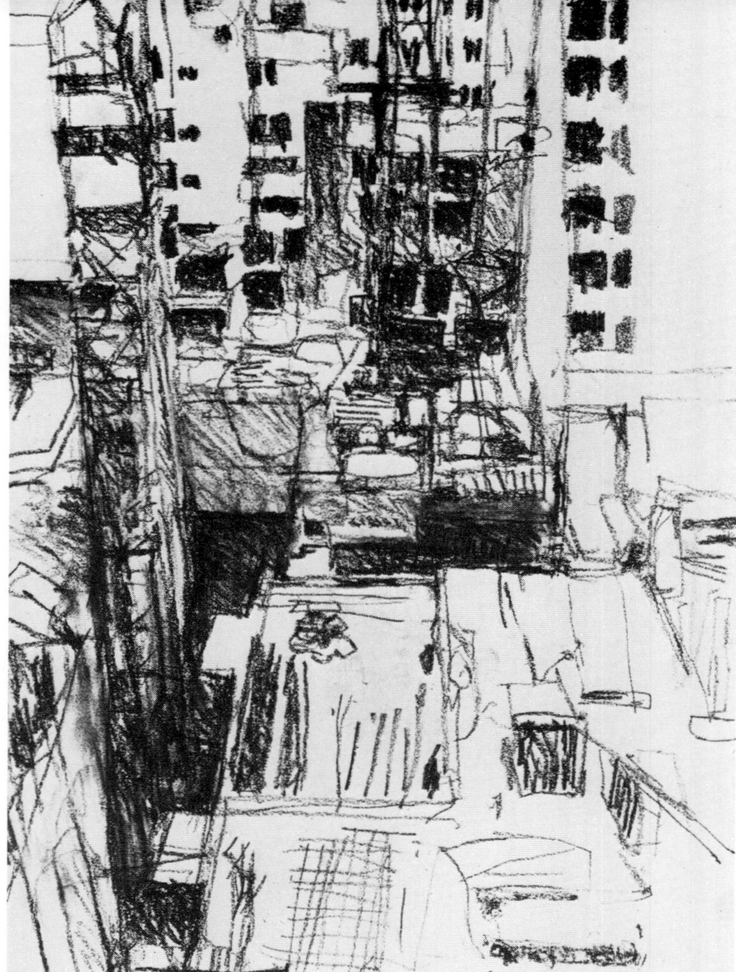

A bird's-eye view of the Paris construction site provided the impetus for this picture. Natapoff had worked with construction sites before, but never from such an angle. She was intrigued by the various internal changes and forms occurring within the larger white shape of the site. Her complex composition was given an organic wholeness and structural unity by the elevated viewpoint.

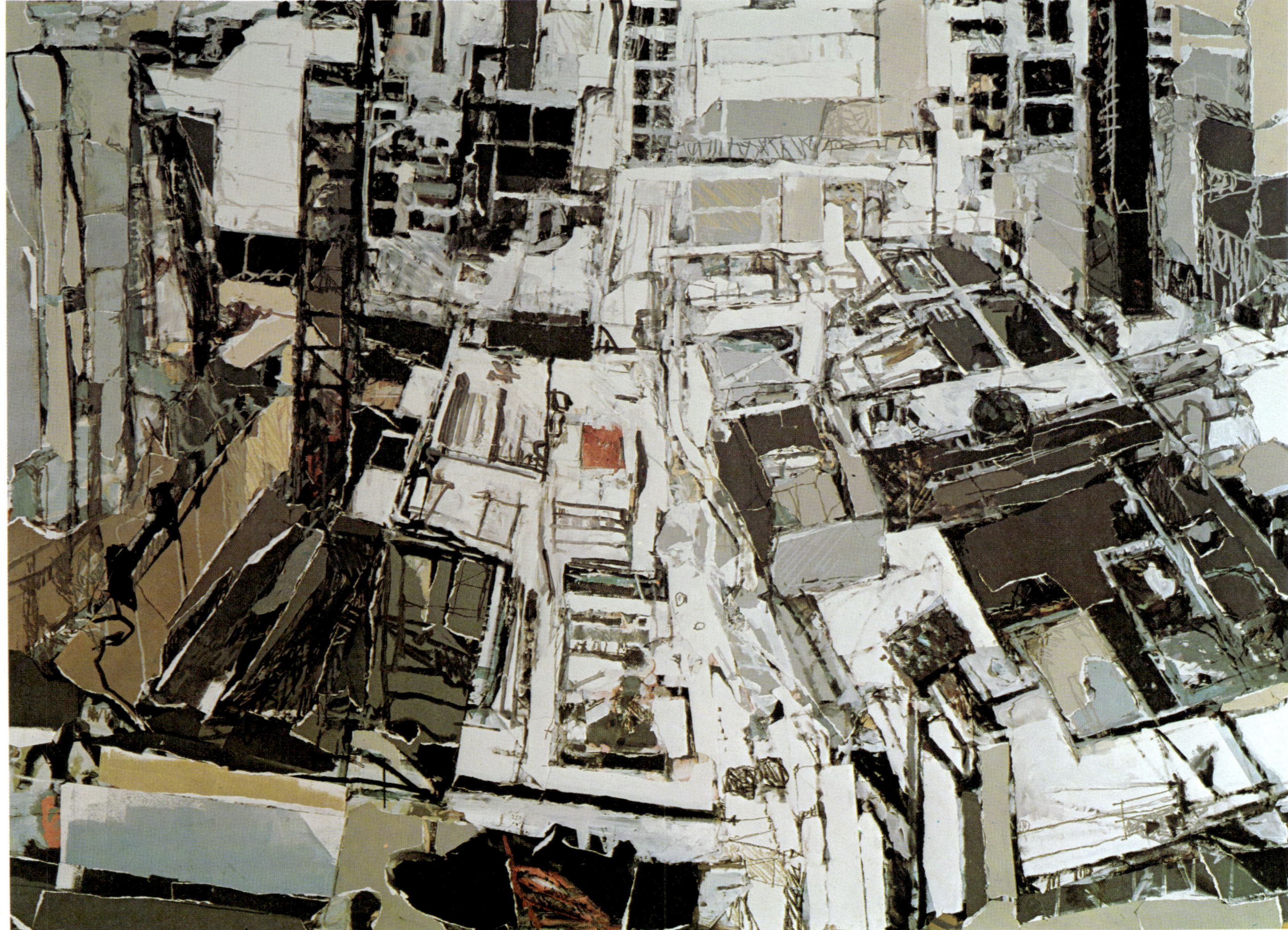

White Site, **1978. Acrylic, pastel, and collage on canvas, 72″ x 97″. Flora Natapoff.**

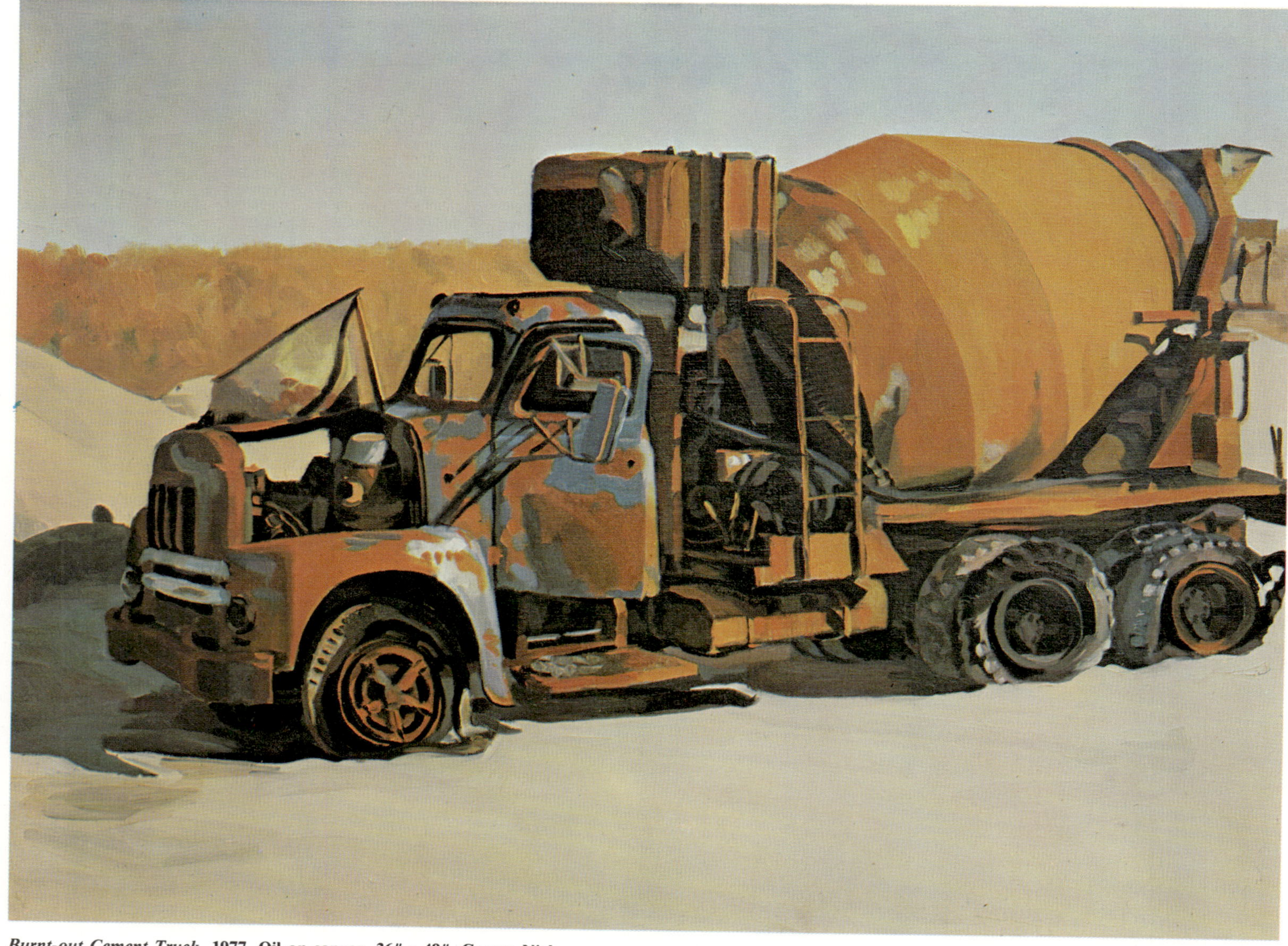

***Burnt-out Cement Truck*, 1977. Oil on canvas, 36″ x 48″. George Nick.**

It took George Nick fifteen sessions of one-and-one-half to two hours each to complete this painting from his mobile studio.

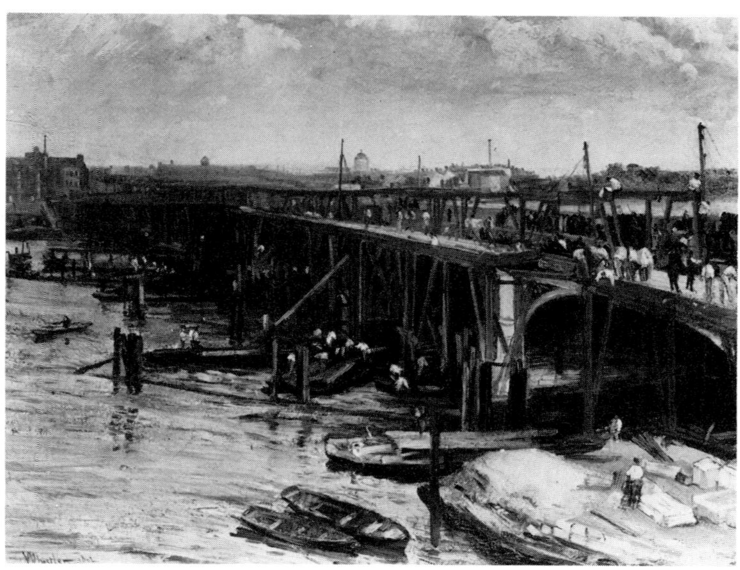

***The Last of Old Westminster*, 1862. Oil, 30⅝" x 23⅞". James Abbot McNeil Whistler. Courtesy, Museum of Fine Arts, Boston, the Abraham Shuman Fund.**

Whistler's long involvement with the river Thames began in 1859. He had taken rooms in Wapping to work on his famous set of etchings of the dockland reaches and the next year he also began to do paintings of the river. In 1863 he settled in Chelsea and ten years later he painted his Thames *Nocturnes.* In this composition of the demolition of the old and the construction of the new Westminster bridge, the first of the seven iron arches of the present span may be seen at the right, just emerging from under the timbers. Whistler shows a panoramic sweep of mud-colored wooden structures receding in a long triangle to the river's south bank. The buildings of Lambeth further recede to the horizon in a cooler bluish band of haze. It is a tonal study in browns: green browns, gray browns, and tans. The workmen's shirts and bits of masonry between the dark timbers show as flecks of light.

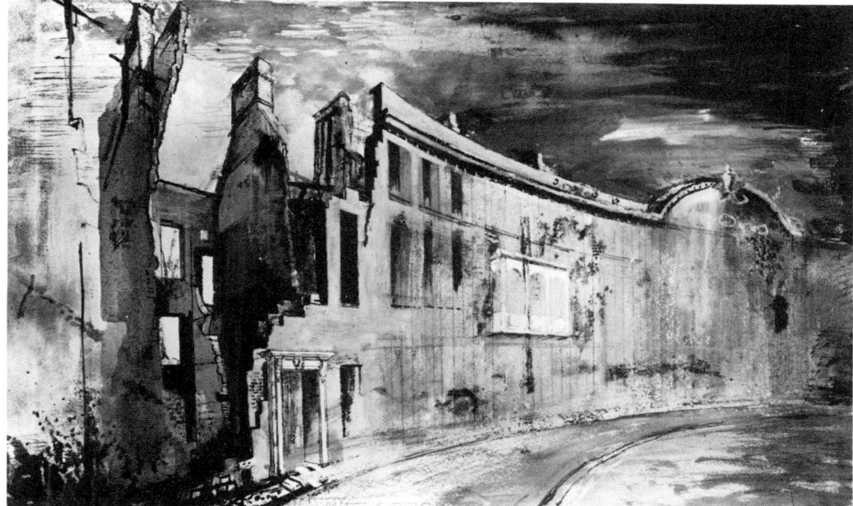

***Somerset Place, Bath*, 1942. Watercolor, 29" x 18". John Piper. Courtesy, Tate Gallery, London.**

In 1942 Piper was appointed an Official War Artist. His job was to record the desecration of buildings caused by World War II. This painting goes beyond recording: it *interprets* the results of one of the Baedecker Raids which damaged some of Britain's architectural treasures.

Piper wrote, "Romantic art is the result of a vision that can see in things something significant beyond ordinary significance; something that for a moment seems to contain the whole world, and, when the moment is past, carries over some comment on life or experience besides the comment on appearances." This sensibility is combined with an abstract painterliness and an architectural awareness which have produced strong topographical paintings. In addition, Piper has written guidebooks and articles such as *Pleasing Decay* and *The Nautical Style* which point out some neglected aspects of the built environment as seen through a painter's eyes.

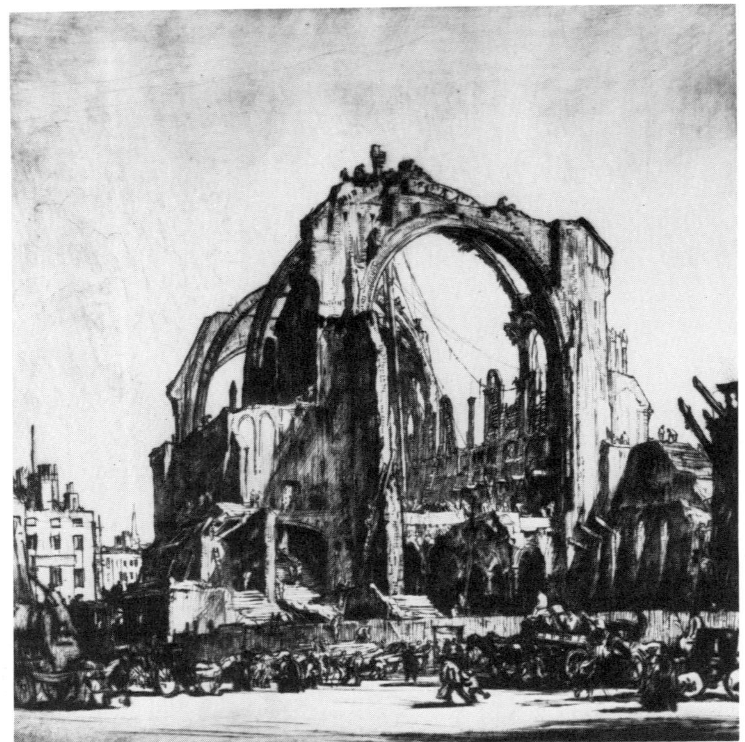

Demolition of St. James Hall, **1907. Drypoint, 11⅞″ x 11½″. Sir Muirhead Bone. Courtesy of the Boston Public Library, Print Department.**

Bone did an exterior and interior view of this subject. In this composition, the ribs of the Gothic arch vault against the sky and resemble the bones of some half-decayed creature. The building has become a vast sculpture, interacting with the sky and articulating the play of sunlight and shadow into a rich pattern. The antlike band of human activity at its base gives the structure monumental scale and grandeur.

The dismantling of part of the Boston Elevated Railway in 1975 for a short time produced a remarkable series of strange cityscapes. Rows of columns and arches which supported nothing lined the suddenly bright streets. Pedestal stations, no longer flanked by the raised lines of tracks that connected them, stood alone. This watercolor was developed from sketches made of the partly demolished City Square station. It became a monstrous structure of girders, columns, braces, stairways, railings, roofs, and tracks forming tunnels, towers, and elaborate bridges.

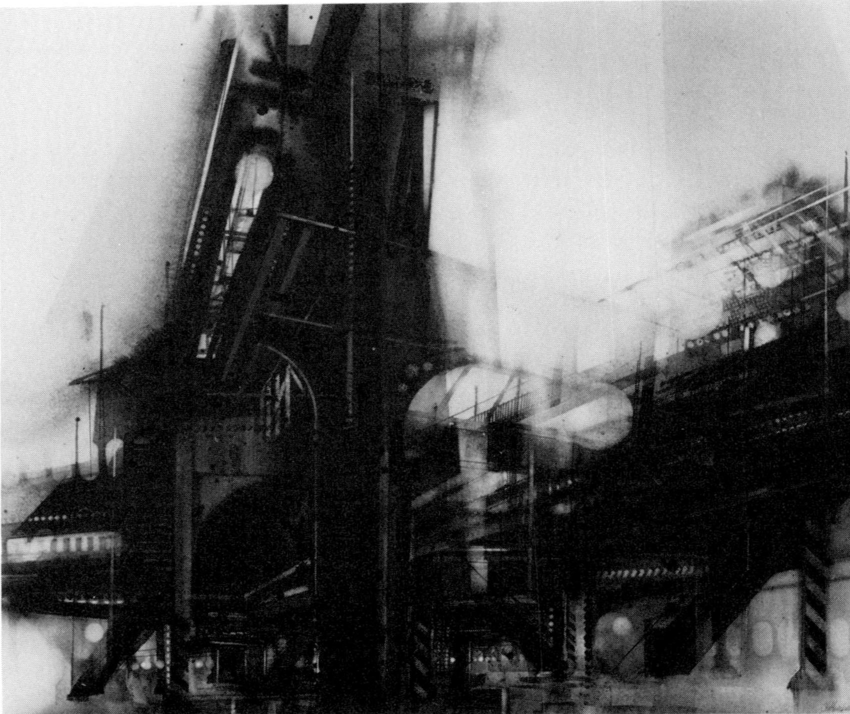

El Station Demolition, **1975. Watercolor and acrylic on paper, 18½″ x 23¼″.**

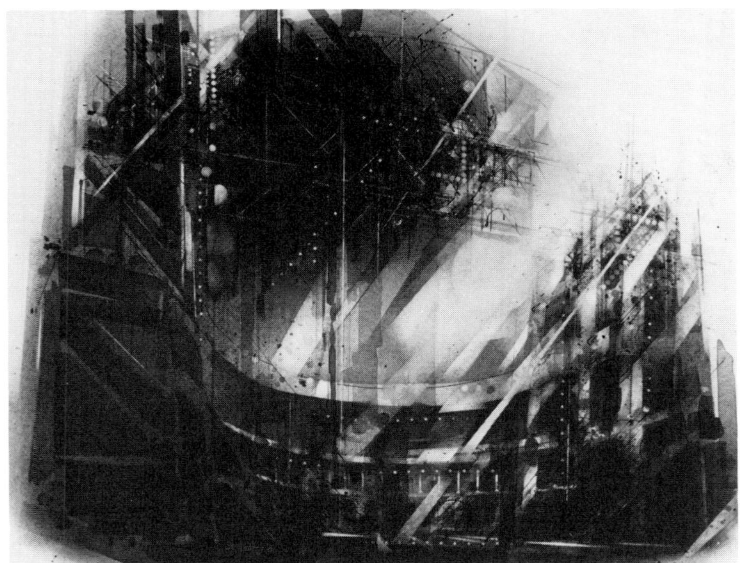

Opera House Ruin, **1978. Watercolor on paper, 20½″ x 26½″.**

When the Boston Opera House was torn down, the interior was exposed to daylight for a few days. In all of its working life, the Opera House had never experienced such a theatrical effect. Shafts of sunlight came through the opened roof, cutting diagonals in the dusty air and picking out in sharp relief the details of the balconies, boxes, and orchestra floor. Because the stage was demolished first, the rest of the building was opened up in a kind of cross-section, creating a wonderful opportunity for painting light-articulated interior/exterior space and structure.

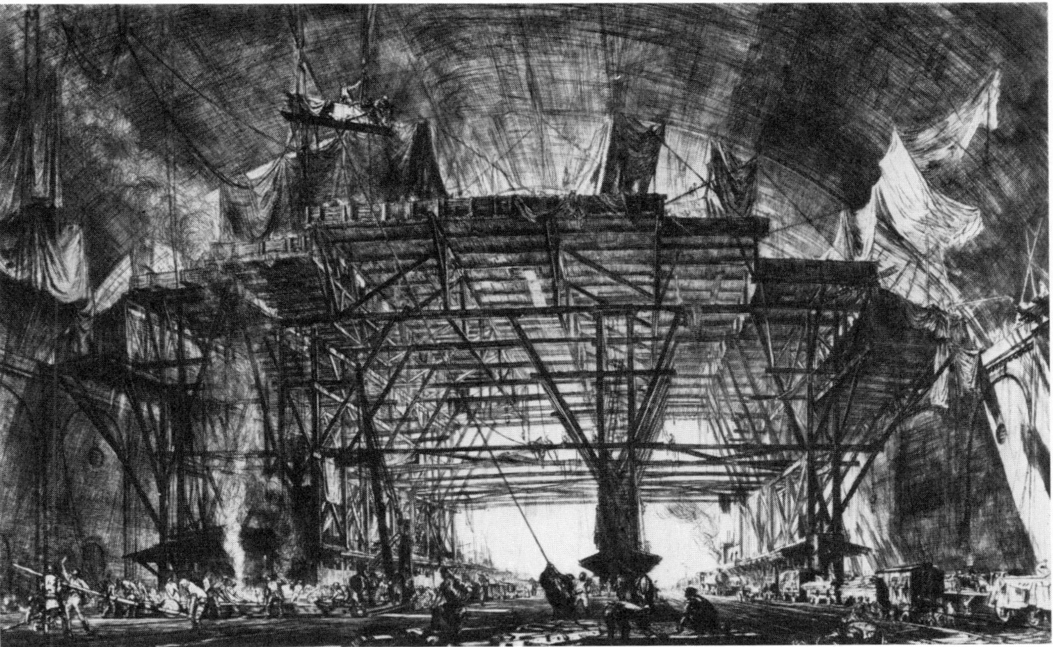

The Great Gantry, Charing Cross Station, **1906. Drypoint, 11″ x 17⅞″. Sir Muirhead Bone. Courtesy of the Boston Public Library, Print Department.**

In 1905 while under repair, a large section of the vaulted glass and iron roof of this London railway station collapsed and killed seven workmen. It seems likely that this print somehow relates to that event.

The artist achieved a tremendous force and heroic scale by using a low horizon and diminished figures and trains. A dramatic back light hits the undersides of the intricate wooden scaffolding. Smoke rises to the enormous arch of the roof and drop cloths, like enormous sails, catch the wind.

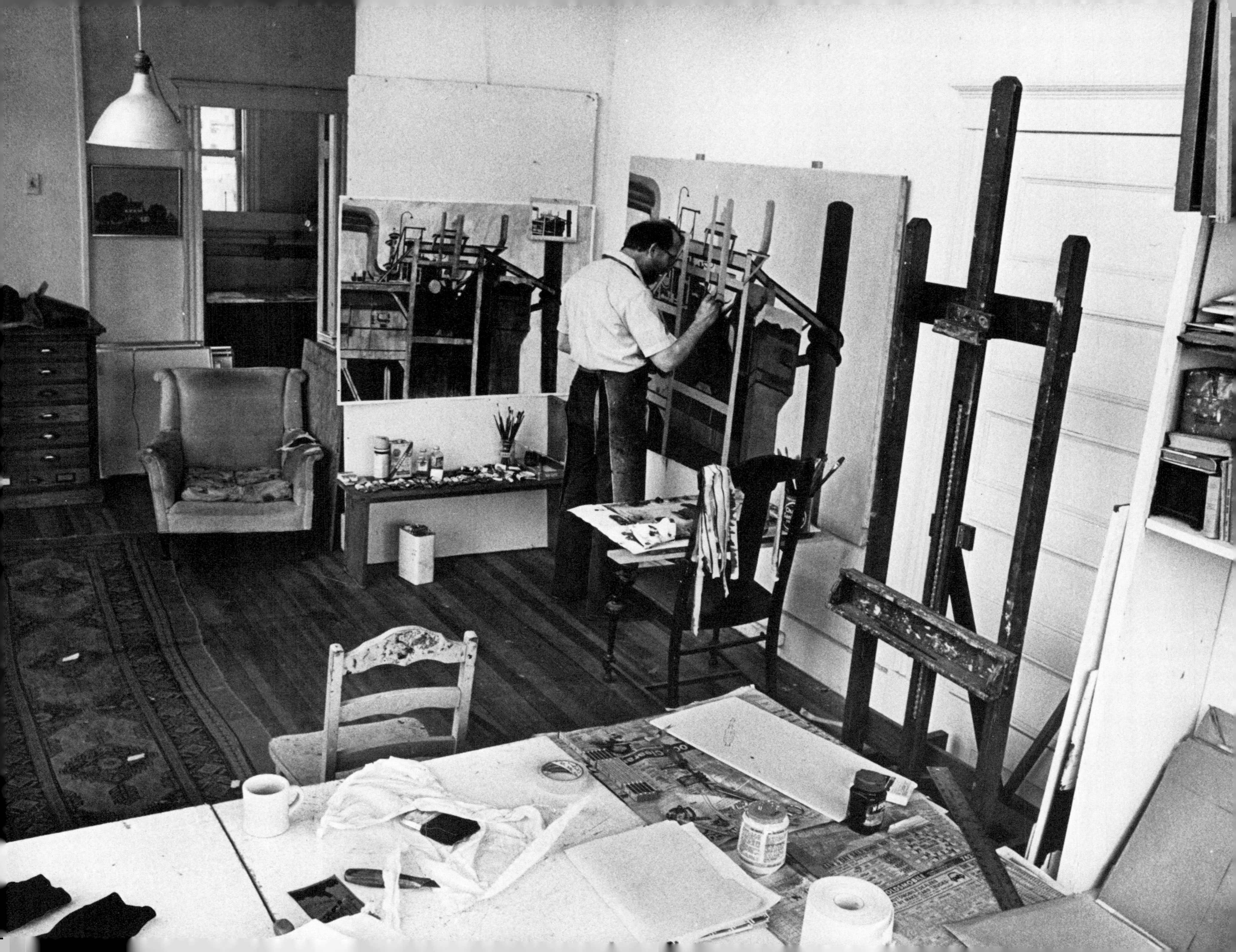

CHAPTER FIVE

Industrial

Sidney Hurwitz was raised in Worcester, Massachusetts, an industrial city where railroad freight yards, coal hoppers, a forging plant, and a leather company were part of his daily experience as he walked to and from school. Years later, when he lived for a time in England, these childhood impressions were recalled by the pipes, ventilators, cranes, and Victorian industrial architecture that he saw along the lower reaches of the Thames river. Using a 35mm single lens reflex camera with black-and-white film, he liberally documented those parts of the riverside which most appealed to him, often photographing from the decks of boats which ply the river from Charing Cross to Greenwich. Selecting the most promising compositions from the contact sheets, he had the photographs enlarged to 8″ x 10″. From these he completed a series of ten large, black-and-white etchings.

Hurwitz continues to explore the industrial theme in printmaking, and has recently expanded into painting which allows for a larger scale and the use of color. What particularly interests him is the strong sculptural qualities of industrial forms and the problem of reducing these to two dimensions.

A view of Hurwitz's studio (opposite) as he completes the painting, *Boiler and Stack.* A large skylight which runs along one side of the room allows an even amount of light to enter the studio.

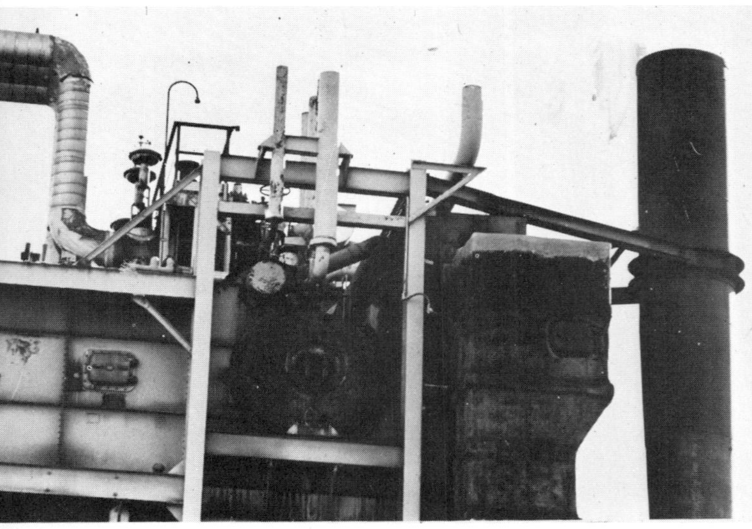

Case study of the painting, *Boiler and Stack*, by Sidney Hurwitz

By contacting officials of the Exxon Corporation, Hurwitz received permission to take photographs within its Everett, Massachusetts oil terminal. He spent several hours examining the complex and then extensively photographed specific structures from different angles. The steam boiler, with its pipes silhouetted against the sky, particularly appealed to Hurwitz. He felt that its steel framework acted as a skeletal structure by organizing the various shapes and textures of the pipes. Although he did not know the function of each part, he felt that there was an unplanned sculptural rightness about the whole.

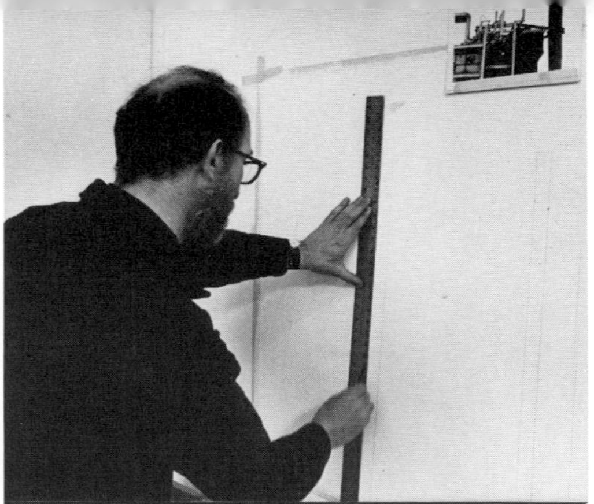

The preliminary line drawing

Hurwitz chose a photograph that combined the qualities he wanted to work with and had an 8″ x 10″ glossy print made of it. This print is mounted on the wall of his studio above a sheet of 100 percent rag paper that has been prepared with two coats of acrylic gesso. The paper is more square than the proportions of the photograph, and this necessitates the inclusion of more of the boiler's lower part than is seen in the photo. The drawing will mainly involve selection rather than distortion, and the different proportions will emphasize the vertical lines of the subject. It will also stress the contrast of large forms at the bottom to small detail at the top of the photograph. The drawing is begun with a soft charcoal pencil and a straight edge. Proportions are measured by eye and erasures and adjustments are made where necessary.

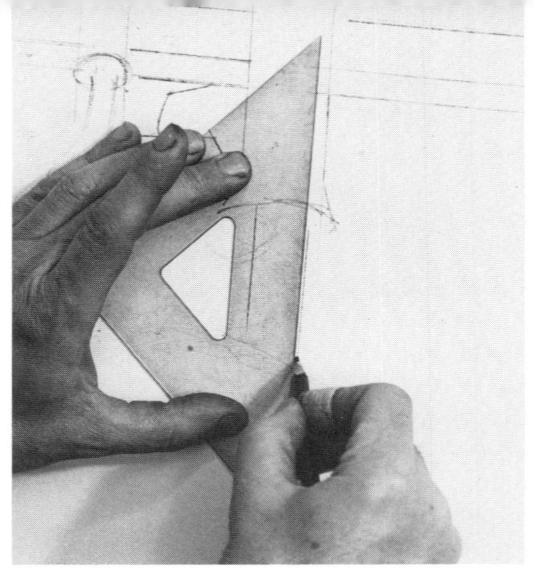

A triangle is used for the shorter lines.

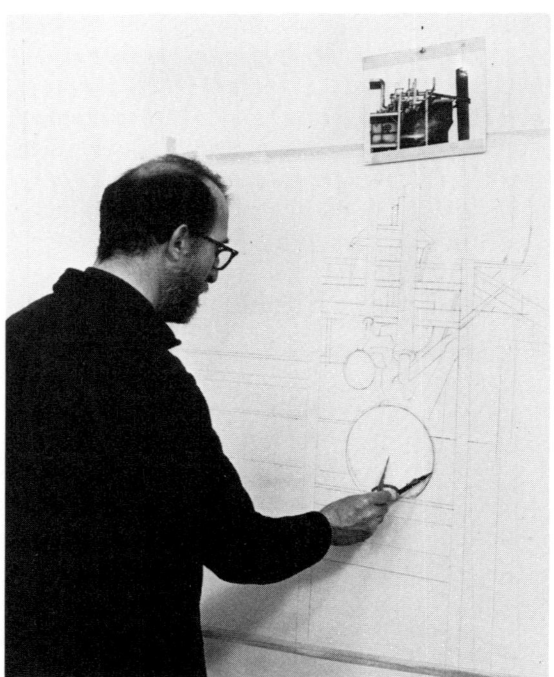

Crisp arcs and circles are drawn with a pencil compass.

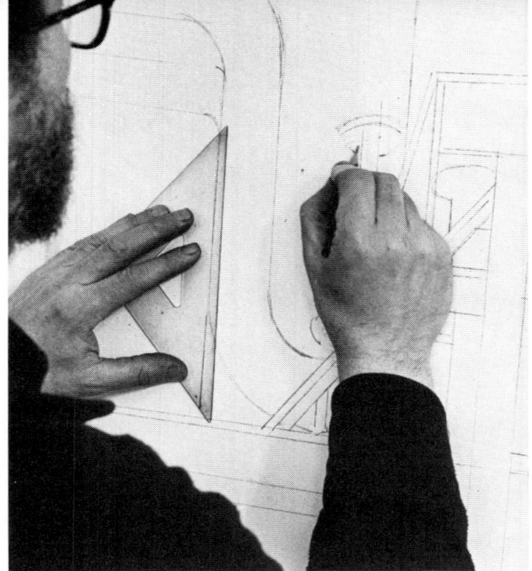

Smaller details are drawn freehand. If fine detail or areas are not clearly shown in the photograph, Hurwitz simplifies or rearranges the forms.

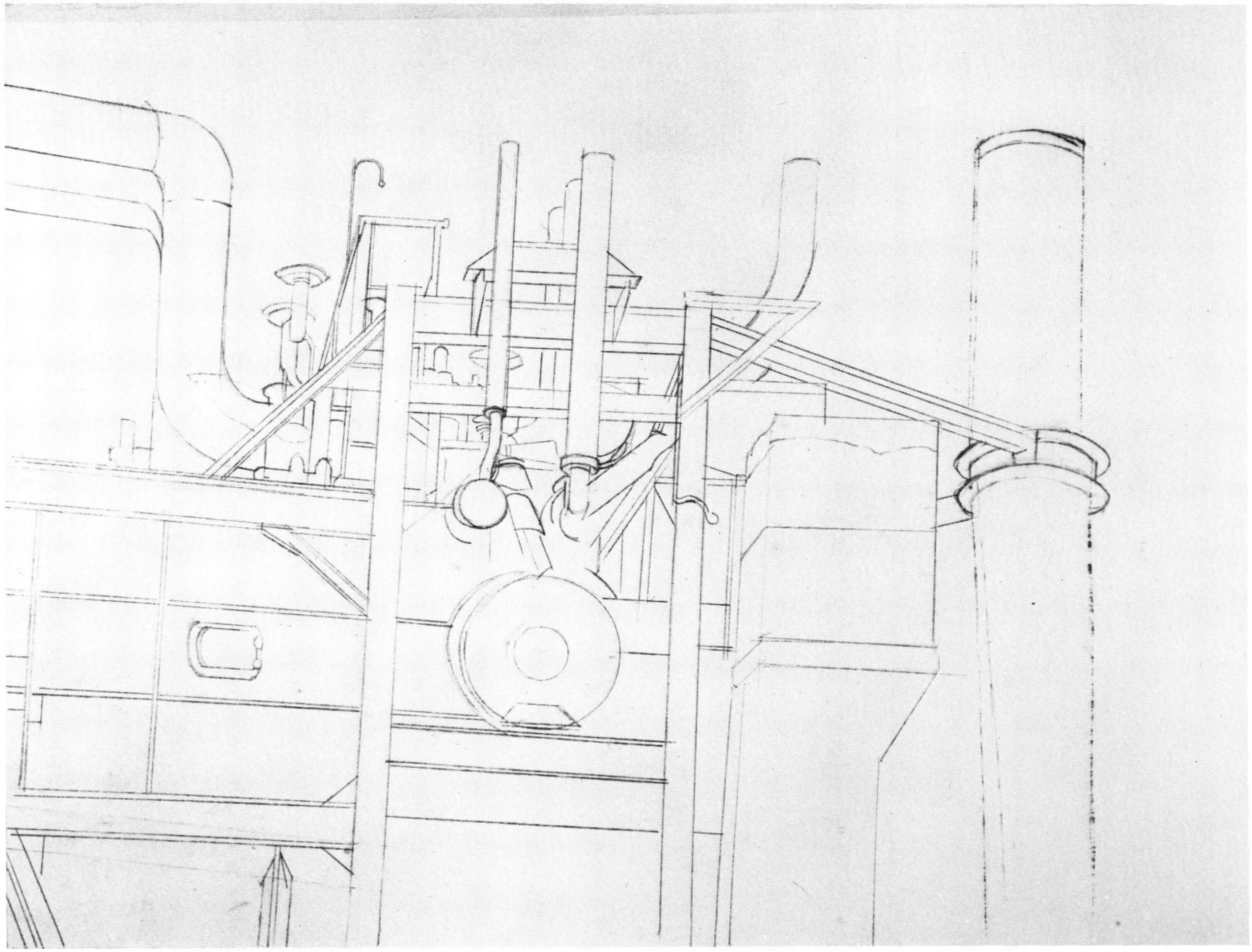

The finished line drawing, sprayed with fixative.

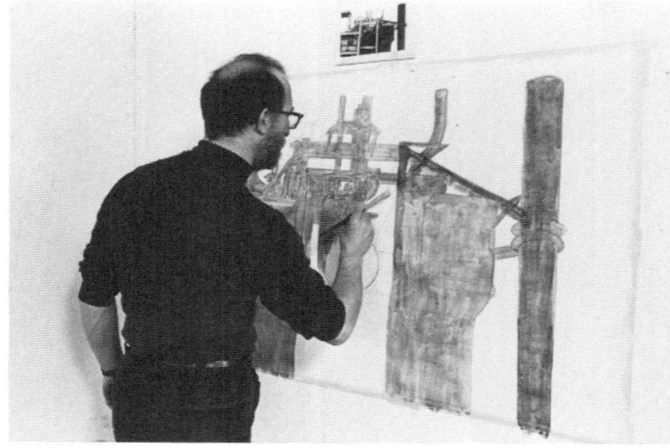

The acrylic wash drawing
Raw and burnt umber are mixed with water for an acrylic wash. This is applied with a flat brush to begin the buildup of tones. The drawing remains visible from underneath this wash.

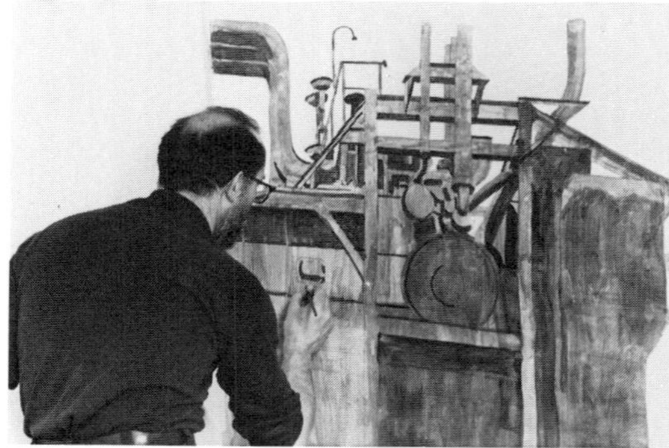

Acrylic mars black is added to make a darker wash which is used for the shadow areas. Hurwitz generally works from light to dark to define forms. He retains the drawn lines in places where they mark the edges of contrasting areas.

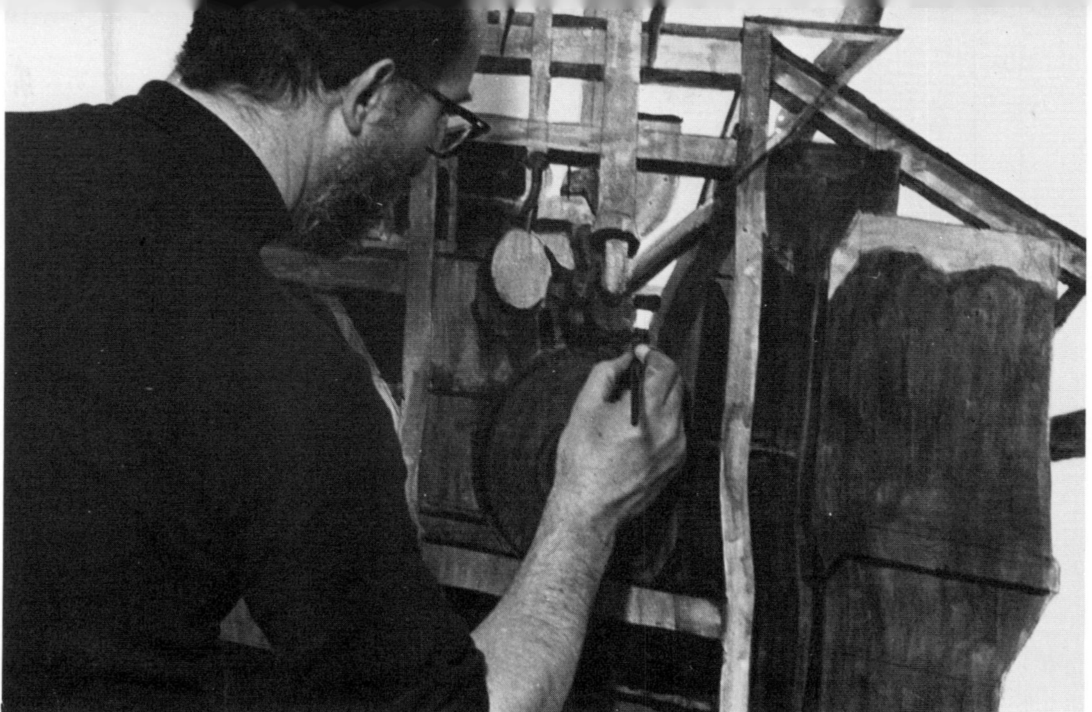

The center of the composition is worked in a darker, shadowed mass and begins to be a focus. The problem is, should the large circle at the center become a bull's-eye or be played down in importance? Hurwitz decides that since it is already prominent by virtue of its shape and position, he will tonally deemphasize it, making it nearer in value to its surroundings.

Detail is applied as the preliminary wash drawing nears completion. At this point, Hurwitz decides to tone the sky area to pull together the composition. The white sky in the photograph tended to make the steam boiler read as a strong silhouette. By darkening it in the painting, the eye is brought into the structure. The purpose of the preliminary drawing is to work out certain problems before starting the final painting. He eliminated the rings on the large pipes at upper left so that the eye is not interrupted in the sweeping movement made by these pipes.

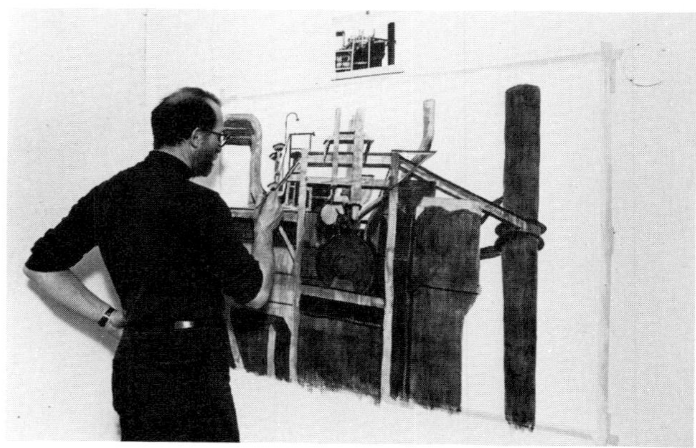

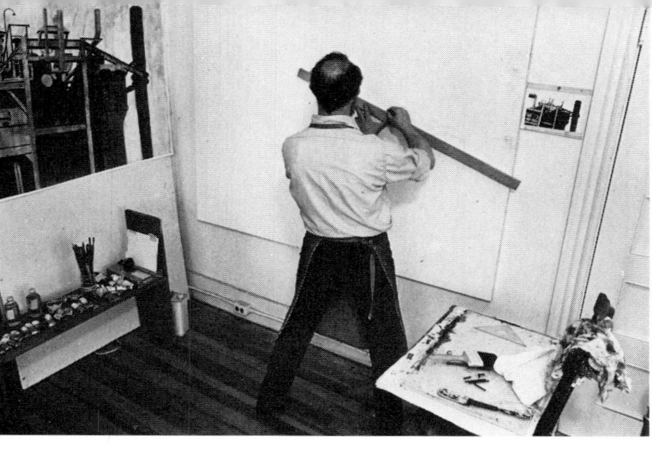

The oil painting

Working in a corner of his studio, Hurwitz has hung a 54″ x 72″ stretched canvas prepared with two coats of acrylic gesso on the wall. Just to his right is the photograph of the steam boiler. To his left is the preliminary wash drawing. Using a conte pencil, he is drawing the now familiar image on the canvas. Adjustments and revisions from the acrylic drawing are considered: the scale is enlarged, less sky is allowed for, and the effect of sloping off to the right that was in the original photograph but lost in the drawing is brought back.

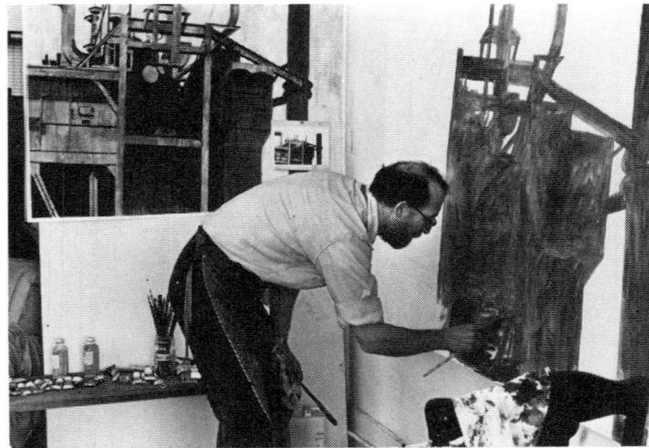

A wash or raw and burnt umber oil paint and turpentine is applied with a #14 flat brush.

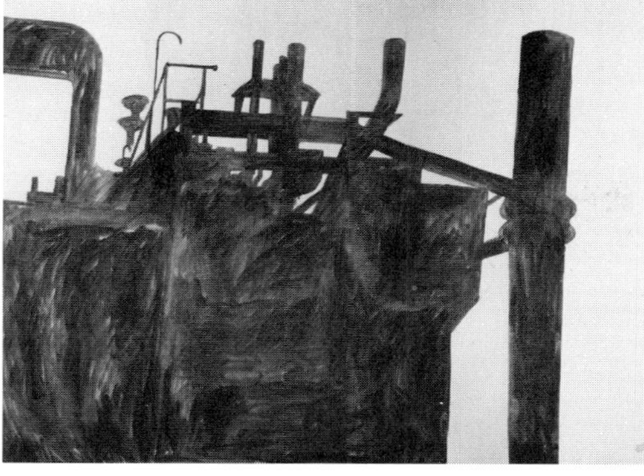

The completed base tone. The line drawing can still be seen underneath it.

Hurwitz uses a #10 soft flat brush to add darker washes for the shadows.

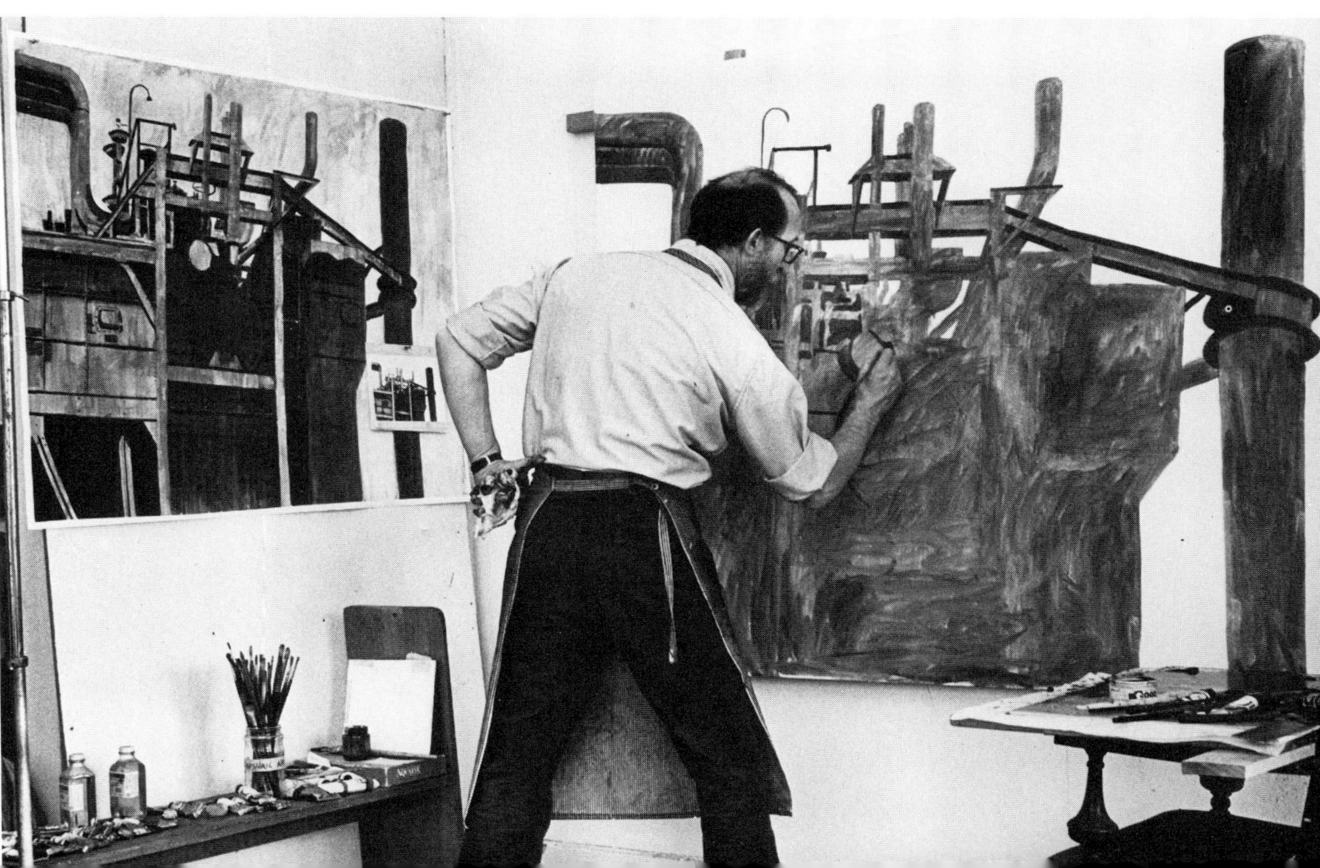

Close-up showing the beginning of the large circle at the center of the composition. Note the soft texture of the cotton duck canvas under the brushwork. Some of this might be retained in the finished painting.

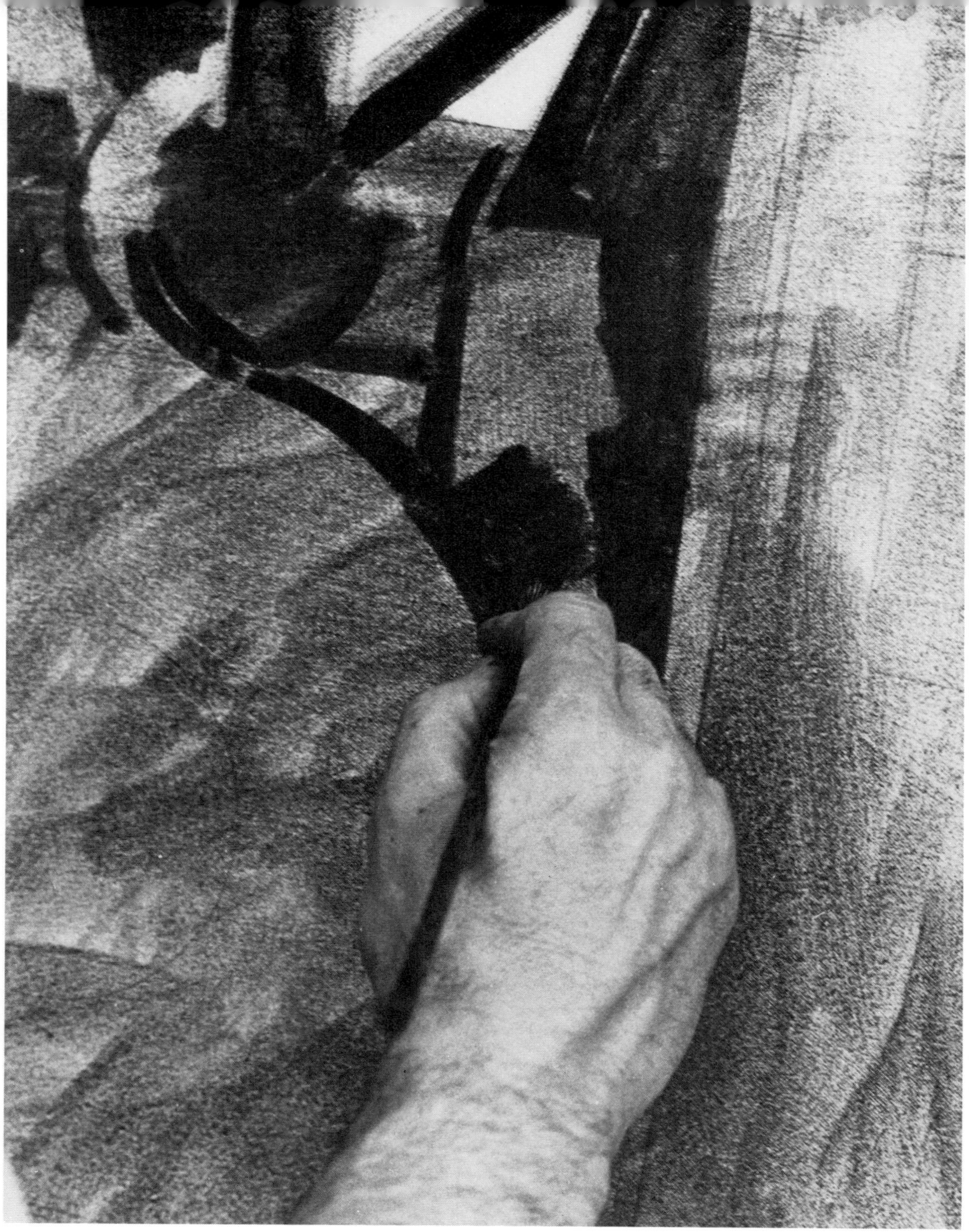

Detail and form are worked into the large wash area.

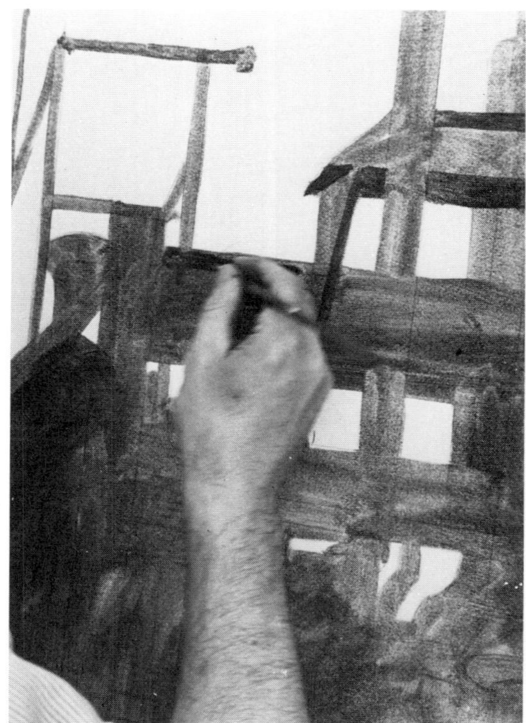

The underpainting after two hours of work.

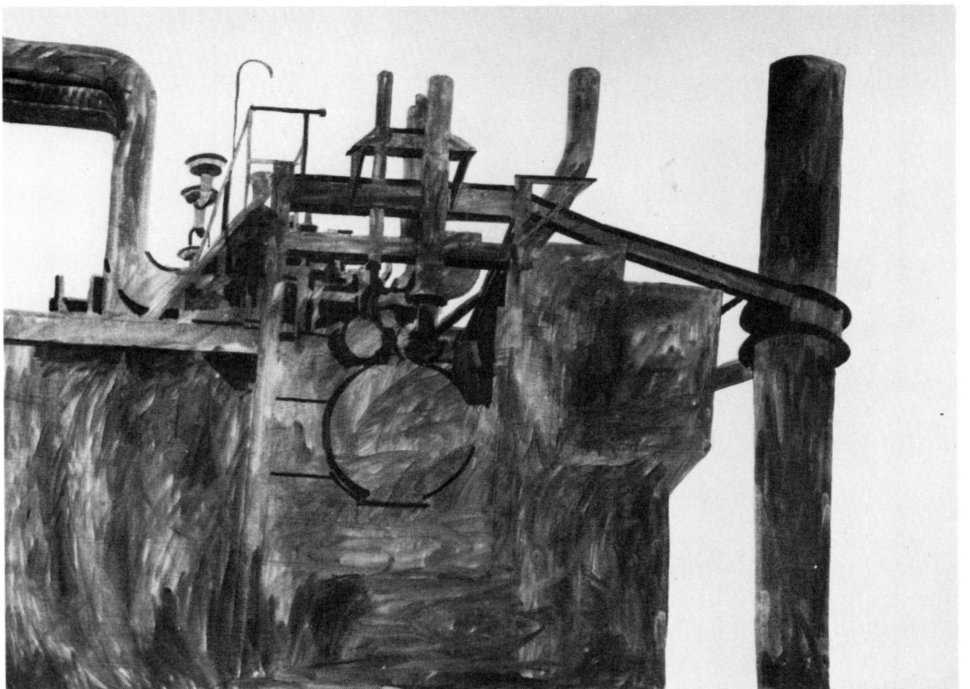

The turpentine wash underpainting is complete. There is a close resemblance to the acrylic drawing, but the brushwork is somewhat looser, there is less detail, and there are fewer value differences.

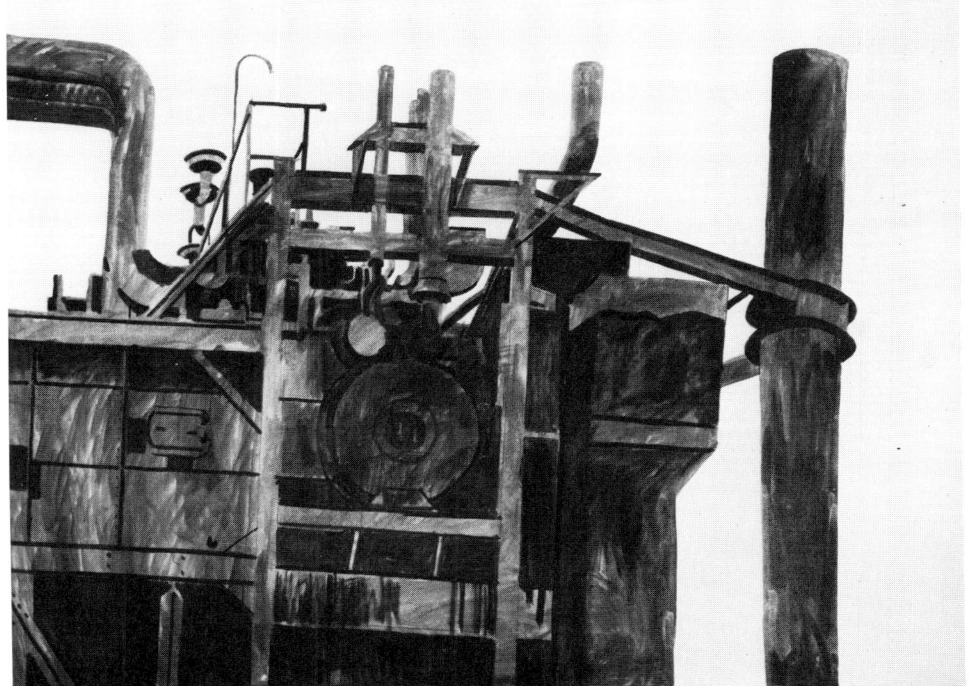

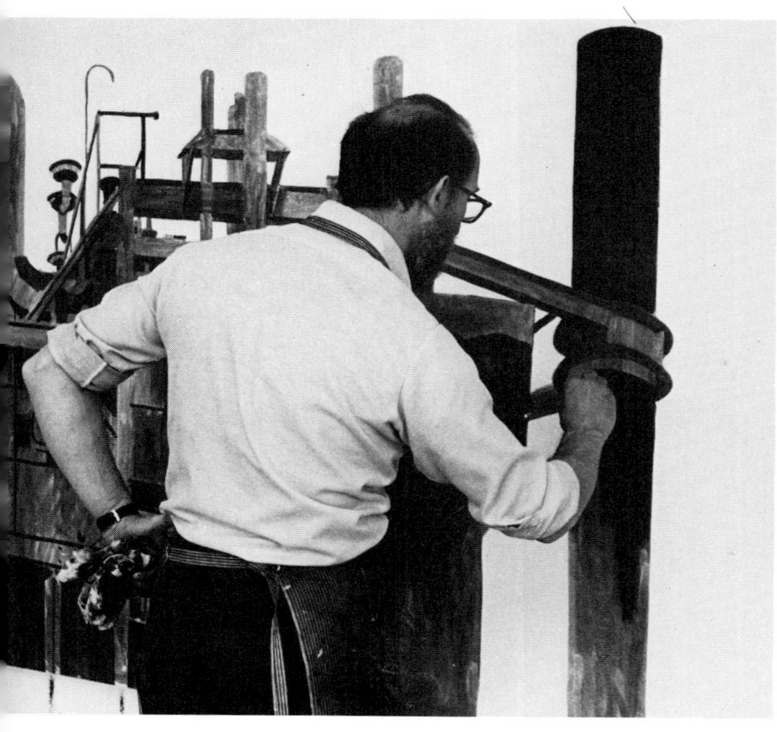

The next phase involves the application of more opaque tones. A mixture of burnt umber, burnt sienna, and mars black oil paint is added to a medium of one-third mineral spirits, one-third damar varnish, and one-third linseed oil.

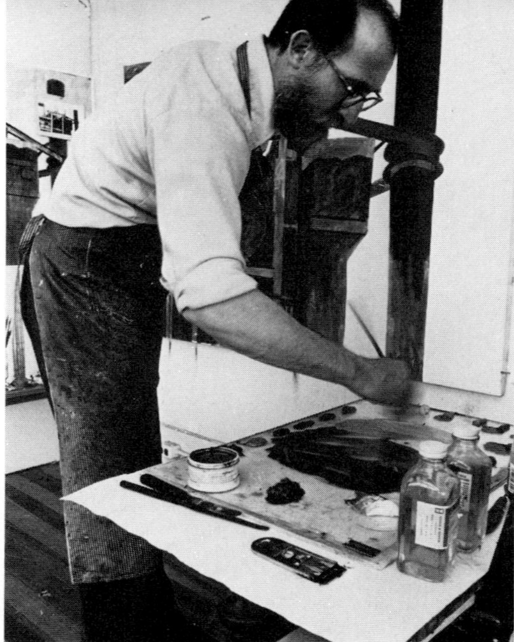

Mixing a lighter opaque tone of yellow ochre, white, and raw umber on a glass palette.

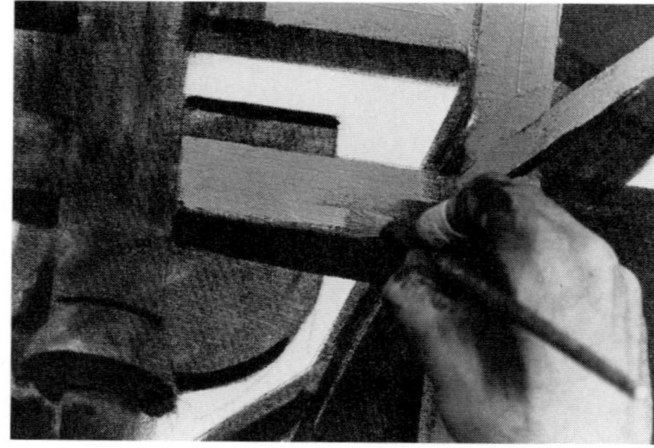

This close-up shows the effect of the light opaque paint covering the darker wash underpainting. The colors are generally variations of grays, moving toward warm or cool. They are invented, rather than based on the colors of the structure itself.

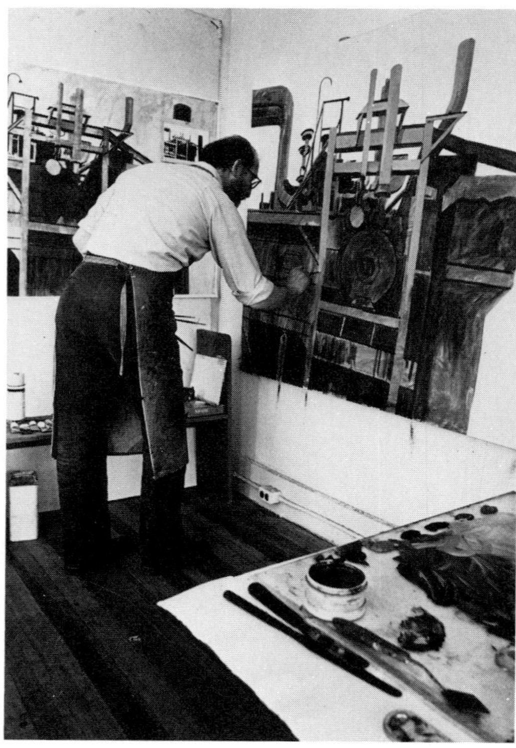

The lighter tone is used to pick out the framework.

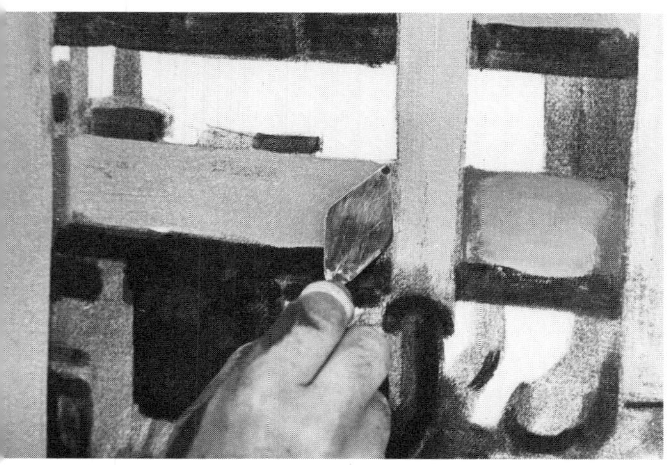

A diamond-shaped painting knife is used to simulate the surface texture of the actual material.

The palette knife is sometimes used to smooth paint surfaces after the color has been brushed on and creates a contrast to the brush strokes.

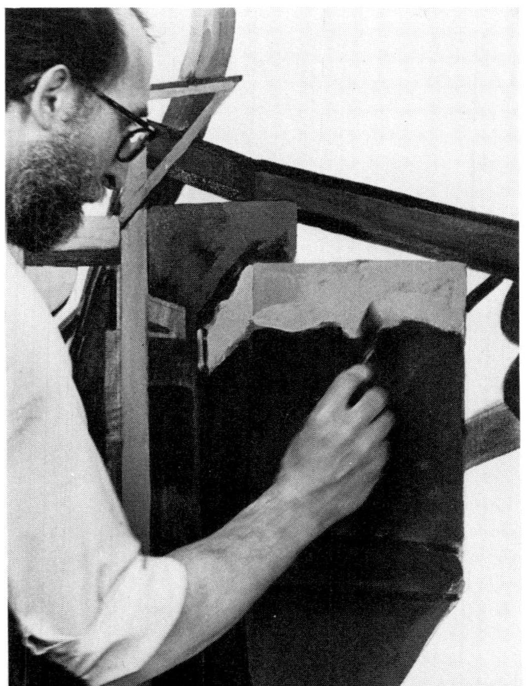

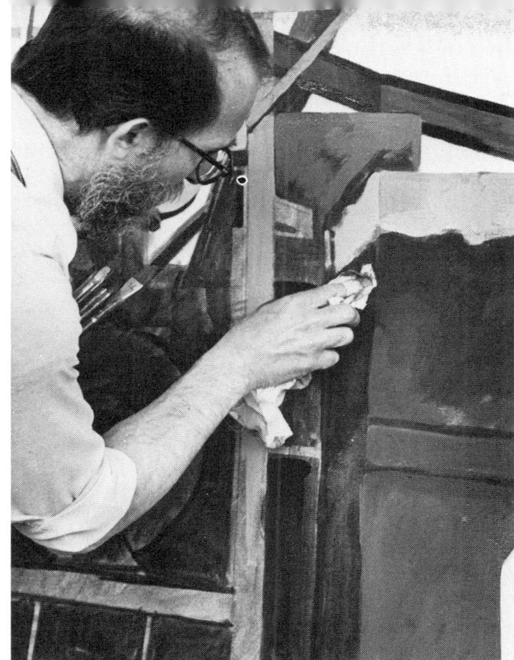

Using a cloth to remove a tone that is too dark. It will then be repainted a lighter tone.

A detail of the top center of the painting. This shows the contrast between the opaque and the wash areas.

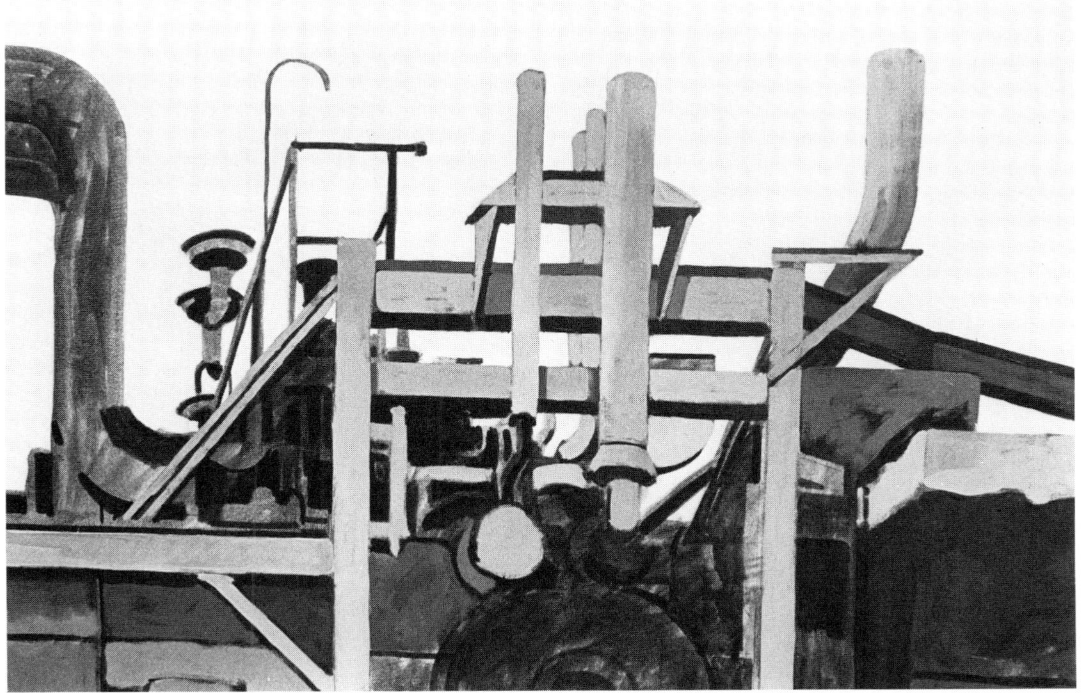

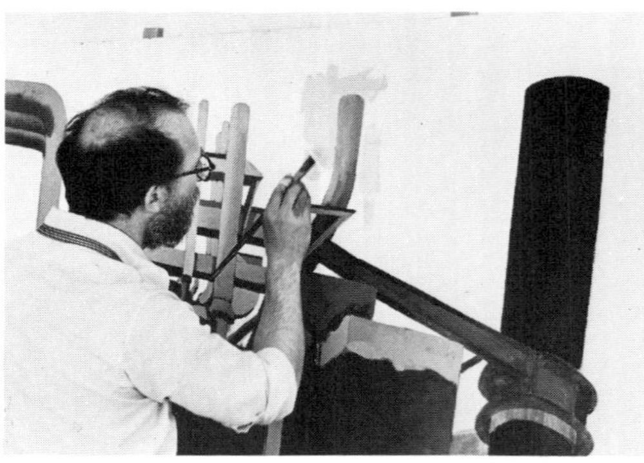

A mixture of white, ultramarine blue, cobalt blue, and raw umber is brushed onto the sky area with a #14 soft flat brush.

Islands of sky in the superstructure are toned with the same opaque, cool, blue gray.

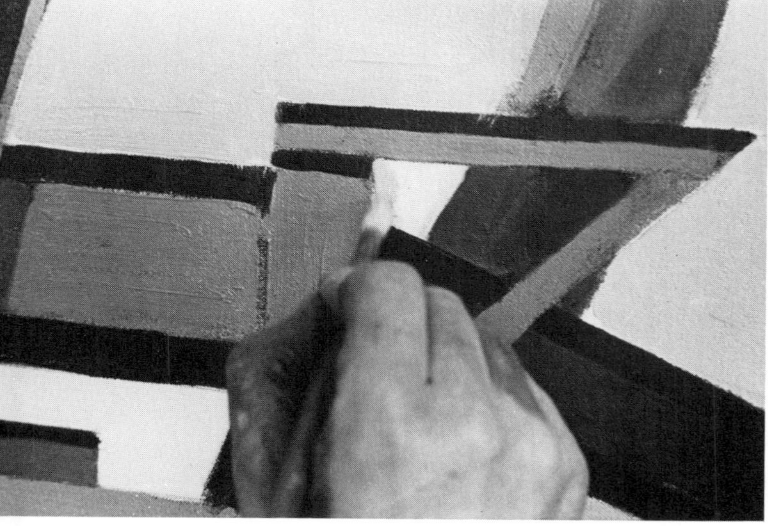

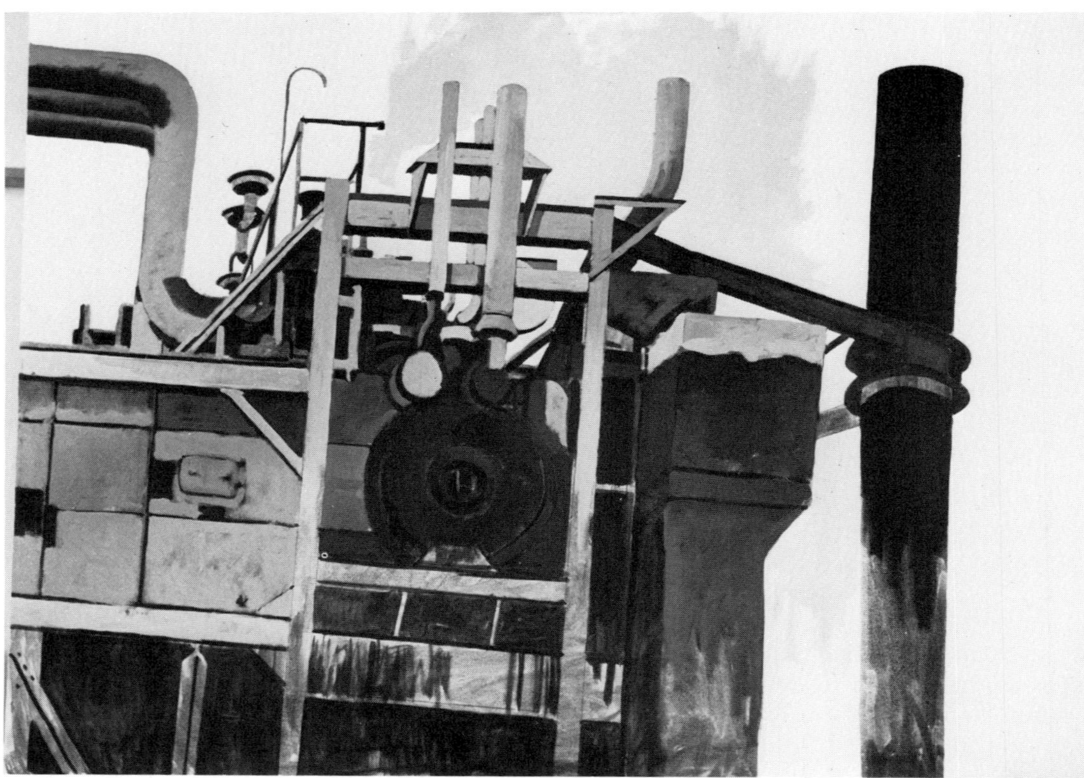

The entire painting showing the effect of the partially painted sky.

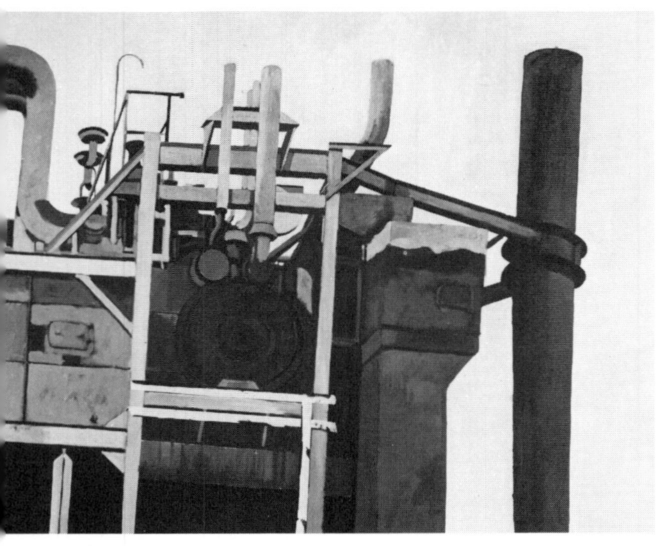

The painting after approximately forty hours of work. The masking tape strips in the lower center are in preparation for another technique.

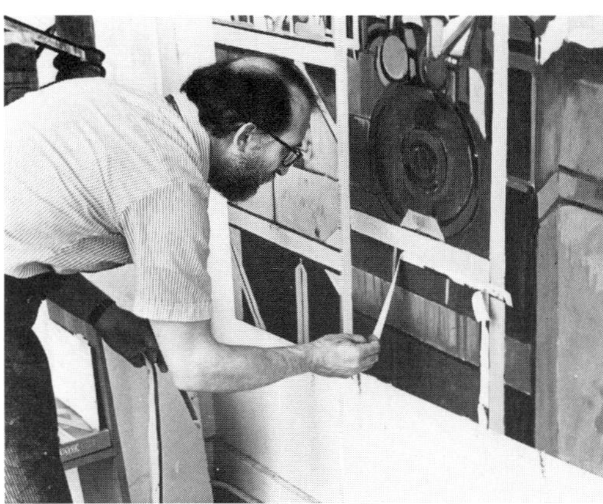

Hurwitz peels off the tape, leaving a sharp edge. This contrasts to the softer edges in most of the painting.

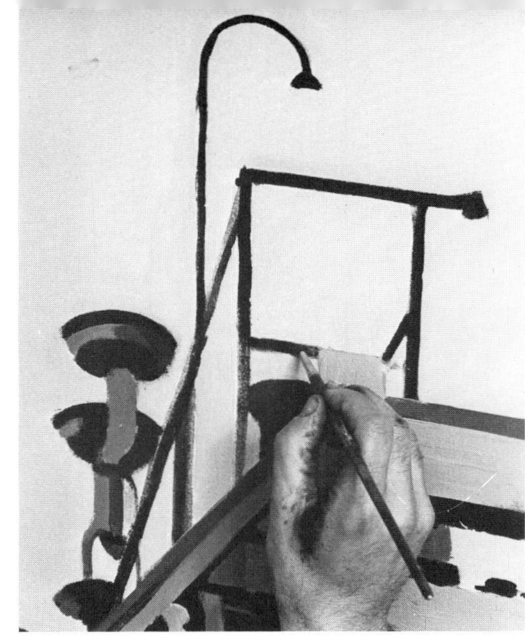

Detail in the upper part of the superstructure is painted in last. This illustrates the pattern of a railing being strengthened.

A horizontal member of the framework is widened by masking off the surrounding dark areas and applying an opaque light tone.

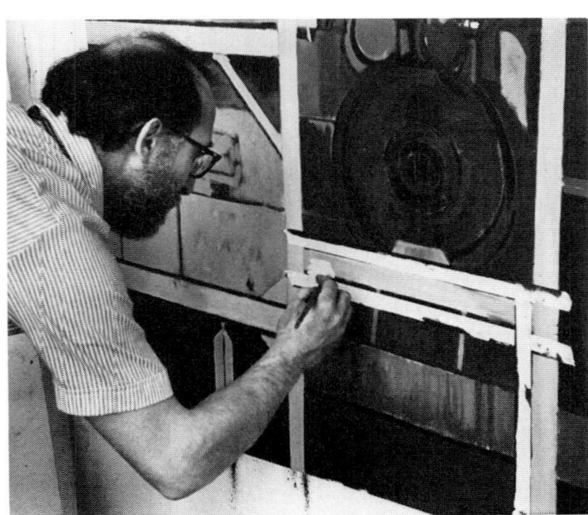

A #10 soft round brush is used to add dots of pigment which represent a line of bolts.

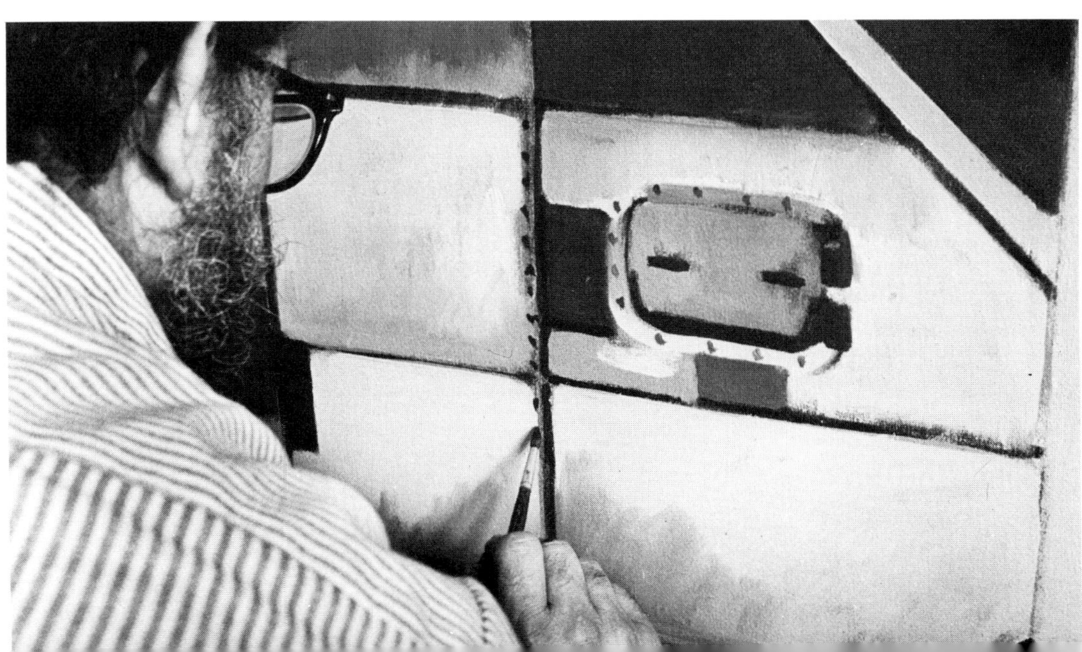

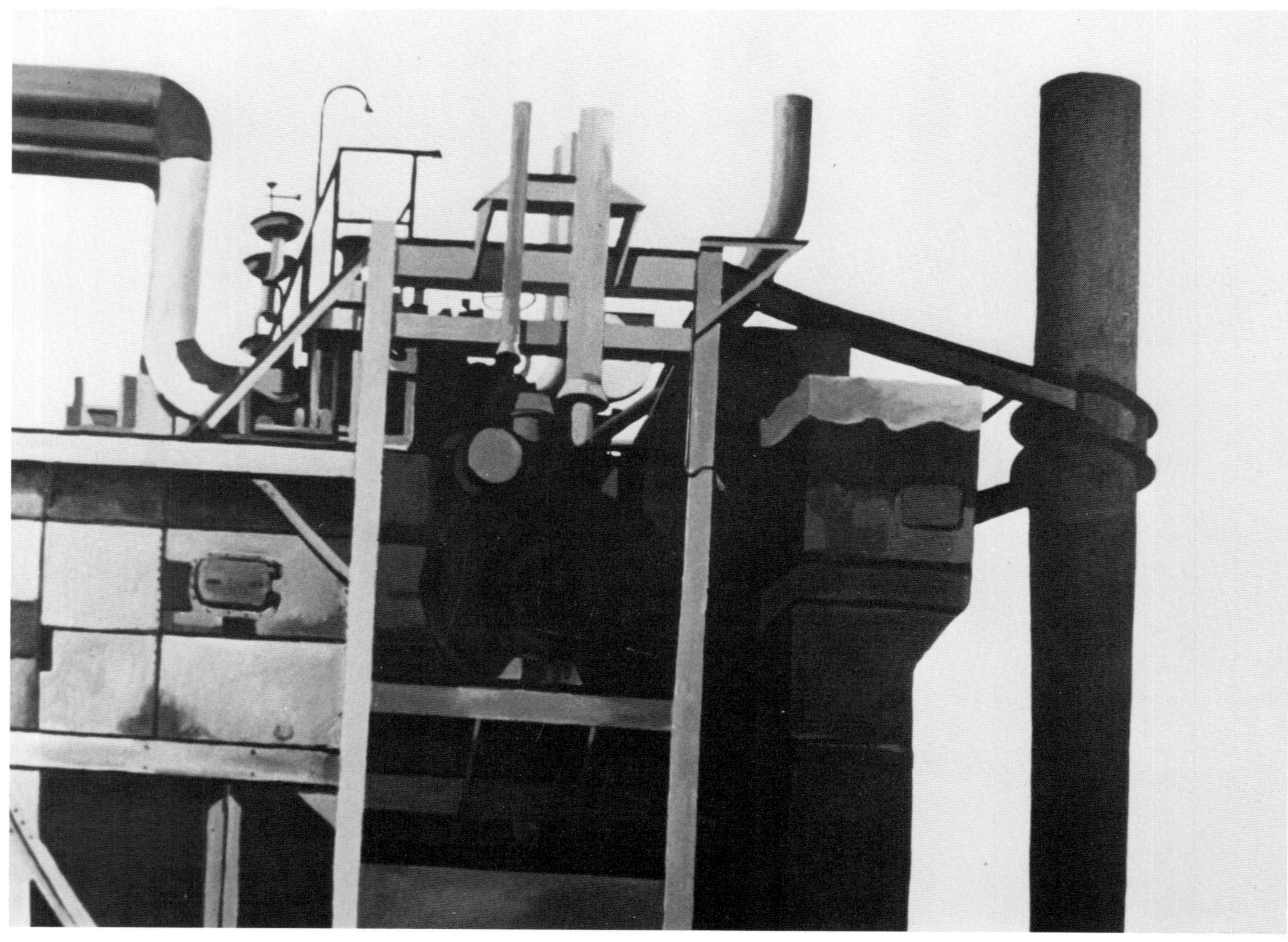

Boiler and Stack, **1978. Oil on canvas, 54" x 72". Sidney Hurwitz.**

Boiler and Stack in its final state. Hurwitz said in explaining his use of color, "I spent a lot of time keeping the colors as close to the pure neutral as possible, trying to maintain the structure as seen in a certain light."

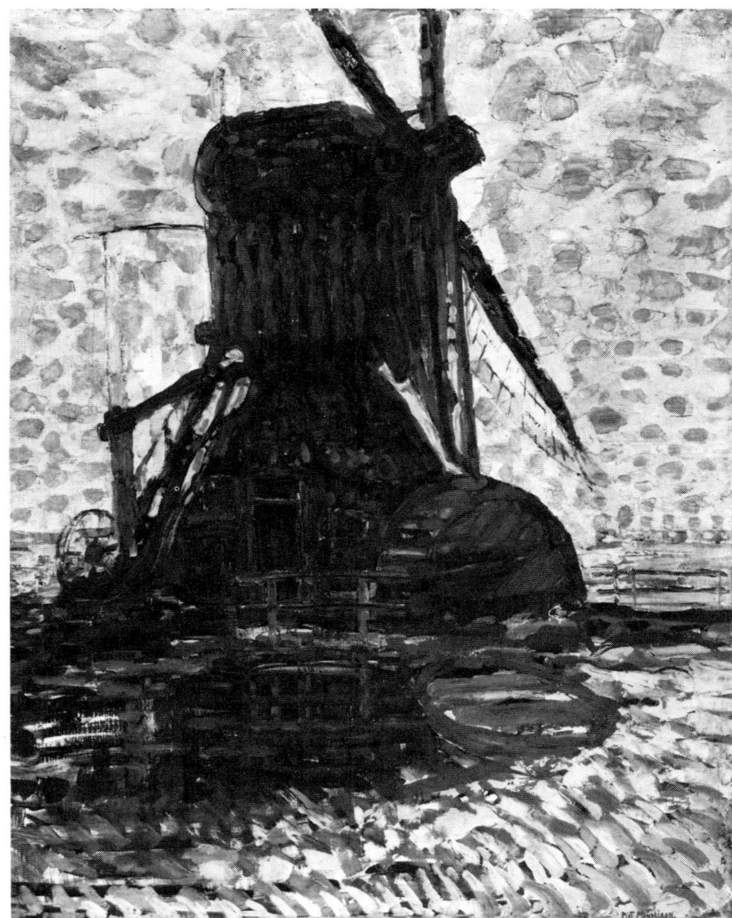

Windmill in Sunlight, c. 1911. Oil on canvas, 34⅞" x 45⅝". Piet Mondrian. Courtesy, Haags Gemeentemuseum, The Hague.

European windmills date back to the twelfth century and are probably the first large industrial forms to appear in the landscape. Akin to sailing ships in that they also use sails to harness the driving power of the wind, they clearly show their function in their outward form. Their picturesque appearance has fascinated and inspired artists through the centuries. Piet Mondrian painted this Dutch post mill in a combination of Impressionist and Fauve manners which he had briefly adopted while searching for his own style. The painting is vibrant in intense primary colors which have been applied to the canvas in strokes and patches.

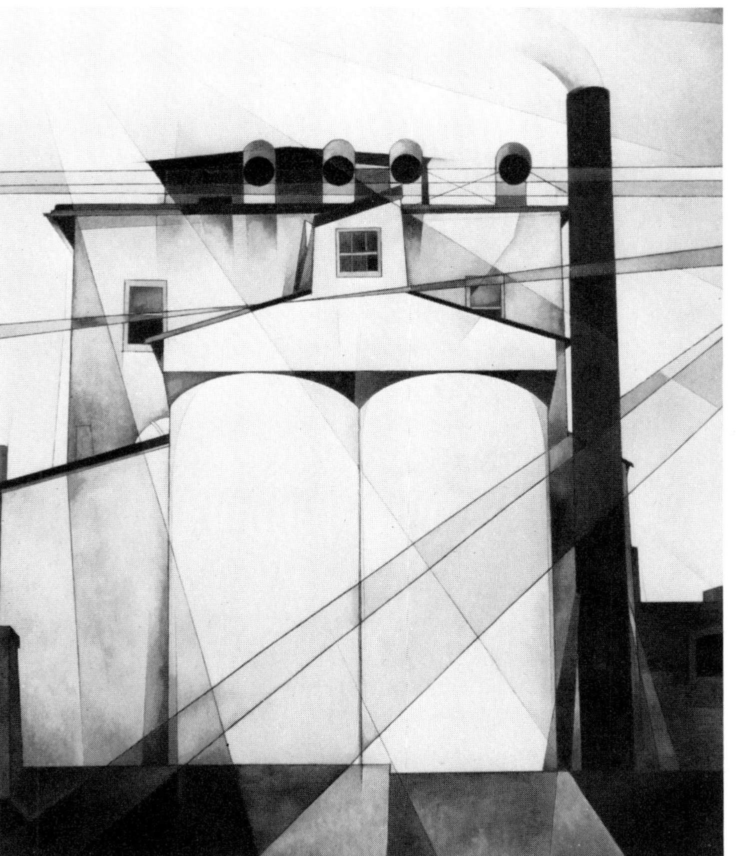

My Egypt, 1927. Oil on composition board, 35¾" x 30". Charles Demuth. Collection of Whitney Museum of American Art, New York. Photograph by Geoffrey Clements, Staten Island, New York.

Between 1907 and 1915 Charles Demuth spent much of his time in Paris, learning what he could about the avant-garde, and especially the Cubist analysis of form. He then refined these techniques to suit his own temperament. Among the subjects he tackled is a notable series of industrial scenes. *My Egypt* has the crisp treatment that gave rise to terms such as *Immaculates* or *Precisionists* which described artists such as Demuth and Charles Sheeler. Raylike shafts cut diagonally across the composition, supporting it and breaking it into a faceted structure of tonal steps that builds to dazzling light and deep, rich dark tones.

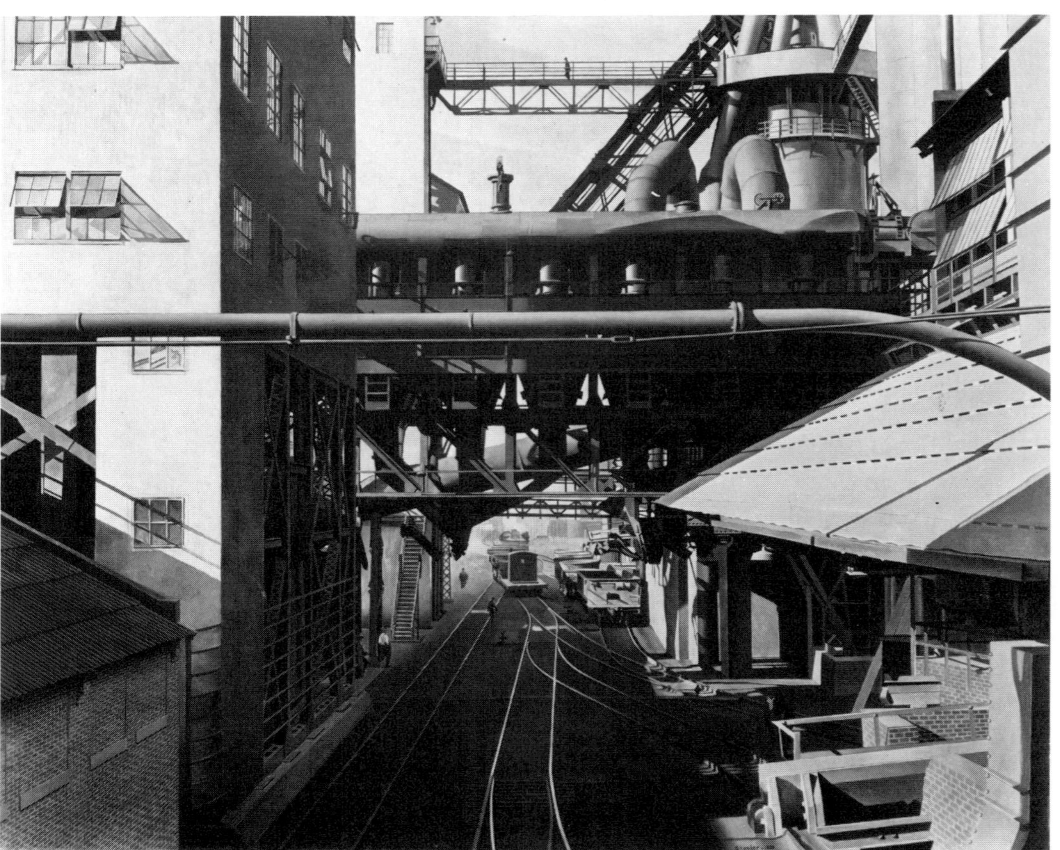

***City Interior*, 1936. Painting on fiberboard, 22⅛" x 27". Charles Sheeler. Courtesy of the Worcester Art Museum, Worcester, Massachusetts.**

City Interior was carefully planned, then drawn on the canvas, each area independently completed. When it was almost half finished, work was interrupted for more than eight months. When Sheeler resumed work, no revisions were required and the painting was completed without a break.

Sheeler said, "I can't go out and find something to paint. Something seen keeps recurring in memory with an insistence increasingly vivid and with attributes added which escaped observation on first acquaintance. Gradually, a mental image is built up which takes on a personal identity. The picture attains a mental existence that is complete, within the limits of my capabilities, before the actual work of putting it down begins. Since the value of the mental picture can be determined only by the degree of response it arouses in other persons, it must be restated in physical terms—hence the painting."

As can be seen, *City Interior* has a remarkable finish. There is no evidence of struggle or the physical marks of paint application. "For I favor the picture which arrives at its destination without the evidence of a trying journey, rather than one which shows the marks of battle. An efficient army buries its dead."

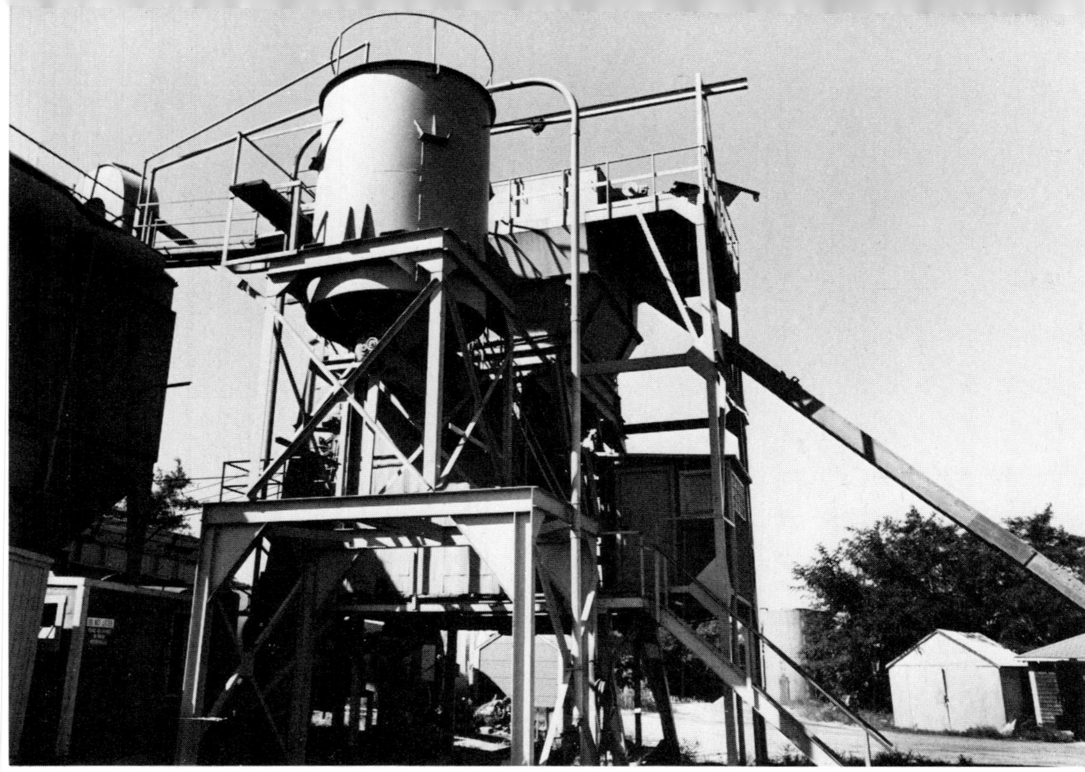

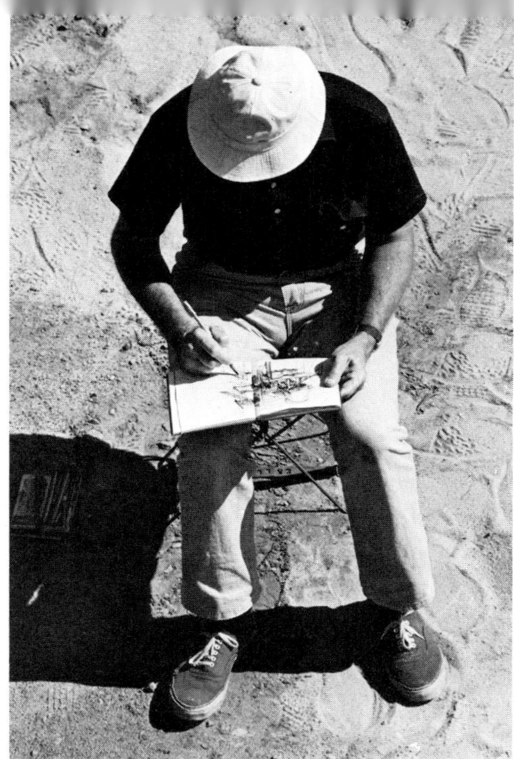

On-site drawing of the *Concrete Plant*

I chose this point of view because from the close, low angle, the plant builds into a triangular mass. The triangle is endlessly repeated by the diagonal braces, corner reinforcers, patterns of sun and shadow, and the way that the sky is cut by the long trough and stairway. I was attracted by this pyramidal mass and the light triangles that glittered against the black shadows.

For larger, more complex drawings, a folding camp stool can be most welcome. Working on location means less than ideal conditions. An example is trying to get the essentials of a subject as seen from a safety island in the middle of a busy street on a cold, windy day. A minimum amount of equipment is used: a small sketchbook held firmly with one hand while the basic lines and tones are sketched in with the other hand. Another example is lying on one's stomach in order to get the lowest angle at which a subject best composes itself. As uncomfortable as these situations are, the results are worth the trouble and there is satisfaction in achieving one's purpose against such odds. If the sketching situation is extremely difficult, the drawing can be roughly worked and then completed in more comfortable conditions while the memory of the subject is still fresh. Occasionally, a really impossible situation arises, such as a moving subject or a viewpoint that cannot be maintained for more than a moment. Then the snapshot is the only recourse. Even when it is possible to do a comprehensive drawing on the spot, a few photographs might be helpful for later reference.

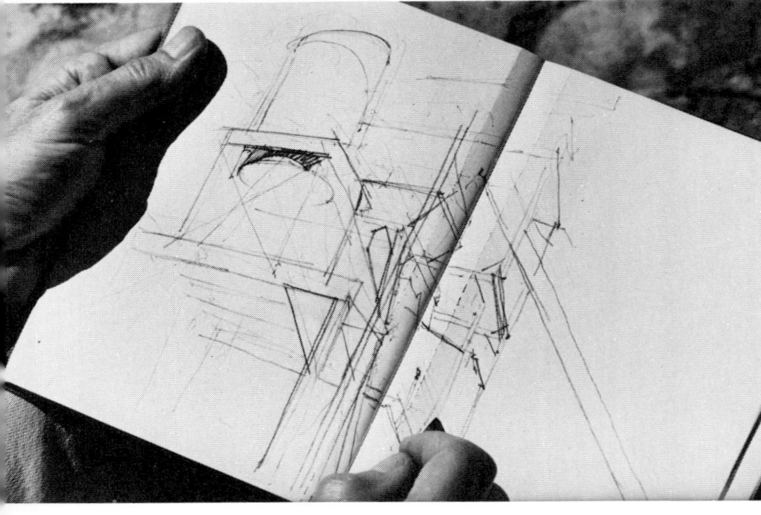

The sketchbook's double page spread is used for maximum detail. I decided to compose the triangular mass as large as possible and include the entire structure from top to bottom. The apex of the lopsided triangle is at the top left, its two sides running down to the bottom corners of the paper. The main body of the drawing is placed on the left page and the trough forms a long arm down to the lower right-hand corner of the second page. This makes a more dynamic balance than if the mass had been centered. As a result, the busiest area of the complicated structure, and therefore the center of interest, will be at left center. The first light web of lines is sketched in with this in mind.

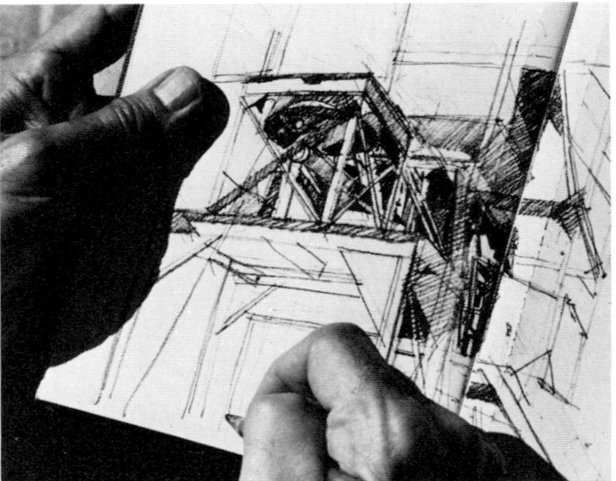

Tones are hatched in with a soft (4B) charcoal pencil. I concentrate on the tonal work in the crucial center of the structure because as time passes, the dark and light patterns are rapidly changing.

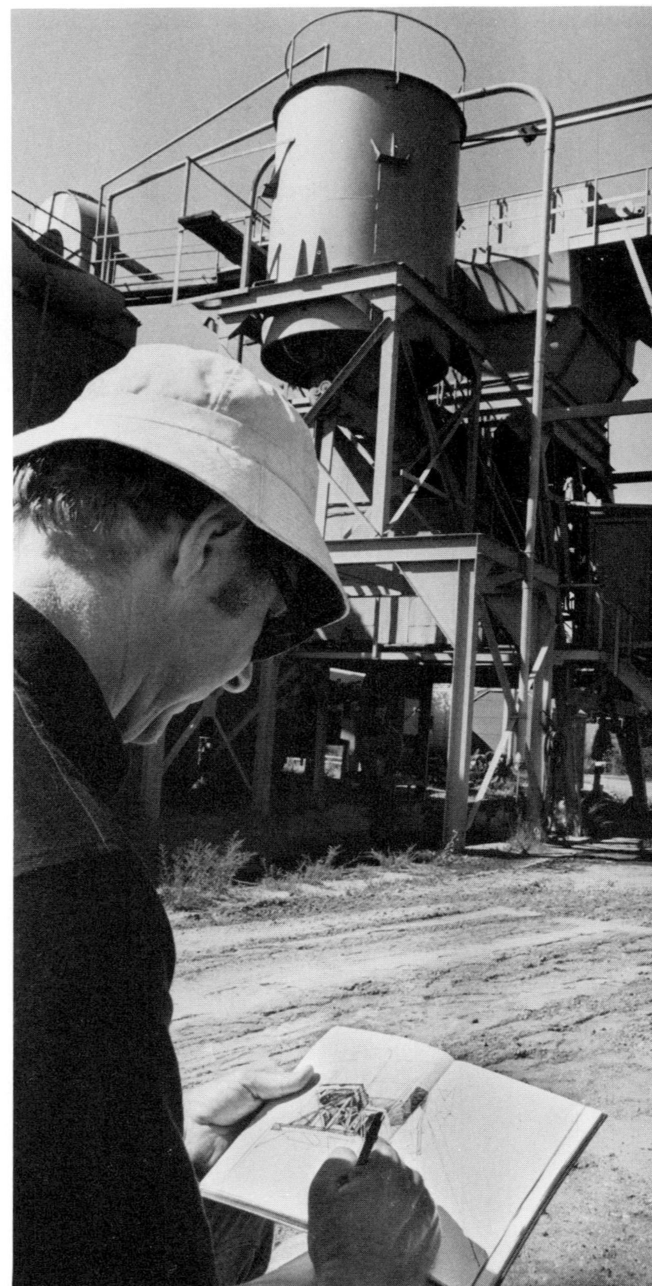

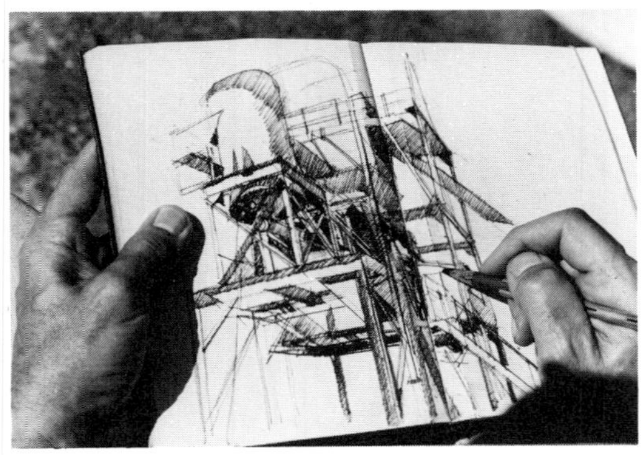

Shadows are gradually extended out from the center in a floating pattern of angular shapes.

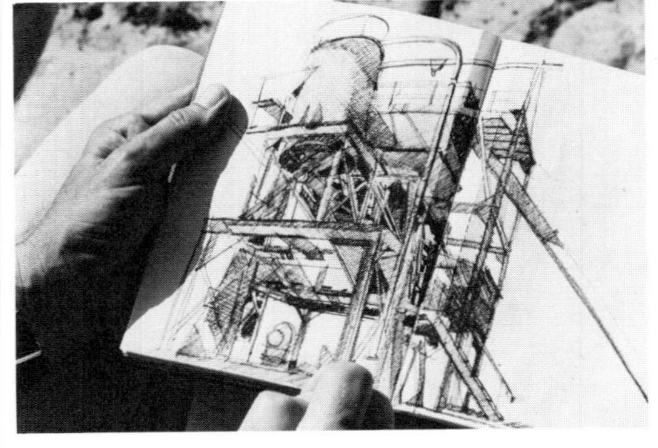

At this point, the essential values *as seen* are in, but the drawing is far from complete. I will rework the tones, trying to attain the same impact of the initial observation.

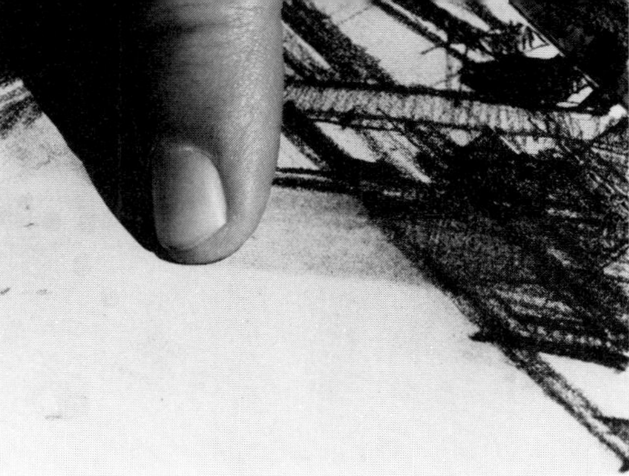

Finger smudging part of the drawing produces subtle tones that are impossible to achieve with only a charcoal pencil.

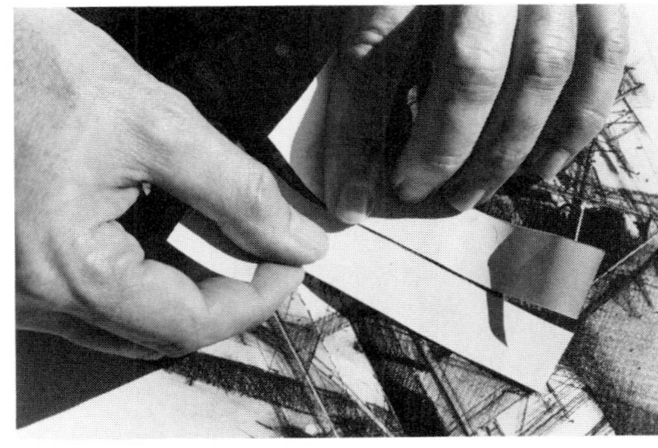

An eraser and mask can put light back into dark areas. Two strips of paper are put down in preparation for making a light line, the edge of a girder.

Holding the masks in place, the eraser removes the charcoal that is exposed between the paper strips.

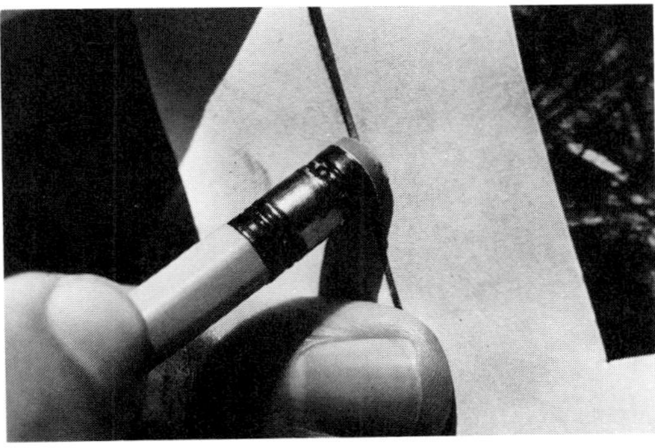

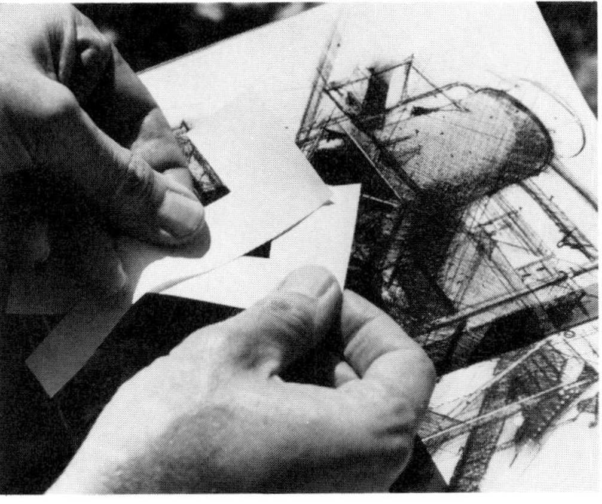

A light, triangular shape will be erased from a dark part of the drawing.

A kneaded eraser removes the triangle of charcoal.

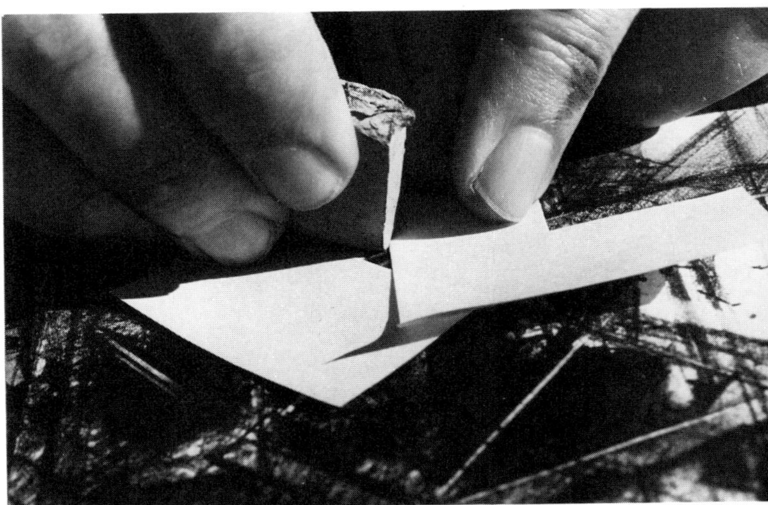

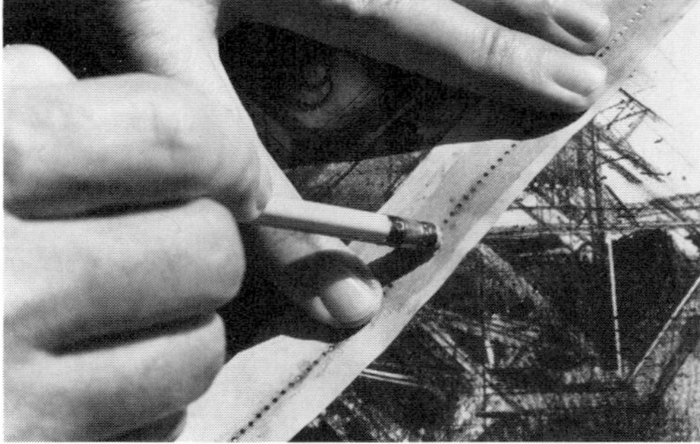

A strip of computer tape used as a mask.

The result is a line of white dots in the drawing.

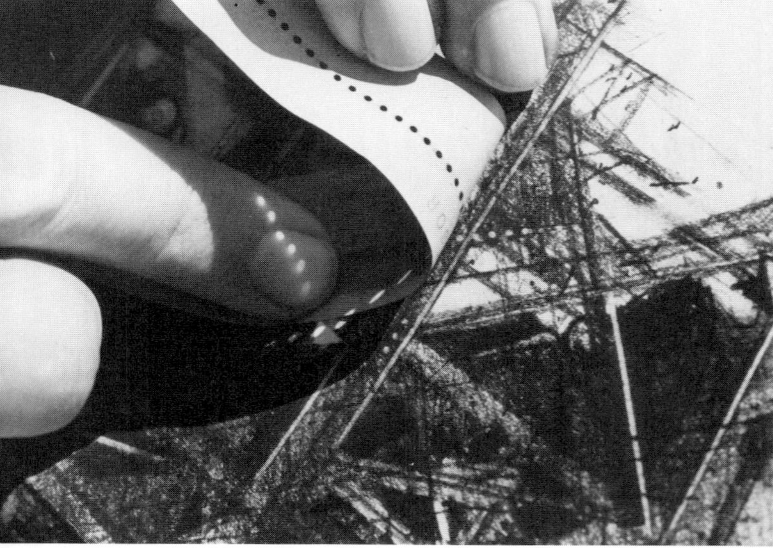

An enlarged section of the drawing shows the results of charcoal pencil hatching, crosshatching with smudging, and spots and patches of light produced by erasing through masks.

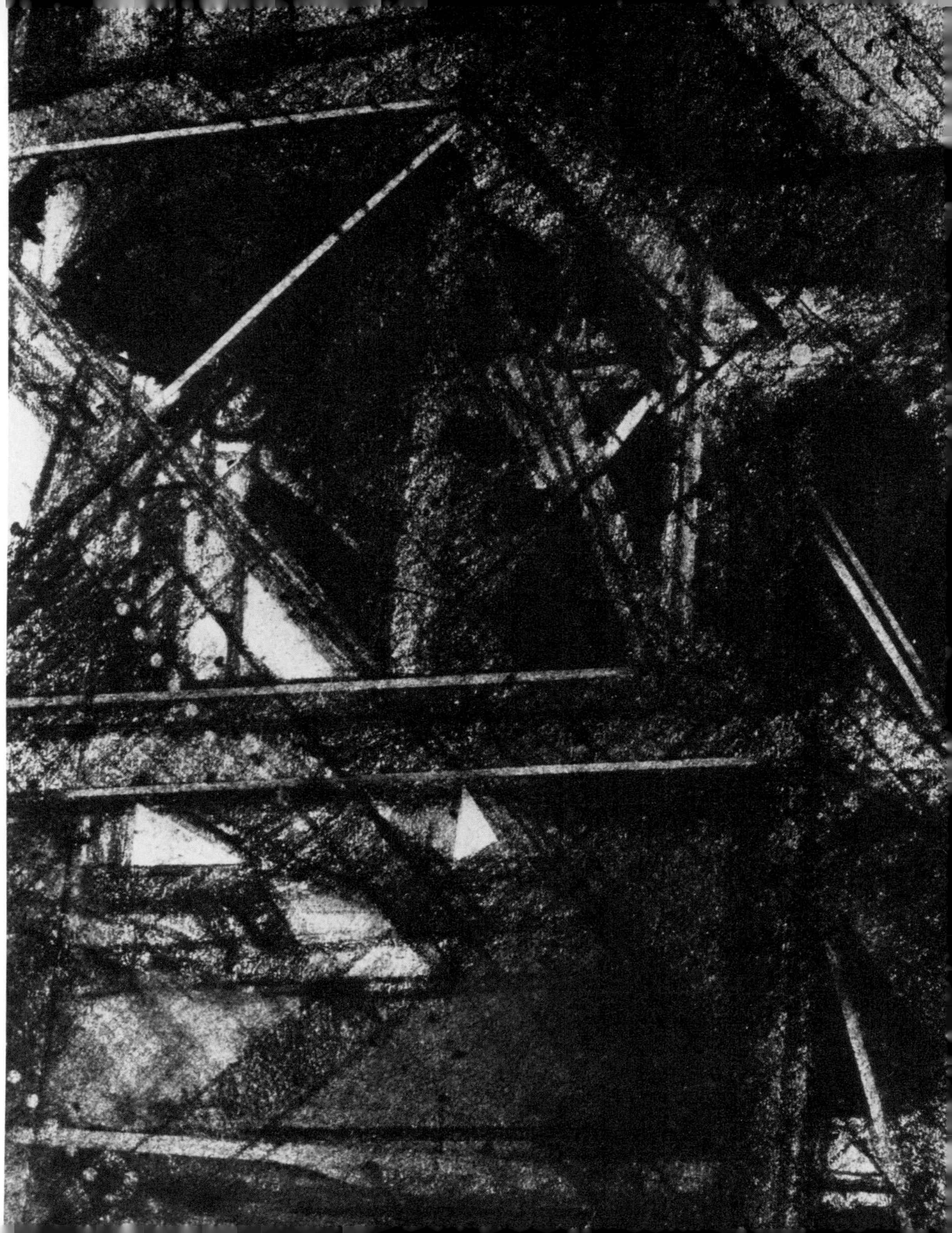

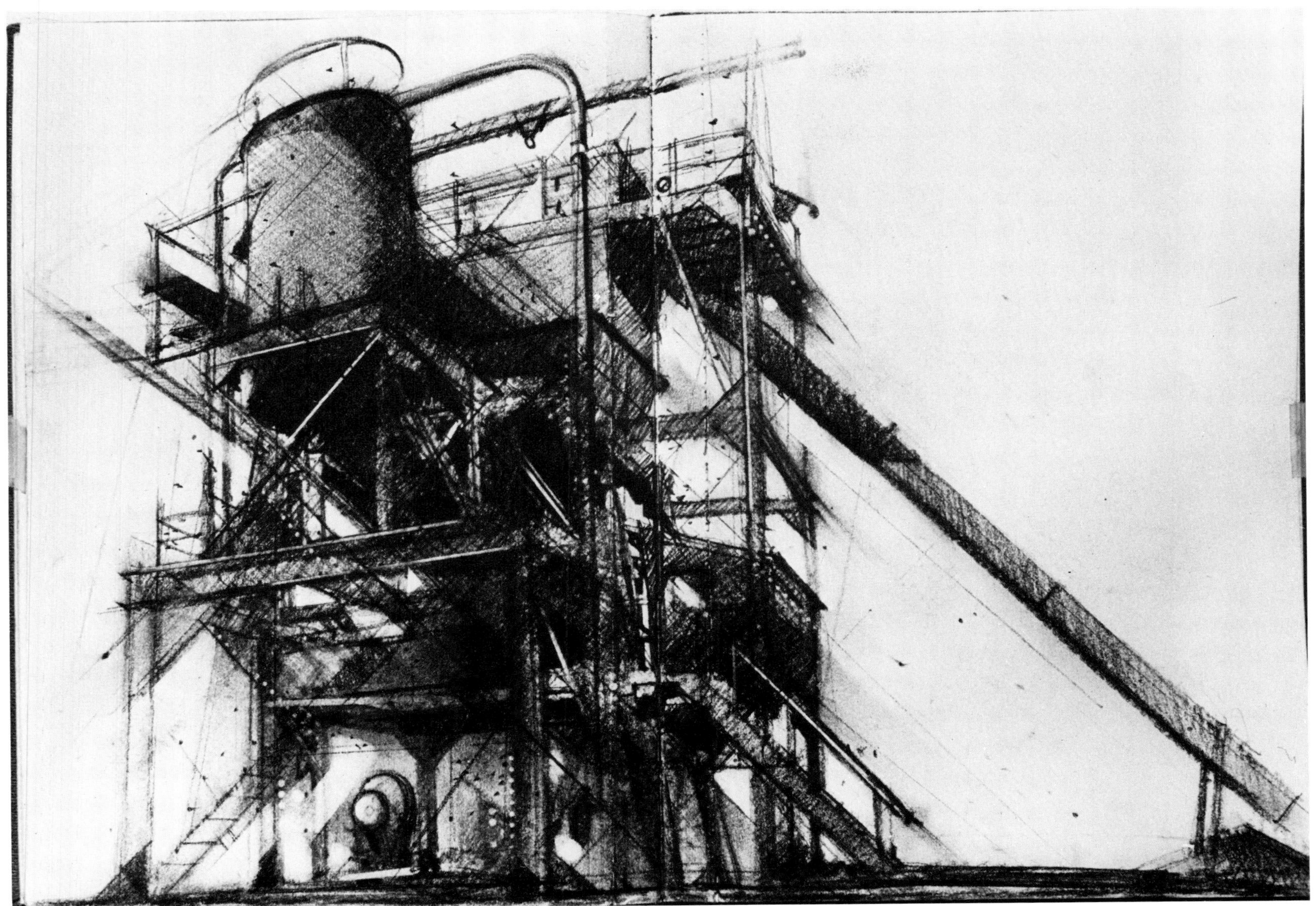

Concrete Plant, 1978. Charcoal, 8¼″ x 11¾″.

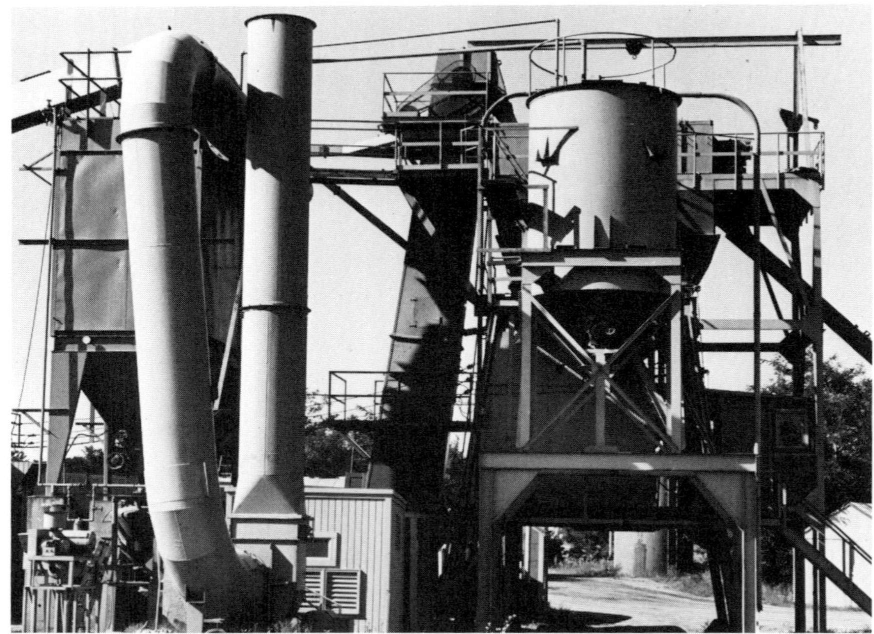

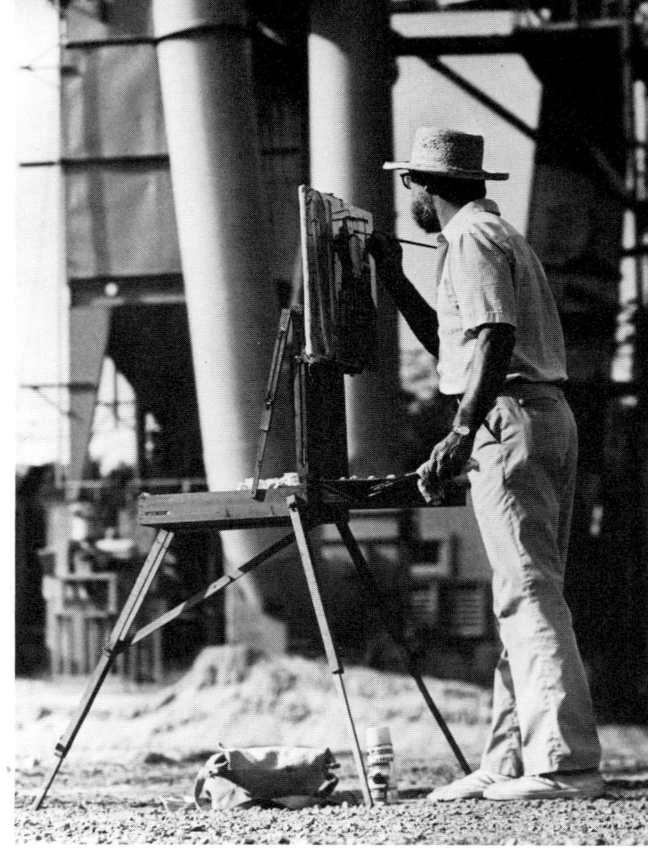

On-site painting of a concrete plant by Sidney Hurwitz

The first session

This concrete plant on Cape Cod offered special opportunities for on-site work. It stands in a rural setting with open space on all sides to permit a wide choice of viewpoints. It also provided a chance for Hurwitz to directly paint forms that were very similar to some he had explored exclusively through photographs. After scouting the plant from all sides, he chose this elevation because he liked the way it separated into two masses: the two, large, vertical pipes at left and the tank with supporting structure at right center. From this angle, the thin pipes and braces at the top and right naturally framed the entire composition into a rectangle. The early afternoon light from the left strongly modeled the two large vertical pipes and the tank in half-light and half-shade. The sun picked out the linear supporting structure with shadows behind it under the tank. This light also created a pattern of shadows from the catwalk and its railings on the tank.

The on-site painting was done in two three-hour sessions with some studio work to finish it.

Hurwitz used a portable French easel which contains paints, palette, brushes, solvents, drawing implements, and an 18″ x 22″ stretched linen canvas. He had previously primed the canvas with white lead and had toned it with a wash of raw sienna oil paint and turpentine. Hurwitz set up about one o'clock on a Saturday in late summer. His first step was to make a preliminary drawing on the canvas with a vine charcoal stick. He decided that the structure should fill the canvas, so he drew in the tank at right center, expanded it, letting the supporting legs and the large pipes at left run off the bottom edge. Hurwitz used the braces and pipes at top and right as an interior frame, leaving an inverted, L-shaped band of sky around it.

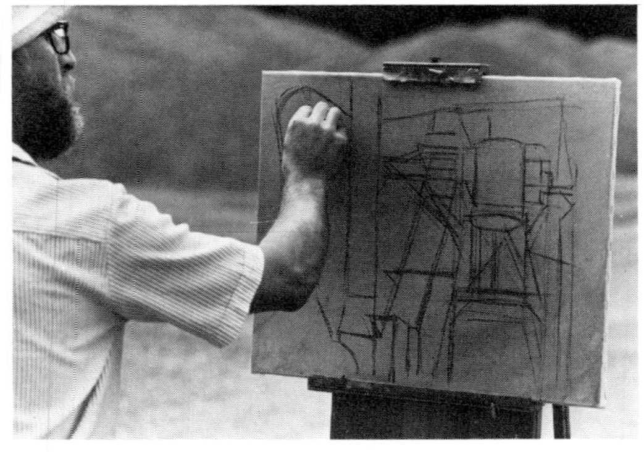

Because Hurwitz did not want sky around all the edges of the painting, he let the edge of the canvas cut off the flat tank behind the vertical pipes at left. His main interest was in the sculptural forms of the plant; the sky serves only as background. The completed charcoal drawing was sprayed with fixative.

Using a small, pointed brush and a wash of mineral spirits and burnt umber, the drawing is reinforced and elaborated on with the introduction of some shadows.

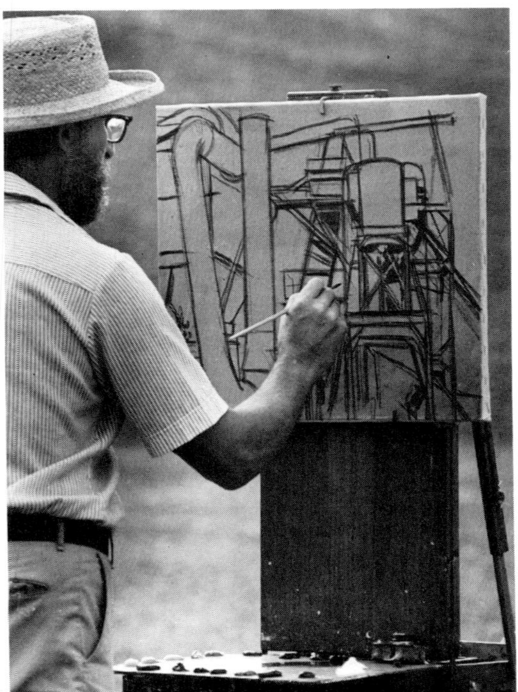

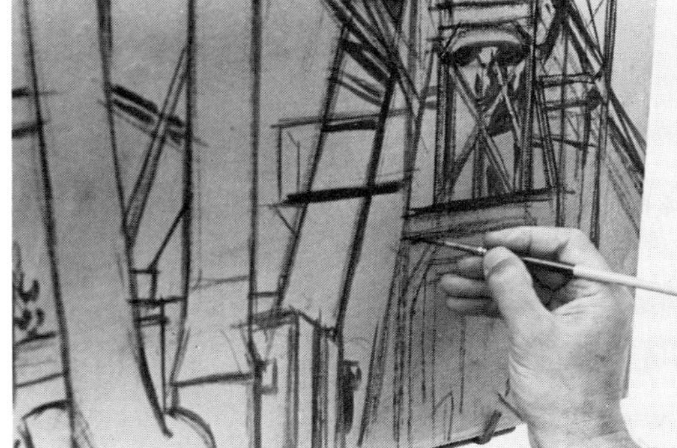

After about three-quarters of an hour's work, the skeleton of lines that defines the composition and structure is well established.

The completed preliminary drawing.

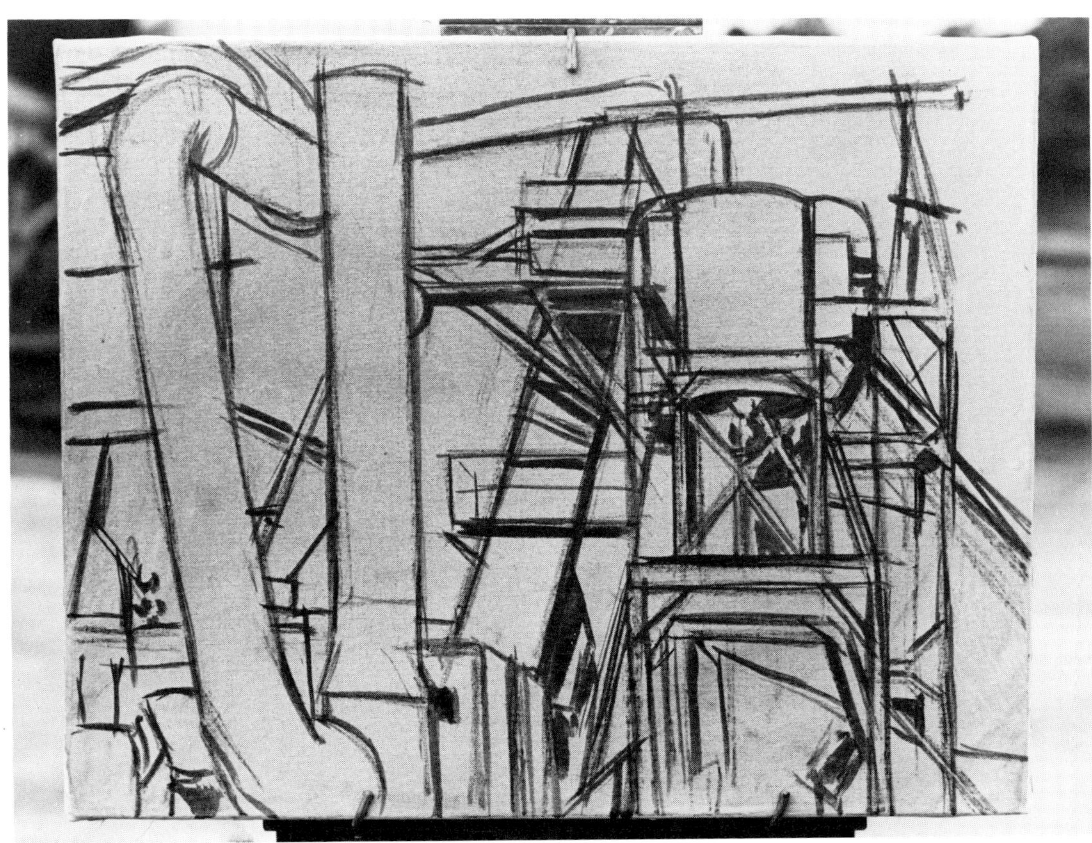

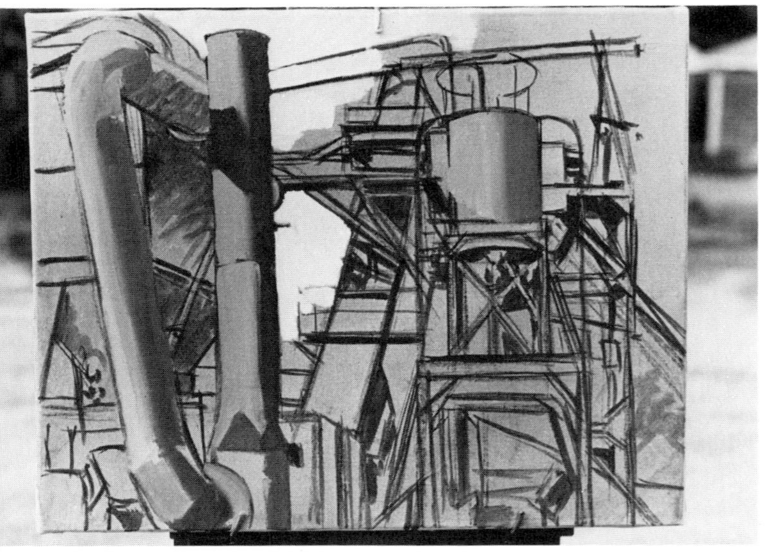

The palette is laid out. Blues to greens to yellows to browns are placed around the edge. There is also a larger gob of white and two cups. The first cup contains a mixture of equal parts mineral spirits, damar varnish, and linseed oil. The second cup contains only mineral spirits.

Light blue has been worked into the sky areas at top center. Modeling in tones of light and dark blue gray has begun on the pipes and tank.

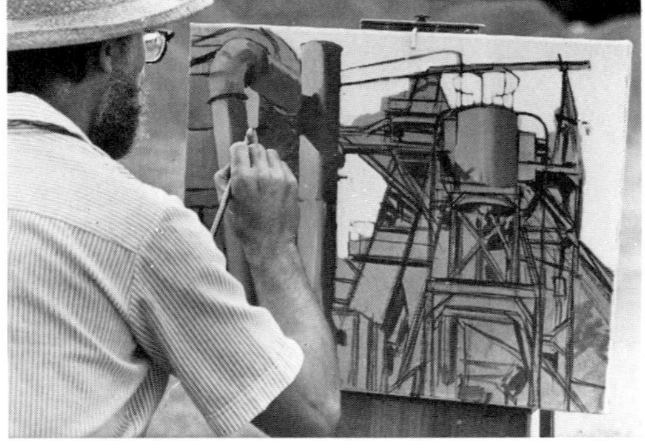

More sky has been painted around the drawn forms. By this time, the afternoon sky had become partly cloudy and Hurwitz spent the sunny periods working on crucial light and shadow modeling. He built up linear detail when it became cloudy.

The painting at the end of the first session. The larger forms are modeled against the sky and a pattern of shadows is beginning to emerge.

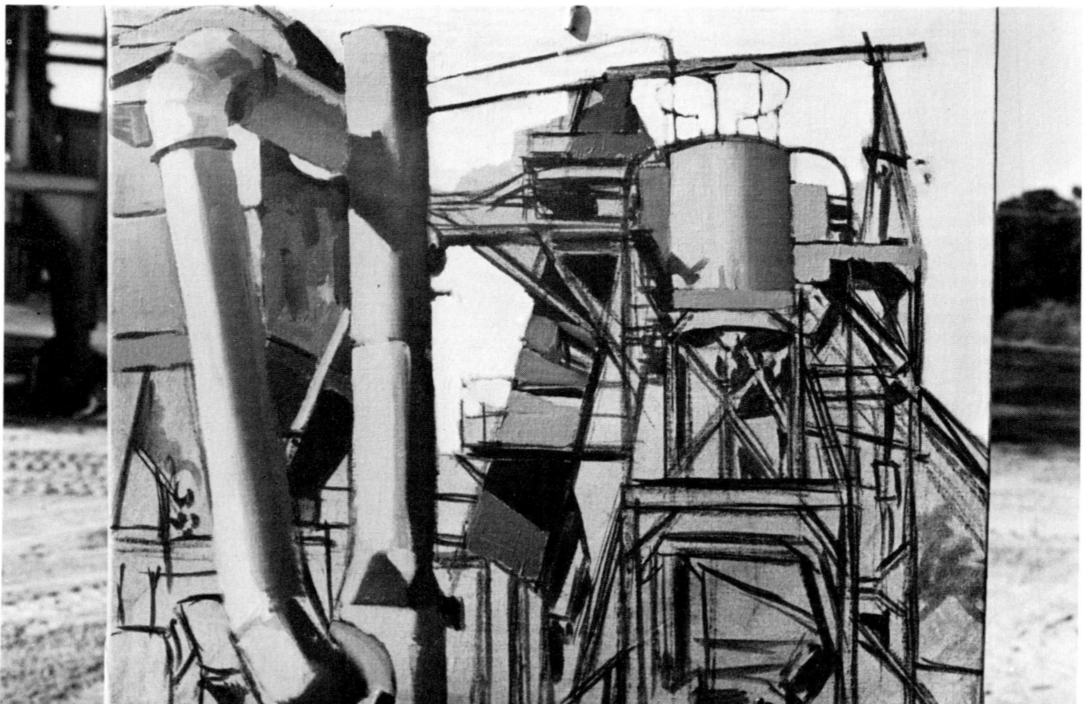

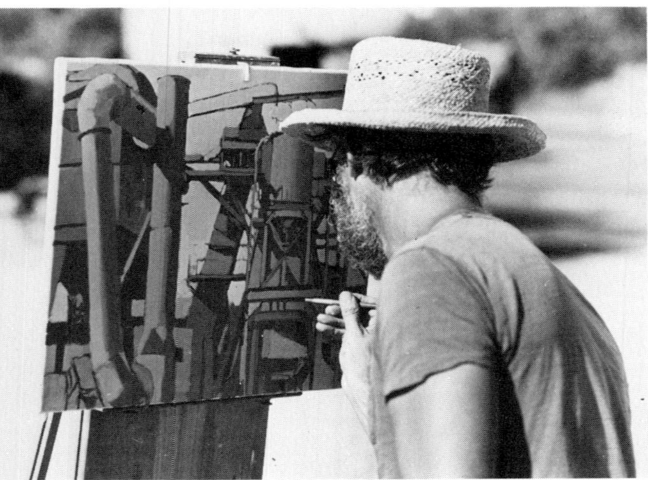

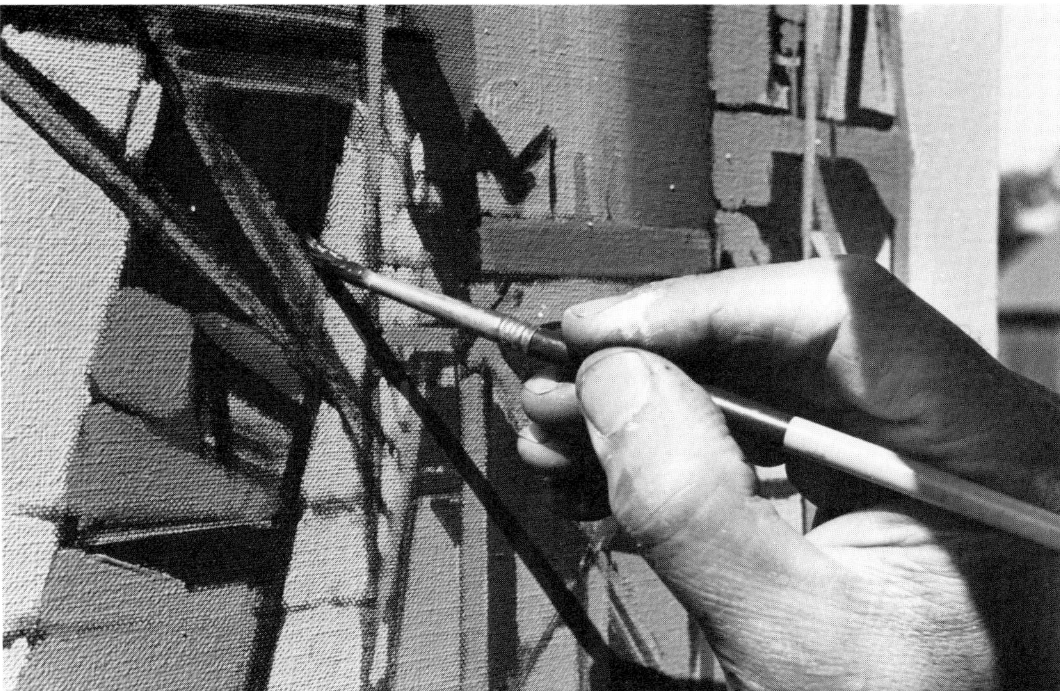

The second session

The entire sky has been painted in, breaking into and defining parts of the structural mass. Blue has been intensified because the original pale blue now seems too weak. This session was devoted to putting in opaque tones of various blue gray values to further build up the forms.

The drawing has gradually disappeared underneath the flat tones. Hurwitz uses a dark blue gray to repaint some of them to bring them back to the surface. Others will remain merely as line traces.

Deepest shadows are put in with dark blue gray.

Close-up views show the textural qualities of paints and canvas as the top edge of the tank is redefined. This looser, less detailed technique is characteristic of on-location work where speed and simplification are required. Hurwitz finds that outdoor work forces him to develop quick metaphors, simplifications for complicated subjects. More is done by implication or generalization than by spelling out. Paradoxically, while on location the artist has the maximum amount of available information: direct contact, many viewpoints, light and color details. However, working conditions often prevent making the greatest use of this information.

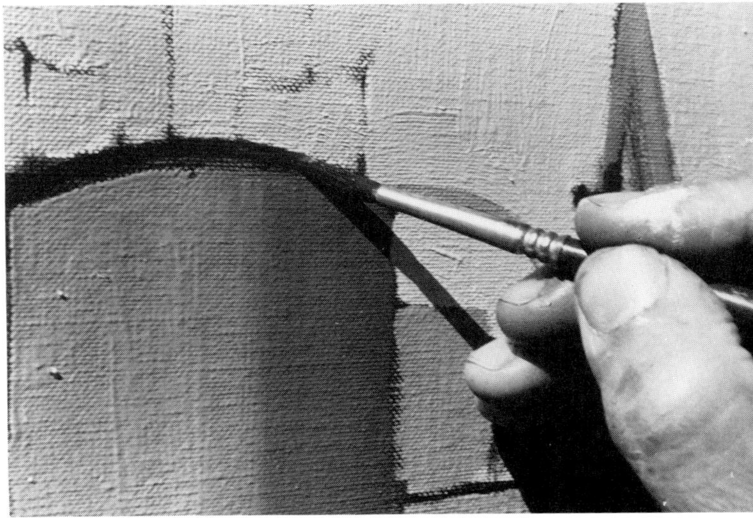

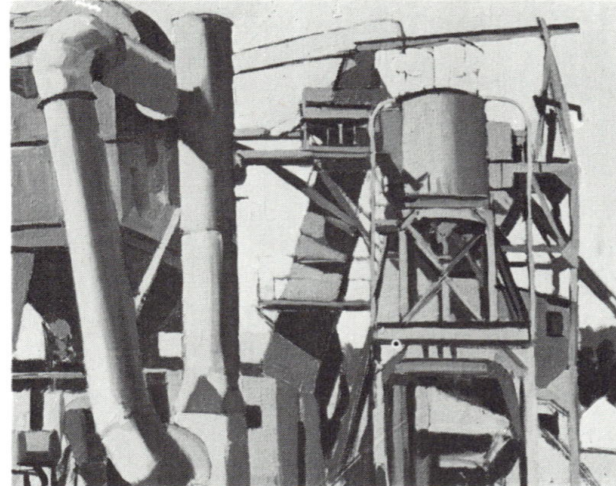

The painting at the end of the two outdoor sessions (six hours). Most of the information is in place and the work is perhaps eighty percent completed. The tunnel under the supporting structure is unresolved and the lower left corner is incomplete. Realizing he might be unable to finish the painting on location, Hurwitz took a series of 35mm color slides of various details for future reference.

In his studio, the indoor light showed the blue sky to be too intense, so Hurwitz toned it down to better relate to the rest of the composition. He straightened some of the drawing which had a tendency to lean to the left, and he sharpened some of the forms under the tank.

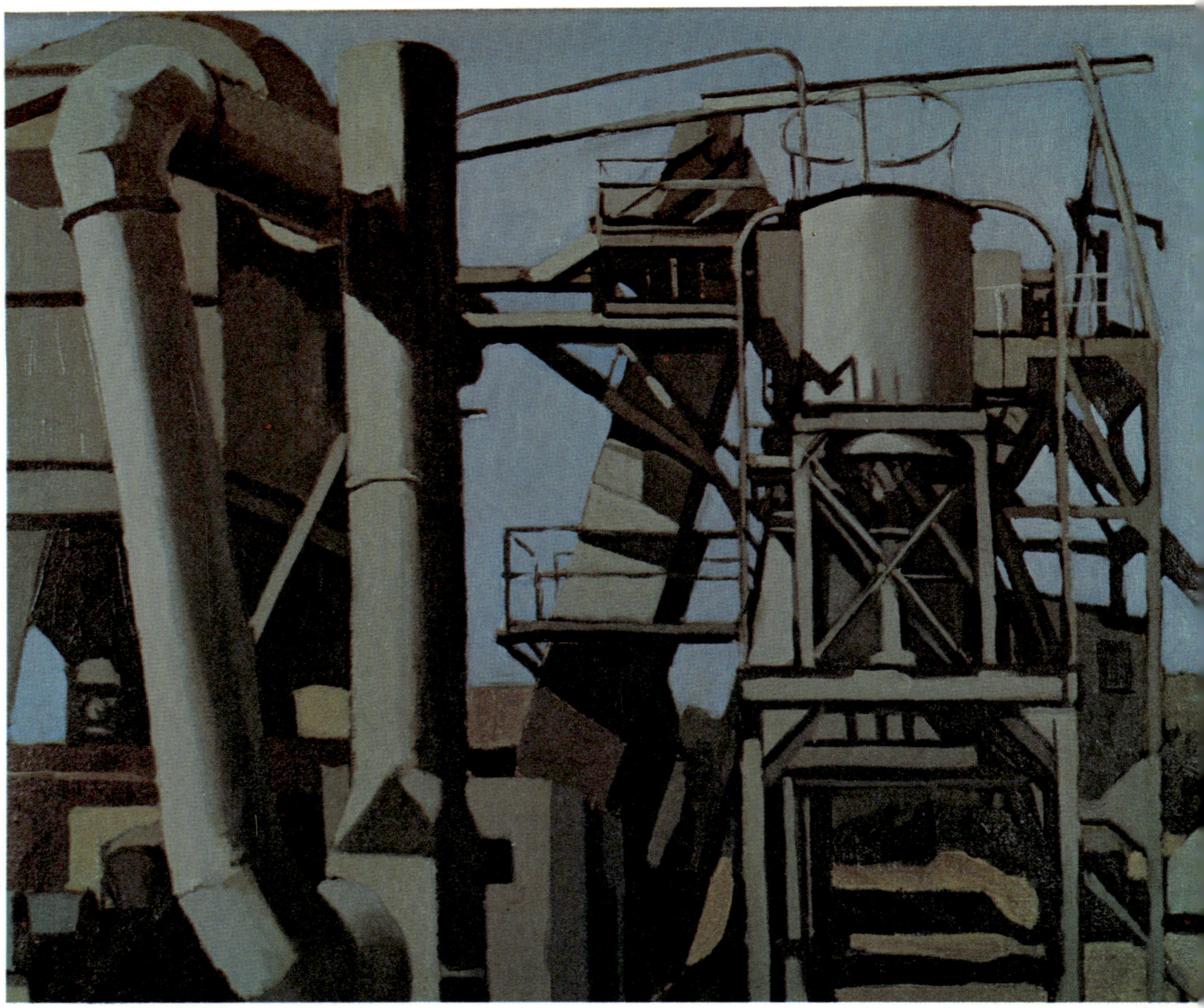

***The Concrete Plant*, 1978. Oil on canvas, 18'' X 22''. Sidney Hurwitz.**

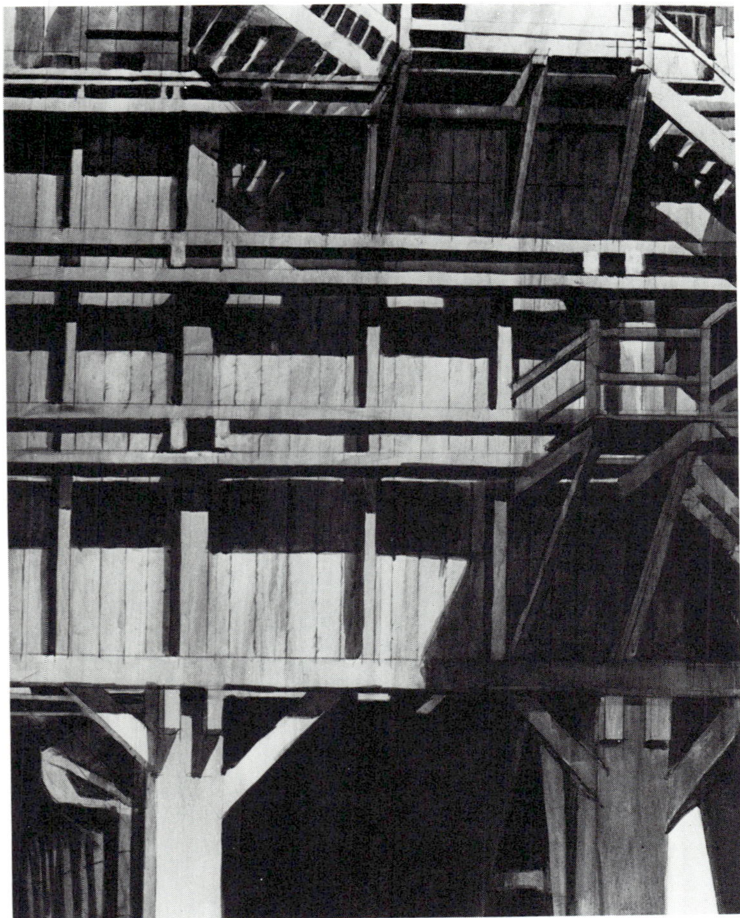

***Coal Dock*, 1978. Acrylic drawing on paper, 19″ x 26″. Sidney Hurwitz.**

This massive, timbered structure is located on Boston's waterfront. When Hurwitz saw it in strong sunlight, it interested him for its pattern of diagonal shadows which echoed the wooden braces and contrasted to the strong, sculptural, vertical/horizontal grid of the dock.

***Compressor*, 1978. Oil on paper, 48″ x 36½″. Sidney Hurwitz.**

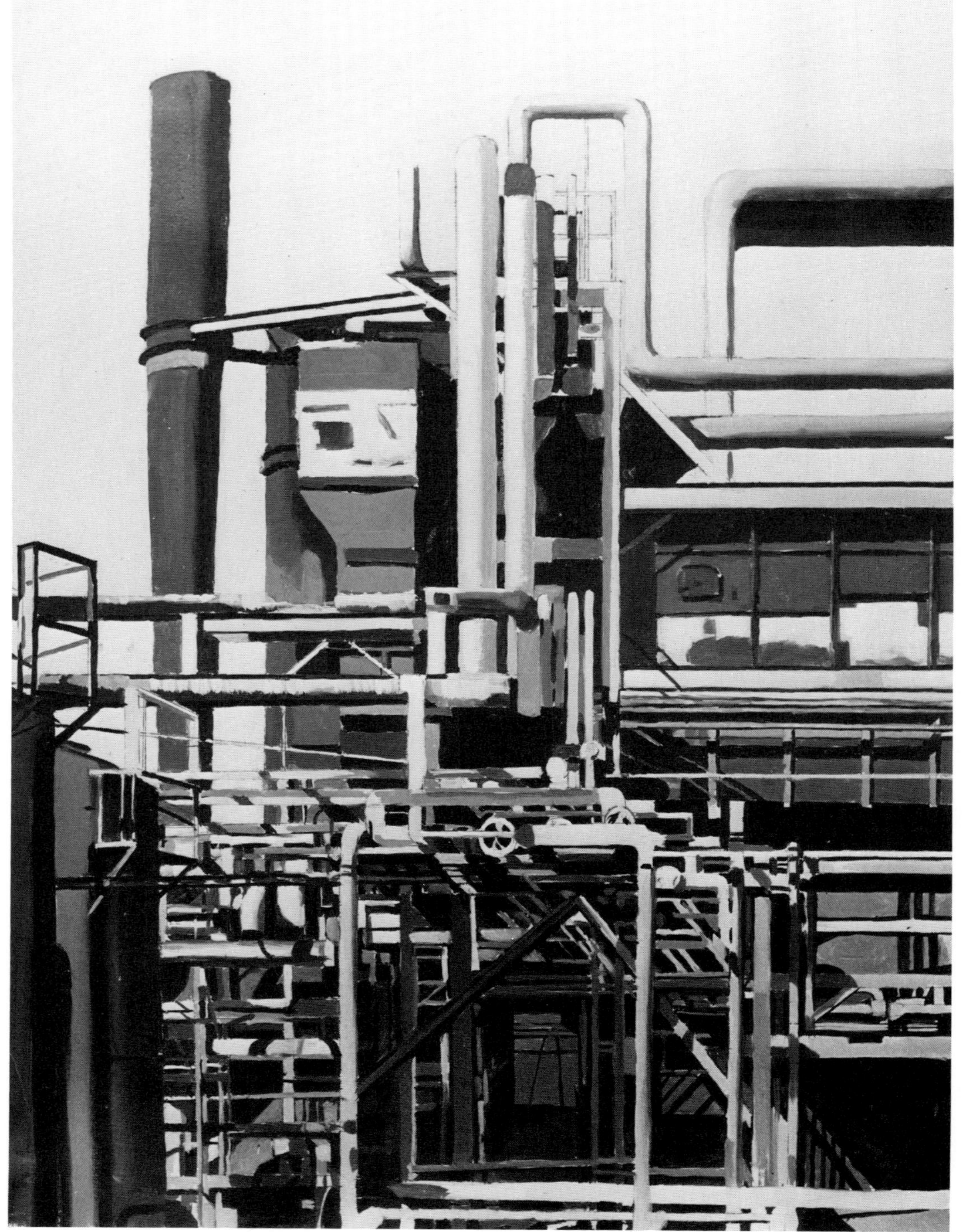

Boiler Complex, 1978. Oil on paper, 29″ x 21″. Sidney Hurwitz.

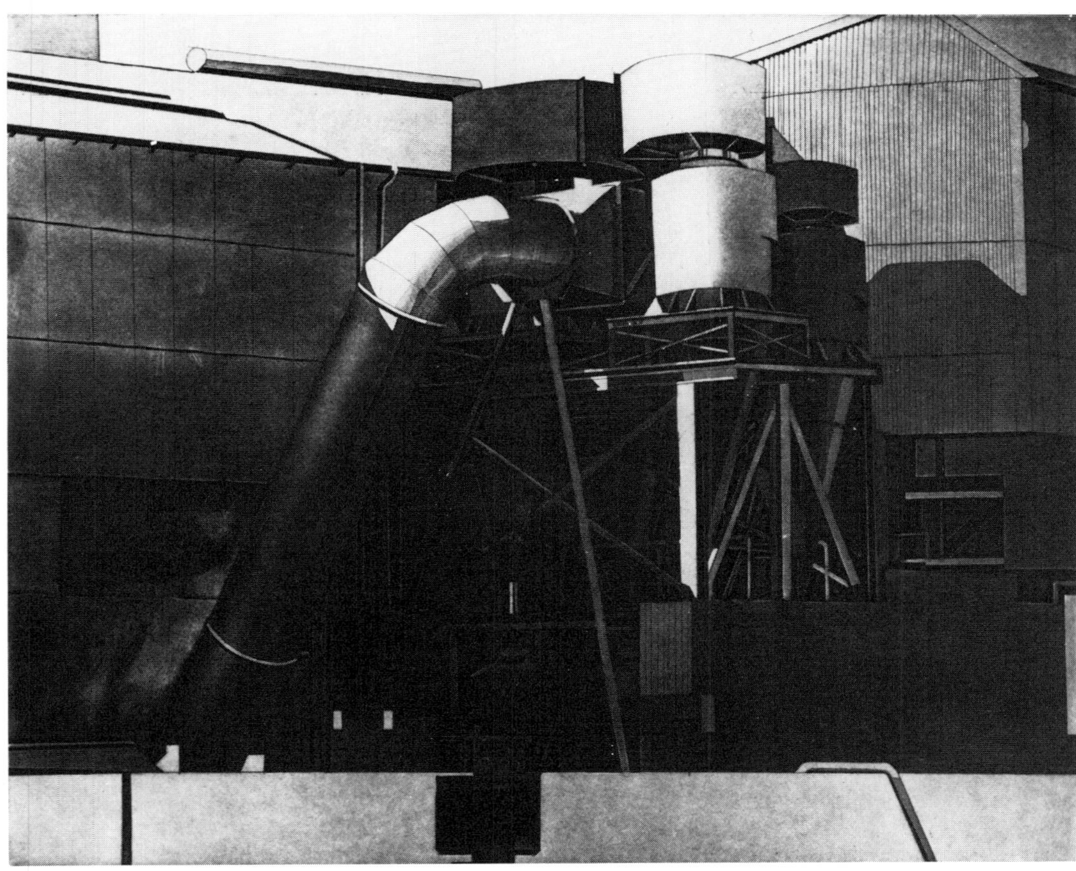

***Refinery*, 1976. Etching and aquatint on paper, 20" x 24". Sidney Hurwitz.**

In this print, Hurwitz plays the complicated dark structure in the center against the simpler, flat shapes surrounding it. He works out the interaction of a few strong light areas within a predominantly dark composition.

CHAPTER SIX

Transportation

Railroads

The steam locomotive

Railway mania was at its height in the 1840s when Turner, himself a rail enthusiast, painted this picture. It is a celebration of the Railway Age and, in particular, the opening of the Bristol and Exeter extension of the Great Western Railway. It was built in 1844 and decreased travel time from London to Bristol from twelve to four hours. Isambard Kingdom Brunel, the great Victorian engineer, was responsible for the design of the G.W.R., from its huge seven-foot gauge, innumerable bridges and tunnels, to its splendid glass-roofed London terminus, Paddington Station. In the right foreground of the painting is the Maidenhead Railway Bridge, an audacious structure of two, flat, elliptical arches designed by Brunel in 1839.

Painted by Turner near the end of his life, this work combines the motion, steam, and fire of the industrial engine with the natural forces of wind, water, clouds, and fog in a swirling image of light and power. It is a document of the early Industrial Revolution, inspiring English author William Makepeace Thackeray to say, "The world has never seen anything like this picture."

***Rain, Steam, and Speed: The Great Western Railway*, 1844. Oil on canvas, 48″ x 35¾″. Joseph Mallord William Turner. Courtesy, the National Gallery, London.**

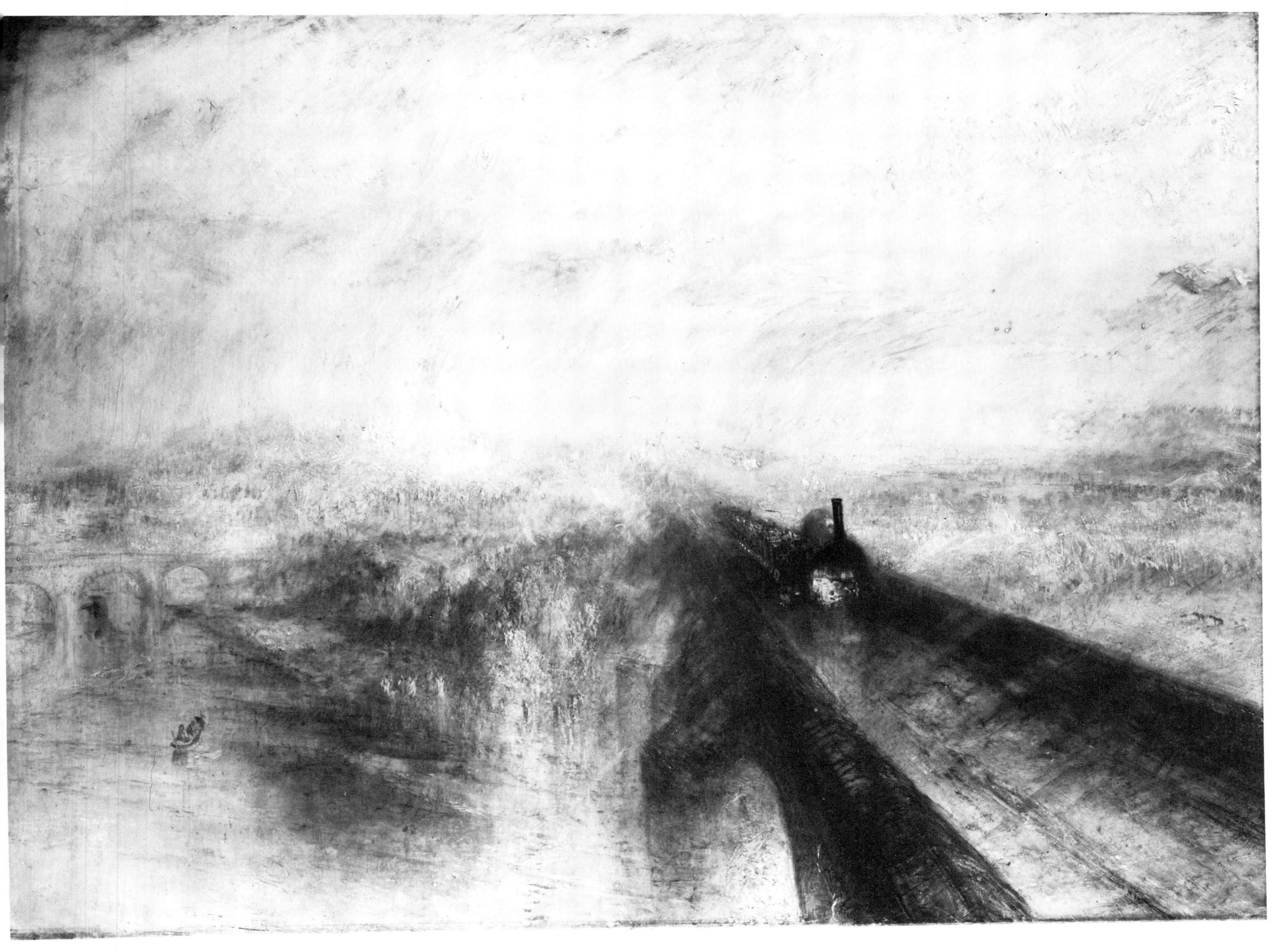

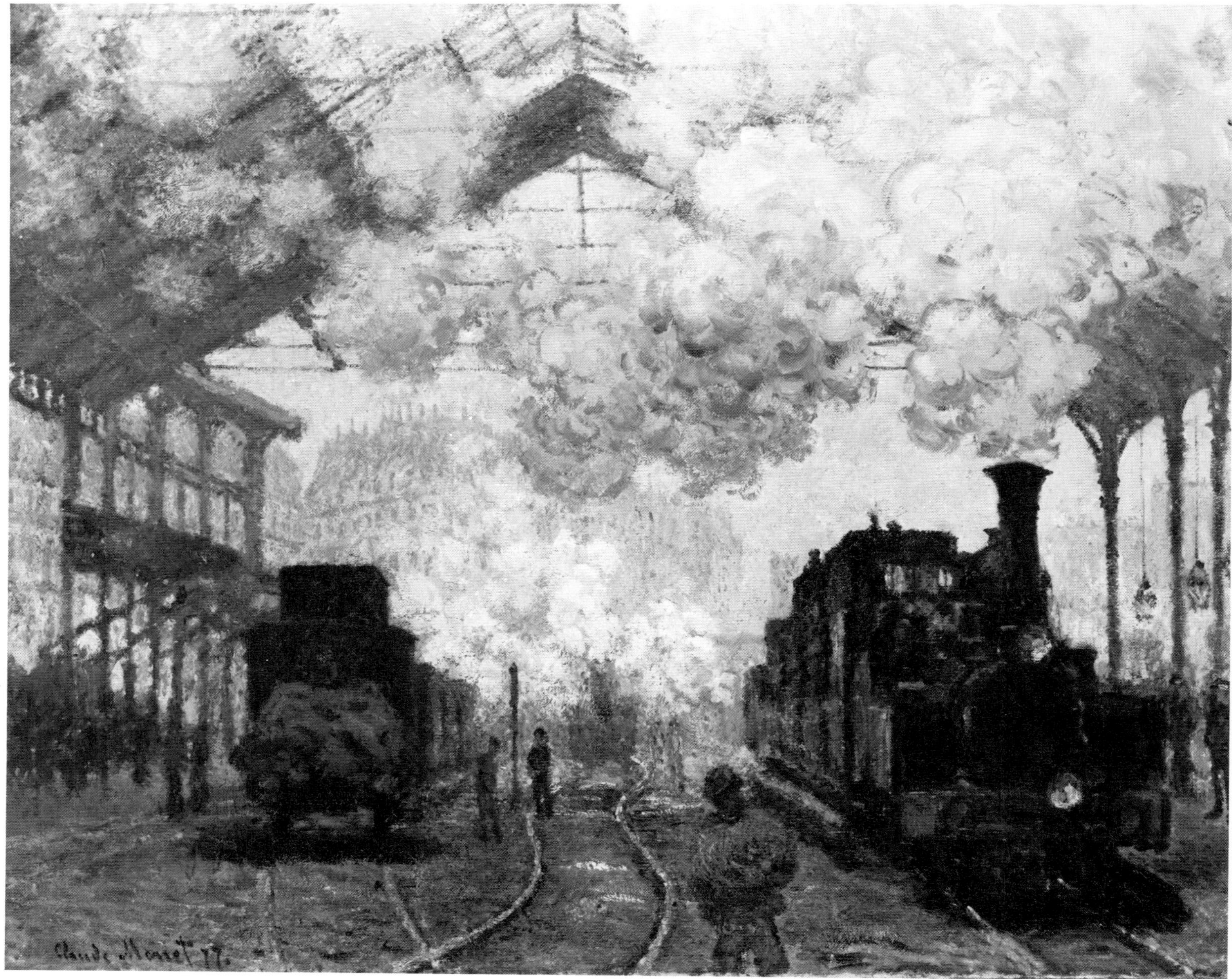

Gare Saint Lazare, Paris, 1877. Oil on canvas, 32¼" x 39¾". Claude Monet.
The Fogg Art Museum, Harvard University, Cambridge, Massachusetts.
Bequest—Collections of Maurice Wertheim.

Claude Monet was a pioneer in on-location painting and in using industrial subject matter. He insisted upon working on the spot to capture the fleeting impression of nature. He said that he wished he could have come into the world blind and then recovered his eyesight so as to have no a priori knowledge of objects; to stand all at once before appearances with a virgin eye. He also believed in painting series of the same subject to explore the changing effects of light through the use of broken color. This work (opposite) is but one of many he painted of the interior of the Saint Lazare railway station. These pictures allowed Monet to study the contrast of the steam locomotive to the changing atmospheric conditions of sun, puffing smoke, rising vapor, and steam against the great enclosure. The buildings of Paris under a luminous sky can be seen beyond the open end of the glass-roofed train shed.

While in Bulgaria during the summer of 1977, George Nick did a number of oil sketches and paintings of steam locomotives, some of which are still operational. The four small oil paintings, none more than a foot square, were done in a rail yard at Shoumen. Painted on four consecutive days, each took about one and one-half hours to complete.

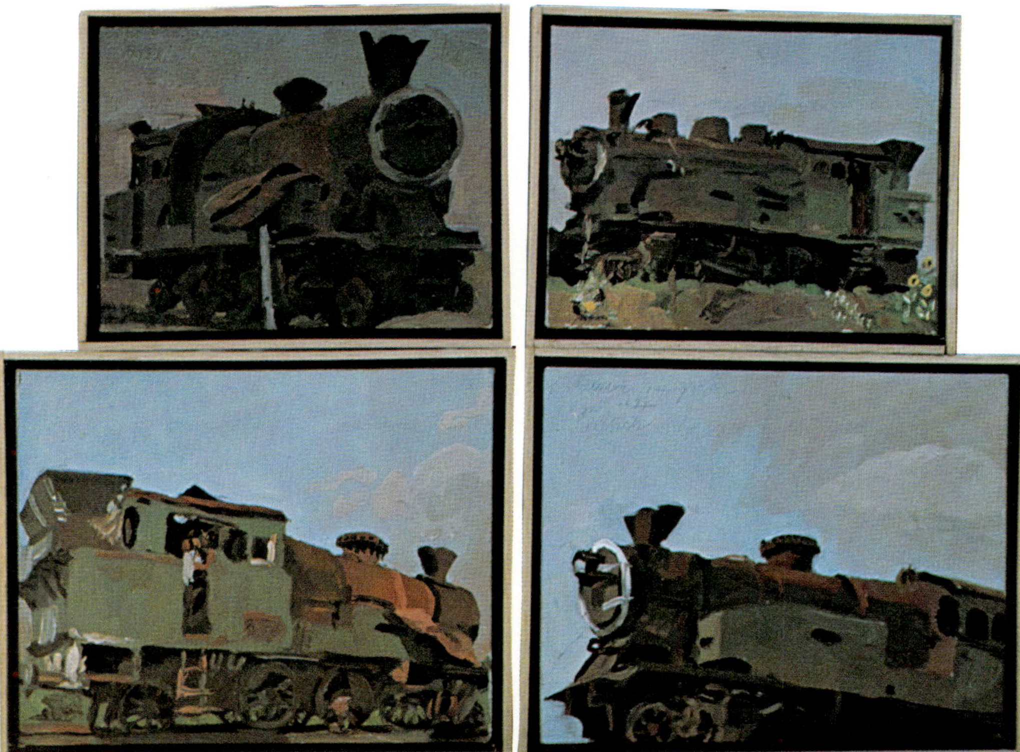

***Steam Locomotives*, 1977. Oil. George Nick.**

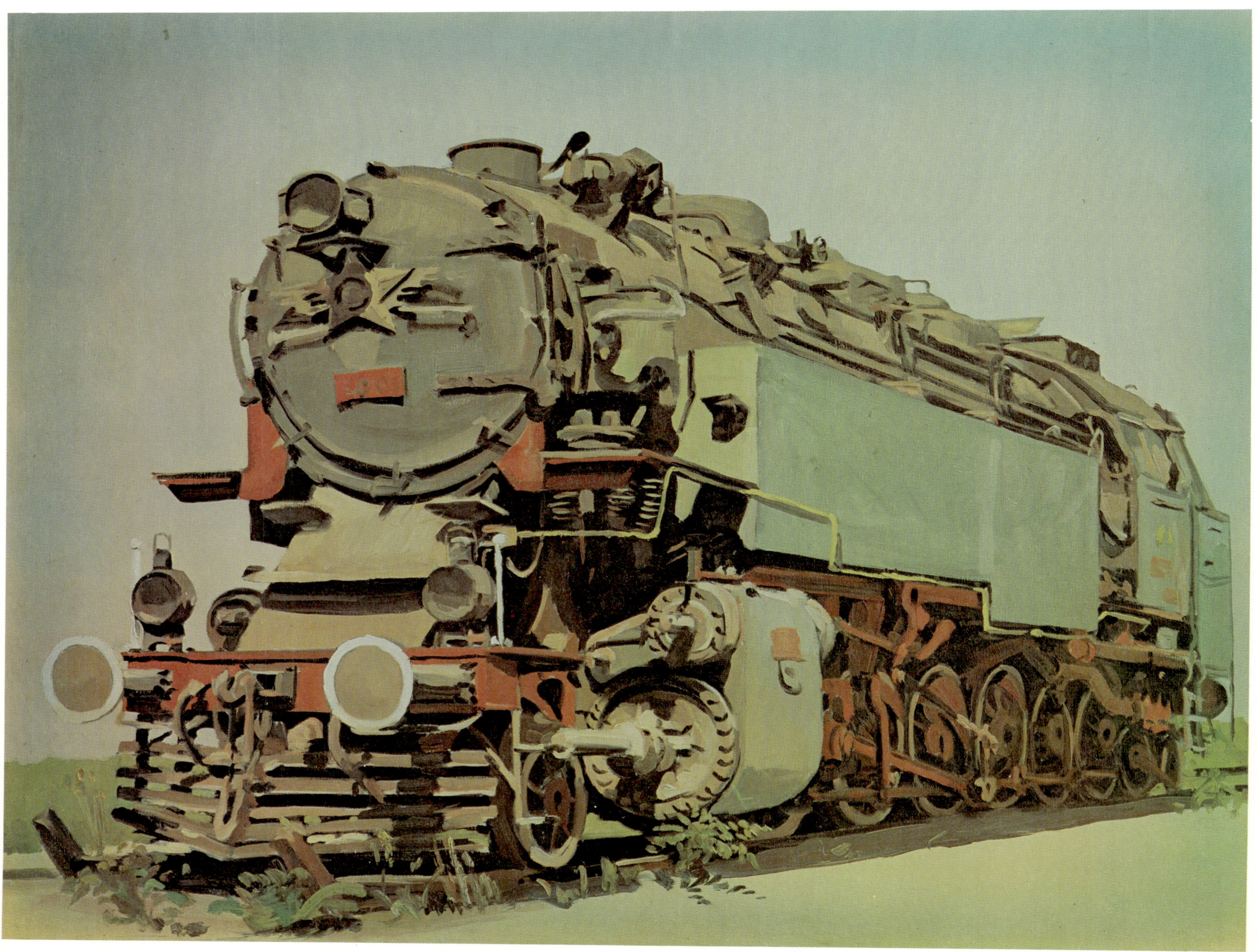

The large oil painting opposite depicts the Czar's Locomotive #231—Poznan which Nick found in the Sofia Railroad Station's repair yard. During the first few days, Nick completed a preliminary drawing of it. He finished the painting in twenty sessions of two hours each.

Perhaps more than any other built object, the steam locomotive expressed purpose and power in its external form. Each element of the complicated whole contributed to the total effect of force and motion. The myriad parts combined to make an organic mass that seemed to have a presence beyond that of the merely mechanical. Various artistic interpretations of it are shown here.

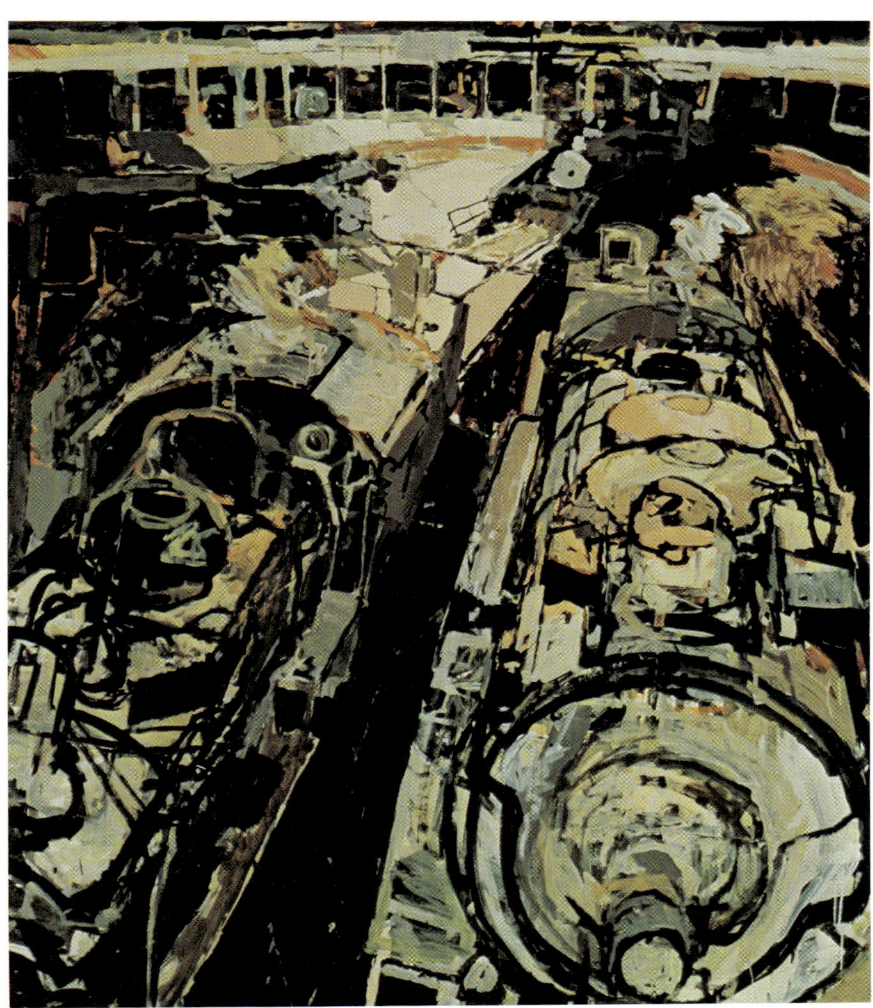

Trains, 1974. Acrylic collage on canvas, 61½″ x 72″. Flora Natapoff. Collection, Museum of Fine Arts, Boston.

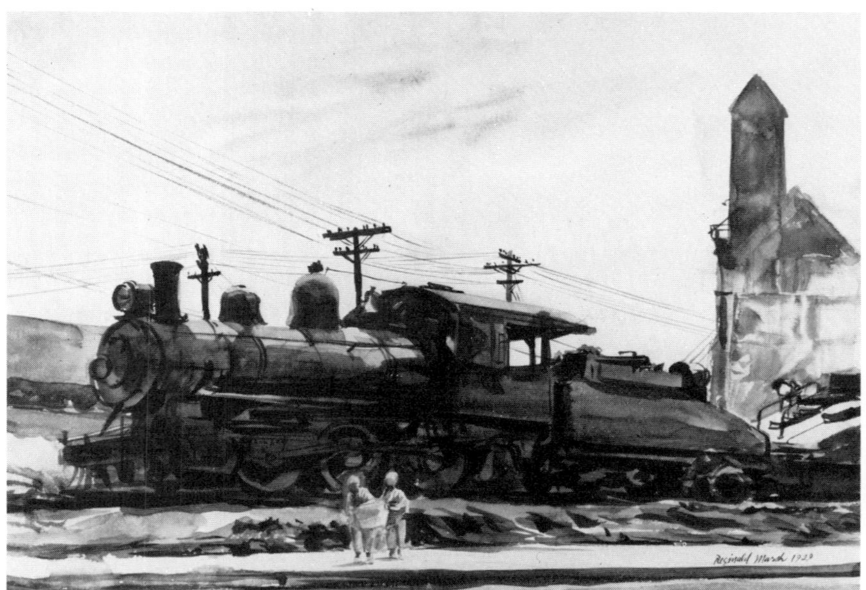

Locomotive, Number 2, 1929. Watercolor on paper, 13½″ x 19½″. Reginald Marsh. Collection of the Whitney Museum of American Art, New York.

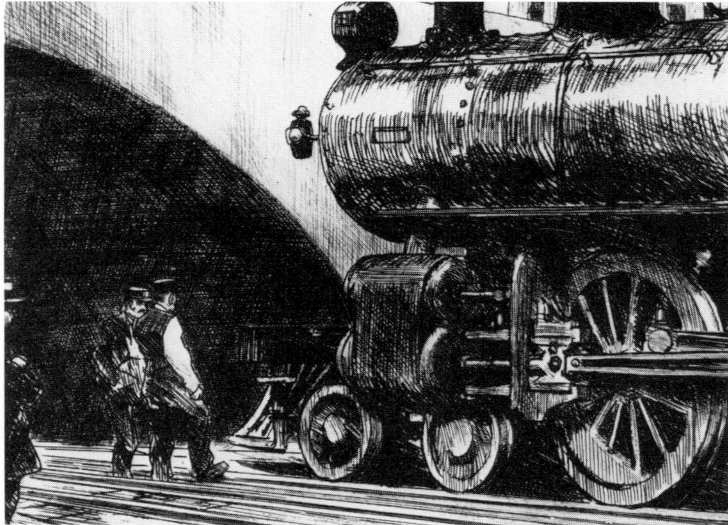

The Locomotive, 1922. Etching on paper, 13⁷⁄₁₆″ x 16⅛″ (sheet). Edward Hopper. Courtesy of the Whitney Museum of American Art, New York. Bequest of Josephine N. Hopper.

Although Reginald Marsh was best known for his studies of urban humanity, on occasion his work did go in other directions. Here is a very lively watercolor of a steam locomotive done in a loose, but authoritative manner.

This painting (right) moves in the direction of sculpture. Discs of smooth-coated canvas, areas of marble dust, metal washers, snaps and grommets, contact numbers, and rings of thread and cord were incorporated into the acrylic underpainting. The oil paint was then washed, sponged, and brushed on. The aim was to approximate the texture and strong, sculptural character of the engine. Care was taken to integrate the collage materials so that they remained subordinate to the total image.

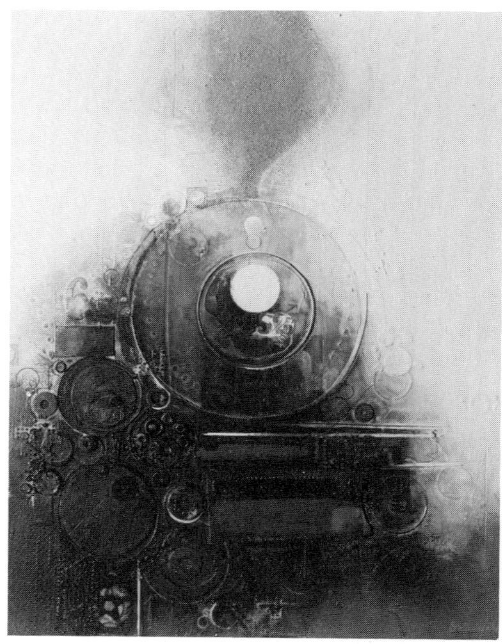

Locomotive, 1969. Acrylic, collage, and oil on canvas, 15″ x 12″.

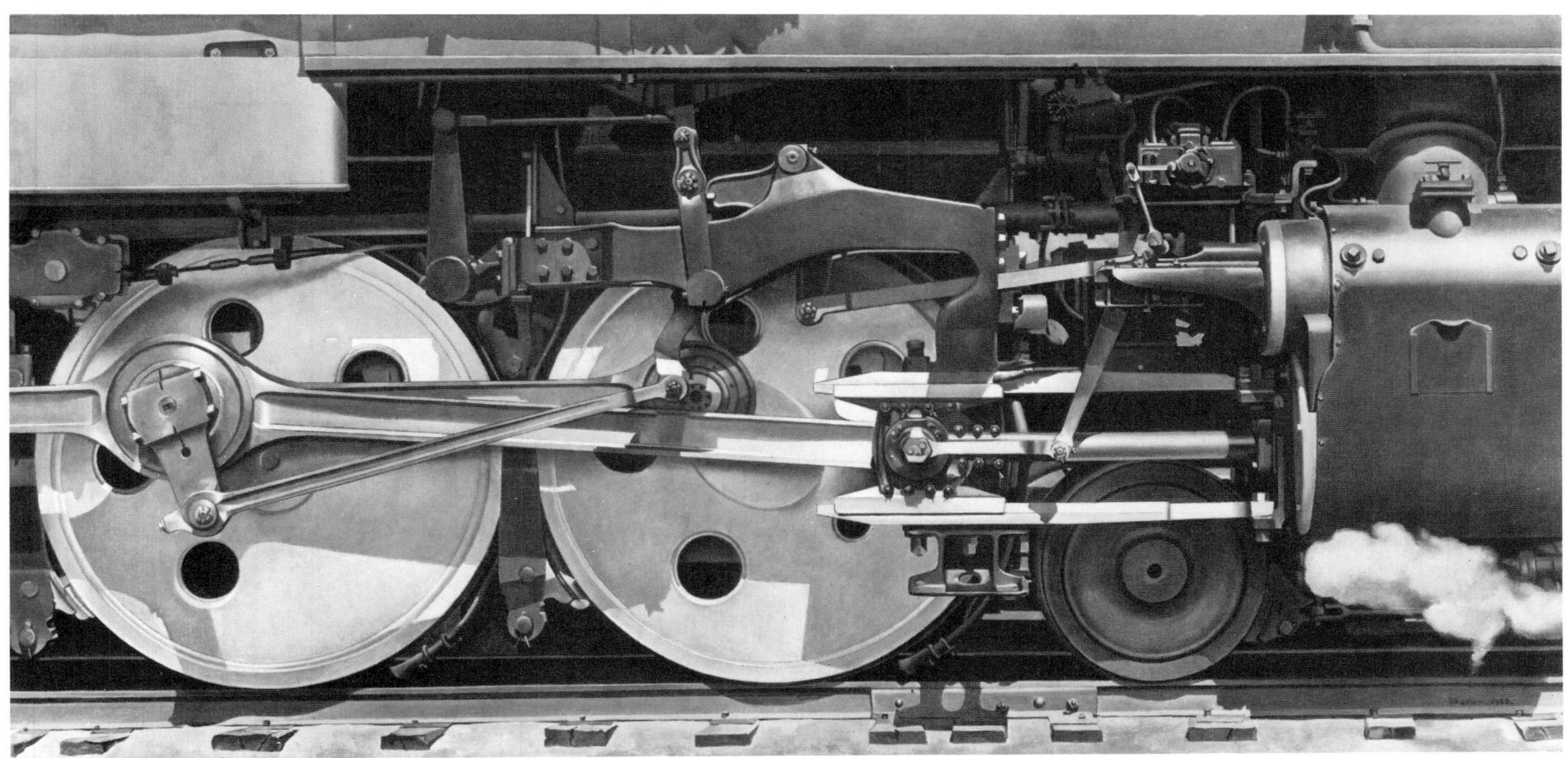

***Rolling Power*, 1939. Oil on canvas, 15″ x 30″. Charles Sheeler. Smith College Museum of Art, Northampton, Massachusetts.**

In 1939 Sheeler took *Wheels*, a photograph of a streamlined steam locomotive in Harmon, New York. Much that is obscure in the photograph becomes articulate in the painting, which took three months to complete. The oil streaks, grease, and corrosion that appear in *Wheels* are not in *Rolling Power.* The latter is a clean, idealized version of modern machinery. Sheeler believed in industrial technology and his work is a celebration of it.

Hopper wrote of Charles Burchfield: "His work is most decidedly founded, not on art, but on life, and the life that he knows and loves best. From what is to the mediocre artist and unseeing layman the boredom of everyday existence in a provincial community, he has extracted a quality that we may call poetic, romantic, lyric, or what you will. By sympathy with the particular he has made it epic and universal. No mood has been so mean as to seem unworthy of interpretation: the look of an asphalt road as it lies in the broiling sun at noon, cars and locomotives lying in God-forsaken railway yards, the steaming summer rain that can fill us with such hopeless boredom, the blank concrete walls and steel constructions of modern industry, mid-summer streets with the acid green of close-cut lawns, the dusty Fords and gilded movies—all the sweltering, tawdry life of the American small town, and behind all, the sad desolation of our surburban landscape. He derives daily stimulus from these, that others flee from or pass with indifference." Hopper might have been describing himself.

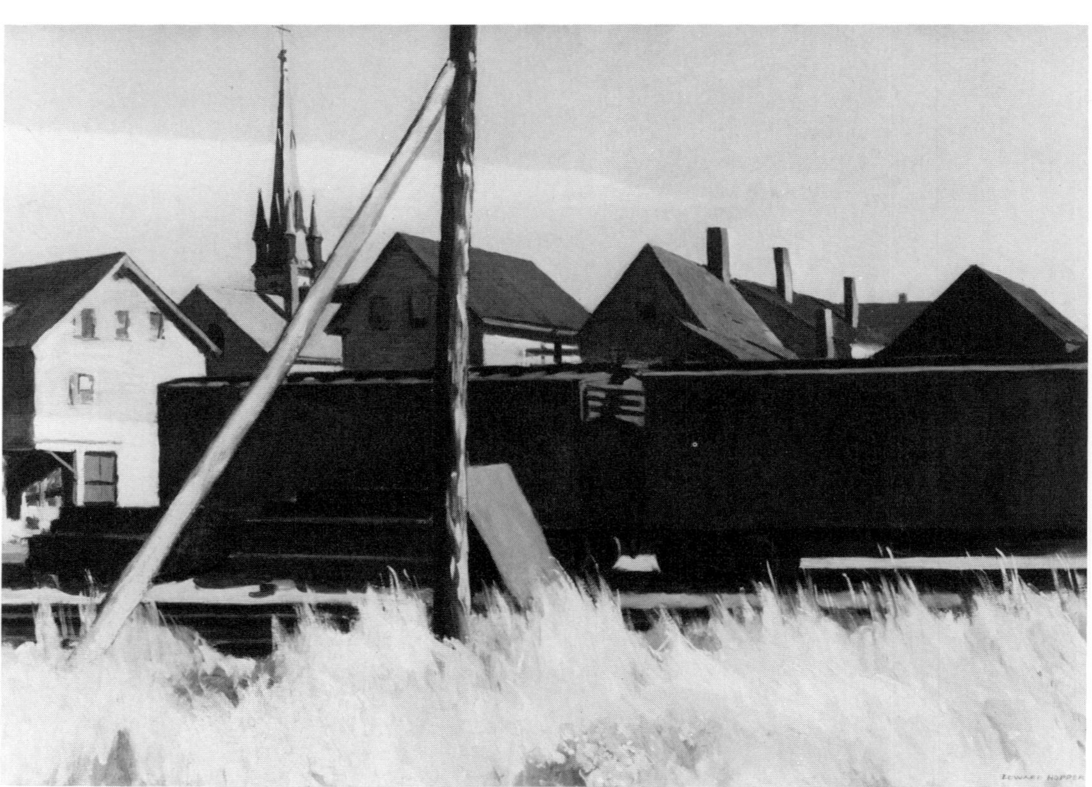

***Freight Cars, Gloucester*, 1928. Oil, 29″ x 40″. Edward Hopper. The Addison Gallery of American Art, Phillips Academy, Andover, Massachusetts.**

Marine

Warship paintings by Flora Natapoff

A view of Flora Natapoff's studio in what was once a factory. To the right, not visible in the photograph, is a row of windows which looks out at rooftops over a railroad cutting yard five floors below. Natapoff is seated at upper center, looking at the warship collage paintings on the long, white wall. These assemblages of paper, acrylic paint, and pastel have been mounted on cotton duck canvas so that they can eventually be stretched for hanging. Behind her are two more works and in the foreground is a stack of acrylic drawings that relate to the same subject. The large roll of paper at the center of the photograph is the base material upon which the collage paintings are done. All around the studio are the raw materials she employs: the piles of snapshots, colored collage papers, jars and tubes of acrylic paint, adhesives, pens, brushes, and pastels.

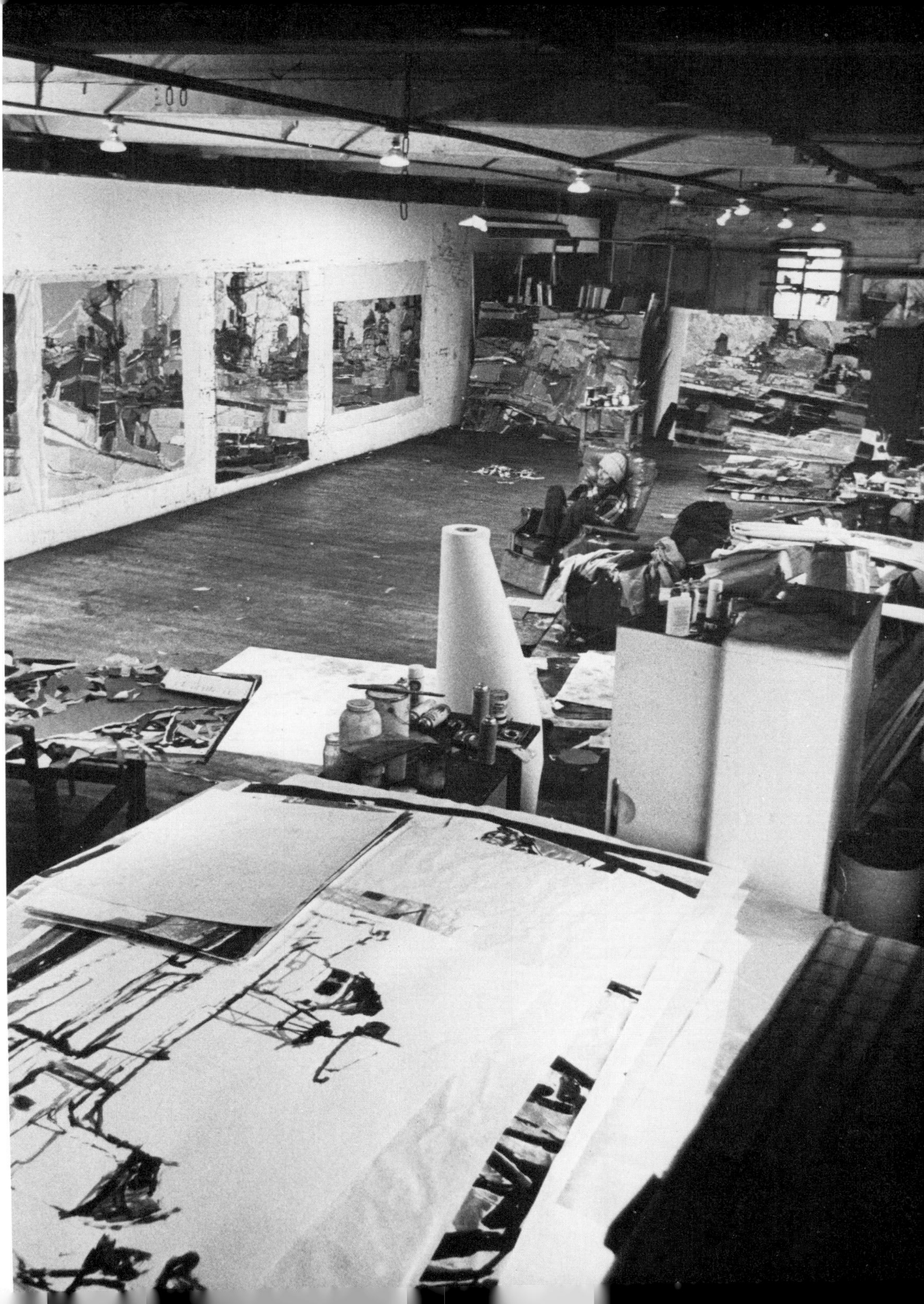

Flora Natapoff feels that the built environment is *The* landscape of today, the one we identify with and best understand. Some years ago, while under the influence of Breughel, she did the painting, *Tower of Babel*, a cutaway of a building that is a mass of cubicles. At that time, she was watching the construction of a new building in Cambridge, Massachusetts, and she had a revelation of what she was really doing in the tower painting: the "multiplicity of exits and entrances" parallel life's experiences. She expresses "metaphors for life" by painting "structures that almost hold" the parts that seem to be falling away.

From the *Tower of Babel* Natapoff went on to construction sites, factories being demolished, bridges and waterfront structures, railroad trains and stations, and more recently, warships. In each she explores her subject through a series of works that begin with on-location sketches, snapshots, drawing studies. She then progresses to the studio work of larger-scaled acrylic drawings and collage paintings. The entire process involves simultaneously working on a number of pieces, many of which will be discarded when no longer relevant. She believes in "giving the work its head to go where it will." It is the continuing process rather than the products of painting that interests her. That process is in a continual state of flux. "The minute a process becomes habitual, I change it." She works back and forth between formal or abstract considerations and descriptive ones, using snapshots only when she is in need of forms.

The most notable feature of her working process is the way in which images are built up in a variety of materials. The transformation from what appears at close range to be totally abstract and fragmented assemblages of colored chalks, painted strokes, and torn colored papers into the dynamic, coherent forms of the subject is a dramatic one. The work suggests constant change, an unfinished state of movement from one stage to another. Her sources, the photographs and sketches, become points of departure throughout the complex process.

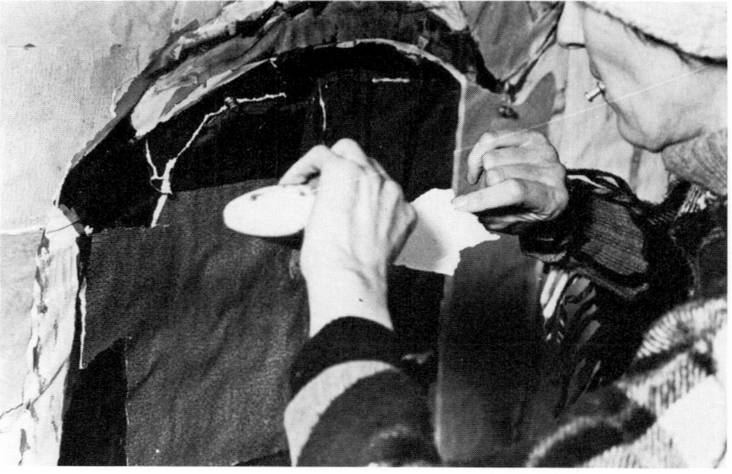

Applying adhesive to the back of a piece of torn, colored paper. The adhesive is a special glue recommended by the paper conservator at Harvard University's Fogg Museum. She also uses it for mounting successful works to canvas.

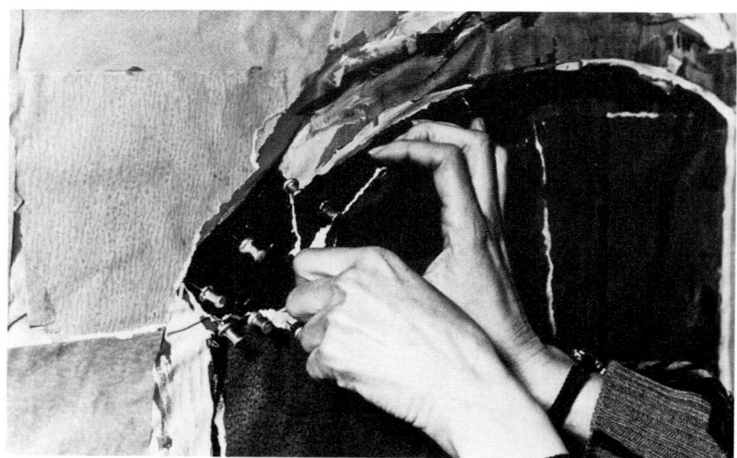

Pushpins are used to try out possible colored paper relationships and, after a choice has been made, for holding the papers in place until the adhesive dries.

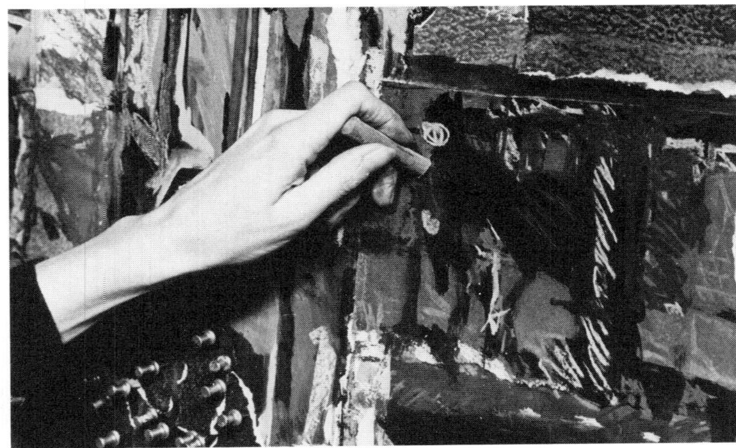

The artist adds variety to the textures and reinforces the drawing with pastel chalks.

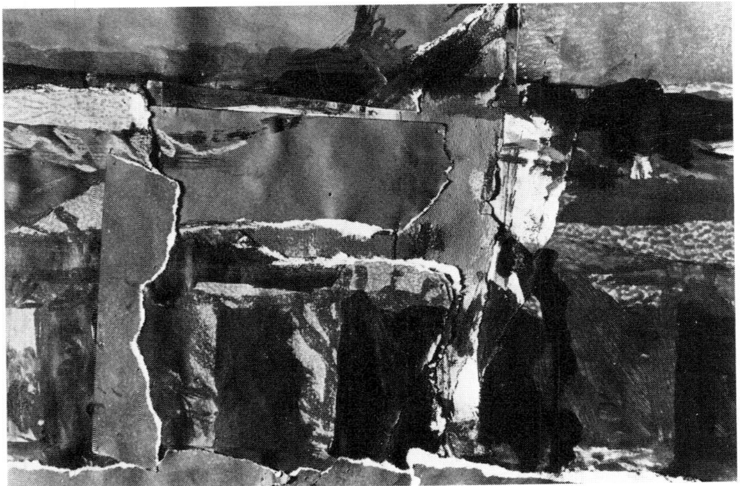

A close-up of a section of one of the warship collages showing the combination of paint, pastel, and torn paper.

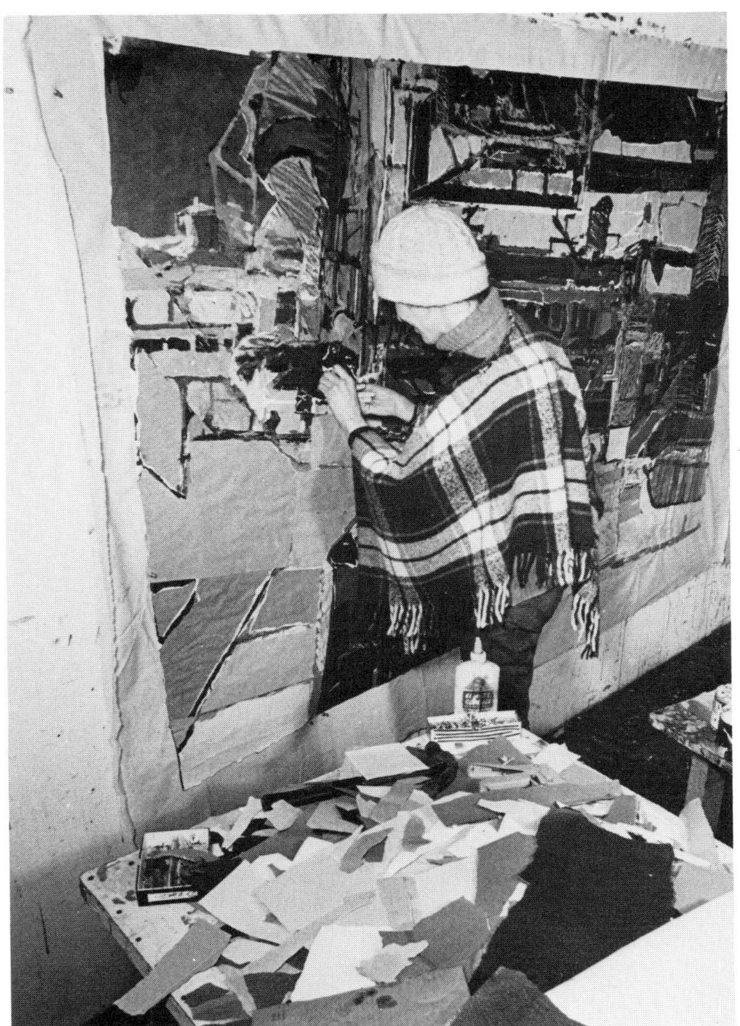

The artist working on one of her warship pieces. A large sheet of rag paper has been pinned to the wall and forms the surface on which the paint, pastels, and pieces of colored paper are mounted in alternating stages. The table in the foreground holds a variety of colored papers. Natapoff began with colored Canson paper in her earlier works, but now has an assistant who makes a greater color range by rolling acrylic paints onto sheets of white process paper.

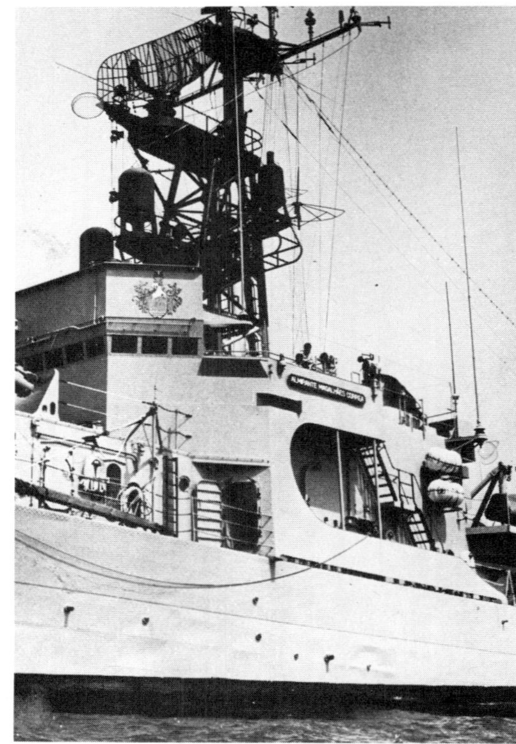

Natapoff's snapshot of the midsection of a Portuguese guided missile destroyer.

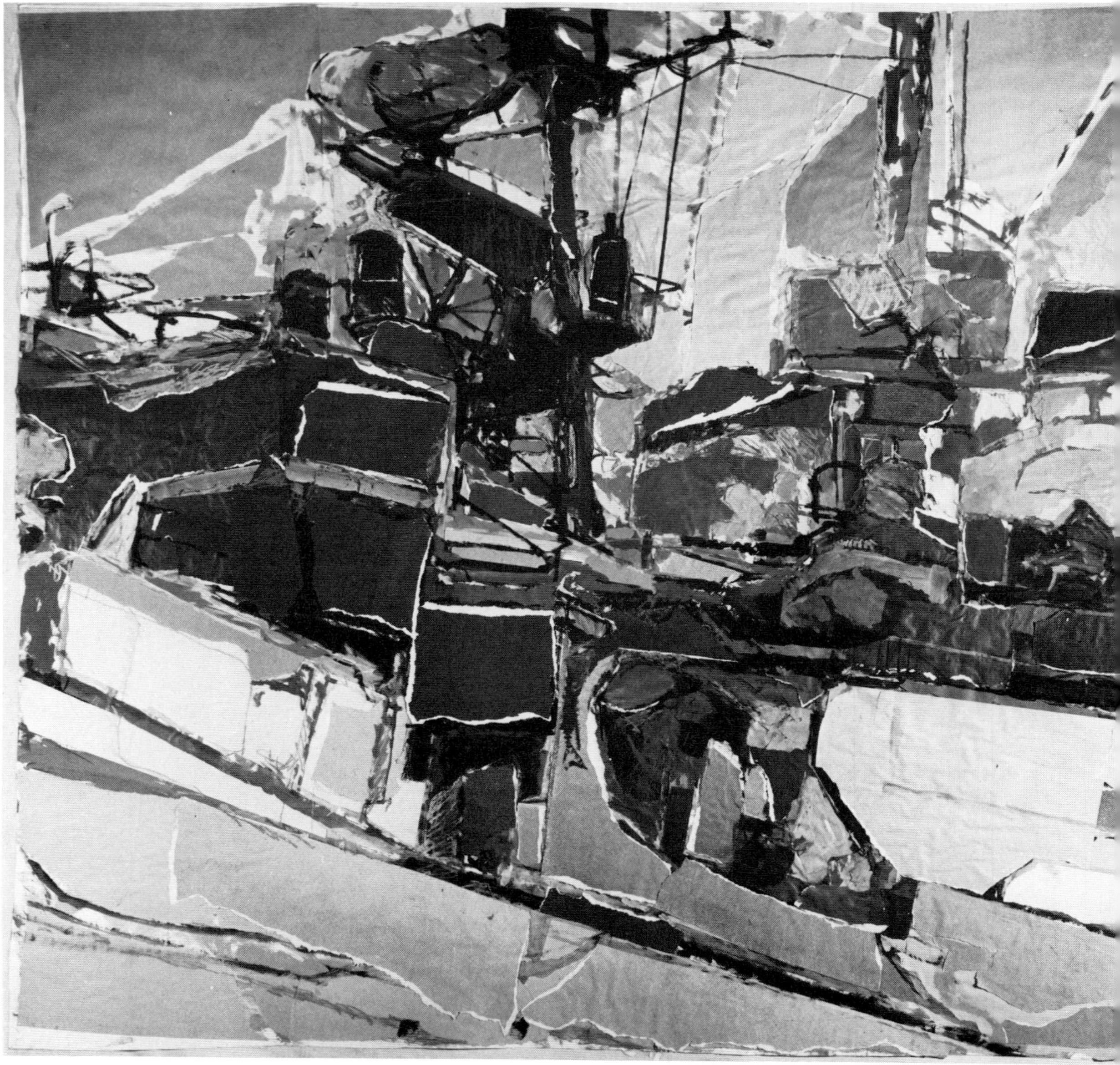

***Portuguese Destroyer*, 1978. Acrylic, pastel, and collage on canvas. 72″ x 74″. Flora Natapoff.**

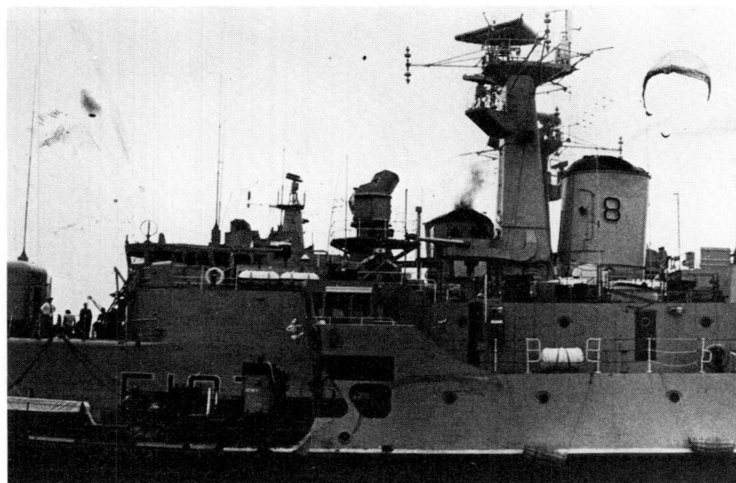

A snapshot of two British warships docked next to one another in Portsmouth Harbor, England. Numerous drawings and collage paintings came from the photographs of the warships that met for the Silver Jubilee Fleet Review in June 1977. Flora Natapoff uses only snapshots that she has taken, for she finds that only they provide the raw material that she needs.

The collage painting (left) shows the combination of distortion and invention that Natapoff employs in the development of a major work. Visual material from the photograph has been taken apart and synthesized until it relates back to the subject in a new interpretation. In the painting, the tightly knit forms of the warship have been exploded so that they slide and move against one another to set up a lively and dynamic tension that avoids static equilibrium.

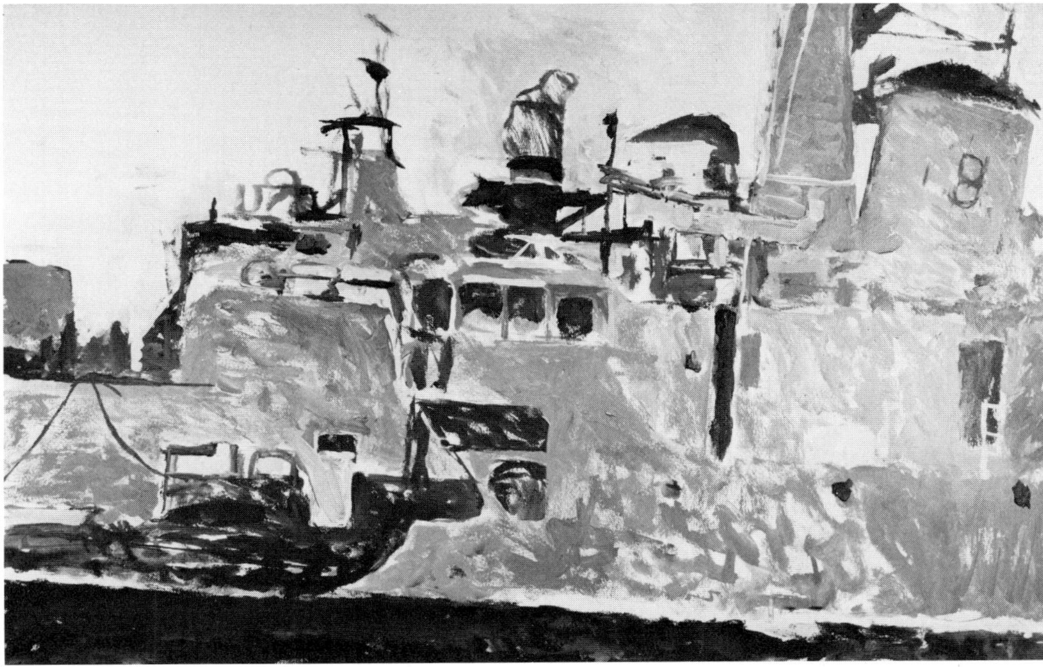

The acrylic drawing made from the snapshot. Here is the transformation of visual material: The railings, rigging, and other linear detail have been eliminated. The superstructure mass has been distorted and condensed to a more vertical shape. The sky has been emphasized as part of the whole drawing, not just as background. Her textured brushwork activates the entire surface and brings in atmosphere and tension. Natapoff has closed in on the ships, eliminating much of the sky, the mast top, and everything to the right of the funnel.

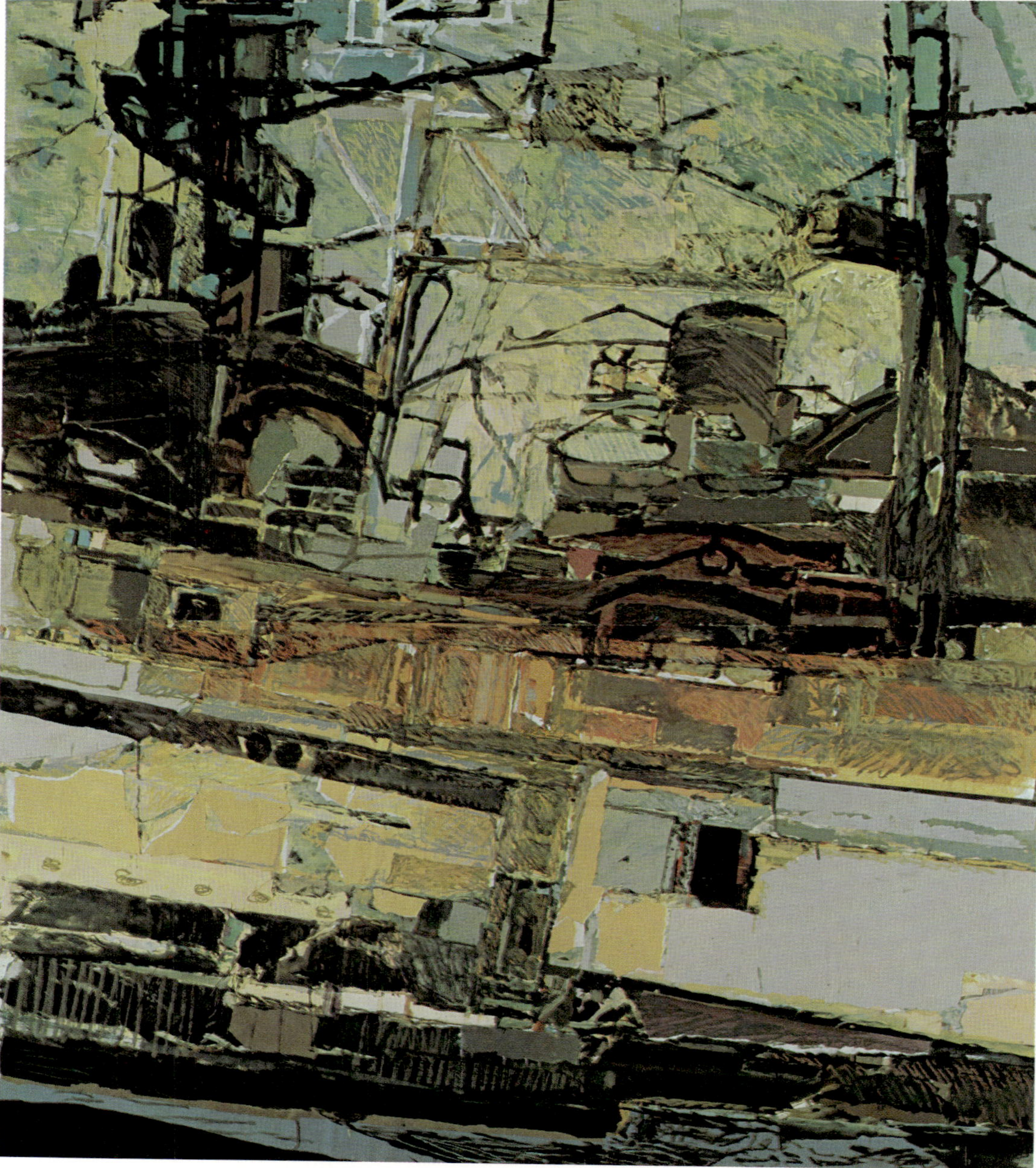

Radar, 1978. Acrylic, pastel, and collage on canvas, 86″ x 72″. Flora Natapoff. Photograph by Greg Heins.

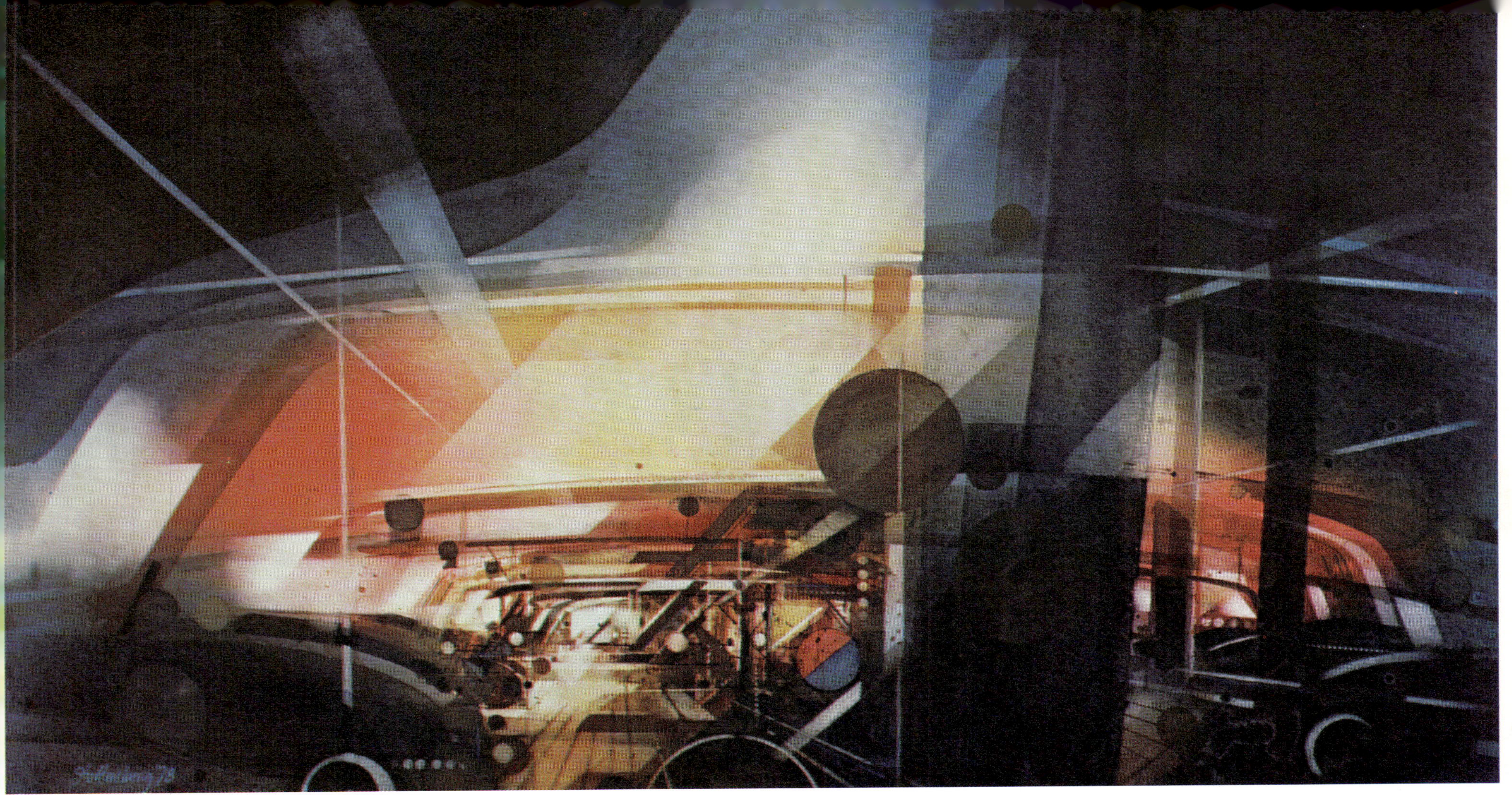

This painting began because of my familiarity with the museum ships U.S.S. *Constitution, Constellation*, and the H.M.S. *Victory*, relics of the wooden navies of the eighteenth and nineteenth centuries. The immediate impulse was a visit on board the *Constellation* in Baltimore. The impression was of a deep, arched, horizontal space with light flooding the deck from the open hatches. Diagonal shafts of light were echoed in the ladders, timber knees, and the sloping sides of the ship.

***Gun Deck*, 1978. Watercolor on Arches paper, 15½″ x 28″.**

The composition was worked out with a series of trial pastel and charcoal thumbnail sketches. Watercolor was floated on a wet, stretched paper and after drying, sponges and masks were used to scrub out the light areas. Tunnellike depth was achieved by the repetition of forms in decreasing scale towards the lower center.

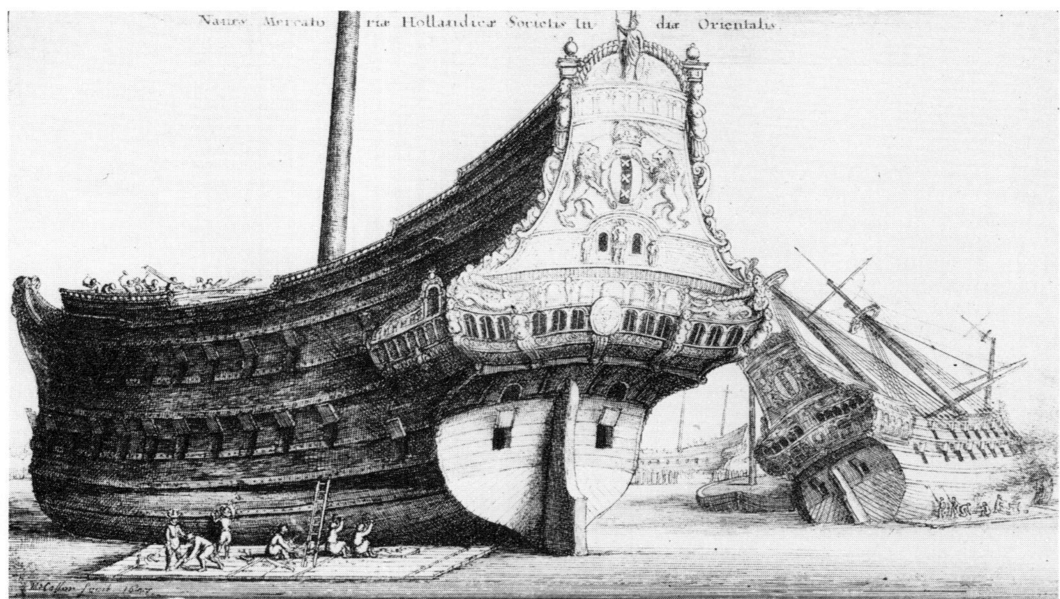

Amsterdam Indiaman Caulking, **c. 1640. Etching, 9½″ x 5½″. Wenceslaus Hollar. Courtesy of The National Maritime Museum, London.**

For over five decades, Hollar recorded the topography of seventeenth century England and Europe. Wherever he traveled, his pencil, notebook, and occasionally his watercolors were ready. He made prints of the great cities of central Europe and profiles of London before and after the great fire of 1666. Ships interested him throughout his life and he drew them with accuracy and clarity. Done while Holland was enjoying a brief but glorious period of supremacy on the seas, this composition shows the ship at right careened to be tarred and calked below the waterline. The strong sculptural forms of the ships are emphasized by the artist's skillful use of chiaroscuro.

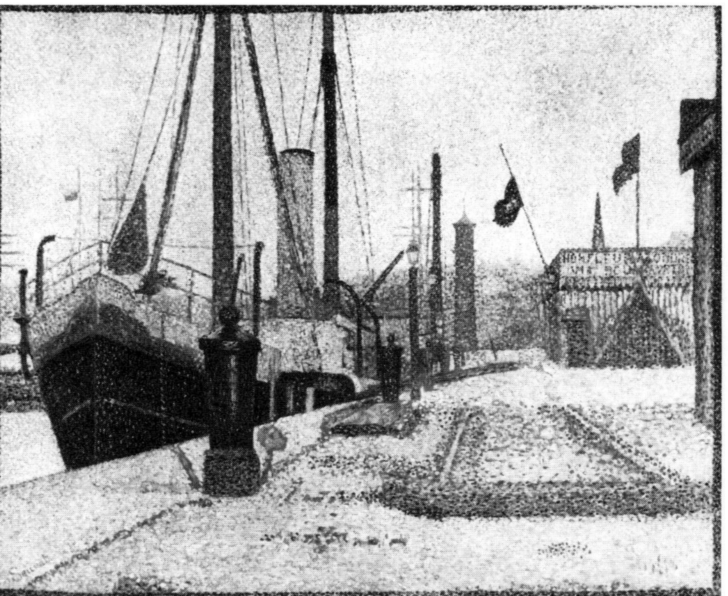

La Maria a Honfleur, **1886. Oil on canvas, 25⅝″ x 21 7/16″. Georges Seurat. Courtesy, Museum of Modern Art, Prague.**

Working at Honfleur in 1886, at Port-en-Bessin in 1888, and at Gravelines in 1890, Seurat produced a series of some of the most masterfully organized marine compositions ever painted. Employing a scientific divisionist color technique which gained luminosity by allowing adjacent dots of color to mix in the viewer's eye rather than being premixed on the canvas, he carefully built up designs in which exact color, tone, and positioning of shapes are crucial.

In this example, bollards, masts, stanchions, davits, flagpoles, and rigging set up a play of strong verticals that contrasts with the diagonals and horizontals of the quay, roofs, railings, and ships' yards. The small, irregular, but extremely important, flag shapes add a playful counterpoint to the classic stability which marks all of Seurat's work.

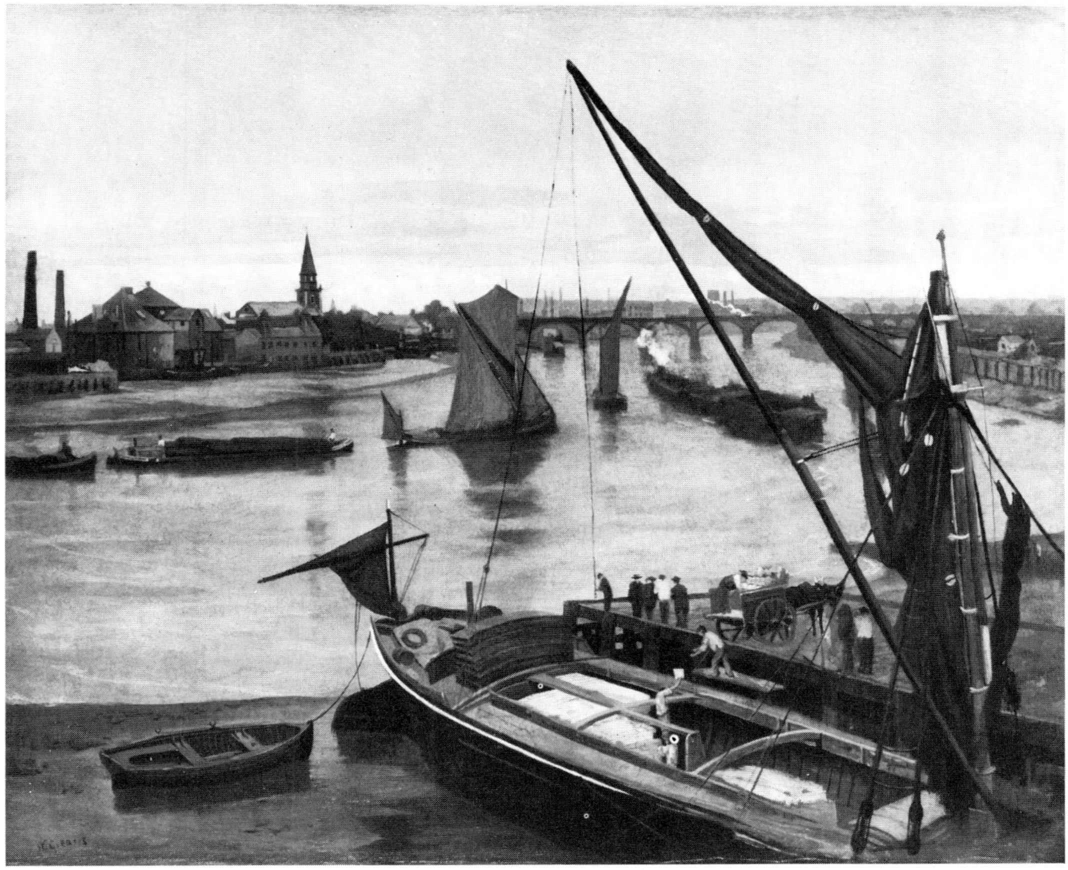

***Battersea Reach*, 1870. Oil on canvas, 25¼" x 30¼". Walter Greaves. The Tate Gallery, London.**

Walter Greaves, the son of a Chelsea waterman and boatbuilder, also worked on the river Thames. When Whistler moved to Chelsea in 1863, Greaves and his brother Henry took Whistler out on the river and introduced him to the subject which became so important to his work. A self-taught painter, Greaves came under Whistler's influence, but remained a painter of things rather than of moods. He knew Chelsea and the river intimately, understood it, and painted it with affection. This view with the spritsail barges shows the Thames when its upper reaches were still active with commercial traffic, before the wide, granite embankments tamed it.

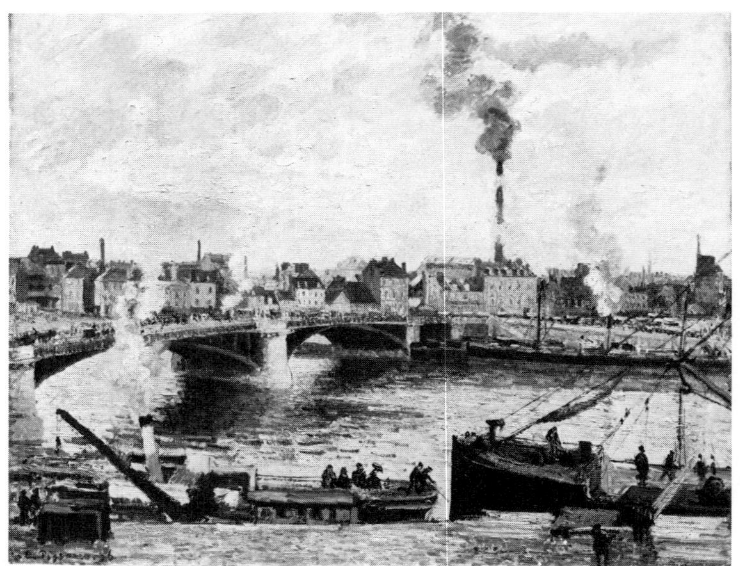

The Great Bridge at Rouen, **1896. Oil on canvas, 29″ x 36″. Camille Pissarro. Courtesy of the Museum of Art, Carnegie Institute, Pittsburgh, Pennsylvania.**

Determined to exactly reproduce the motif before him, Pissarro also brought sensibility and poetry to this scene of riverfront Rouen at the end of the last century. Carefully drawn and firmly constructed, it documents a time and place and is a lively study in Impressionist light and color.

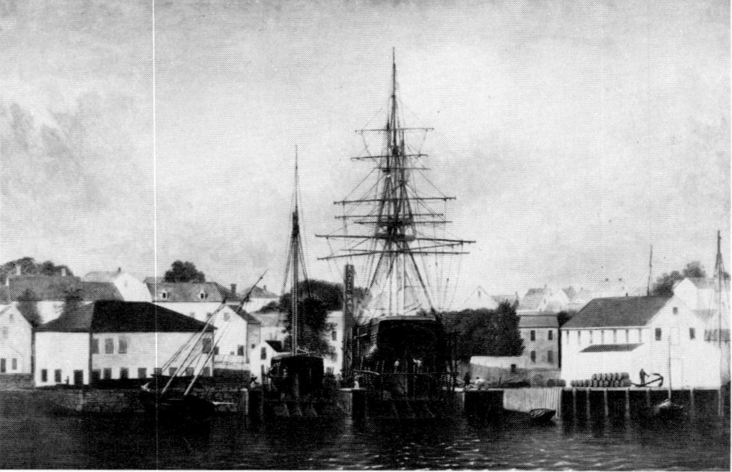

***Three Master on the Gloucester Railways*, 1855. Oil on canvas, 39¼″ x 59¼″. Fitz Hugh Lane. Courtesy, the Cape Ann Scientific, Literary, and Historical Association, Gloucester, Massachusetts.**

Gloucester, Massachusetts, with its harbor, ships, and coastal light was Fitz Hugh Lane's territory. He served it well in a lifetime of observing and depicting it in hundreds of paintings and lithographs. This work, executed as a poster-sign to be hung over a paint shop, shows his keen eye for the structure and detail of ships. Especially sensitive to climatic and seasonal atmospheric effects, he is numbered among the American luminist painters of the nineteenth century.

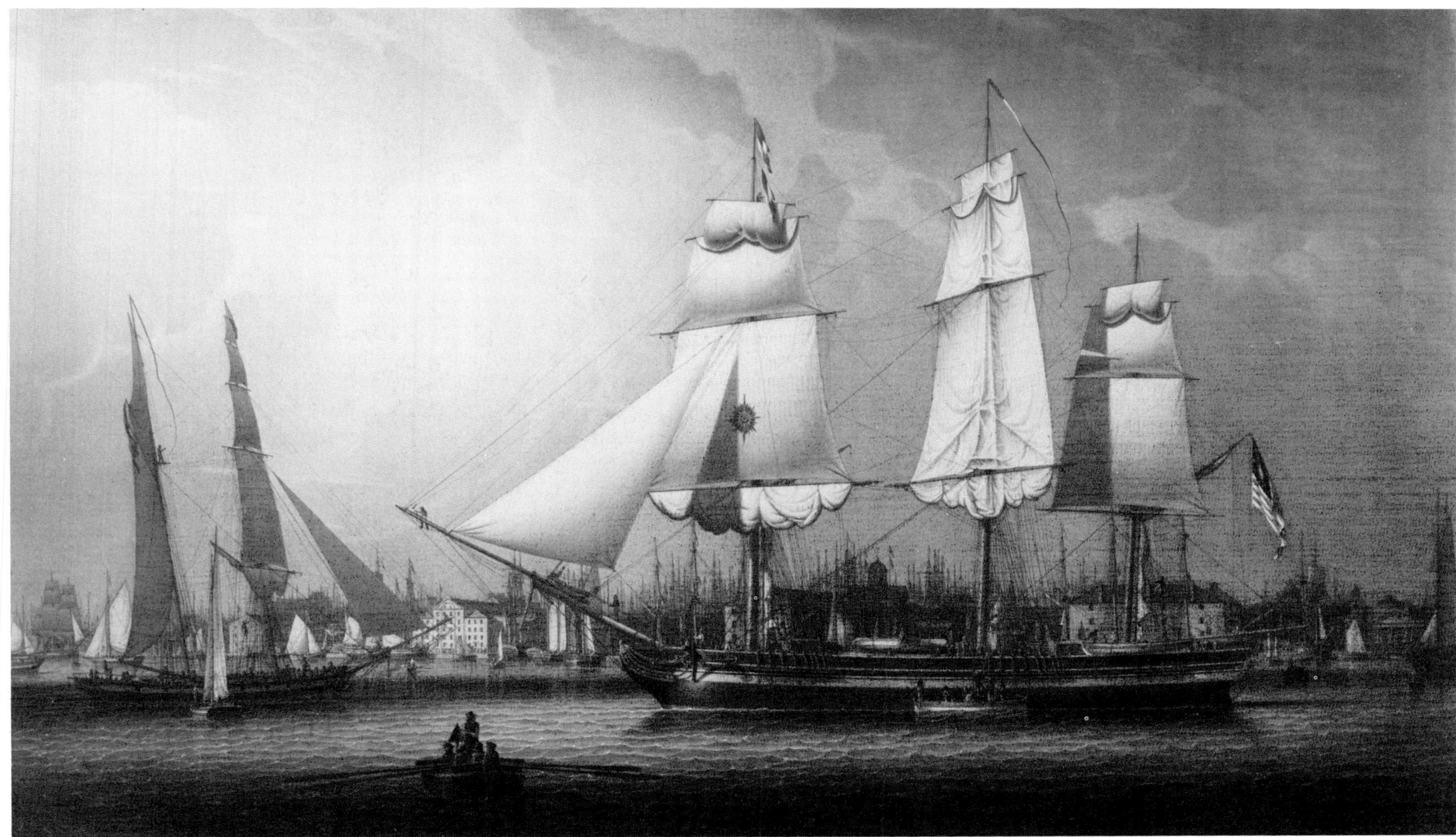

***Wharves of Boston*, 1829. Oil on canvas, 40″ x 68″. Robert Salmon. The Bostonian Society, Boston, Massachusetts.**

In his early fifties, Robert Salmon came to America. A marine painter in England, he now established his studio on a Boston wharf and spent the next fifteen years documenting the growth and shipping of that port. His clear, crisp style owes much to Canaletto. He carefully and accurately delineated his subjects and painted them faithfully with a wealth of detail unified by striking atmospheric and tonal control. This portrait of Boston Harbor is of interest historically as a topographic record (some of the buildings still exist) and for its painterly qualities. He created atmospheric depth through the use of receding bands of light and shadow moving towards a low horizon. Light is concentrated in the upper left sky and is picked up again in the large and small sails and in the distant buildings. The contrasting darks, so carefully worked out, add drama and mystery to the composition.

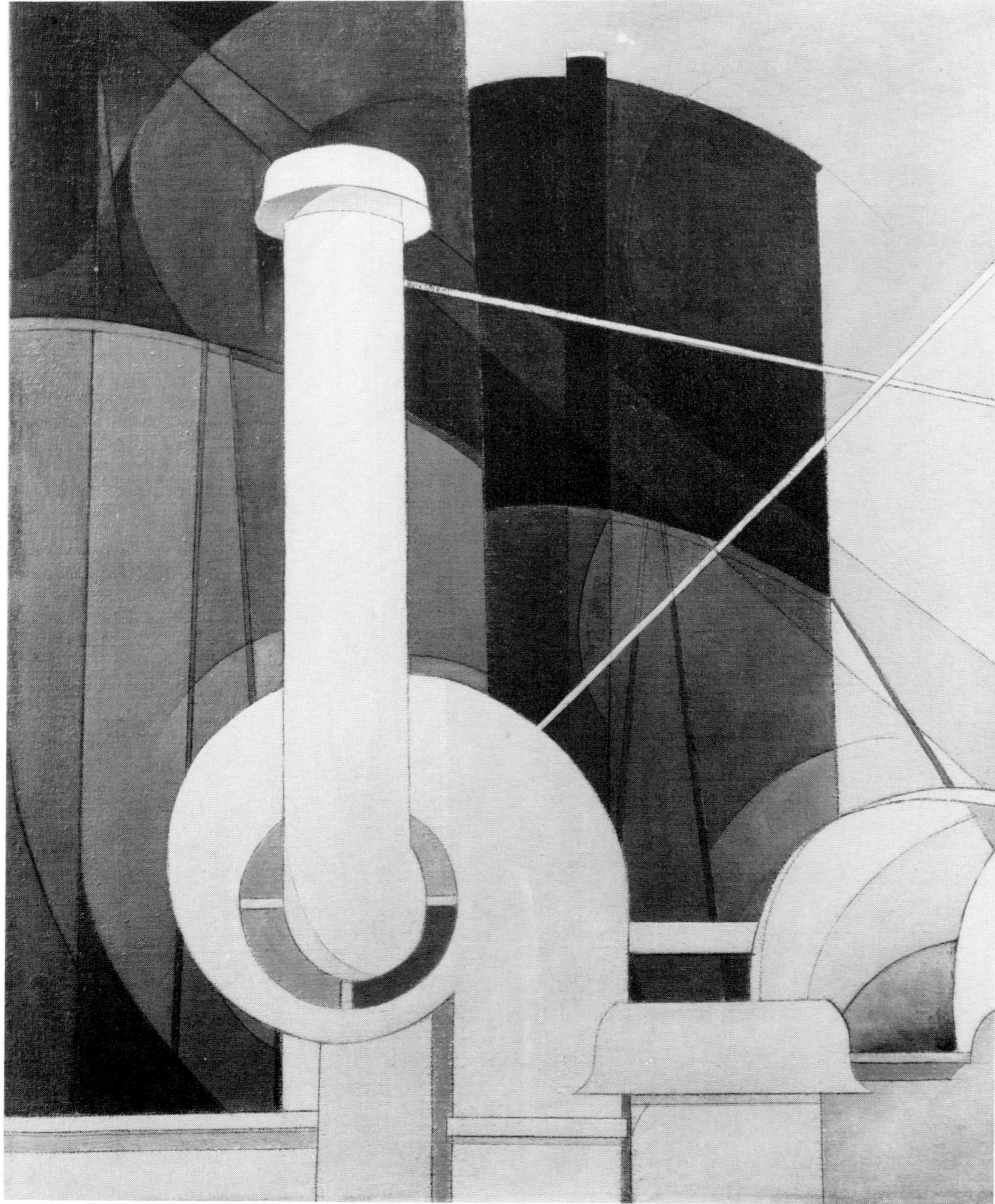

The French line's S.S. *Paris* was the ultimate in clean, modern technology when Demuth crossed the Atlantic on it in 1921. He made pencil sketches of the superstructure which were later developed into this oil painting. It shows parts of two of the ship's three red and black funnels, white ventilators, and guy wires against a blue sky. These elements are articulated into planes defined by subtle shadows and repeated contours. It is an intense fragment that speaks of the character of the whole ship.

***Paquebot Paris*, 1921-1922. Oil on canvas, 24½" x 19⁷⁄₁₆". Charles Demuth. The Columbus Museum of Art, Ohio: Gift of Ferdinand Howald.**

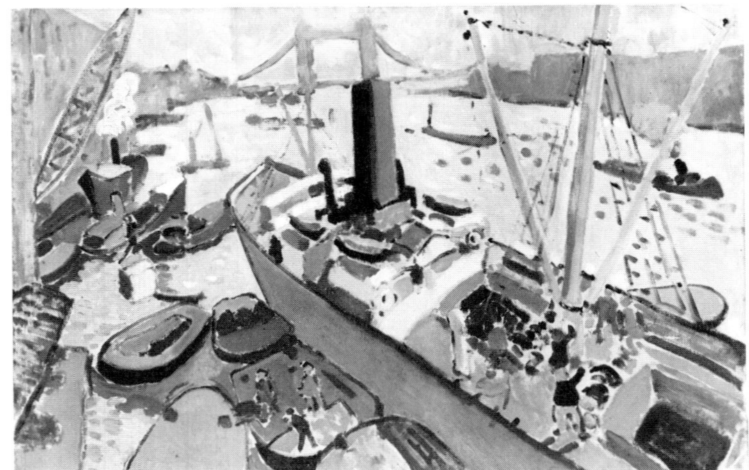

***The Pool of London*, 1906. Oil on canvas, 25⅞" x 39". Andre Derain. Courtesy of The Tate Gallery, London.**

When he came to London in the spring of 1906, Fauve painter Andre Derain was dazzled by the brilliant colors of the shipping, barges, and warehouses on the river Thames. The Fauves loved color; singing, shouting, sun-drenched, liberated color. With this attitude, Derain produced a series of paintings based upon the down river view from London Bridge towards Tower Bridge that explode with chromatic vitality. In this painting, the shapes are simple and the forms are broken down into blocks of color which float against one another on the surface of the canvas. The result is that the composition is an equivalent experience of the scene, rather than a description of it. Color and light are stepped up to their highest intensity, making for a truly vivid expression of London's river life.

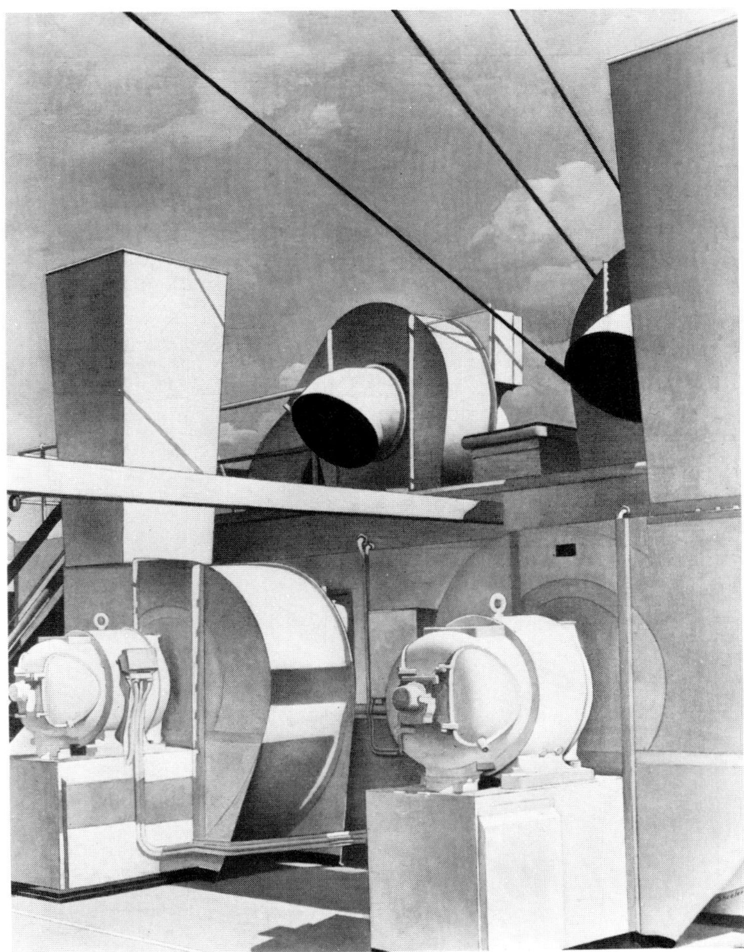

***Upper Deck*, 1929. Oil on canvas, 29⅛" x 22⅛". Charles Sheeler. Courtesy of the Fogg Art Museum, Harvard University, Cambridge, Massachusetts. Purchase—Louise E. Bettens Fund.**

The S.S. *Majestic* was the largest passenger liner afloat in 1929. Photographic studies of it by Sheeler were the basis for this painting, a landmark in precisionist art. Sheeler was attracted to the subject because its ''forms existed on their own terms; for use. Their disposition is utilitarian.'' He felt that it was an important work in his development: ''This is what I have been getting ready for. I had come to feel that a picture could have incorporated in it the structural design implied in abstraction and be presented in a wholly realistic manner. I sought to reduce natural forms to the borderline of abstraction retaining only those forms which I believed to be indispensable to the design of the picture.''

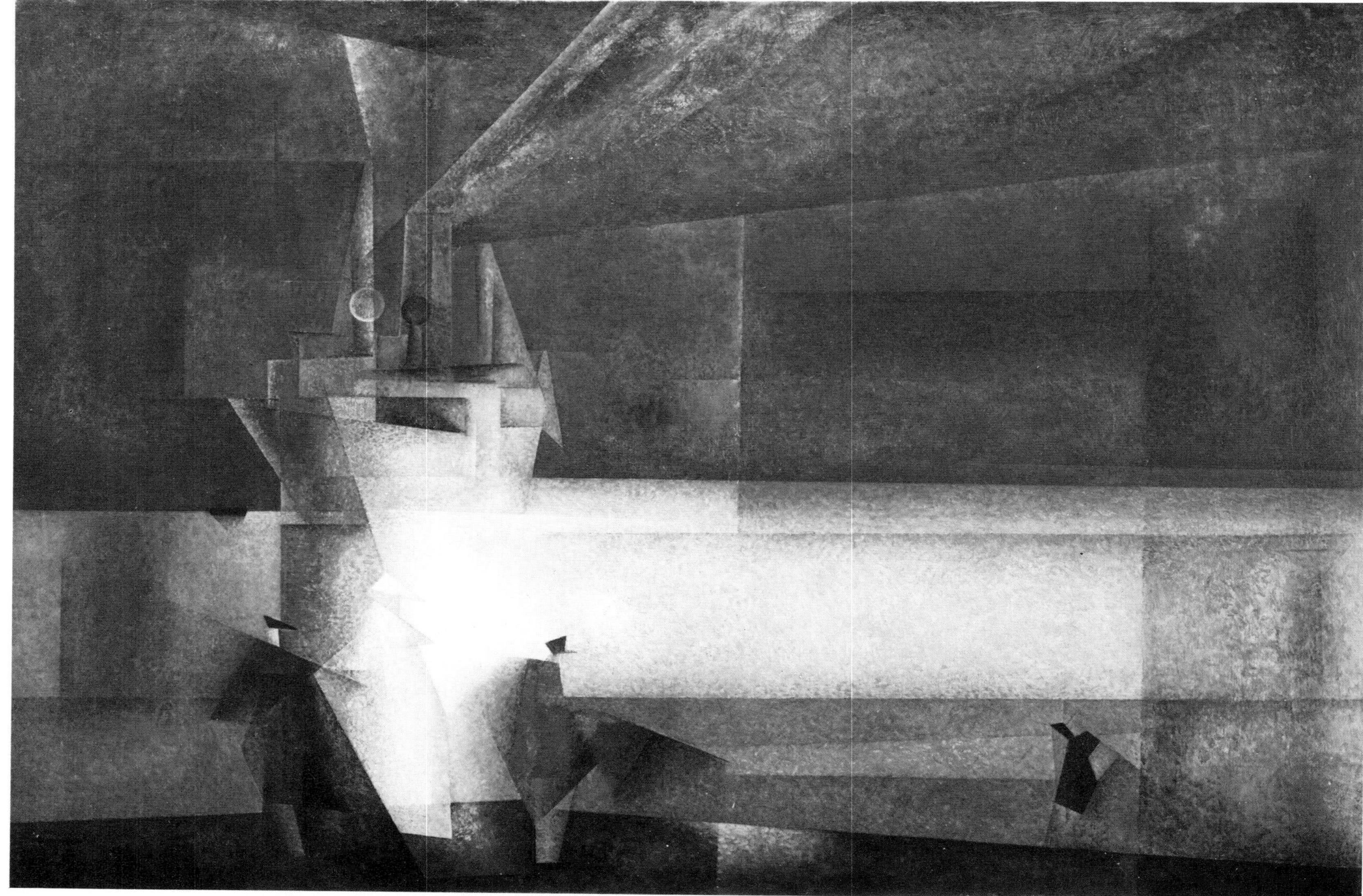

The Steamer, Odin II, 1927. Oil, 26½" x 39½". Lyonel Feininger. Courtesy of the Museum of Modern Art, New York, acquired through the Lillie P. Bliss Bequest.

Opposite is just one example of the many ships and boats under sail and steam which figured in Feininger's work during the long period he was active in Germany and America. From observation and through drawings, paintings, and prints, he transformed reality into a prismatic vision of light and color.

"I draw quite spontaneously and almost instantaneously whatever interests me; however, never with the intention of making paintings out of these drawings. No, first the irresistible longing for a particular composition must manifest itself in me and *then*, sometimes years later, there may be a painting which for me represents reality as I experienced it—while the *real reality*, if by chance I encounter the same situation again, in contrast to my picture looks very dreary to me and contaminated with unsympathetic associations. Paintings have to sing, must enrapture, and must not stop at portraying an episode."

Sheeler did a much smaller version of this picture in tempera on Plexiglas called *Fisherman's Wharf, San Francisco*. Although loosely painted, it is nearly identical in composition and is probably a sketch in which the design, values, and color arrangements for this later painting were worked out. The superimposition of two similar photographic negatives, a double view of a boat's foredeck, is the basis for this composition. All traces of round modeling, weathering, or texture are eliminated as shapes, values, and colors are abstracted from the subject to make a purified, classic, and timeless statement.

***San Francisco*, 1956. Oil on canvas, 32″ x 22″. Charles Sheeler. Courtesy of Terry Dintenfass, Inc., New York.**

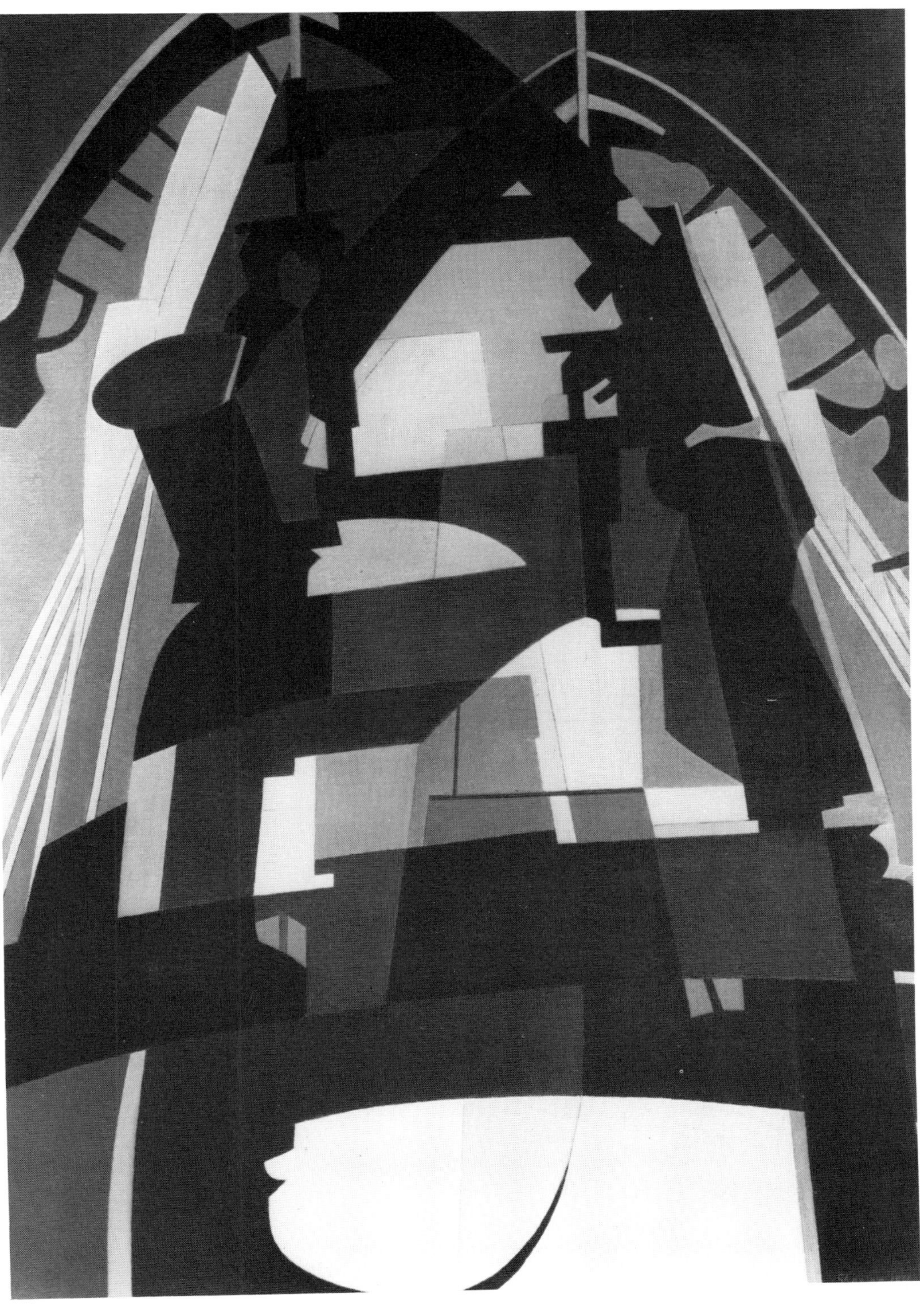

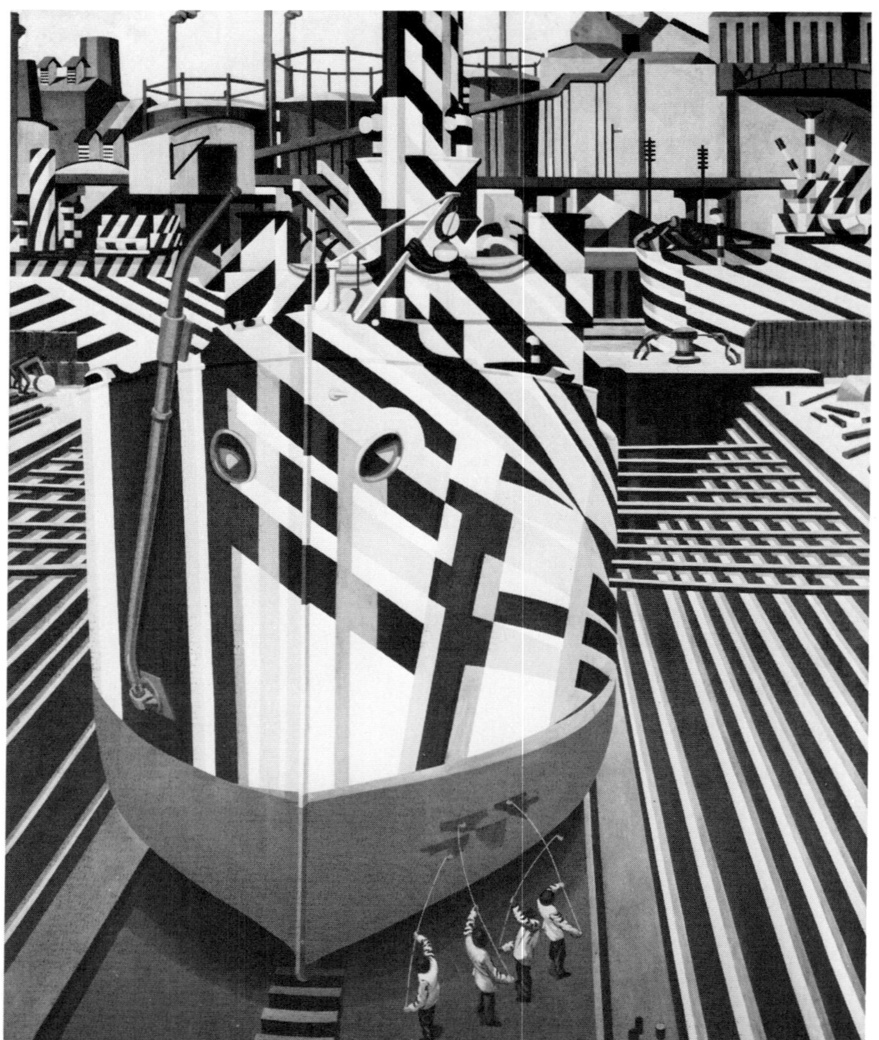

Dazzle-Ships in Drydock at Liverpool, 1919. Oil on canvas, 119½" x 96". Edward Wadsworth. The National Gallery of Canada, Ottawa.

The dazzle-camouflage painting of ships was developed in England during the latter part of the First World War. Various schemes were tried on scale models, not to make the ships invisible, but to confuse an attacker as to the direction, speed, and character of a ship under way. Among the artists chosen to do this work was the Vorticist painter, Edward Wadsworth.

Vorticism, an English movement somewhat related to French Cubism and Italian Futurism, stated that, "A machine is in greater or lesser degree a living thing. Its lines and masses imply force and action." It adopted an aesthetic of "bareness and hardness" and produced works which expressed force and energy through sharp opposition of lights and darks. The movement did not survive the First World War, but its effects persisted in the work of Wadsworth and others.

In this painting, Wadsworth successfully applied Vorticist principals to a realistic theme. Taking his cue from the hard-edge, dazzle pattern on the ships, he has treated the drydock and the industrial forms in the same sharp, patterned way. There are few graded tonal areas; each shape is clearly defined. Subtlety is used only in the close values of adjacent shapes, as in the tanks in the upper distance. As in dazzle-camouflage, the painted shapes in this oil fight with, rather than help describe the drawn forms. The result is extraordinary tension as the eye attempts to distinguish the real contours of form from the painted surface shapes.

The painting (right) suggests an aircraft's tenuous relation to the earth; how the connecting elements—wheels, fueling hoses, steps, and ladders—interrupt the thin band of light between the plane and the field. This creates a focus for all of the directions and lines of force in the painting.

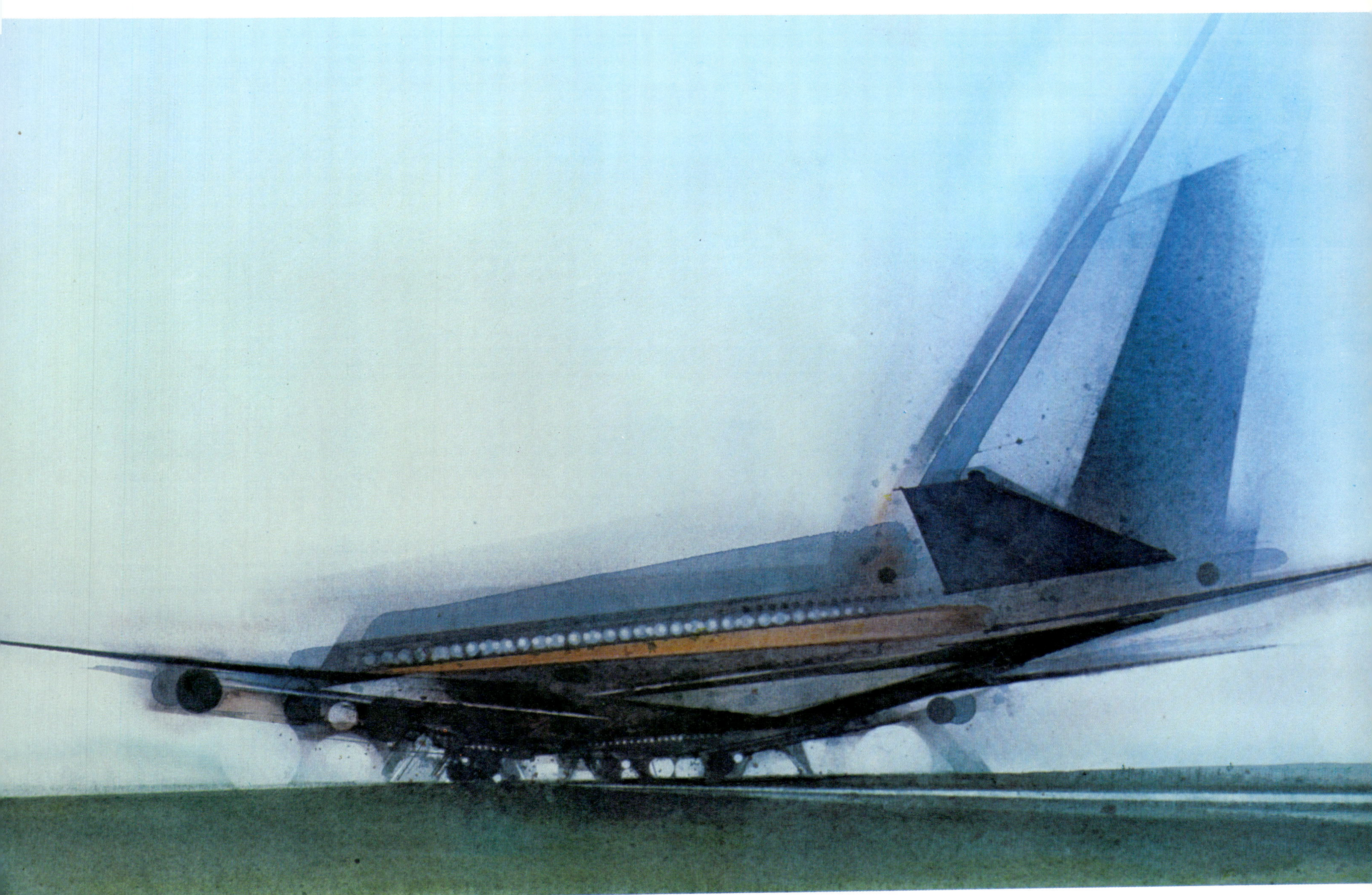

Airliner, 1979. Watercolor, 12½″ x 21″.

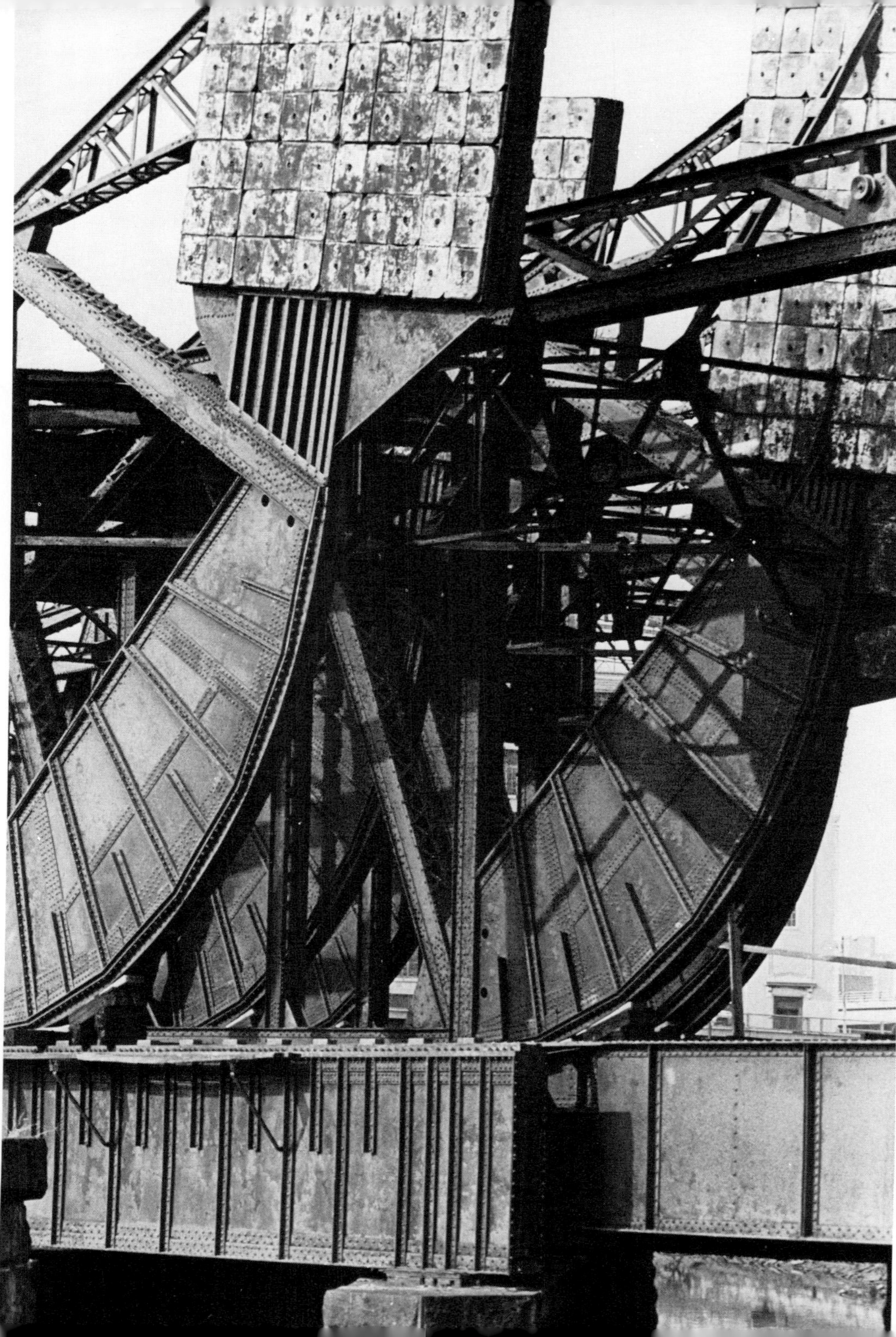

CHAPTER SEVEN

Bridges

The Fort Point Channel Railroad Bridge

Crossing the murky waters of Fort Point Channel in Boston are the massive, twin bascule railroad bridges that carry the main lines south and west from the city. These complicated steel structures, with huge, concrete counterweights, have long held a fascination for area artists. It was not difficult, therefore, to find various interpretations of it, some of which are shown here.

Photograph by Larry Webster.

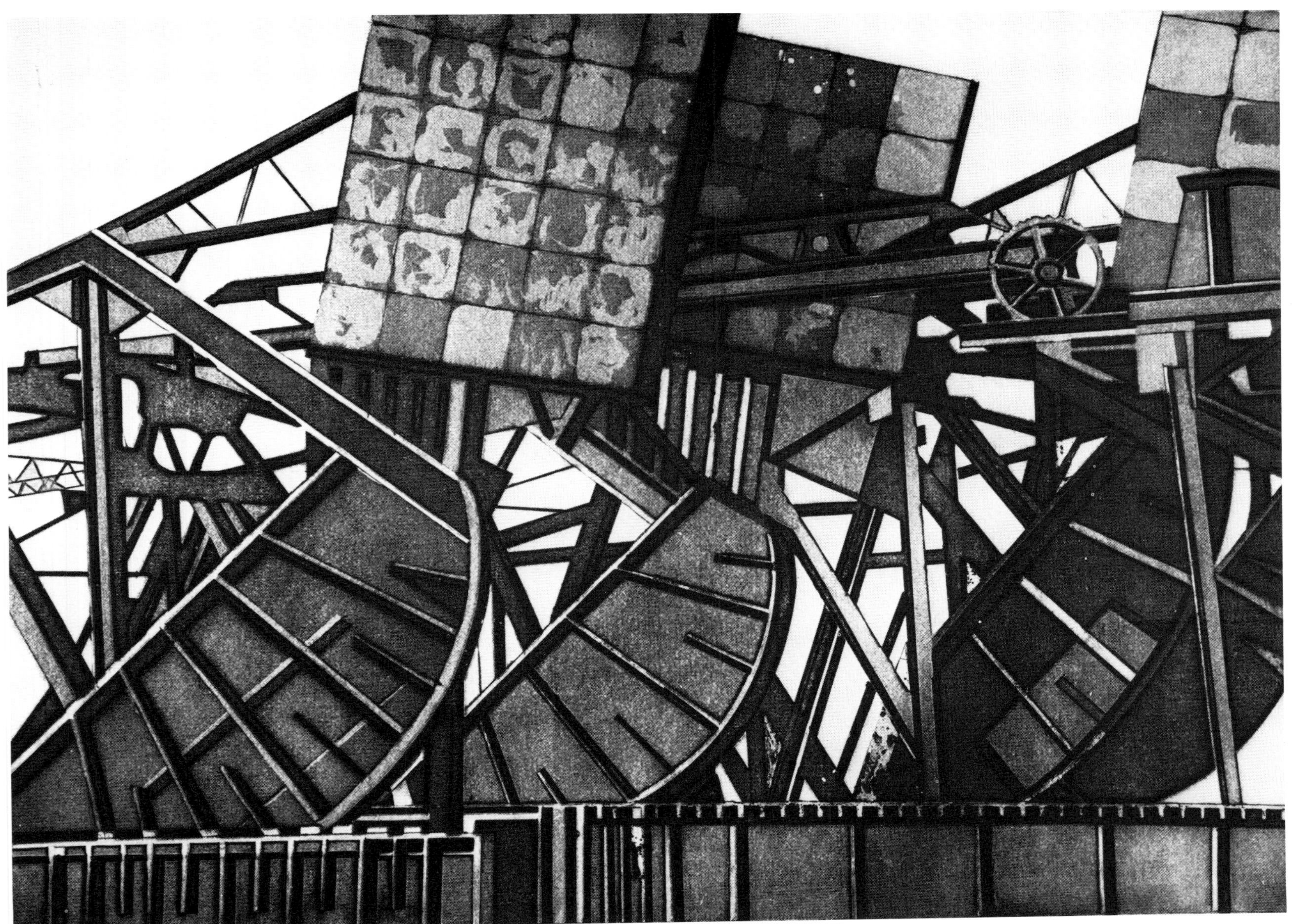

Fort Point Channel Bridge I, II, and III, 1974. 17½″ x 23½″, Etching and aquatint, Sidney Hurwitz. (See also p. 128.)

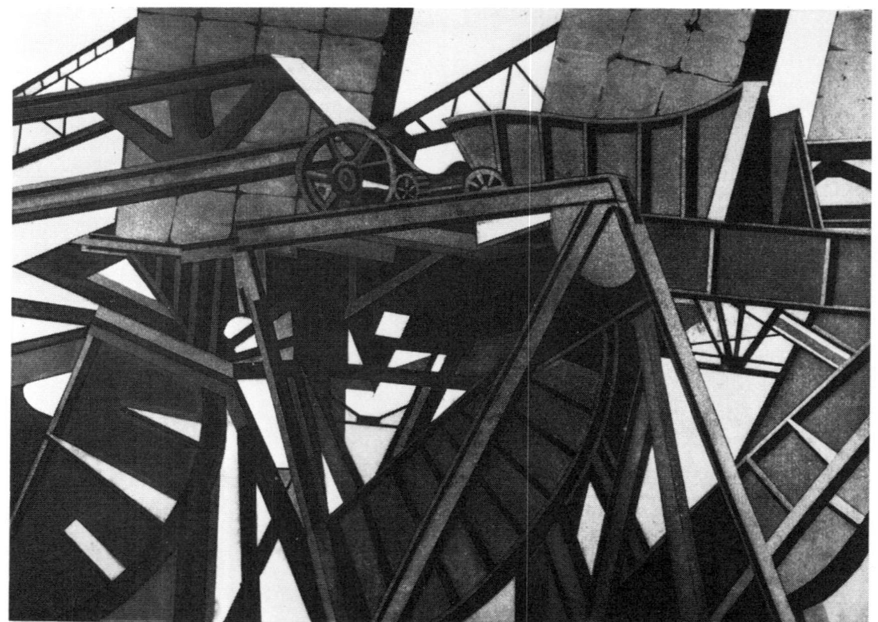

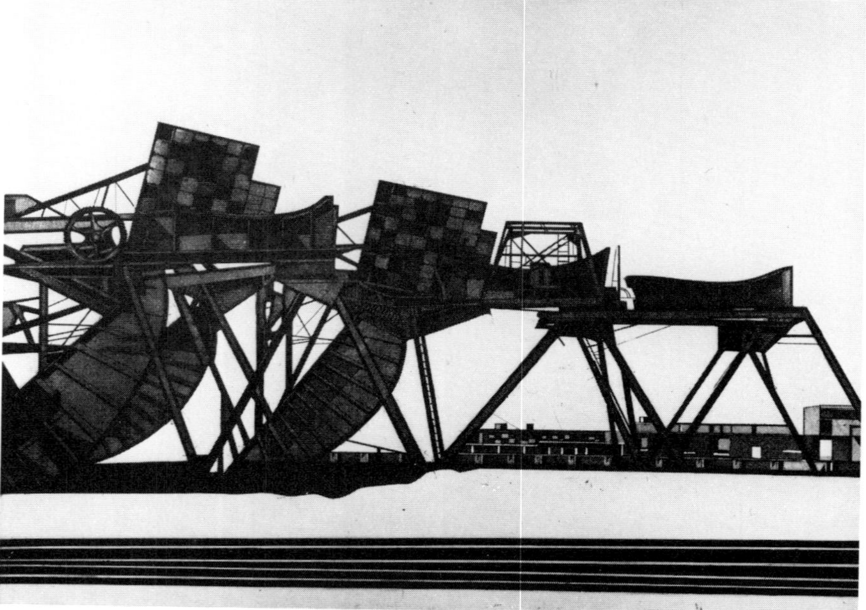

The grainy quality of intaglio (etching-aquatint) printing resembles the surface textures of weathered steel and concrete. Note the emphasis on the sky that is cut into crisp patterns by the complicated, angular structure.

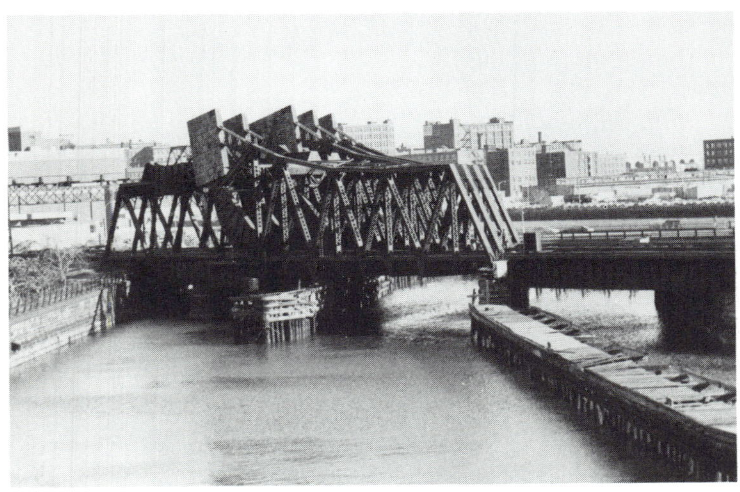

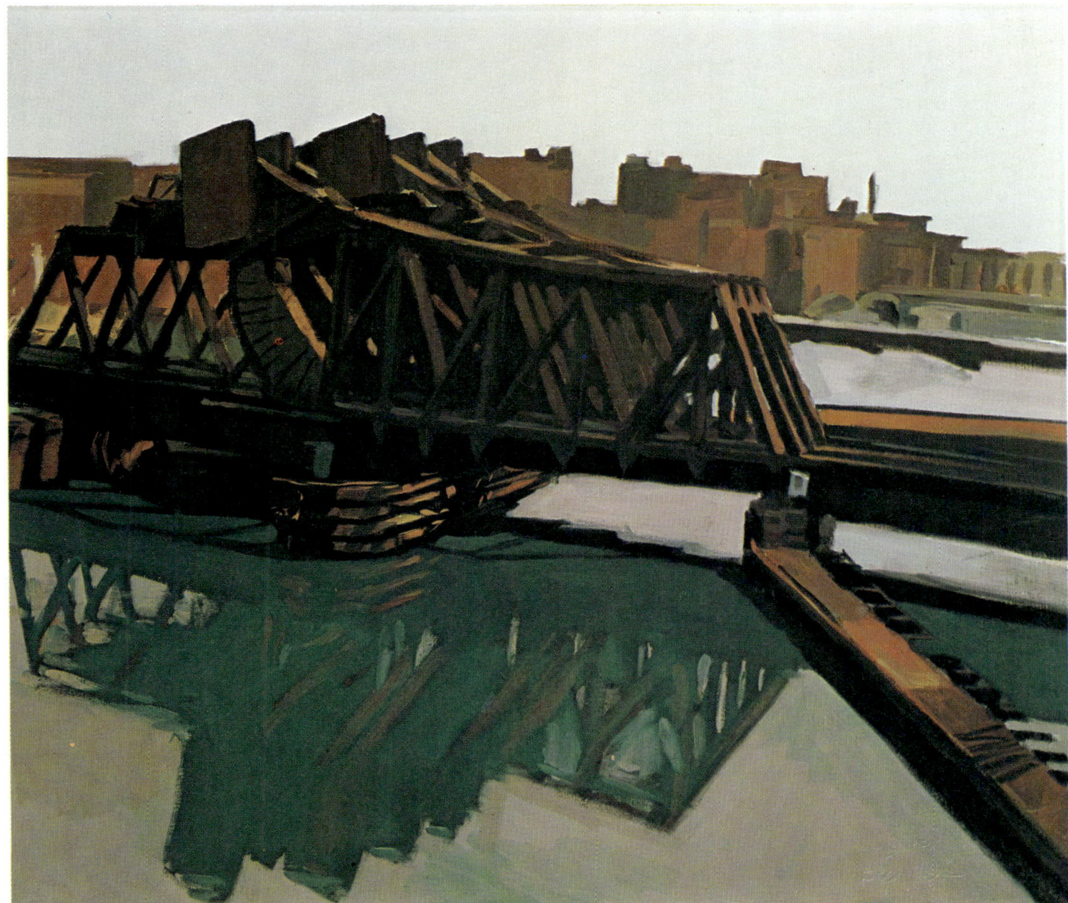

Railroad Lift Bridge, Boston, 1978. Oil on canvas, 30″ x 34″. George Nick.

The viewpoint of George Nick's painting is from another bridge that crosses the channel. Its roadway is higher and allows for a mirror reflection to be seen in the calm, green water. A comparison with the photograph taken from the same location shows the simplification of detail with the resultant intensification of mood.

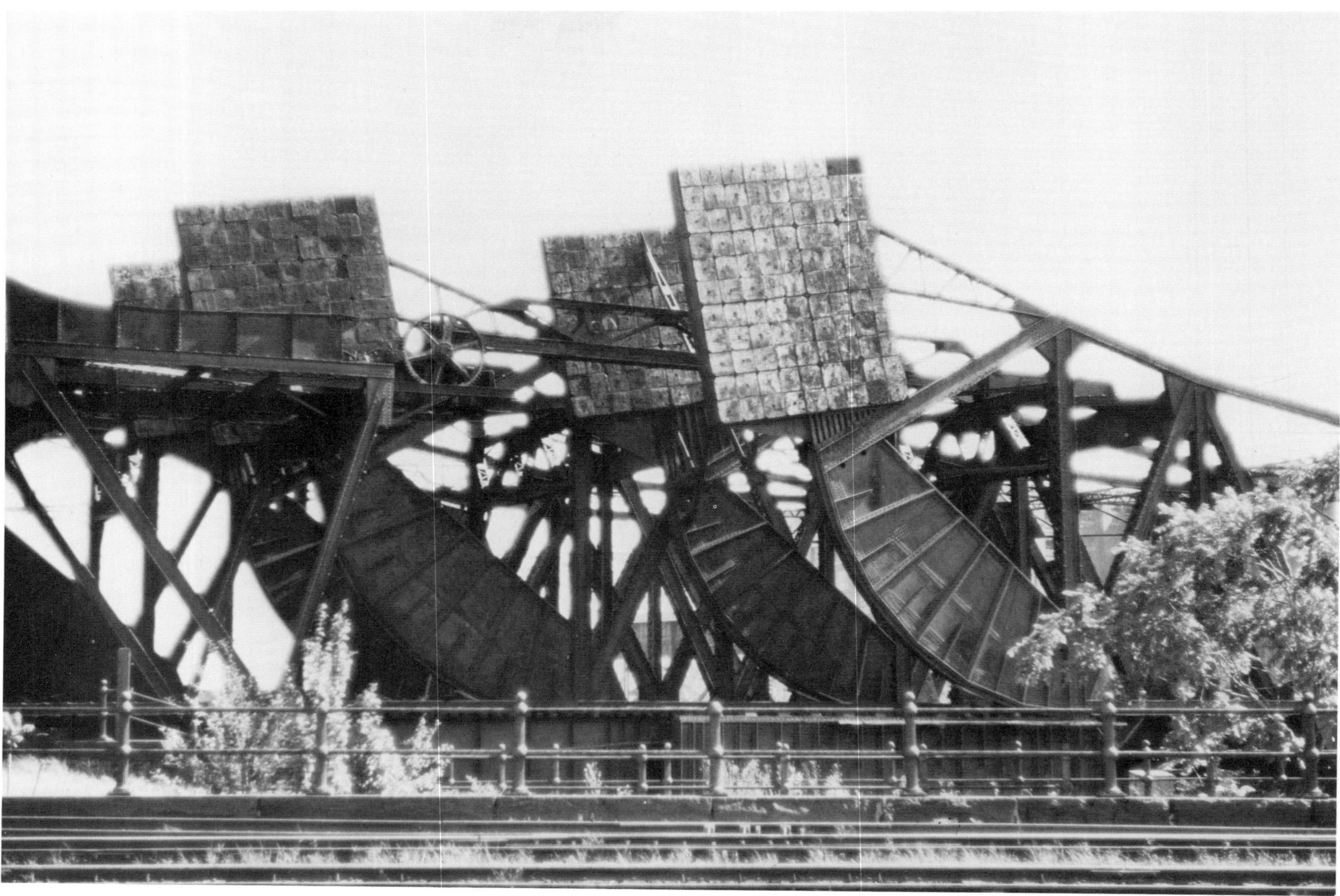

Fort Point Channel Bridge. Photograph by Sidney Hurwitz.

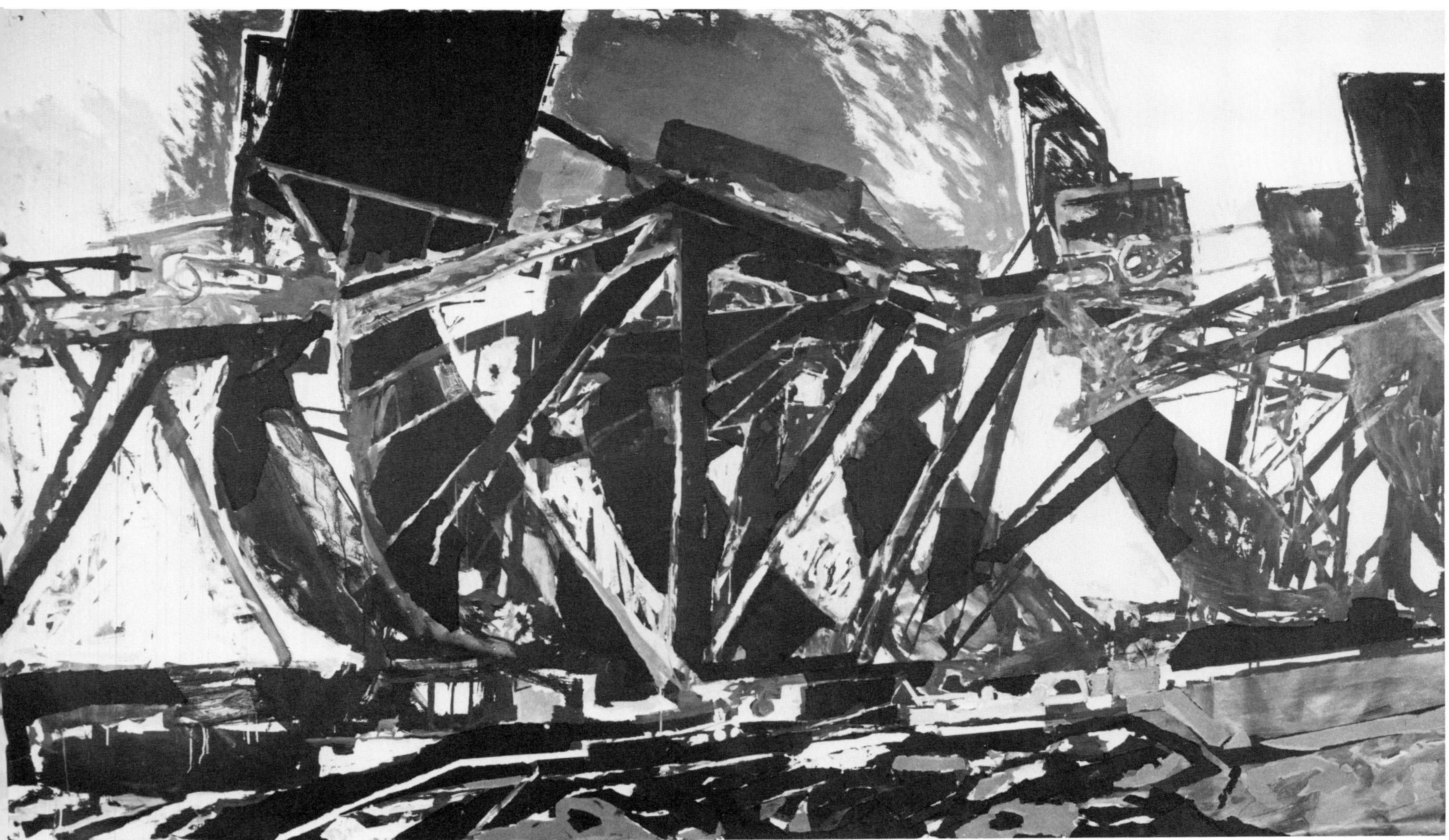

Fort Point Channel Bridge. **Flora Natapoff.**

Flora Natapoff's acrylic, collage painting emphasizes the shattering effect of the girders, counterweights, and rockers against the sky. The direct and reflected light from the girders and tracks is fragmented into hundreds of sharp, hard-edged shapes.

Motion, however, is the overriding quality in this interpretation; the motion that is inherent in the parts that move when the bridge is lifted; the surging, jumbled motion of diagonals that seems to rise and fall in a rhythmic march from one edge of the composition to the other.

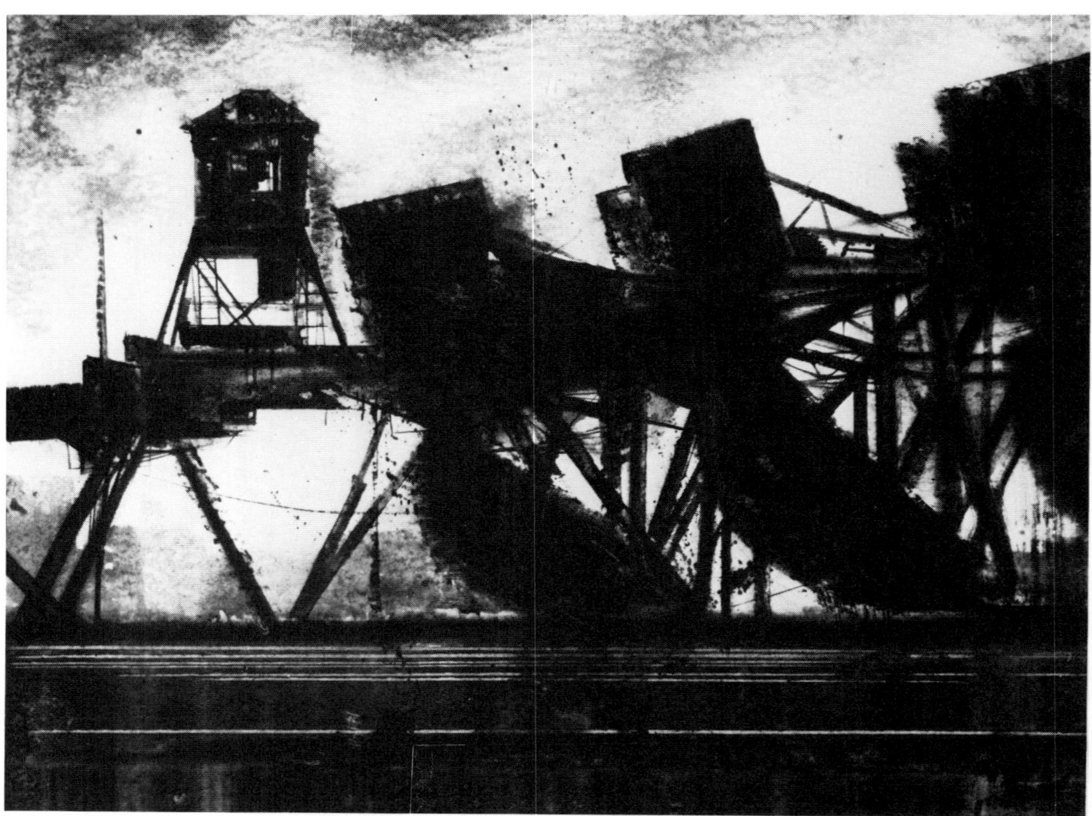

Case study of the painting, *Superstructure* #3, by Larry Webster

Larry Webster is a watercolor painter who has a strong interest in machines and industrial structure. To him, the bridge over Fort Point Channel is an old friend. For years he rode over it in a commuter train twice a day. Before attempting this watercolor, he had painted it twice. In his first effort in 1964, he chose its high-perched control house (since removed) as the center of interest. In 1967 he used a flat elevation with tracks in the foreground (see illustration). So, it was with considerable familiarity and experience that he approached painting the bridge for the third time.

He explored the area on foot with a sketchbook and a Nikkormat 35mm single lens reflex camera loaded with black-and-white film. In the hazy, morning sun, numerous photographs were taken from various angles: inside and outside of the structure, from the tracks, and from the

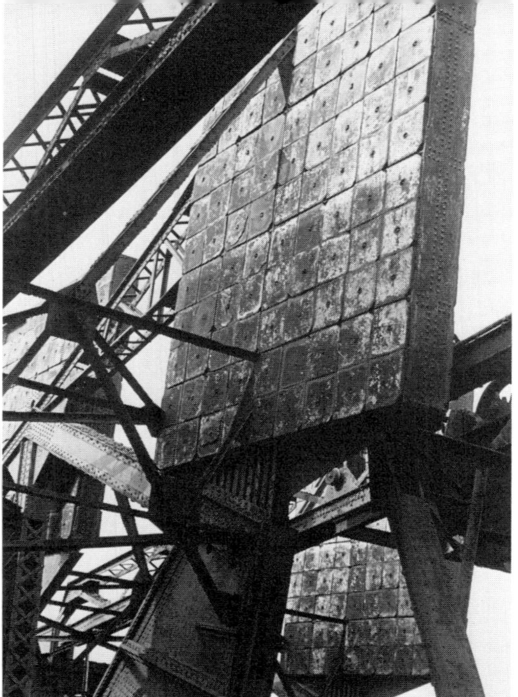

sloping bank along the channel. The pencil drawings were also done at this time. Webster decided to do a detail of the bridge rather than the entire structure to best emphasize the tremendous contrast of large masses to the light structure. He also liked the repetition of arcs and circles of the gears and rockers that opposed the straight lines of the bridge, and the texture and earthy color of the rusty metal and stained concrete. All of these qualities came together from the embankment just below the level of the tracks. From this low angle, the power and thrust were most evident.

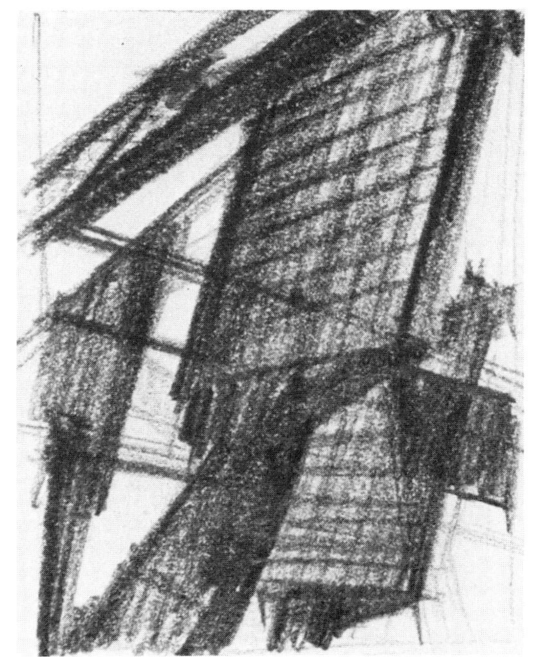

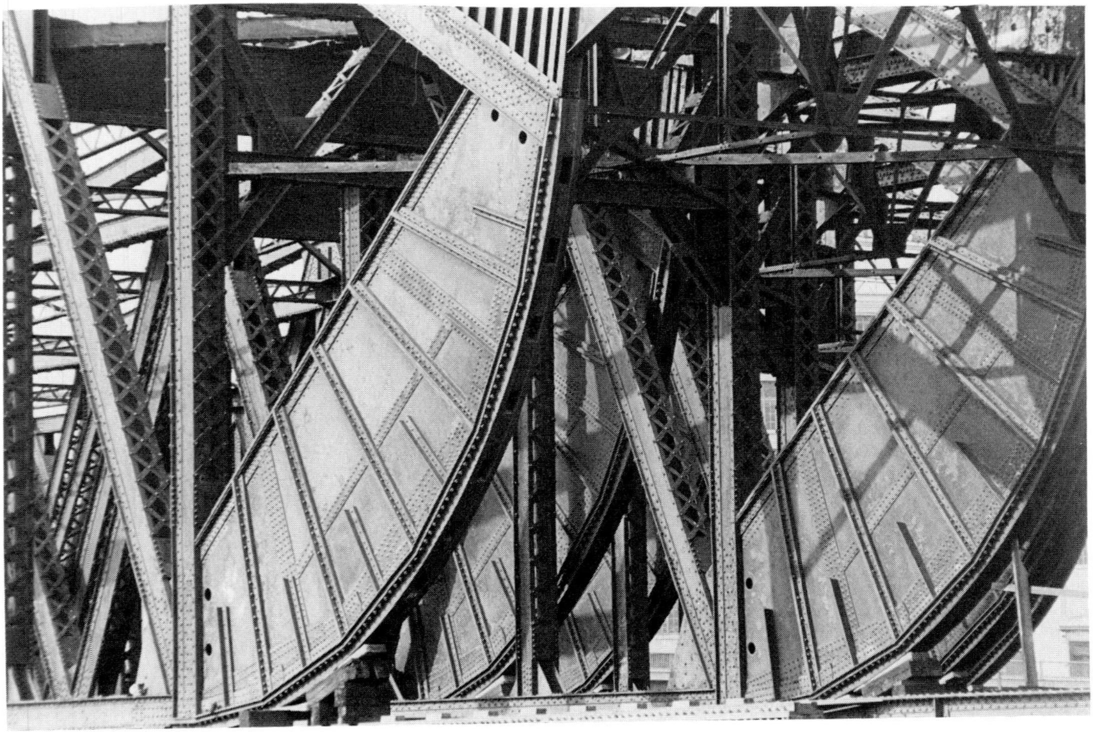

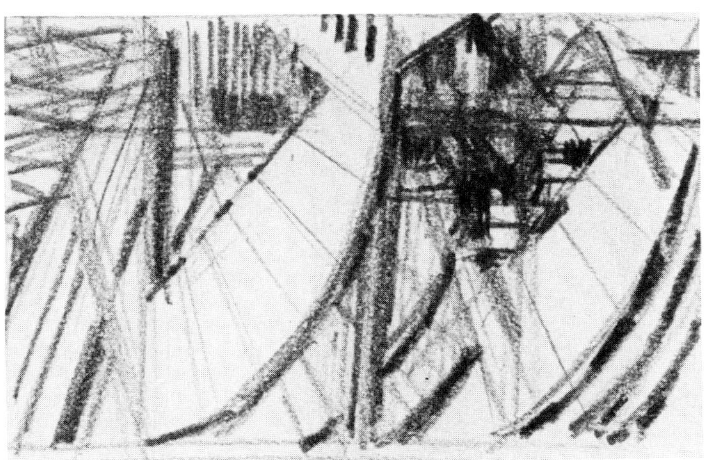

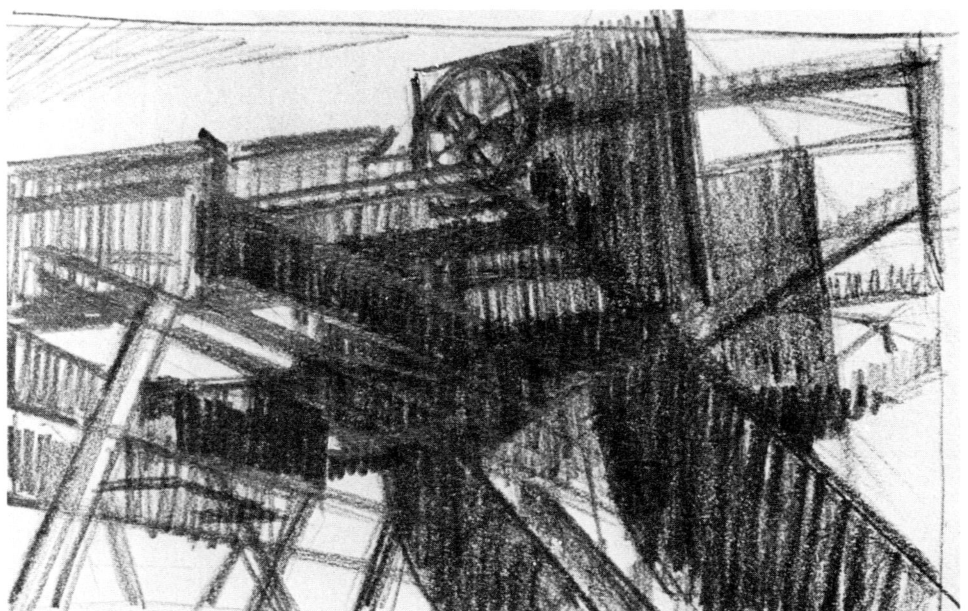

The largest pencil sketch shows the bridge segment that Webster chose for the composition. Bascially, it is a T-shape that tips up to the right. The concrete counterweights take a strong, sloping, horizontal direction and the rockers make a downward, thrusting diagonal. A fan of secondary diagonals is formed by the cross braces that go off into perspective. Emphasis is on the pattern of dark, positive shapes.

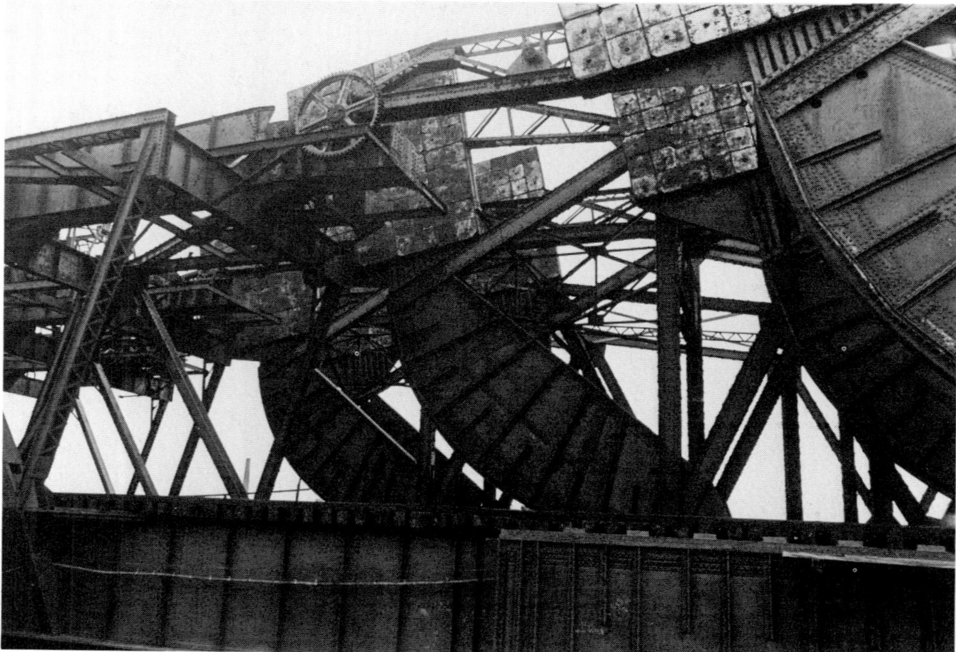

Photograph of the bridge taken by Webster from the spot where the painting will be done.

Webster returned to the bridge on a soft, sunny Sunday morning, a day similar to his earlier visit. The light was behind the bridge and simplified the values within the structure into a close range of darks. About two hours were spent laying out the design of shapes on paper.

Webster's equipment. The brushes include a one- and a two-inch flat bristle, a ¾-inch flat sable, #6, #8, and #12 rounds, and a #4 round rigger. The tube paints are burnt and raw sienna, burnt and raw umber, French ultramarine blue, Winsor blue, cerulean blue, paynes gray, black, alizarin crimson, cadmium red medium, brown madder, yellow ochre, and new gamboge. In the metal paint box, which has shallow depressions for mixing puddles of color, are a sponge, paper tissue, a palette, and a jackknife. A 30½" x 22¼" sheet of 300 lb Fabriano Classico cold press paper is shown mounted with masking tape to a slightly larger piece of plywood. The plastic container at left will be fastened with a clip to the bottom edge of the plywood and is used to hold brushes and knives. The coffee can is filled with water and will be hung from the center of the board support of the folding, wooden watercolor easel (not shown). The pliers are for firmly tightening the adjustable easel to control the angle at which the board is held. The drawing in the sketchbook has established the composition, the massing of lights and darks.

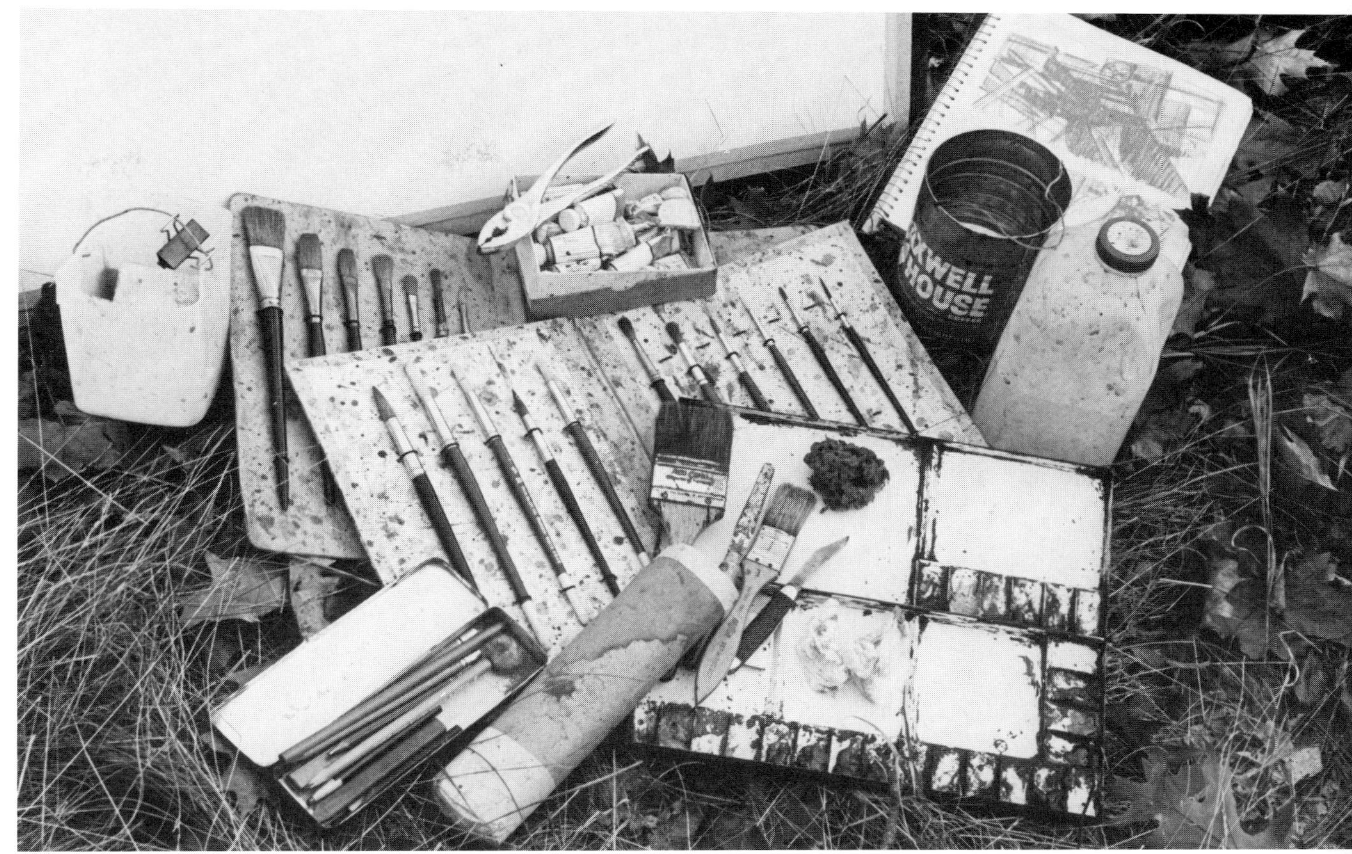

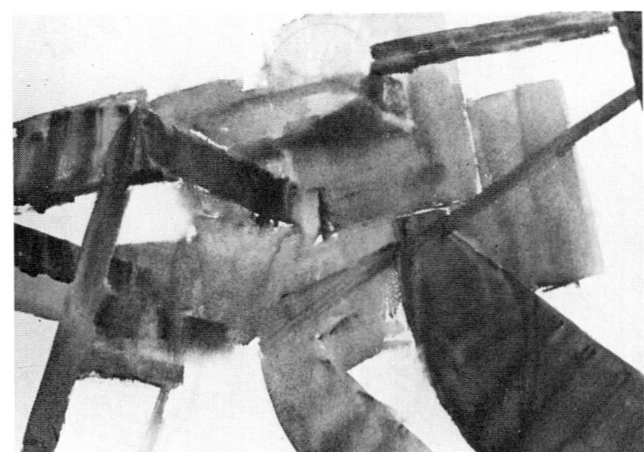

After mixing a gray wash composed of raw umber, alizarin crimson, and ultramarine blue in the cover of the paint box, initial tones were put in with a two-inch flat bristle brush.

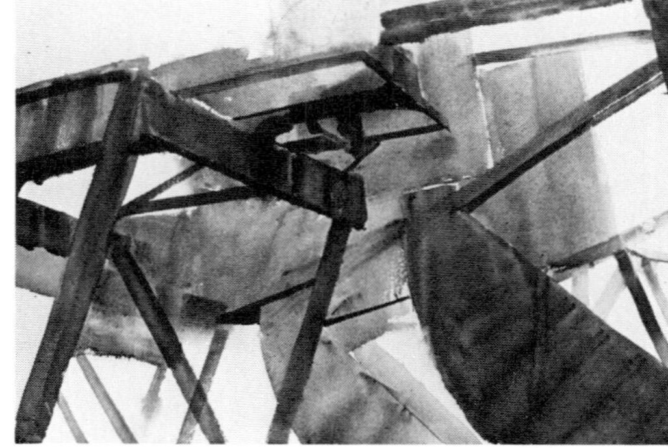

Using a #1 bristle brush and smaller flats, Webster added raw and burnt sienna for a warm tone, and worked in more definition and value contrast.

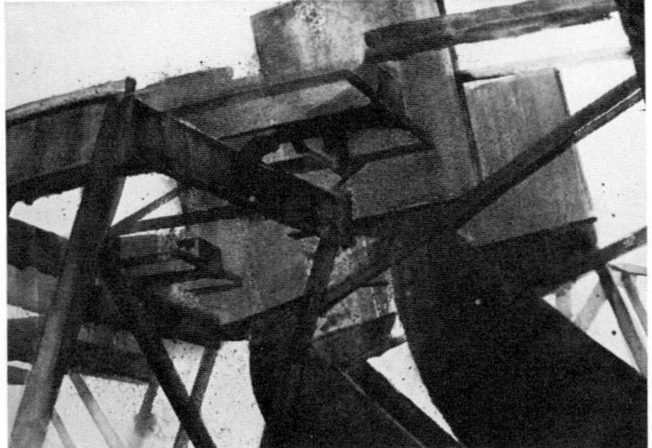

More tones were added to bring the watercolor to the point at which it contains all of the basic shapes. Almost all of the work has been additive, with very little sponging out. Four hours have been spent on location and three hours of further work will be done from memory and the black-and-white photographs in Webster's studio.

A #6 round brush is used to define the gear wheel which becomes the composition's focus. The pattern of thin cross braces at right is put in with the same brush. The process of articulating and defining continues, but some of it is now done subtractively. For the zigzag braces in the vertical beam at left, two cards are used to mask the dark areas and the light lines are sponged out. These cards are also used as straight edges when needed. A rigger is used to make the grid lines which define the blocks of cement in the counterweights. Spattering is done at this stage to create surface texture or to eliminate brush strokes.

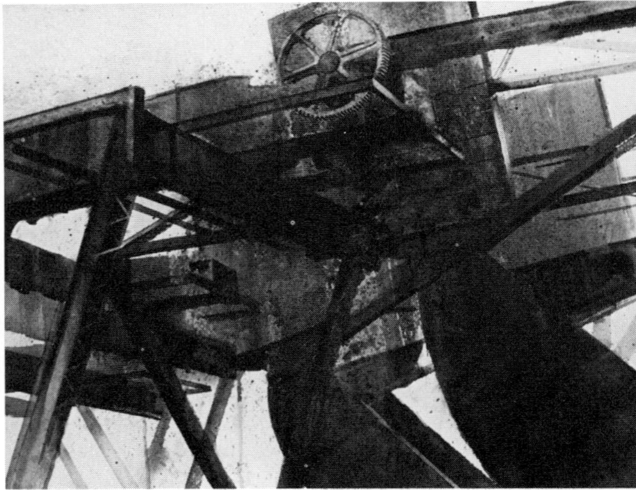

If an edge becomes too strong, as in the upper left corner, water is thrown at it and paint is spattered on it with a #1 flat bristle brush. The continual process of strengthening and weakening is done through painting, spattering, and wiping out. Detail, such as the row of rivets along the beam at lower left, is added with a #6 round brush.

Finally, cerulean blue is brushed or spattered onto areas for cool light while brown madder is added to other areas to create rusty warmth. The finished watercolor shows how light has been allowed to filter through the structure to give it an airy quality in spite of its heavy, metallic character.

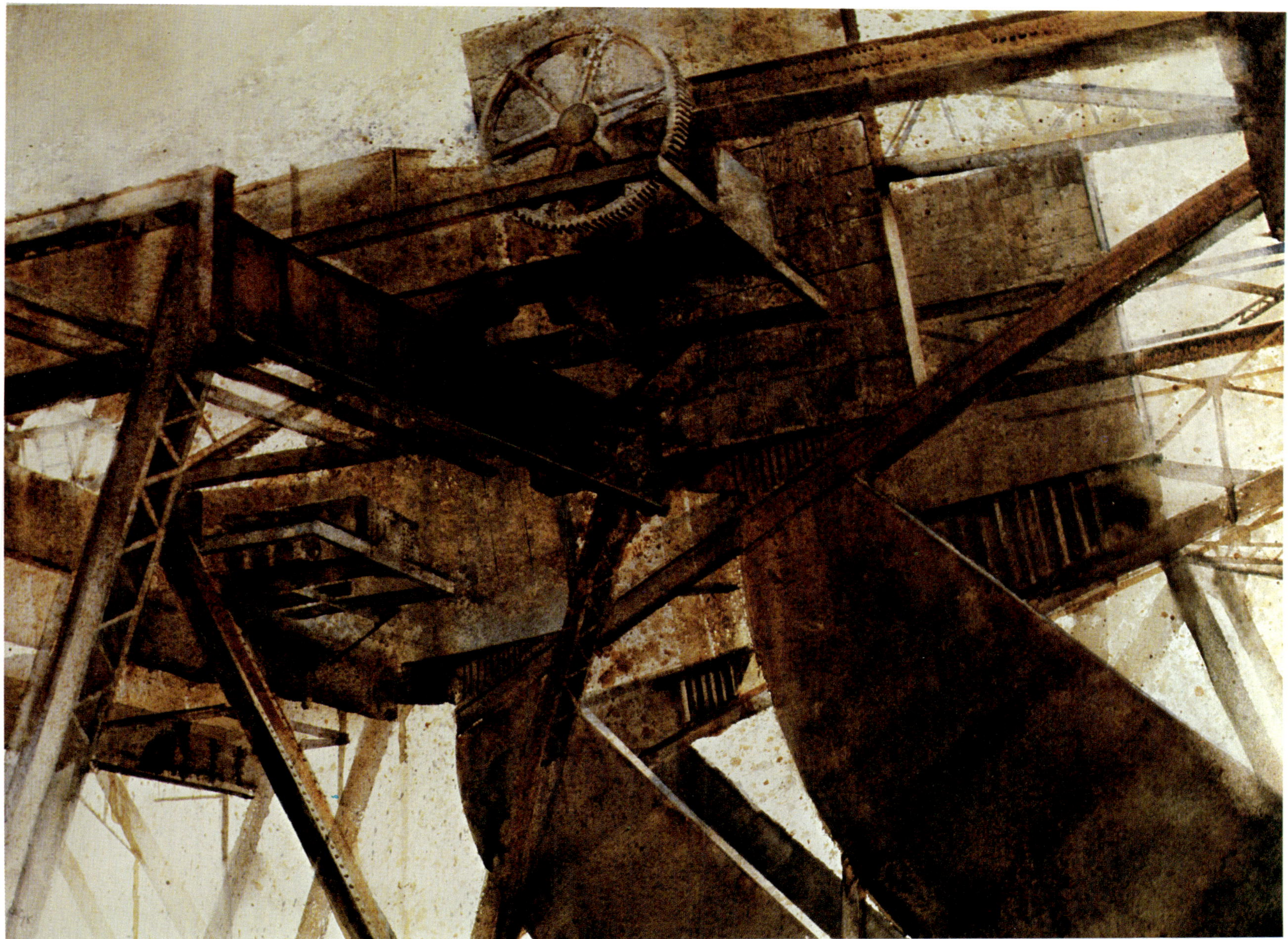

Superstructure #3, 1978. Watercolor, 21″ x 29½″. Larry Webster.

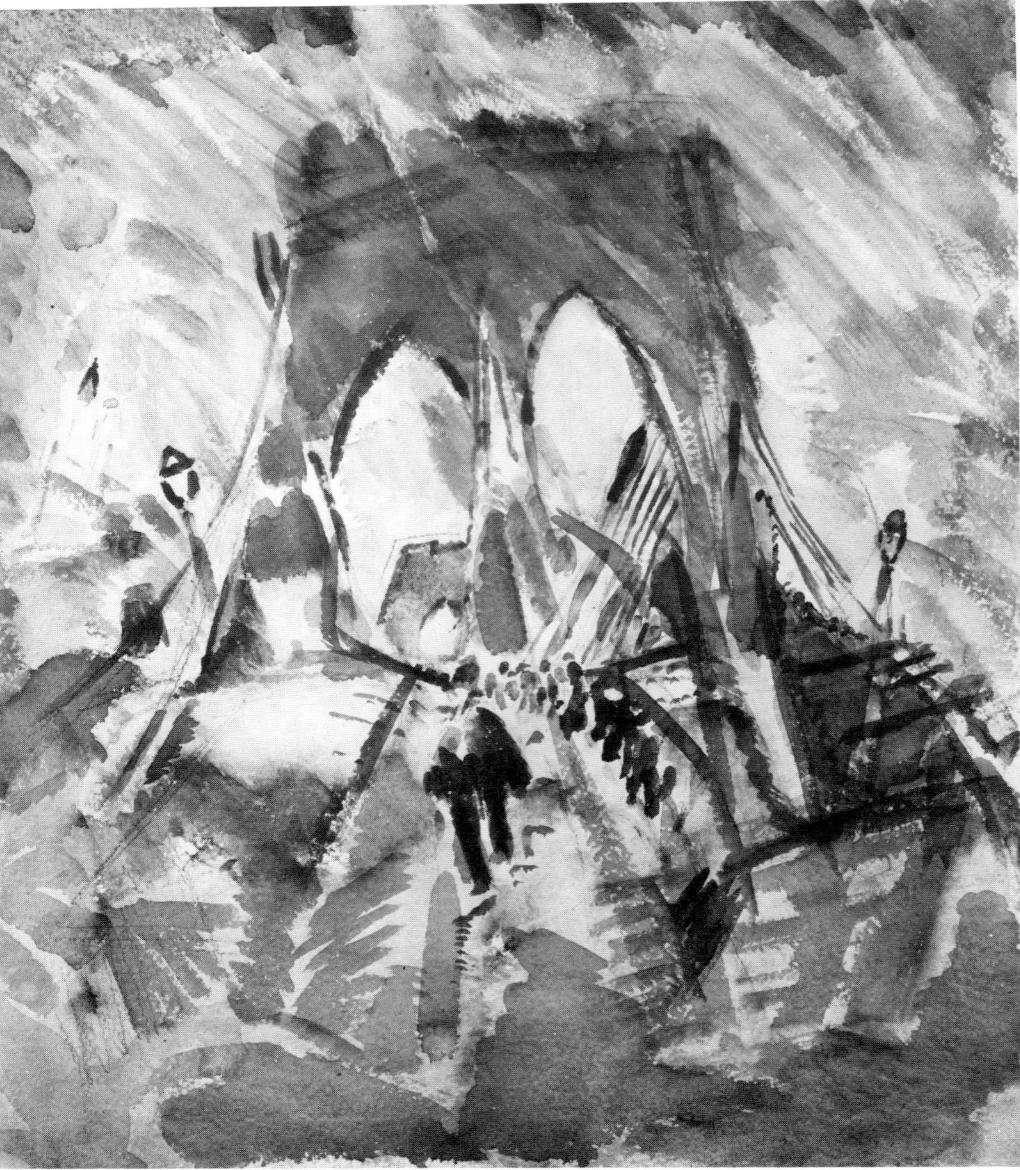

Brooklyn Bridge, 1910. Watercolor, 18½" x 15½". John Marin. The Metropolitan Museum of Art, New York. The Alfred Stieglitz Collection.

Bridges

This painting (left) vibrates with explosive energy. Marin's response to the masonry and metal structure emphasizes the tensions of the diagonal bracing, the surging of the traffic, and the soaring roadways. Sometimes painting with both hands, he infused the entire surface of the paper with pulsating form and color, using slashing lines and splashes of paint. It is a dynamic interpretation of the urban scene, bursting with nervous vitality.

An Expressionist interpretation of the bridge (right), this painting is a subjective transformation with simplified forms that are brutally painted to express strength and power. Arcs cut the sky into harsh shapes and the bridge almost seems to be alive, distorted in its effort to span the river.

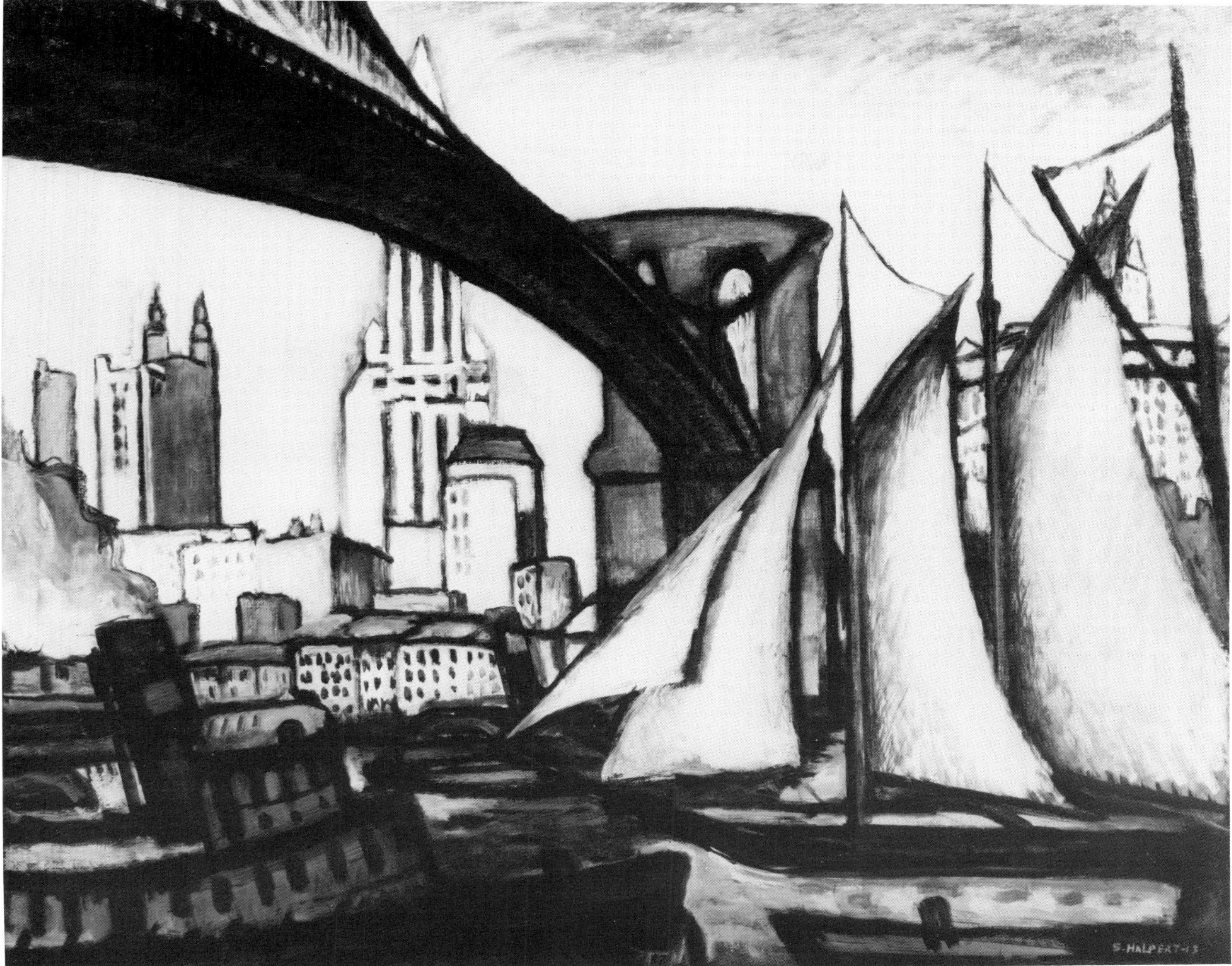

Brooklyn Bridge, 1913. Oil on canvas, 34″ x 42″. Samuel Halpert. Collection of Whitney Museum of American Art, New York. Gift of Mr. and Mrs. Benjamin Halpert.

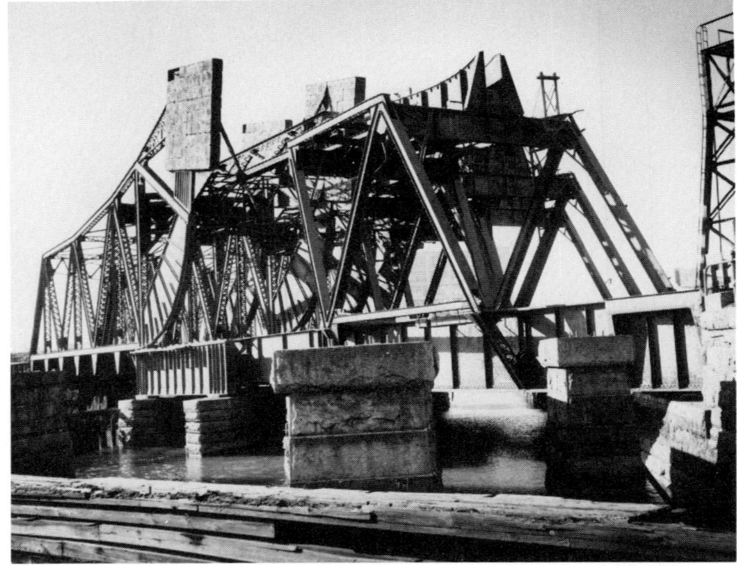

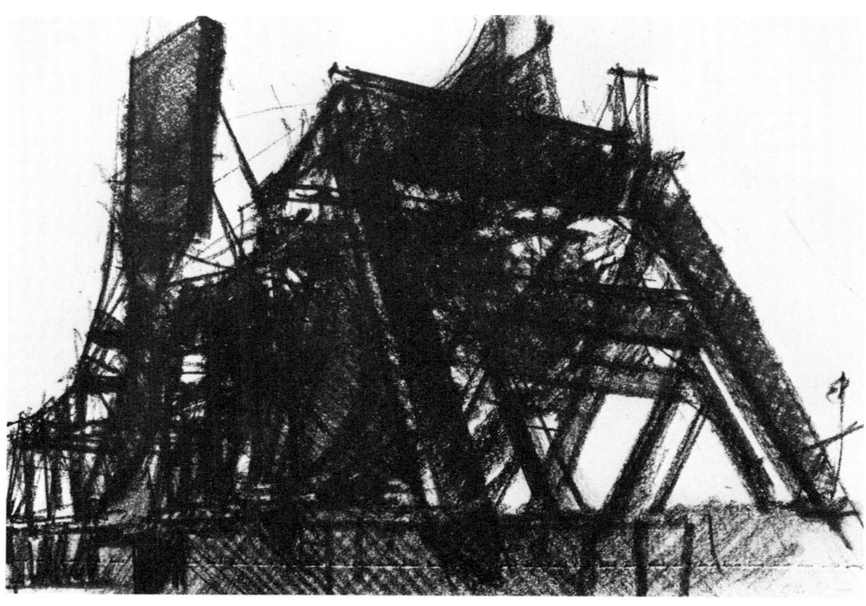

The basic element in this painting is the diagonal. It is forcefully apparent in the photograph as the basic component of the strongly braced structure. By making the drawing from a closer point of view, exaggerating the height, and compacting the form, the triangularity is firmly established. The oil painting carries the idea a step further by more distortion: the diagonal braces are thickened and their directions of thrust are emphasized. The massiveness of the bridge is stressed by slablike patches of red brown paint and is relieved by allowing blue sky to penetrate the spaces between them. The light, airy, linear character of the distant part of the bridge at lower left acts as a contrast.

***Fort Point Channel Bridge*, 1977. Acrylic and oil on canvas, 24″ x 30″.**

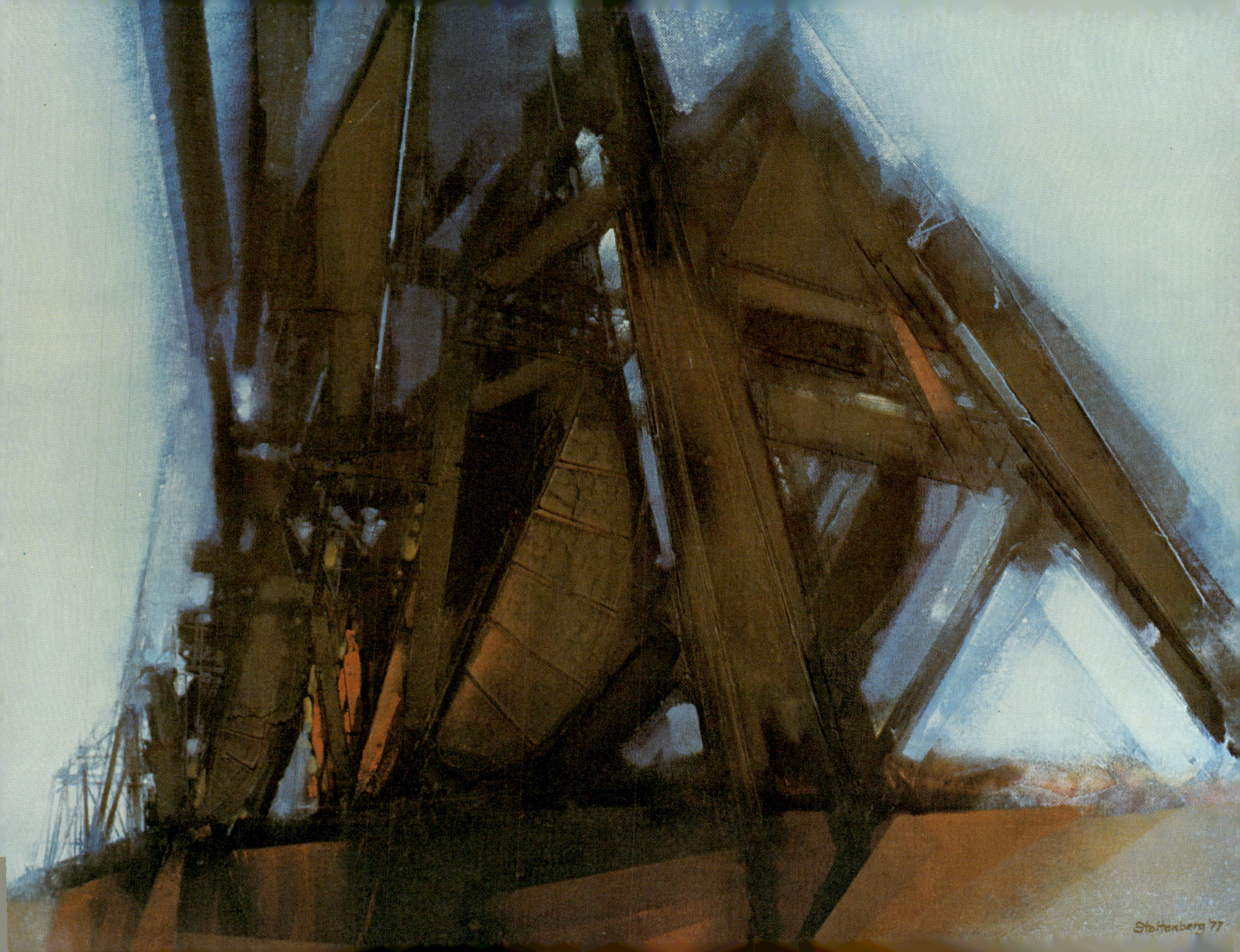
Stoltenberg '77

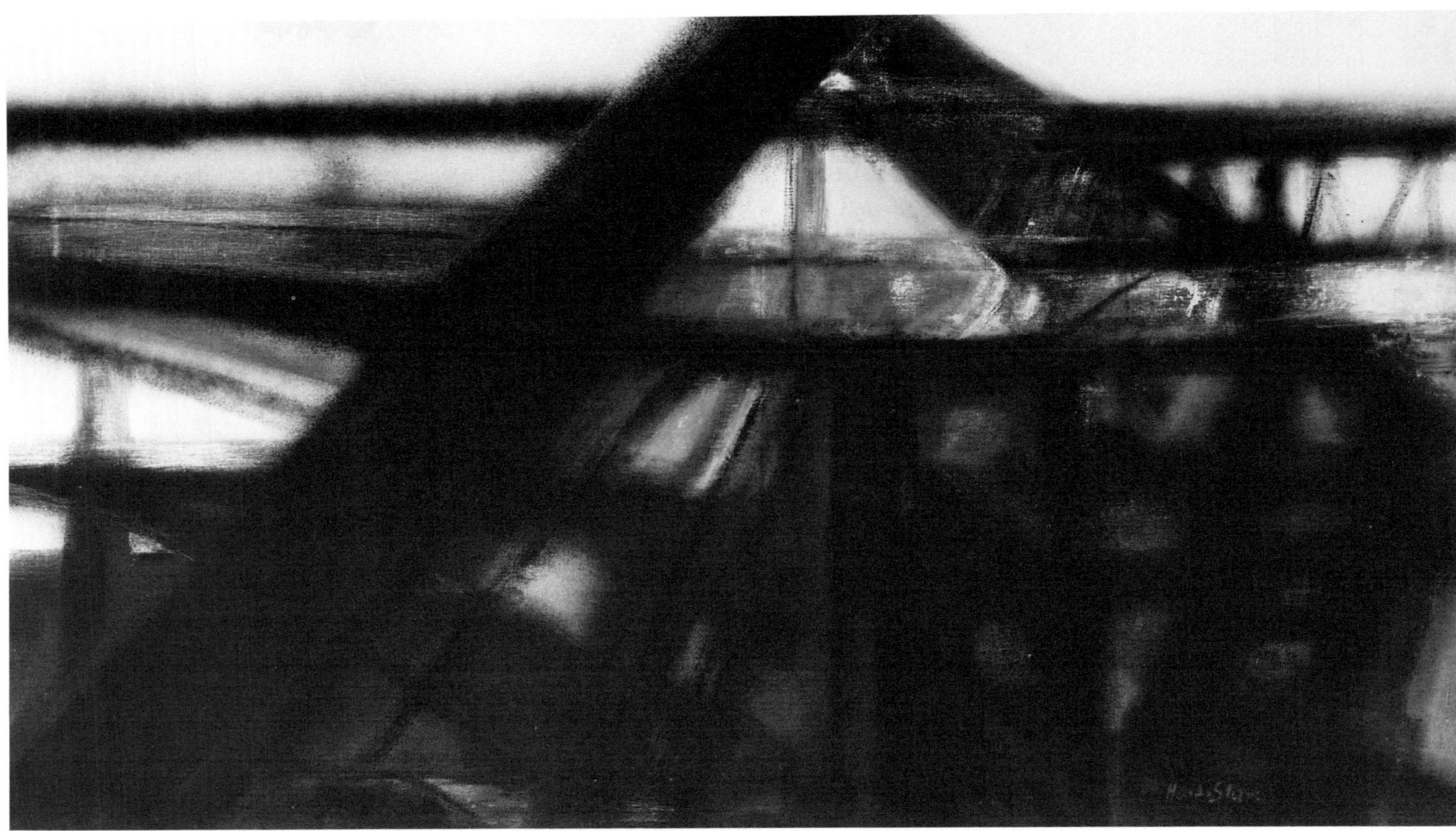

Brooklyn Bridge, **1954. Oil on canvas, 60″ x 35″. Hedda Sterne. Courtesy, Betty Parsons Gallery, New York. Photograph by Oliver Baker.**

Painted with verve in soft, blurred focus, Sterne uses just a fragment of the bridge to express another of its qualities—movement—crossing the bridge at high speeds, allowing only fleeting perceptions of its roadway structure. Spray paint, applied in rapid strokes, is particularly appropriate to the character of the painting.

The Erie and New York Central Railroad bridges (right) over the Buffalo River of which Burchfield said, "I had observed and admired the two bridges for many years—a wonderful structure of blackness even on the sunniest day, but on a gray day the epitome of sinister darkness. . . . Even the stream below, polluted as it was with various chemicals and oily substances, seemed to be made of liquid black iron."

***Black Iron*, 1935. Watercolor on paper, 41″ x 29″. Charles Burchfield. Courtesy, Kennedy Galleries, Inc., New York.**

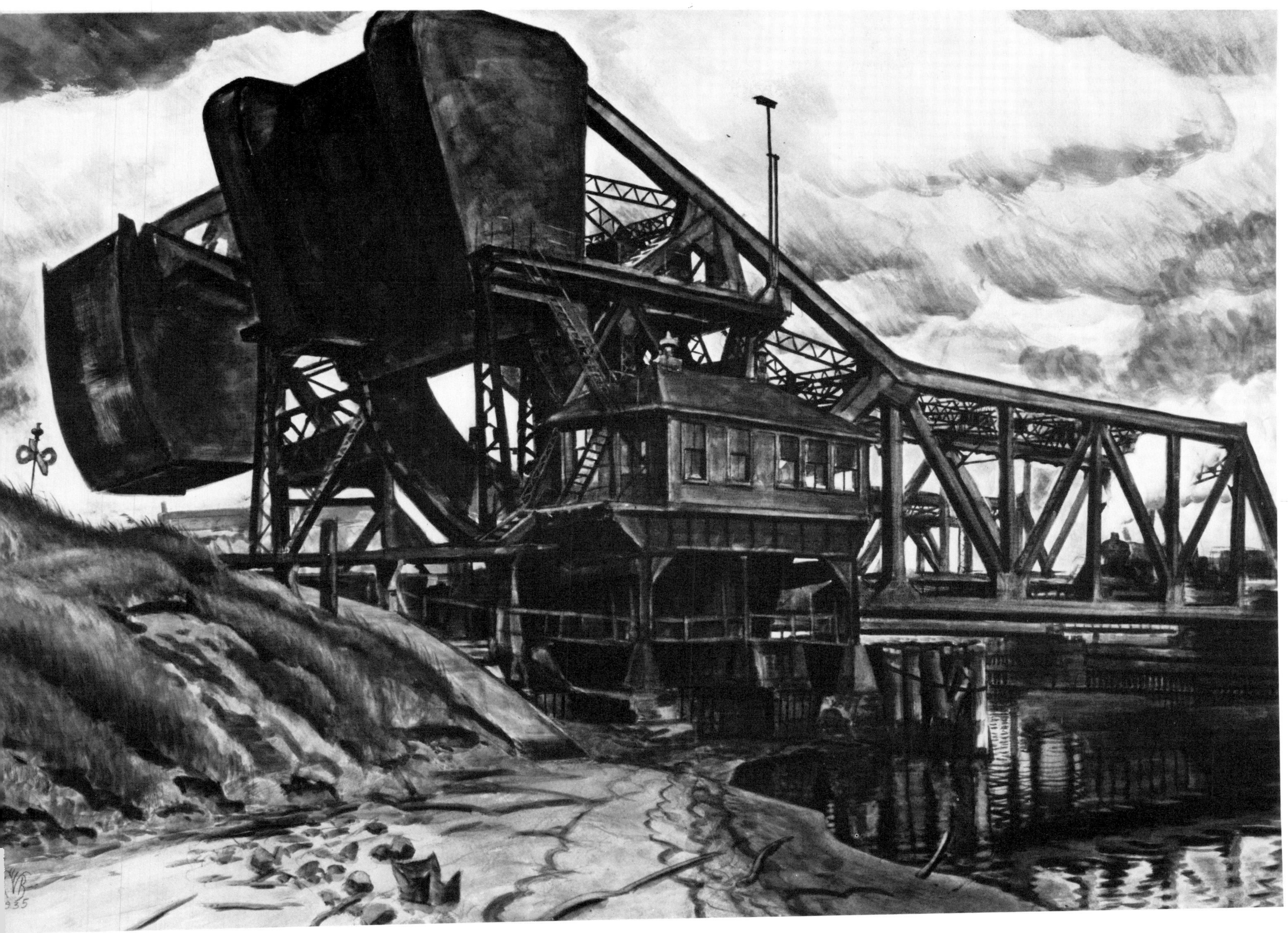

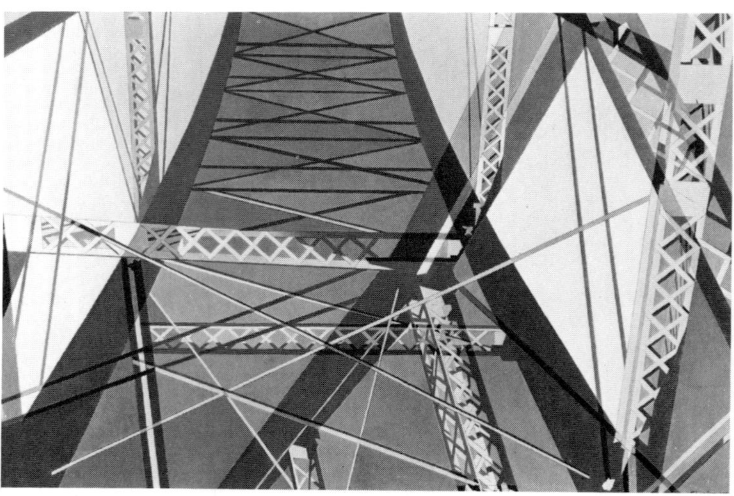

Steel—Croton, **1953. Oil on canvas, 16″ x 24″. Charles Sheeler. The Virginia Museum of Fine Arts, Richmond. Purchased by the John Payne Fund.**

A composite of bridge parts seen as it is being crossed might describe this painting by Charles Sheeler. As in much of his later work, superimposed photographic images play an important part in the conception. Brown and tan openwork girders, tie-rods, and braces create geometric patterns and break up the sky into blue toned triangles. As Sheeler said, this is all done with "craftsmanship so adequate as to be unobstrusive."

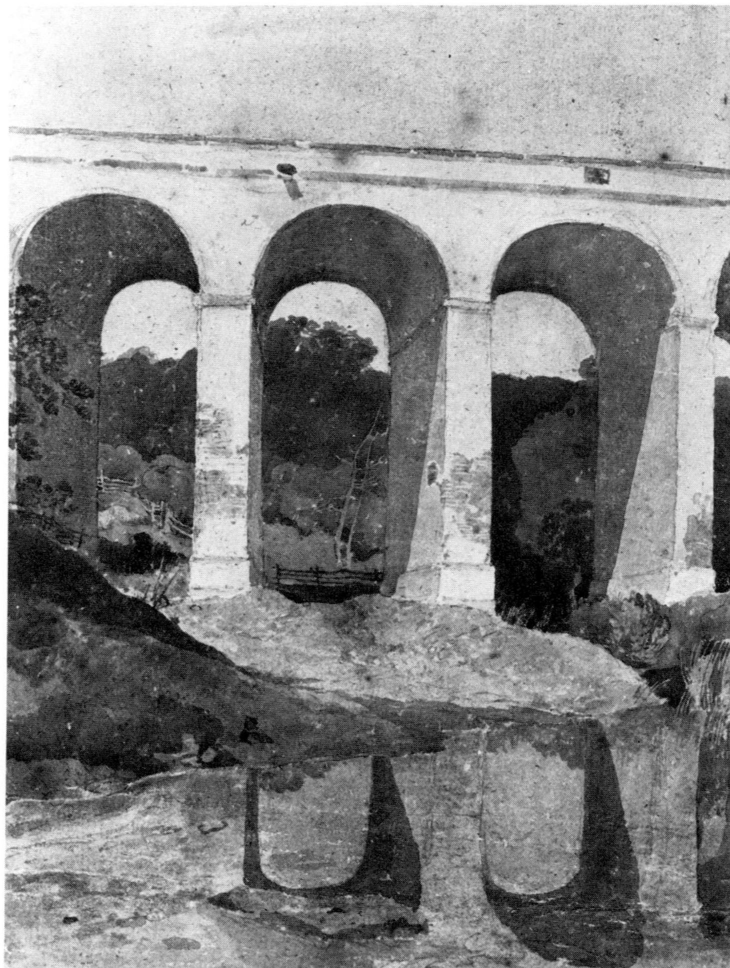

Chirk Aqueduct, **c. 1804. Pencil and watercolor on paper, 9⅛″ x 12½″. John Sell Cotman. Courtesy, Victoria and Albert Museum, London.**

Seventy feet high, Chirk Aqueduct carries the Ellesmere Canal over the Ceriog Valley in Wales. It was built from 1796 to 1801 and was designed by the great engineer Thomas Telford. It is one of the most striking achievements of the Canal Age. Cotman has used three of its ten huge arches in this firm, pictorial structure. His remarkable control of flat watercolor washes describes the deep sculptural volumes of the masonry while making the softer, natural forms below and beyond it act as foils.

It is interesting to compare this painting with John Cotman's *Chirk Aqueduct.* Painted more than a century apart, they are products of vastly different sensibilities.

Not allowing the eye to deeply penetrate through the arches, Feininger has kept his painting surface conscious. He has broken the motif into planes of light and shadow that recede or advance, contrary to their actual positions. This creates a tension as the eye engages in sorting out this painted world of shifting, transparent, and interpenetrating planes.

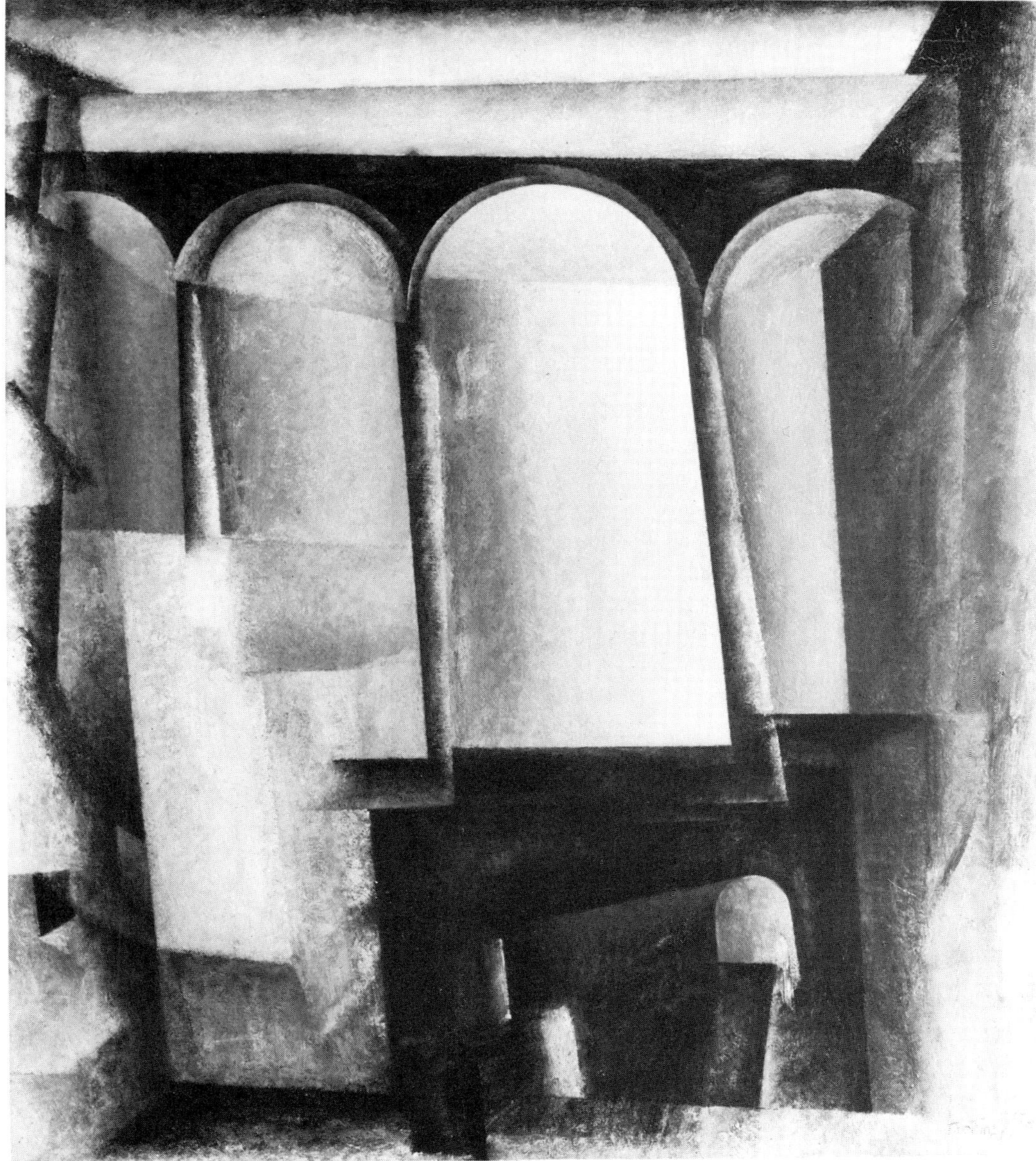

***Viaduct*, 1920. Oil on canvas, 39¾" x 33¾". Lyonel Feininger. Collection, The Museum of Modern Art, New York. Acquired through the Lillie P. Bliss Bequest.**

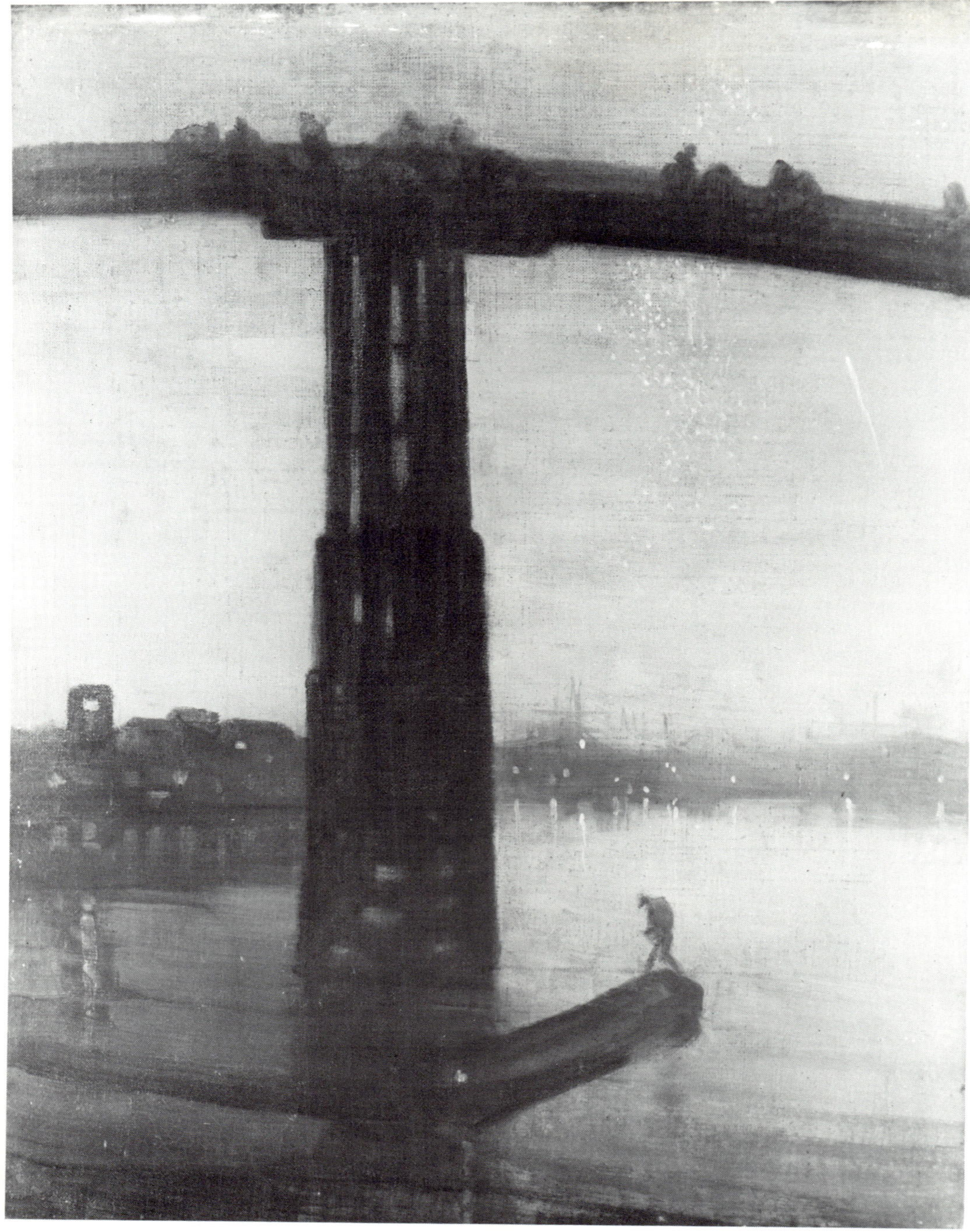

Built in the eighteenth century to cross the Thames at Chelsea, Old Battersea Bridge was a massive structure of bolted timbers that formed nineteen spans. As seen from the river at low tide, this section of the roadway and the tall pier form a strong T-shape. There is a soft, tonal, and poetic mood reminiscent of the Japanese prints he admired. The fleeting character of the evening light that he painted forced him to train his visual memory. He would stare at a scene for several minutes, mentally noting values, proportions, and salient details that would be painted in his studio the next morning. His blue nocturnes were done over a red ground, an underpainting, or a mahogany wood panel. His paints were mixed with linseed oil and turpentine to such a fluid consistency that at times the paintings had to be laid on the floor to prevent the oils from running. Regarding color, he once wrote, "The same color ought to appear in the picture continually here and there, in the same way that a thread appears in an embroidery . . . in this way the whole will form a harmony."

***Nocturne in Blue and Gold: Old Battersea Bridge*, 1872-1875. Oil on canvas, 20" x 64¾". James Abbot McNeil Whistler. Courtesy, Tate Gallery, London.**

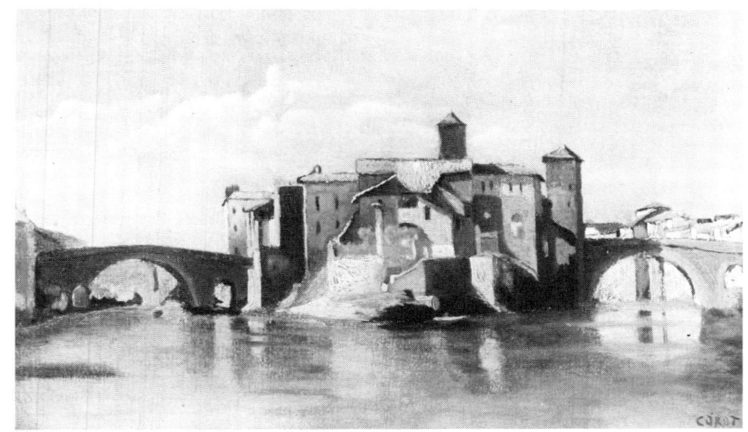

***Island of San Bartolomeo, Roma.* Oil on canvas, 17″ x 10½″. Camille Corot. Courtesy, Museum of Fine Arts, Boston, The Harriet Otis Croft Fund.**

This island in the Tiber (Isola Tiberina) suggests a ship. In Roman times, stonework which resembled a prow was erected on its shore. In the mid-eighteenth century, Piranesi featured this stonework in one of his etchings. However, by the time Corot painted this view, additional buildings had changed the island's appearance. More recently, a wide quay has been built which further diminishes its shiplike character. The two ancient bridges, Ponte Cestio on the left and Ponte Fabricio on the right, connect the island to mainland Rome. Corot has combined the island and its bridges to form a horizontal band of Cubistlike planes painted in a wide value range of warm, earth tones.

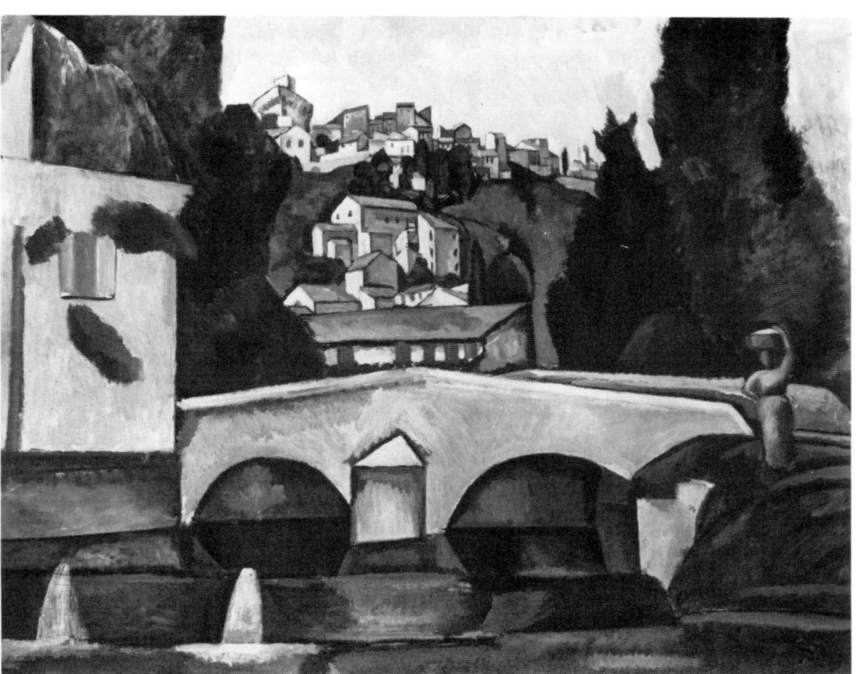

***The Old Bridge*, c. 1910. Oil on canvas, 31⅞″ x 39½″. Andre Derain. National Gallery of Art, Washington, D.C., the Chester Dale Collection.**

Painted by Derain while he was under the influence of Cezanne, this view of a masonry bridge in the French town of Cagnes is handled in the firm, architectonic manner of that master. The painting is constructed of planes which repeat in character but decrease in size. The disparate qualities of masonry, water, foliage, and sky are painted in the same boldly modeled way to produce a unified and solidly built composition.

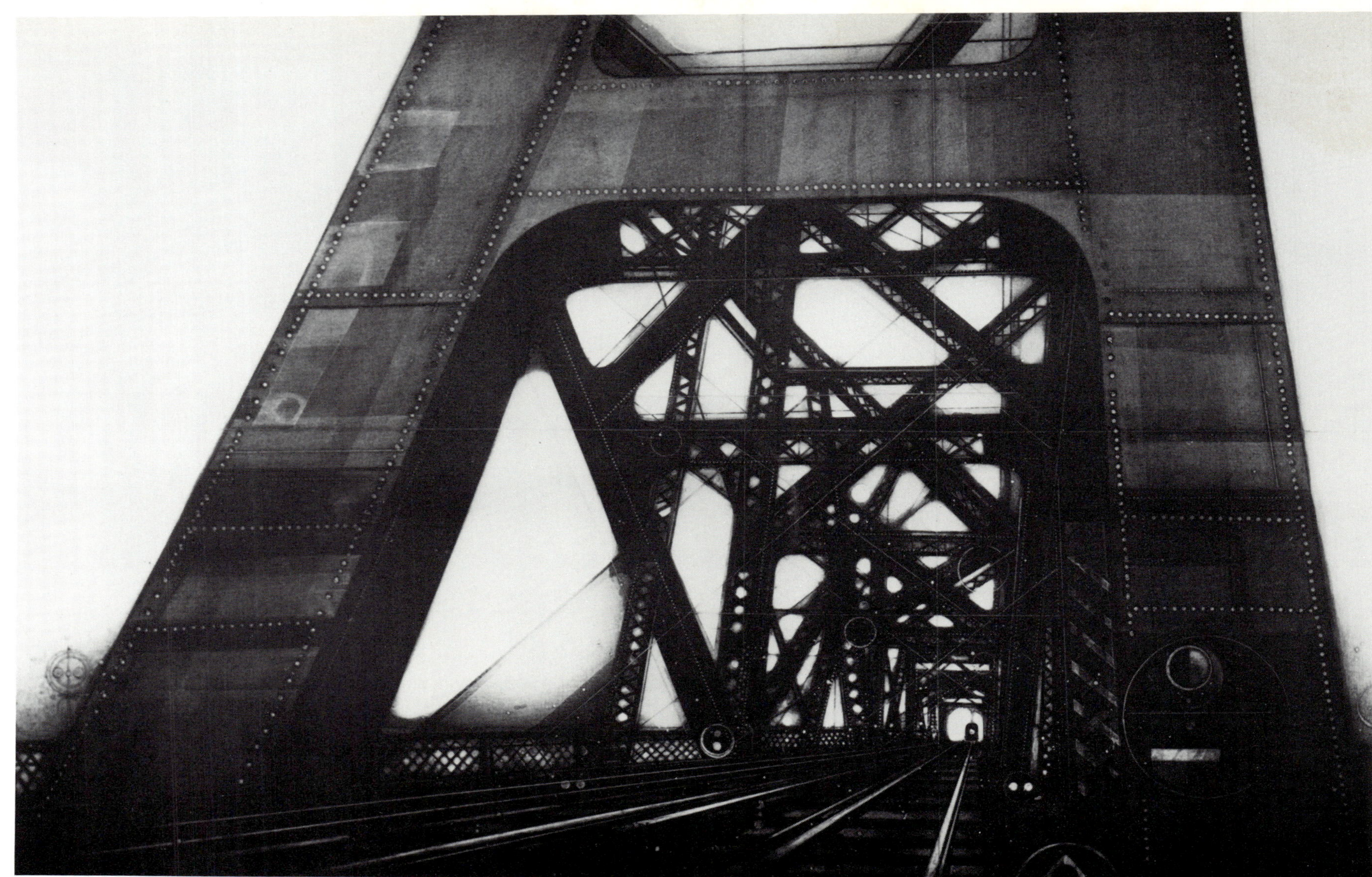

Rail Bridge, 1979. Collagraph print on paper, 35¾" x 23⅝".

It took a composite of several views to achieve the feeling of the massive, powerful, steel structure in this print. Even when undecorated, older engineering works are often rich in functional detail: jungles of small cross braces and patterns of rivets and bolts contrast with sheets of rusted, weathered steel. The dominating H-shape acts as a doorway or arch. The interior space of the bridge recedes to the far opening where the train works as a small, but very important, focus of attention.

Bibliography

Baigell, Matthew. *Charles Burchfield.* New York: Watson-Guptill Publications, Inc., 1976.

Cooper, Douglas. *The Cubist Epoch.* New York: E. P. Dutton (Phaidon), 1971.

Crespell, J. P. *Utrillo—Churches.* New York: Tudor Publishing Co., 1960.

Davidson, Marshall B. *The Artists America.* New York: American Heritage Publishing Co., Inc., 1973.

Eeles, Adrain. *Canaletto.* London: Paul Hamlyn, Limited, 1967.

Elgar, Frank. *Mondrian.* New York: Praeger Publishers, 1968.

Ellis, C. Hamilton. *Railway Art.* Boston: New York Graphic Society, 1977.

Friedman, Martin. *Charles Sheeler.* New York: Watson-Guptill Publications, Inc., 1975.

Gage, John. *Turner: Rain, Steam and Speed.* New York: Viking Press, Inc. (Art in Context Series), 1972.

Gindertael, R. von. *De Stael.* Boston: Museum of Fine Arts, 1965.

Goodrich, Lloyd. *Edward Hopper.* New York: Harry N. Abrams, Inc., 1977.

Gould, Cecil. *Corot.* Catalogue for an exhibition arranged by the Arts Council of Great Britain, 1965.

Hazan, Fernand. *Dictionary of Modern Painting.* New York: Paris Book Center, Inc., 1956.

Hess, Thomas B. *Abstract Painting.* New York: The Viking Press, Inc., 1951.

Kinnear, Katherine. *The Thames in Art.* Catalogue for an exhibition arranged by the Arts Council of Great Britain, 1967.

Leymarie, Jean, editor. *Graphic Works of the Impressionists: The Complete Prints of Manet, Pissaro, Renoir, Cezanne, Sisley.* New York: Harry N. Abrams, Inc., 1971.

Lieberman, William S. *Lyonel Feininger—The Ruin by the Sea.* New York: The Museum of Modern Art, 1968.

Links, J. G. *Townscape Painting and Drawing.* New York: Harper & Row, 1972.

McBride, Henry, et al. *John Marin.* New York: Museum of Modern Art, 1936.

Ness, June L. *Lyonel Feininger.* New York: Praeger Publishers, 1974.

Piranesi, Giovanni B. and Levit, Herschel. *Views of Rome Then and Now: 41 Etchings with Corresponding Photos and Text.* Magnolia, Massachusetts: Peter Smith Publisher, Inc.

Pocock, Tom. *Chelsea Reach: The Brutal Friendship of Whistler and Walter Greaves.* Mystic, Connecticut: Lawrence Verry, Inc., 1971.

Raynal, Maurice. *Modern Painting.* Geneva, Switzerland: Skira Inc., 1953.

Reynolds, Graham. *A Concise History of Watercolors.* New York: Harry N. Abrams, Inc., 1971.

Rienaecker, Victor. *John Sell Cotman.* England: F. Lewis Publishers, Ltd., 1953.

Ritchie, Andrew Carnduff. *Charles Demuth.* New York: Museum of Modern Art, 1950.

Robbins, Daniel, editor. *Jacques Villon.* Cambridge, Massachusetts: Fogg Art Museum, 1976.

Rourke, Constance. *Charles Sheeler.* New York: Harcourt, Brace, Jovanovich, 1938.

Russell, John. *Seurat.* New York: Praeger Publishers, 1965.

Seitz, William C. *Claude Monet: Seasons and Moments.* New York: Museum of Modern Art, 1960.

Sutton, Denys. *Andre Derain.* New York: E. P. Dutton (Phaidon), 1959.

Tralbaut, Marc Edo. *Vincent Van Gogh.* New York: The Viking Press, Inc., 1969.

Van Eerde, Katherine S. *Wenceslaus Hollar: Delineator of His Time.* Charlottesville, Virginia: The University of Virginia, 1970.

Wilmerding, John. *Robert Salmon: The First Major Exhibition.* Lincoln, Massachusetts: The DeCordova Museum, 1967.

______. *Fitz Hugh Lane: 1804-1865 American Marine Painter.* Salem, Massachusetts: The Essex Institute, 1964.

Woods, S. John. *John Piper.* New York: Curt Valentin, 1955.

Young, Mahonri Sharp. *Early American Moderns.* New York: Watson-Guptill, 1974.

Index